New Explor

Critical N

ON PRESCRIBED POETRY FOR THE 2008 EXAMINATION
(HIGHER AND ORDINARY LEVEL)

EDITED BY
John G. Fahy

CONTRIBUTORS
Carole Scully
Bernard Connolly
Marie Dunne
John G. Fahy
Ann Hyland
Mary Shine Thompson
John McCarthy
David Keogh

GILL & MACMILLAN

Gill & Macmillan Ltd
Hume Avenue
Park West
Dublin 12
with associated companies throughout the world
www.gillmacmillan.ie

ISBN-13: 978 07171 4055 8
ISBN–10: 0 7171 4055 5

Design and print origination in Ireland by O'K Graphic Design, Dublin

The paper used in this book is made from the wood pulp of managed forests. For every tree felled, at least one tree is planted, thereby renewing natural resources.

Acknowledgments

Harcourt Publishers for 'The Figure a Poem Makes' by Robert Frost, which was published as an introduction for *The Collected Poems of Robert Frost.*

Faber and Faber Ltd for 'Self's the Man' from *Collected Poems* by Philip Larkin;

Carcanet Press for complete poems and extracts from other poems by Eavan Boland from her *Collected Poems*, and also for extracts from her autobiography *Object Lessons: The Life of the Woman and the Poet in our Time* (1995).

CONTENTS

P = poem also prescribed for Ordinary Level 2008 Exam

P = POEM ALSO PRESCRIBED FOR ORDINARY LEVEL 2008 EXAM

P = poem also prescribed for Ordinary Level 2008 Exam

P = POEM ALSO PRESCRIBED FOR ORDINARY LEVEL 2008 EXAM

1 *John* DONNE

Carole Scully

The quest for certainty

John Donne was born in 1572 in Bread Street, London, into a family that was prosperous, educated and, as Catholics, part of an unpopular religious minority. He was the third of six children. His father, also called John, was a successful merchant and a prominent member of the Company of Ironmongers. His mother, Elizabeth, a devout Catholic, was the daughter of John Heywood and the granddaughter of John Rastell, both popular writers in their time; even more significantly, she was the grandniece of Sir Thomas More, who had been beheaded by King Henry VIII in 1535 because he would not swear the oath accepting Henry as supreme head of the church. More had famously declared on the scaffold: 'I die the King's good servant, but God's servant first.'

This staunch religious devotion in the face of oppression was very much in evidence in Elizabeth's family. Two of her brothers, Donne's uncles, became members of the Jesuit order – an extremely dangerous choice of career, as Jesuits were considered, with some justification, to be the main leaders of the Catholic revolt against English Protestantism. It was treason, punishable by horrific forms of death, to be a Catholic priest, or even to help a Catholic priest. One of Donne's uncles, Jasper, led a secret Jesuit mission to England between 1581 and 1583; he was caught and sentenced to death, but this sentence was reduced to imprisonment and exile. There have been suggestions that the young Donne accompanied his mother to visit Jasper in the Tower of London, but there is no proof of this. In all likelihood, Donne was fully aware of his uncle's situation, as he was about eleven years old at the time and still living at home with his mother and stepfather.

Donne's father had died when Donne was four years old, leaving about £3,500 to his wife and six children – a large fortune at the time. About six months later Donne's mother, still only in her thirties, had married Dr John Syminges, a wealthy widower with three children. At one time Syminges had been president of the Royal College of Physicians; more significantly, he was a Catholic. Donne continued to live, therefore, in a family where education was valued, affordable, and Catholic.

Education

Donne was educated at home with his brother Henry for the early years of his life. There are strong indications that the boys' teachers were Jesuits. In later years Donne wrote of these men: 'I had my first breeding and conversation with men of suppressed and afflicted religion, accustomed to the despite of death and hungry of an imagined martyrdom.' This early exposure to religious intensity had a profound effect on Donne and may partly explain his constant intellectual struggle to find some evidence of certainty in existence. Izaak Walton, Donne's first biographer, relates how Donne, at the age of twelve, entered the University of Oxford with his younger brother, Henry. By starting university at a slightly younger age, Catholic boys could finish early; in this way they left before taking a degree, as that involved swearing the Oath of Supremacy, which declared the English monarch, and not the Pope, to be head of the church. The boys attended Hart Hall, a college with Catholic sympathies, for three years. There are suggestions that they then transferred to the other great university town of Cambridge. Even though he was still unable to take a degree, Donne benefited from this time spent in studies and in mixing with the intellectual group that lived around the colleges.

The world's pleasures

At some time in his youth, most probably between 1589 and 1591, Donne appears to have travelled on the Continent. Travel was very much a part of a young gentleman's education at this time. He seems to have been fluent in Italian and Spanish, and in later years he kept a great many Spanish books in his library; indeed at about this time he chose a Spanish motto for himself, *Antes muerto que mudado* (Sooner dead than changed). The dramatic nature of this motto expresses the type of young man Donne was, or at least wished to be. An early portrait shows him beautifully dressed, with long, dark, curly hair, his intelligent, educated gaze looking into the future while his hand grasps a sword. He is the epitome of the Elizabethan gentleman. Perhaps Donne had discovered, as so many of us do, that there is a comforting certainty in belonging to a recognisable group.

In 1592 Donne was admitted to study law at Lincoln's Inn, London. In this he was following the strong family tradition on his mother's side. However, as the student lawyers were from wealthy families, they spent more of their time pursuing the pleasures of London life than in studying law. A friend of Donne's from this time, Sir Richard Baker, described him as 'not dissolute but very neat: a great visitor of ladies, a great frequenter of plays, a great writer of conceited verses'.

At this point in his life the twenty-year-old Donne was living a life that was radically different from the one he had learnt from his Jesuit teachers and his family. He was Master of the Revels (the title explains his role) for the Christmas celebrations at Lincoln's Inn. His poetry was circulated, with much praise, among the learned of London. He went to the theatre and socialised with fashionable women; he was on the way to becoming a popular celebrity. This may simply have been the natural rebellion of a young man against the beliefs of the older generation, or it may have been a reaction to seeing his younger brother, Henry, die from the plague while imprisoned in Newgate prison for helping a Catholic priest. It could have been another attempt to find the elusive certainty in life. Whatever the reason, Donne gave himself up to living the life of a gentleman about town and expressing his view of the world in bright, clever, sensual poetry:

> Put forth, put forth that warm balm-breathing thigh,
> Which when next time you in these sheets will smother
> There it must meet another.

Gradually, he drifted away from the law. In 1596 he joined a band of volunteers, under the leadership of Robert Devereux, Earl of Essex, and Sir Walter Raleigh and sailed to Cádiz. He experienced a violent sea battle and wrote with grim honesty of the terrible scenes he witnessed: 'They in the sea being burnt, they in the burnt ship drowned.' He returned to England briefly, but in 1597 he joined another expedition under the command of the Earl of Essex, sailing to the Azores with the aim of capturing the Spanish treasure fleet.

It was socially acceptable for young men from the upper classes to take part in these expeditions. At the time relations between England and Spain were uneasy. As recently as 1588 English forces had narrowly defeated the Spanish Armada, more by luck than by design. Queen Elizabeth, though officially disapproving of her subjects' attacks on Spanish vessels and territories, was perfectly happy to receive a share of the booty. Certainly the sense of drama and adventure seems to have appealed to Donne, as can be seen in his poetry:

> Here take my picture, though I bid farewell;
> Thine, in my heart, where my soul dwells, shall dwell.

The trip to the Azores was not a success, with violent storms battering the ships. Donne described the damage vividly:

> And from our tattered sails, rags drop down so,
> As from one hanged in chains, a year ago.

There is a feeling that Donne may have gone on these voyages hoping to find that elusive certainty he craved, but came home with the realisation that it was not to be found in the role of adventurer.

The world of politics

On his return to England, Donne, who by now had largely exhausted his finances, became a rather lowly member of Queen Elizabeth's court. He was twenty-five years old, charmingly ambitious, entertainingly educated, and had proved his valour on military expeditions. Not surprisingly, his fortunes soon improved. In 1598 he was offered a post by the father of one of his fellow-volunteers to Cádiz, and he became private secretary to Sir Thomas Egerton, Lord Keeper of the Great Seal. This was a great opportunity for Donne, as he now had steady employment and a clear connection with an important member of the court. The Lord Keeper presided over the House of Lords and the Court of the Star Chamber, where religious trials were conducted, and he organised the Court of Chancery. As was customary, the Lord Keeper lived at York House; so Donne came to live in a large palace with beautiful gardens that swept down to the Thames. He became part of Egerton's extended family group, which included his fourteen-year-old niece Ann More.

There is no doubt that Egerton was very fond of Donne. When his son died of his wounds in Dublin Castle while serving with Essex in Ireland, Egerton asked Donne to carry his son's sword in the funeral procession at Chester Cathedral. In 1601 he made Donne member of Parliament for one of the boroughs that he controlled. It seemed as if John Donne was destined to play an important role in the world of Elizabethan politics. Perhaps he had found his certainty at last.

The religious difficulty

In all likelihood it was about this time that Donne began to move towards the Church of England. He had already considerably loosened his connections with the Catholic Church. In his pursuit of certainty he had been drawn to study the religious controversies that abounded at the time, and he seems to have developed the view that the different religions were simply different representations of the one truth:

> As women do in divers countries go
> In divers habits, yet are still one kind,
> So doth, so is religion.

By taking up the post with Sir Thomas Egerton, Donne in effect committed himself to practising the religion of the court: it would have been impossible for a Catholic to act as a private secretary to one of Queen Elizabeth's more senior courtiers. There is no doubt that Donne was fully aware of the opportunity he now had. A man could advance himself at court if he came to the attention of those in power. Donne carried out his duties diligently and enthusiastically.

Marriage and its consequences

In December 1601, in what could be seen as a foolish and impulsive action or as yet another attempt to find certainty, Donne, now twenty-nine years old, eloped with Ann More, who was seventeen. Ann's father, Sir George More, was a man known for his violent temper. When the couple finally confessed the marriage to him he was furious that his daughter had tied herself to a penniless private secretary. Donne was instantly dismissed from his post by Egerton, Ann's uncle, and was for a time imprisoned. Sir George More used his influence to ensure that Donne was unable to find employment to support his new wife. Donne, with his customary honesty, summed up his situation in six words: 'John Donne, Ann Donne, Un-done.'

Luckily, Ann's cousin, Sir Francis Wolley, offered the couple shelter in his home in Surrey. For the next few years Donne struggled to provide for his growing family. By 1608 Ann had given birth to five children. He spent some time assisting Thomas Morton, a chaplain, who was fiercely anti-Catholic. Indeed there are some indications that Donne may have collaborated with Morton on a number of writings against the Catholic Church, though his name does not appear on any of them.

When Morton was made Dean of Gloucester in 1607, he tried to persuade Donne to take holy orders in the Church of England. Donne's letter of refusal expresses a change in his approach to life. He appears to be ashamed of the heady days of his youth:

> . . . Some irregularities of my life have been visible to some men, and though I have, I thank God, made my peace with Him . . . yet this, which God knows to be so, is not so visible to man, as to free me from their censures and it may be that sacred calling from a dishonour.

Donne may have been using his past life as an excuse to avoid taking holy orders, because he was not yet fully convinced of the religious doctrines of the Church of England. Perhaps he still harboured the desire to succeed in Elizabethan politics. Or it could simply have been that Donne was not sure whether he could make an adequate living in the religious world to support his ever-increasing family. Nevertheless, whatever their motive, these are the words of a man who has sought certainty but has yet to find it.

Happily, in 1608 relations between Donne and his father-in-law improved, and Ann finally received her dowry. They were able to move to a small house in

Mitcham that was, to Donne's delight, convenient to London and his old friends.

There has been a great deal of debate about the nature of Donne's relationship with his wife. On the one hand, he seems to have felt extremely guilty about the way in which their marriage changed her life. He wrote to a friend, describing himself sitting

> in the noise of three gamesome children, and by the side of her whom I transplanted into a wretched fortune, I must labour to disguise that from her by all such honest devices, as giving her my company and discourse.

On the other hand, he wanted to escape from the house at Mitcham, calling it a 'prison' and a 'dungeon'.

Donne travelled extensively on the Continent with Sir Robert Drury and his family between 1611 and 1612. Ann remained in England with their seven children. Finally, in 1615, as a result of continual urging from King James I, Donne broke from the Catholic Church when he was ordained deacon and priest at St Paul's Cathedral, London, and became a royal chaplain. He quickly became known for his brilliant and moving sermons.

The death of his wife

In 1617 Ann died, a few days after giving birth to a stillborn child. She had borne twelve children in fifteen years, seven of whom lived; the eldest was fourteen, the youngest only twelve months. Donne was devastated. Walton describes how he 'became crucified to the world . . . a commensurable grief took as full possession of him as joy had done . . . .' When he wrote a sonnet in her memory Donne clearly stated that he intended to channel all his passion into his life as a cleric and his new religion:

> Since she whom I loved hath paid her last debt
> To nature, and to hers, and my good is dead,
> And her soul early into heaven ravished,
> Wholly in heavenly things my mind is set.

He did indeed become extremely successful in his new religion. In 1625 he preached a sermon at the lying in state of King James I, and then another for the new king, Charles I. His sermons were noted for their use of striking metaphors. In the 'Sermon of Valediction' he challenged his parishioners to consider their relationship with God in the following terms:

> No man would present a lame horse, a disordered clock, a torn book to a king . . . . Thy body is thy beast; and wilt thou present that to God, when it is lam'd and tir'd with excess of wantonness? When thy clock . . . is disordered with passions . . . when thy book . . . is torn . . . wilt thou then present thy self thus defac'd and mangled to almighty God?

Donne was by this time deeply ashamed of his youthful adventures, and he adjusted his life story so that the biography written by his contemporary, Izaak Walton, largely omits his early years. Nevertheless he was sympathetic towards the extremes of youth:

> An old man wonders then how an arrow from an eye could wound him when he was young, and how love could make him do those things which he did then.

He came to believe that his difficulties in supporting his family were part of God's plan for him:

> . . . And looking back on my past life, I now plainly see it was his hand that prevented me from all temporal employment; and that it was his will I should never settle nor thrive till I entered into the ministry.

His sermons were popular because they were filled with a sense of the common humanity of mankind:

> No man is an island, entire of itself; every man is a piece of the continent, a part of the main . . . . Any man's death diminishes me, because I am involved in mankind. And therefore never send to know for whom the bell tolls. It tolls for thee.

The final quest

In 1631, having got out of his sick-bed, Donne delivered his last sermon, entitled 'Death's Duell'. He spoke of the interconnection of life and death, once again using vivid images to convey his message:

> Wee have a winding sheet in our Mother's womb, which grows with us from our conception, and wee come into the world, bound up in that winding sheet, for wee come to seek a grave.

In a gesture that recalls his youthful fondness for the dramatic, Donne ordered a large carved wooden urn to be brought to his room. He stood on it wrapped in his own shroud while an artist made the life-size sketch that was later used for a stone figure.

It is generally agreed that had Donne not died when he did, on 31 March 1631, he would have become a bishop. He was buried in St Paul's Cathedral.

Donne's apostasy

There has been much debate about Donne's apostasy (giving up his religion) and the sincerity of his conversion to the Church of England. Perhaps he was motivated by the desire to succeed in a world where Catholics were definitely second-class citizens. There is no doubt that King James greatly influenced his decision to be ordained by refusing to grant him a secular appointment. Or it may have been that his early experiences led him to rebel against the religion that had caused so much distress in his family. Interestingly, his mother, who was always a staunch Catholic, came to live with Donne and his family in the Deanery at St Paul's. Was his change of religion simply another attempt to find that emotional and intellectual certainty he so badly craved?

Whatever his motivation, Donne's conversion did not end his quest for certainty. His sermons may have expressed an unwavering faith in God, but his poetry still trembled with uncertainty. In his final poem, 'A Hymn to God the Father', Donne begs God for mercy. There is a poignancy in the uncertainty that still haunts his very being after all his years of searching. Yet behind the overwhelming need and the religious language there is still the glimmer of the man who, in spite of the terrible uncertainty he could see, lived life with a passion, the man who was made Master of the Revels, sailed the seas, married impulsively and preached inspiringly, the man who even at the last could not resist punning on his own name:

> But swear by thy self, that at my death thy son
> Shall shine as he shines now, and heretofore;
> And, having done that, thou hast done,
> I fear no more.

Perhaps he did find his certainty after all.

John Donne and metaphysical poetry

John Donne wrote poetry throughout his life. Whether he was on land, at sea, at court, in prison, Catholic or Protestant, single or married, Donne wrote poetry. But, surprising as it may seem, he did not write for publication. For Donne lived at a time when the writing of poetry was considered to be the accomplishment of a true gentleman. Rather like mastering fencing, it was a skill that defined a man's social status. A gentleman wrote to amuse, to impress and even to seduce, but he never wrote to publish. Donne circulated his poetry among a select group of friends and patrons. His point of exhibition and distribution was generally the Mitre, an inn frequented by intellectual gentlemen. He rarely dated his work and all too often did not keep copies of the poems he had written. But although Donne followed the customs of the day in the way he viewed his poetry, he was rigorously individual in the way he wrote.

It is ironic that the term 'metaphysical', applied so often to Donne's style of writing, was first thrown at him as a term of critical abuse. In 1693, some sixty years after Donne's death, John Dryden wrote that he

> affects the metaphysics, not only in his satires, where nature only should reign, but perplexes the minds of the fair sex with nice speculations of philosophy, when he should engage their hearts, and entertain them with the softnesses of love.

In truth, this passage says more about Dryden's expectations of poetry than it does about metaphysical poetry; but his use of the word 'metaphysics' is important, because it captures in one word an essential aspect of Donne's poetry: his desire to go beyond the physical confines of existence. When Donne wrote about love he did not list his beloved's physical qualities, as was customary with traditional poets: instead he ignored these 'softnesses of love' and told her of the ways in which she filled his emotions, his mind and his every waking moment. Donne united the intellect and the emotions in a way that had never been done before. As T. S. Eliot put it, 'A thought to Donne was an experience; it modified his sensibility.'

In an effort to communicate this unified experience of thought and emotion, Donne made use of the *conceit*. Conceits, in the form of far-fetched comparisons, had long been used in traditional love poetry as a device for emphasising the beauty of the poet's beloved. But Donne discarded the traditional in favour of his own unique approach. Once again it is a negative interpretation by a critic that provides the key to what Donne was attempting to do. Samuel Johnson famously commented that in metaphysical poetry 'The most heterogeneous ideas are yoked together by violence; nature and art are ransacked for illustrations, comparisons and illusions. . . .' His use of the words 'violence' and 'ransacked', though intended to be a reproach, suggest the uncompromising way in which Donne combined ideas in his poetry. He disregarded convention, both in thought and taste. He can use the image of a flea in a love poem and urge God to ravish him in a religious one.

Because he was trying to communicate an incredibly complex experience, Donne used the conceit as a device whereby he could connect apparently unconnected images in such a way that the gradual uncovering of a connectedness between them conveys both an intellectual and an emotional message. T. S. Eliot called it a 'telescoping of images and multiplied associations . . .' It is a way of dramatically and rapidly communicating complexity of both feeling and thinking. So Donne could summarise the essence of Elizabeth Drury's being in three words: 'Her body thought.' As readers we can react to this statement on an instinctive level. By combining two images that are accepted as relating to two distinctly different aspects of human existence, Donne succeeds in communicating a unity of message. The three words, and the mental images they carry, amalgamate into a new and complex concept that simultaneously appeals to the intellect, the emotions and the spirit. There is an instinctive quality to our reaction to Donne's conceits that arises out of this challenging combination, a quality all too often lacking in more logical and expected comparisons. In his writing Donne released himself from the accepted norms of appropriateness; in our reading of his work we should endeavour to do the same.

To be able to make these connections, the metaphysical poet had to be finely tuned in every fibre of his being. Here again, those who were suspicious of metaphysical poetry regarded this as a weakness. Johnson rather huffily pronounced that 'The metaphysical poets were men of learning, and to show their learning was their whole endeavour . . . .' In a way, Johnson both hit and missed the point with this statement. The metaphysical poets, and Donne in particular, were indeed men who had benefited from the privilege of education; but instead of simply exhibiting their education by reproducing skilful copies of what they had previously studied, they confronted the very foundations of that education: they questioned the logic they had been taught and tested the substance of the rhetoric they had practised. In this way Donne takes the framework of the traditional Petrarchan sonnet and subjects it to the stresses of unexpected conceits; he fills the dramatic opening, so long the poet's comfortable starting point, with a tension of contradiction, and rejects the conventionally artificial language and rhythm of poetry for the words of everyday speech and the rhythm that comes from the sense of these words.

To be able to do all this, he had to have 'wit' – not in the simplistic sense in which we use that word today but, in the words of the critic Josef Lederer, as 'a brilliant result of long study, a quintessence of deep learning'. Samuel Taylor Coleridge expresses his view in more detail:

> Wonder-exciting vigour, intenseness and peculiarity of thought, using at will the most boundless stores of a capacious memory, and exercised on subjects where we have no right to expect it – this is the wit of Donne!

Of course the fundamental question with Donne is whether his poetry grew out of some inner, inescapable urge that demanded expression or was the calculated posturing of a man who was ambitious for fame and fortune. Did Donne possess a mind that was, in T. S. Eliot's words, 'perfectly equipped for its work' of 'constantly amalgamating disparate experience'? Was this mind tormented by the vision of the uncertainty of existence and forever searching for some evidence of certainty? Do his unconventional conceits and 'wit' simply represent the spiritual, intellectual and emotional insecurity that Donne felt throughout his life? Or was his poetry merely a brilliant exercise in self-advertisement, a cynical publicity stunt to attract the applause and admiration of his peers?

The Flea

Text of poem: New Explorations Anthology page 2

[*Note: This poem is also prescribed for Ordinary Level 2008 exam*]

One of the difficulties with Donne's poetry is that he never made any attempt to keep his poems together, or to organise them in chronological order. Izaak Walton deeply regretted this attitude, commenting that Donne's pieces 'were loosely, God knows too loosely scattered in his youth'. Publication did not appeal to Donne, and on the rare occasion when he allowed the 'Anniversaries' to be printed he wrote to a friend: 'The fault that I acknowledge in myself is to have descended to print anything in verse.' It was not until 1633, two years after his death, that the first collected edition of Donne's verse appeared. The order and grouping of the poems was largely a matter of guesswork on the part of his friends.

It has been said that 'The Flea' was one of Donne's most celebrated and most widely known poems while he was alive. Though there is no definite evidence to support this, there are indications that it was translated into Dutch.

A reading of the poem

Donne opens the poem in a dramatic fashion. He is talking to his lover, but it is definitely a one-sided conversation. It is almost as if he is lecturing her. His use of the image of the flea, though a common poetic device in the seventeenth century, adds to the drama and the tension. There is a feeling that Donne has already tried a number of arguments and has been rejected. Perhaps somewhat at a loss in the face of constant refusal, his eyes wander around the room and suddenly light upon the flea, and inspiration strikes.

The first line appears to be a casual comment on the appearance of a flea. We can imagine how it would catch his lover's attention, how she would probably feel rather puzzled at this sudden change of topic. But the second line quickly undercuts this apparent simplicity. Donne uses the flea to make a very important point to his lover. She is denying him something he wants, but so far he does not specify what it is.

In the next two lines he returns to his comments on the flea. He describes how the flea has bitten both himself and his lover, and their blood is now mixed together in the flea. A basic physicality is suggested in his use of the blood image, which prepares us for the sixth line. Donne's use of the word 'maidenhead', along with 'sin' and 'shame', leaves little doubt about what it is his lover is denying him.

Donne reinforces the connection between himself and the flea in the final three lines of the first stanza. Unlike Donne himself, the flea is able to enjoy an intimate relationship with this woman, even though it has not gone through the rituals of courtship. The use of the word 'pampered' implies a feeling of contentment and satisfaction – two states that Donne most certainly does not feel. The suggestion is that he has played the wooing game according to the rules, and he feels that, in all fairness, his lover should play her part in the game.

It is evident from reading this first stanza that how this poem is interpreted, and what reaction we experience to it, depend on how we view the tone of the piece. Donne would probably have read this poem aloud to a small group and in this way could have coloured the tone. But our interpretation has to develop as a result of careful reading and rereading. If we consider Donne to be approaching his lover in a mock-dramatic or charmingly pathetic manner, we can react with amusement; we can join in the joke that is trembling between Donne and his lady. But if we think he is behaving in a thoroughly unpleasant fashion, exerting considerable emotional blackmail on his lover with his selfish, adolescent whingeing, we are bound to feel anger and annoyance.

Finally, it may be that Donne deliberately wove this ambiguity into the poem as a way of adding a sense of danger. He knows he is skating on thin ice, and so do we. In this way he deliberately moves away from the safety of creating straightforward amusement and into the perils of humour that challenges our preconceptions.

Donne ended the first stanza on an extremely dramatic note, lamenting in mock-heroic terms – evident in the use of the word 'alas' – the fact that he and his lover have not experienced physical intimacy. He continues this approach in the second stanza. His dramatic plea, 'Oh stay,' asking her to not to squash the flea, carries with it a wealth of understated comedy. In an age when fleas and their destruction were commonplace, the drama Donne attaches to this incident can only be interpreted as humorous. He asks that the flea's life be spared, because in killing it his lover will destroy the flea's life and, because it contains their blood, her life and Donne's. He urges her to remember that the mingling of their blood is intimate and special: it is like their 'marriage bed' and their 'marriage temple'. Here again Donne overstates the situation in a humorous way: linking the image of a temple with a flea is patently ridiculous. Donne races on, carried forward by his own eloquence and perhaps by his lover's lack of response despite his best efforts. Nevertheless, in the midst of all these theatricals he produces a stunningly vivid image of their blood within the flea, 'cloistered in these living walls of jet.' Barely pausing for breath, he launches another argument at his lover. If she is unmoved by his death and that of the flea, then she must be concerned about causing her own suicide and thereby committing a sin to add to that of two murders.

Donne uses religious language in this stanza to provide a framework for his argument. His implication is that he regards physical intimacy with his lover as something sacred and special; but there is an undercutting awareness of the humorous incompatibility that lies in linking a flea sucking blood with religion.

Though Donne's lover never speaks, we can clearly visualise her reaction to his arguments in the way that she behaves. She may be verbally inactive but she is far from being passive. The third stanza opens with the death of the flea. Donne is horrified by her action. It is 'cruel and sudden,' perhaps as cruel and sudden as her rejection of his advances. She has spilled the 'blood of innocence'. The clear suggestion is that the woman is callous and cruel in her behaviour towards the innocent flea, just as she is with the innocent Donne. This, of course, is obviously ridiculous. Donne is far from innocent in his desires. He continues this line of thought, stating that she triumphs in the flea's death because she has proved the arguments that Donne put forward in the second stanza to be wrong.

At this point it appears that Donne is completely beaten. He gives the impression that his lover has outwitted him. But he is simply lulling her into a false sense of security. The last three lines of the poem are produced with a magician's flourish. Donne concedes that the woman is absolutely right: she has lost nothing with the death of the flea. But, in a breathtaking reversal of the balance of power, he tells her that, in exactly the same way, her yielding to his advances will not cause her to lose her honour. He is, in effect, using the well-worn argument that he will respect her in the morning!

Style

Donne uses a popular device from sixteenth-century love poetry as the framework on which to hang his poem. The linking of a male lover with a flea had been used in Greek, Latin, French, Spanish and Italian poetry. The image was usually developed along very bawdy lines, with the flea wandering over the woman's body; the death of the flea at the hands of the woman was regarded as ultimately blissful.

This poem could be viewed as Donne testing the limitations of the device not simply to achieve a humorous effect, but to challenge the conventionality that the device represented.

Alternatively
Samuel Johnson wrote of the metaphysicals: 'Whatever is improper or vicious is produced from nature in pursuit of something new and strange; the writers fail to give delight by their desire to excite admiration.'

This piece may be nothing more than the poetic equivalent of a dirty joke. It causes a reaction simply because it uses rude images. Donne takes an 'improper' idea in the belief that he will be able to give it a new slant, purely in an attempt to impress his friends at the Mitre. It is neither 'new' nor 'strange', nor does it 'excite admiration' or 'delight'. In short, it is the perfect piece to be read in a dimly lit room filled with immature men.

Song: Go, and catch a falling star

Text of poem: New Explorations Anthology page 4
[*Note: This poem is also prescribed for Ordinary Level 2008 exam*]

This poem appears to have been written during the time Donne spent at Lincoln's Inn, when he was beginning to make a name for himself as a poet. Poetry at this time was one way in which an educated young man on the fringes of the court could bring himself to the attention of those in power.

Style

The listing of impossible tasks was popular in Petrarchan poetry. This use of *hyperbole* (an exaggerated statement not meant to be taken literally) was a device to emphasise the poet's devotion to his beloved.

There is a strong element of *satire* in this poem. Broadly speaking, satire is used to expose and ridicule folly and shallowness. It is frequently driven by anger, but it is more refined and sophisticated than an angry outburst. The writer generally expresses a one-sided view of his subject, in order to ensure that the satire works. The use of satire suggests that the writer feels superior to those he is satirising, that he can see the folly while others are unaware of it.

A reading of the poem

The first line of this poem has a magical, fairy-tale quality about it. The catching of a 'falling star' belongs to the romantic world of handsome princes and beautiful princesses. Donne deliberately creates specific expectations in the reader by using this as his opening line. However, the second line introduces a sense of unease, as it is a much darker image. The phrase 'get with child' is brutally unromantic. The mandrake is a plant that people at the time believed had human qualities, such as screaming when it was uprooted. Though this image, like that of catching a falling star, is meant to represent an impossible task, it is very much the stuff of nightmares.

The tone changes again with Donne's rather conventional question about the passing of time. But we return to a darker world of images with the question about 'the Devil's foot'. The 'mermaids singing' could belong to the world of falling stars and passing time; however, Donne appears to be deliberately exploiting the ambiguity that existed around the image of the mermaid at this time: while it could refer to a beautiful half-woman, half-fish creature, it could also be used to denote a prostitute. The final image of 'envy's stinging' has a deeply personal feeling about it.

Donne is deliberately playing with his reader's perception of the nature of this poem. He alternates between images usually connected with the Petrarchan view of love and images that are radically and disturbingly opposed to it. He is consciously confusing his reader in order to create tension. All this tension culminates in the final three lines of the stanza, where Donne uses both the sense of his words and their rhythm in a most unsettling way. There is real vehemence in his statement about the lack of success for the 'honest mind'. Does it reflect the frustrations of an ambitious young man not yet able to break into the powerful world of the court? By interrupting the rhythm of the stanza with two lines of only two words, Donne skilfully emphasises this final image.

The second stanza continues this tension but in a slightly different way. Rather than alternate between pleasant traditional images and more unpleasant unconventional ones, Donne remains in the world of the unpleasant. A series of disquieting images is hurled at the reader: being 'born to strange sights,' able to see 'things invisible', riding 'ten thousand days and nights,' hair turning 'snow white' and returning with stories of 'strange wonders'. It is not accidental that Donne repeats the word 'strange' in this stanza, for it is unsettlingly strange.

In a final flourish Donne ends the stanza on the strangest concept of all: the fact that it is impossible to find 'a woman true and fair.' He has propelled us along a roller-coaster ride of emotions, and we are left gasping at the end of this outburst. Are we speechless from shock at the strength of emotion underlying his opinion of women? Or has the tension that fills every word in the poem become unbearable?

The tone of the final stanza is more controlled; it is as if Donne has been emotionally drained by the first two stanzas. There is a sad vulnerability and longing in the line 'If thou find'st one, let me know,' for, despite his best efforts, Donne still yearns for the 'woman true and fair.' Quickly he changes his mind, asking not to be told of such a woman, not even if she were living next door to him. Once again Donne's bitterness returns, perhaps even more effective now that it is more understated in its expression.

In the last five lines of the poem Donne summarises his attitude to women. He no longer rants and raves: he simply states the fact that even if a 'true' woman were to be found she would inevitably turn 'false' in the length of time it would take for a letter to be sent to him while travelling to meet her. It is a shocking ending to the poem; or is it?

As with 'The Flea', this poem is a mass of unresolved ambiguities. Is Donne being serious or not? Is he expressing his real views, his longing for certainty, or is he simply acting out an attitude? Is the 'me' in the poem Donne, or a persona he has taken on? Did he write this poem as a satire? If he intended it to be a satire, what was he satirising? Was he satirising women, perhaps as a result of something he experienced? Or was he drawing attention to the stupidity of the conventional Petrarchan love poem? Was Donne fighting for women to be treated by men as real human beings? It is up to you to decide.

Alternatively

William Hazlitt commented on the metaphysical poets: 'Their chief aim was to make you wonder at the writer, not interest you in the subject . . . .' This poem could be seen as the work of a self-absorbed man. Donne was determined to gain notoriety by being outrageous and controversial. Though this poem may have been written as the words to a song, it is not pleasantly amusing. His images are deliberately disturbing, his views on women are offensive and his tone is nastily pompous. He may pride himself on having an 'honest mind', but on the evidence of this poem it is little wonder that he was unable 'to advance'.

The Sun Rising

Text of poem: New Explorations Anthology page 6

Donne made no attempt during his lifetime to date the majority of his poems, nor to keep them in any kind of order. As very little of his work was published and the poems were simply distributed in manuscript form, we have few indications of when most of the poems were written. In the first printed edition of his poetry, in 1633, the love poems are scattered through the book. However, in 1635, four years after his death, an edition of Donne's poetry grouped all his love poems together under the title 'Songs and Sonnets'. Generally, later editions have stuck to this arrangement, because not enough definite information is available to organise them in any other way.

Style

Donne frequently places himself in a dramatic setting in his love poems. Whether he is attempting to seduce his lover, to remain with her or to leave her behind, the reader is brought into the scene at a very important moment. In this poem Donne uses this drama to give new life and energy to the traditional love-poetry images of royalty and the sun.

A reading of the poem

The opening three lines of this poem are wonderfully dramatic. Donne balances straightforward language and natural speech rhythms to vividly create a sense of immediacy. It is as if we are there with him as he vents his annoyance on the sun. The beams of sun shine in through 'windows' and 'curtains', disturbing Donne and his lover. It is an intrusion into their close intimacy, an unwanted reminder that they will not always be able to exist in this tranquil and contented state. The sun is a reminder to the two lovers of the world outside. Their quietness is emphasised by the frenzied activities, clearly suggested by the rhythm of these lines, of the early morning. In four lines, we see 'late schoolboys' and 'sour prentices' reluctantly going on their way, while courtiers scurry around after the king and farm workers, 'country ants', set about the harvesting. All these people are governed by something outside themselves: the schoolboys by the school day, the apprentices by their work, the courtiers by the whims of the king, and the farm workers by the seasons. However, Donne and his lover are freed from such controls by their love. They have transcended time itself.

The second stanza continues this theme of love triumphant. Donne challenges the power of the sun with his beams 'so reverend and strong'. He states that he could easily blot out these beams by simply shutting his eyes. But he will not do this, because he does not want to miss seeing his beloved for one instant. Therefore, for him his lover is stronger than the sun. This links into the following image, where Donne speaks of her eyes being bright enough to blind the sun. This is a traditional image in love poetry, but Donne places it in a context where the comparison seems to occur naturally and spontaneously. As in the first stanza, he sweeps from the close intimacy of the room to the outside world by his use of vivid images. He challenges the sun further by stating that it may spend the day moving across the world, over the evocative 'Indias of spice and mine' or shining on kings, but the real, true world will be in this room with the two lovers. In this way, love transcends the confines of space.

In the third stanza Donne draws together this central theme of love triumphant. His lover is 'all states' and he is 'all princes'. There is an irresistible quality about Donne's enthusiasm, whatever his motivation. Even if he was only driven by the desire to seduce, it is hard not to be swept along with him. He is emphatic in his belief that the two lovers have everything that matters with them in the room: 'Nothing else is.' The trappings of worldly success, considered so important in the external world, are irrelevant in the world of love. The unlimited power wielded by sixteenth-century royalty is but an imitation of the lovers' power; the rewards of 'honour' are simply amusing imitations, and wealth is useless. The sun, which so rudely wakened them, is pitied by Donne, because its movement is across this external world on its own, whereas Donne and his beloved are two people united in a limitless world of love. Momentarily, he has found some certainty.

In the final four lines of the poem Donne slows the rhythm of his words to underpin the alteration in his emotions. His excited and challenging confidence changes to sympathetic concern for the sun. The sun is old and deserves some respect, particularly from two who have such power. Donne comforts the sun by allowing it to enter into their world, so that in shining on them it will be shining on the true world. Is there a touch of humour in these lines? Could Donne be, once again, practising the art of humorous seduction?

Alternatively

The critic John Carey considers the 'vaunting language' used by Donne in this poem to be a clear indication that he did not feel as confident and contented as he said he did. Rather than feeling better than those involved in the court, or richer than those who had wealth, Carey feels that Donne, who had financial difficulties, was deeply envious of the world of the rich and powerful. He was desperately ambitious to make his mark on the world. Carey's view is that Donne regards the 'private world' he inhabits with his beloved as being only an imitation of the 'public' world he so longs to join. No matter how hard he tries to concentrate on the superiority of love, he is 'irascibly conscious of the rest of the world's activities'.

The Anniversarie

Text of poem: New Explorations Anthology page 8

Background

See the background notes for 'The Sun Rising', pages 16–18.

Style

Donne's poems on love are usually classified as *lyrics*. Though the term 'lyric' is a rather general one, there are certain characteristics that tend to be obvious in a lyrical poem. The nineteenth-century writer John Ruskin defined the lyric as 'the expression by the poet of his own feelings'. There is an undeniable personal quality about the lyric, in that the words are spoken by one person from a personal viewpoint. However, a problem arises regarding exactly who the 'I' of lyrical poetry is. The 'I' could be the poet himself, or it could simply represent a character the poet has created, a persona, to act as a mouthpiece for what he wants to express. Therefore, it is not always clear just how personal 'lyric' poems are.

There has been a great deal of discussion about the reality of the love experiences Donne describes in his love poetry. Some have felt that the 'I' in these poems is not Donne and that the feelings expressed are no more than the wishful thoughts of a frustrated young man. Others believe that Donne based his poems on actual experiences in his life and that the 'I' is very definitely Donne himself. What is undeniable is the fact that when Donne turned to religion he became deeply embarrassed by these poems from his youth.

A reading of the poem

This poem opens on familiar territory, both for the modern reader of Donne and for those few of his contemporaries who were privileged to read his work in manuscript form. The images of the court and the sun were part of the traditional formula of Petrarchan love poetry, which was so popular in Donne's time. For modern readers who have read some of Donne's works these images are familiar because he uses them frequently in his writing. Yet, even though these two groups of readers are separated by more than four hundred years, a common sense of expectancy is stimulated by this opening. Just as Donne's friends might have glanced at each other in anticipation of how Donne was going to follow this beginning, so we are also aware that something will happen in the course of this poem that will not be totally expected.

However, the first stanza continues in a reasonably conservative way. Donne, having noted that everything from the 'kings' to the 'sun' has aged by a year since the lovers first met, states clearly that it is only their shared love that is untouched by time. In the face of 'destruction' and 'decay' their love 'keeps his first, last, everlasting day.'

In the first stanza the concept of time passing is conveyed by fairly unthreatening images. The idea of 'kings', 'beauties', 'wits' and the 'sun itself' ageing by a year is not really disturbing: Donne is simply reproducing the usual formula to suggest the passing of time. Similarly, the line 'Only our love hath no decay' is a common sentiment expressed in love poetry. Love has 'no tomorrow', nor has it a 'yesterday'. This is all fairly unremarkable. But then we meet the line 'Running it never runs from us away,' and the formulaic safety of the opening eight lines begins to tremble slightly. What does Donne mean by this line? He must have felt it was of reasonable importance to use it to interrupt the traditional approach he had followed so far. There is a kind of premeditated intellectualisation in this paradox, a conscious self-awareness that is not present in the previous lines. The verb 'running' is not one that immediately springs to mind in connection with a love affair, yet Donne obviously chose it carefully. Was it simply so that he could construct this clever little paradox to amuse both himself and his friends? Or did he deliberately use 'run' because it was definitely *not* part of the vocabulary of the Petrarchan love poem?

Donne ends this stanza with a line that is beautifully balanced, both in its meaning and its rhythm: 'But truly keeps his first, last, everlasting day.' Love remains untouched by the 'destruction' and 'decay' that haunts everything else.

The second stanza begins with a graphic image of two bodies in separate graves. The threat of death was very real to the Elizabethans, and this would have been a disturbing image, one far removed from the niceties of Petrarchan love poetry. The description of the two lovers lying in the one grave is not totally comforting. Donne continues the royalty image of the first stanza with his comparison between the two lovers and 'princes'. This is an idea that we have met previously with Donne: that mutual love makes two people special, powerful, and set apart – rather like royalty but even better. However, despite their uniqueness the two lovers, along with 'other princes', must inevitably surrender their physical bodies.

It is interesting that there is generally a marked lack of physical details in Donne's poetry: we rarely learn anything about what his lovers look like, even though his love poetry is filled with a sensuous pleasure. Yet here he deliberately writes of the 'eyes' with their 'sweet salt tears' and the 'ears' that were 'oft fed with true oaths'. The first six lines of the second stanza vividly describe the physicality of death, because Donne wants us to feel the overwhelming nature of death, so that love's ability to triumph over it will appear all the more wonderful. For love does triumph. Donne declares that their love has transcended the limitations of mere physical love: it has become a part of their very souls. This spiritual love is able to cheat death: the bodies of the lovers may go 'to their graves,' but the souls will escape to 'there above'. This was provocative stuff in an age when access to Heaven was being fought over by the Catholic and Protestant churches. Both promised eternal life to their followers and damnation to those who rejected them. Yet here is Donne, filled with certainty, saying that love shared between a man and a woman is the way to gain entry into Heaven.

The final stanza opens where the second stanza ends. When the souls of the lovers go up to Heaven they will be 'thoroughly blessed', because their love will be increased by heavenly love. There they will join all the other lovers who have also attained spiritual love, and in this way they will no longer be unique in the way that they are on Earth. However, for the moment they are still here on Earth; they are still 'kings', because their love is true, but they need not fear death. The lovers are safe, because they can be damaged in only one way: by each other. Their love ensures that they are immune to the passing of time and the horrors of death but, ironically, it also makes them profoundly vulnerable to each other. Happily, Donne is so confident in the certainty of their love that he quickly dismisses this possibility. They must simply avoid worrying about 'true and false fears' and live a long life together, secure in the protection of their shared love.

This poem ends in a way that is far removed from the Petrarchan conventions that filled the first stanza. It has travelled from the world of the court to the sun blazing in space, from the darkness of the grave to the light of Heaven. But above all it has declared the power and the certainty of the love that Donne shares with his beloved.

Alternatively
Samuel Taylor Coleridge commented on the metaphysical poets that they 'sacrificed the heart to the head'. Is this poem a sincere expression of Donne's belief in the certainty of his love, or is it simply an intellectual exercise designed to show just how stale and old-fashioned traditional Petrarchan love poetry had become? Did he write from the heart, or did his head make it look as if he was writing from the heart?

Sweetest love, I do not go

Text of poem: New Explorations Anthology page 10

It has been suggested – particularly by Donne's first biographer, Izaak Walton – that Donne wrote this poem, together with 'A Valediction: Forbidding Mourning', to his wife before he left to travel on the Continent in 1611. However, as Donne rarely dated any of his poetry, there is no proof to support this view.

In some manuscripts this poem is in a group entitled 'Songs which were made to certain airs which were made before'. Several seventeenth-century manuscripts contain music for this poem, but again there is no proof that Donne ever intended this poem to be sung.

A READING OF THE POEM

The poem opens in typical Donne style. It is a moment of drama, and we have stumbled upon two people immersed in an intense conversation. But the drama in this poem is far more understated than in much of Donne's other love poetry. There is a sense of true intimacy about the language he uses to express his feelings. He speaks simply and with apparent sincerity. There is little evidence of his sparkling wit and tongue-in-cheek humour; he is simply trying to reassure his beloved. In the very first lines of the poem he emphasises to her that he is not going 'for weariness' of her, nor because he is looking for 'a fitter love'. He then uses gentle humour to try to lighten the moment. After all, he says, he will have to die sometime, and he would rather enjoy life than spend it imagining all the dreadful deaths that might happen to him. We can almost see Donne widening his eyes and giving an appealing smile to emphasise this little joke.

In an effort to carry this lighter tone into the second stanza, Donne then compares himself to the sun. The sun, he tells his beloved, set yesterday but was still able to return. So, he must go away, but he will be back. In a simple little hyperbole he tells her that he will be back more speedily than the sun, because he has the motivation to return to her.

The third stanza approaches the main theme of the poem from a slightly different angle. Donne reflects on the ways humankind deals with life experiences. He comments that we tend to accept the good times for what they are, but when it comes to the bad times we tend to exaggerate how bad they are. He is trying to minimise the 'bad chance' of their parting in an effort to comfort and reassure his beloved.

However, in the fourth stanza he returns to the intensely personal tone of the opening stanza. In a series of beautifully constructed images and rhythms he describes just how deeply connected the two lovers are. Her sadness is so real to him that it actually erodes his life force. Her sighs diminish the strength of his soul; her tears are like a loss of blood to him. Her grief is killing him, and he urges her to remember this, to realise that she is 'the best of me'. This stanza vibrates with a level of sincerity and an emotional openness that are in marked contrast to some of Donne's earlier love poetry. There is no sense that Donne is performing or taking up a position in an effort to impress or amuse. For once, it seems that we are seeing John Donne the man as he really is, filled with the certainty that their love is true.

This emotional intensity sweeps into the final stanza. Donne begs his lover not to imagine all the terrible things that could happen to him when they are parted. He admits the possibility of something dreadful occurring, but he reminds her that they really have no control over destiny. Once again he uses a wonderfully evocative image to convey the depth of his feelings. For lovers such as they, the ultimate terror of death is simply a turning 'aside to sleep'. Their true and certain love enables them to triumph over time and space, and even death itself.

Style

The structure of this poem is deceptively simple. The very appearance of the printed lines on the page implies that this is a poem that should be easily understood, and in many ways it is. Donne uses the simple language of everyday conversation. There are no dramatic exclamations, no witty constructions: just the desire to express sincerity. His occasional movements away from the deeply personal tone (in the second and third stanzas) are not for the purpose of displaying his intellect, but rather are further attempts to relieve the dreadful emotional turmoil the two lovers are experiencing. His use of a light rhythm and a strong rhyme seems to be a deliberate attempt to lighten the intensity of the situation. Similarly, the five eight-line stanzas impose a definite structure on the scene, a structure that is clearly lacking in the reality of the lovers' imminent separation. However, in spite of his best efforts, Donne cannot control the emotional impact of this moment. His true feelings break through rhyme and rhythm. He cannot hide his own vulnerability. The death that he is suffering in this poem is more real and painful than the one he described in 'The Flea', because love is no longer a game.

Alternatively
'In his poems there is often a perfect equilibrium between their exact truth to mood and feeling and their acute awareness of an audience' (Barbara Everett). Is this poem simply another example of Donne using love as a vehicle for his desire to impress his little group of fans? Is he exploiting his lover, once again using their apparent emotional connection as an opportunity to display his 'wit'?

A Valediction: Forbidding Mourning

Text of poem: New Explorations Anthology page 12

As we have seen, Izaak Walton links this poem with 'Sweetest Love, I Do Not Go', suggesting that they were written just before a trip to the Continent in 1611. He comments: 'I beg leave to tell you, that I have heard some critics . . . say, that none of the Greek or Latin poets did equal them.' However, attractive though it may be to connect them to Donne's life, it should be noted that parting or absence from a loved one were traditional themes in love poetry.

A READING OF THE POEM

Donne opens this poem with a vivid image of a death-bed scene. This, coupled with the title – 'A Valediction: Forbidding Mourning' – creates the expectation that this poem will be about the death of someone. It is certainly not an unpleasant death, as the 'virtuous men' are confident of a life after death in Heaven. The atmosphere is one of dignity and composure, with a group of friends present at the gentle passing.

The second stanza links into this idea of a quiet withdrawal. Donne advises his beloved that they should 'melt, and make no noise'. At this point Donne still seems to be dealing with death in its physical sense. But the following three lines have something odd about them. Donne seems to be suggesting that the two lovers should die peacefully. He emphasises the depth and uniqueness of their love by using such religious phrases as 'profanation of our joys' and 'to tell the laity'. Theirs is a love that is wonderfully special and should not involve others. In the light of this intensity it seems odd that he should be advising her to meet their death with 'no tear-floods, nor sigh-tempests'.

The third stanza makes no attempt to resolve this difficulty. Donne seems to deliberately leave the personal and move to the impersonal. He comments on the custom, popular since classical times, of viewing natural occurrences, such as earthquakes, as signs or portents. He sweeps the focus of the poem up into the skies to see the 'trepidation of the spheres', the very planets moving. Gradually this image connects with those in the opening two stanzas: the death of 'virtuous men', Donne's desire for the two lovers to 'melt', and now the 'trepidation of the spheres'. Each of these images is centred on the idea of movement, movement that is profoundly important but is nevertheless a gentle, quiet and 'innocent' movement.

Donne continues his astronomical imagery in the fourth stanza with his reference to 'sublunary lover's love'. This is the type of love that 'the laity' experience. It is a narrow, earthbound type of love that is dependent on physical presence, a love that cannot endure 'absence'. At this point we begin to realise that Donne is not concerned with death in a physical sense but in an emotional sense.

From the fifth stanza on, Donne slowly reveals the reason for his 'valediction'. He expands on the love he shares with his beloved. It is quite unlike that of the 'sublunary lovers'. It has been 'refined', purified, so that all impurities have been removed. Their love is not confined by physical nearness, the presence of 'eyes, lips, and hands': they have achieved an 'inter-assured' love that is founded on connection of the mind rather than of the body. They are able to be careless of the physical presence of each other because they are so confident in each other.

The sixth stanza reaffirms the special quality of their love. Donne has described it as something close to a religious experience, a moving of planets, a shared emotion without imperfections. Now he draws all these images together to represent theirs as a relationship of 'two souls', where a parting, reluctant though it is, is nothing more than 'an expansion'. The central theme of the poem is revealed. Donne and his beloved must face a separation. He is trying to comfort her, to stop her mourning as if it were a death. For, he tells her, physical separation takes their 'refined' love and refines it still further, so that they achieve a connection of exquisite pureness, 'like gold to aery thinness beat.'

These interwoven images of a perfect love are breathtaking; and yet they are not enough for Donne. He has to go beyond the poetically expected, to explore a dimension of imagery that is neither expected nor accepted. He takes the concept of 'connection' and searches for a way to express it further. In the final three stanzas of the poem he rejects the traditional, the quickly recognised, the easily understood, and finds the world of science. For him, the essence of their relationship is captured by the 'twin compasses'. Just as this instrument of measurement is made up of two metal legs joined at a point, so Donne and his beloved are connected in separation. In Donne's case he is the 'foot' that 'far doth roam,' while his beloved is the 'fixed foot' that 'leans, and hearkens after it'. They are mutually dependent, while being independent. So, Donne can declare that she is the certainty in his life; her 'firmness' ensures that his direction is true, and it is she to whom he will return, just as the compasses must inevitably meet together, 'and makes me end, where I begun'. He reassures his beloved that there is no need for her to mourn this separation, because for them it is no separation at all.

Alternatively

In 1837 Henry Hallam wrote of Donne's poetry: 'Few are good for much; the conceits have not even the merit of being intelligible. . . .' This poem is not only confused, it is also confusing. Donne wanders around the early part of the piece in a kind of intellectual haze. Then, in the later part, he pulls out the conceit of the pair of compasses, rather as a bad magician pulls out a bunch of flowers from a pot. There is no real sense to the trick, but it might just impress the audience!

The Dreame

Text of poem: New Explorations Anthology page 14

The idea of the poet's beloved appearing to him while he is dreaming or daydreaming originated in Classical poetry. It was taken up by Renaissance poets and became a very popular topic. Donald Guss holds the view that Donne was in a direct line of influence from the Renaissance: 'Donne sometimes expresses dramatic emotions through the gallant conceits of the Petrarchans.'

Metre

Donne's approach to metre has been the subject of much debate. Though he frequently employed *iambic pentameter* (each line having five stressed and five unstressed syllables), it is generally agreed that the reading of his poetry is controlled more by the sense of the words than by their metre. Coleridge commented on the poetry of Donne that 'In poems where the writer thinks, and expects the reader to do so, the sense must be understood to ascertain the metre.' This view was echoed by Joan Bennett when she wrote: 'Often the rhythm is as intricate as the thought and only reveals itself when the emphasis has been carefully distributed according to the sense.' Any personalised consideration of 'The Dreame' should include an analysis of the way in which Donne links sense and metre to achieve a deceptively natural rhythm.

A reading of the poem

As we have seen, Donne's poetry frequently begins with a moment of drama, where the reader is swept into the piece by a dramatic statement. So, in 'The Flea' we read:

> Mark but this flea, and mark in this,
> How little that which thou deny'st me is . . .

Similarly, with 'Sweetest Love, I Do Not Go':

> Sweetest love, I do not go,
> For weariness of thee . . .

And, perhaps the most dramatic of all openings, that of 'The Sun Rising':

> Busy old fool, unruly sun . . .

However, with 'The Dreame' we encounter a slightly different opening technique. The theatrical statement gives way to a remark that is immediately and intensely intimate and, in many ways, even more dramatic. It is as if we have chanced upon Donne at his most open, caught him in those unguarded seconds between sleep and wakefulness. The very rhythm and sounds of the words in the first two lines of the poem are filled with an unexpected gentleness and emotional vulnerability. Donne tells his beloved that she acted 'wisely' in waking him. His lack of irritation at being disturbed is in marked contrast to the last time we saw Donne being awakened, in 'The Sun Rising'. He speaks to his 'dear love' in a quiet and familiar way, welcoming her arrival. His comment that she 'brok'st not' his dream, but rather continued it, is touching in its sincerity. This Donne is certainly not playing at the game of love. He tells her that she is 'so true' that she makes 'dreams truths, and fables histories'; she embodies the idealised perfection of the worlds of dreams and fairy stories. His invitation to her to 'enter these arms' is a million miles away from his attempt in 'The Flea' to entice his lover to yield to him. A desire to possess and dominate has given way to a longing for mutual submission, for them to finish his dream, to 'act the rest.'

This intense intimacy continues in the second stanza. He tells her that she did not wake him by the noise of her movement, but by the light of her eyes. Here Donne expresses a common feeling among lovers, where a meeting of eyes can have the power to set hearts fluttering and pulses racing. He is so aware of her that her very presence is enough to wake him. The level of their closeness becomes even more apparent as the poem continues. Donne tells her that he thought she was 'an angel', adding with a moving vulnerability that he is telling the truth because she 'lov'st truth'. This is not the Donne who used amusing flattery as an aid to seduction. This relationship is much too serious for anything but the truth; it is based on the certainty of mutual understanding, emotional empathy and a sharing of thoughts. It is no wonder that Donne uses the religious words 'angel' and 'profane' in an effort to convey just how special it is.

In the final stanza Donne gradually becomes more wakeful. He now begins to 'doubt'. On one level, this doubting is simply a question whether his beloved is actually there or not. However, on a deeper level it is indicative of the terrible inner doubt that Donne experienced in all aspects of his life, but particularly when it came to love. Previously, when he did not truly love he had been able to hide this doubt beneath sparklingly witty comments. Now that he does love he must lay his soul bare. He is embarrassed by his own insecurity, admitting that the strength of his love is equalled by the strength of his fear. He speaks for all lovers who know the wonder of truly loving and the terror that it will all suddenly disappear. His beloved is as a light in the overwhelming darkness, with her 'lightning' eyes and her ability to know his heart and his thoughts. She comes into his dream 'to kindle,' to set him on fire with her presence. But even more than that, there is a sense that Donne felt she had come to kindle his very life, to light up the gnawing darkness in his soul that craved some certainty.

The poem closes with an expression of the complexity of Donne's emotions. He longs to return to 'dream that hope again' with such intensity that if he cannot do so he will die. This is more than poetic over-dramatisation, or the role of the charmingly pathetic lover. Instead it is an admission of dependence: he needs to experience true love again, he needs to be close to his beloved, he needs to feel that certainty.

Alternatively
Mario Praz felt that Donne's 'sole preoccupation is with the whole effect'. In this poem Donne simply reproduces a popular poetic device so that he can, once again, display himself. For him, the 'whole effect' of this piece rests on his willingness to be the centre of attention, to describe and analyse his emotional viewpoint. To this end he sacrifices coherent structure, disciplined metre and intellectual resolution. It is undeniable that the 'whole effect' of this piece is impressive, but it is equally undeniable that it is based on a structure of shifting sands.

Batter my heart

Text of poem: New Explorations Anthology page 16

As always with Donne, the dating of this poem is the subject of much debate. Some critics like to view Donne's poetic output as occurring in two phases, which represent two distinct parts of his life. The first phase is that of his youth and marriage and traces his growth from a young man desiring adventure and romantic conquests to a mature man, who shares a deep love with his wife but is profoundly frustrated with his position in life. The second phase is seen as occurring in his later life, after his ordination and his wife's death, when Donne gave himself up to his new religion but was still tormented by doubt.

In this scheme the three sonnets 'Batter My Heart', 'At the Round Earth's Imagined Corners' and 'Thou Hast Made Me' would be seen as belonging to the second phase, while the other seven poems under consideration would belong to the first phase.

However, this is a rather simplistic view of both Donne's life and his poetry. Life is not lived in distinct phases, and poetry is more than just a rhyming diary of day-to-day events. Donne was a highly intelligent and complex man, who was fully aware of the limitations of the human condition and the profound uncertainty of existence. His life was spent in a continuous search for some evidence of certainty in the many aspects of his experience. The world of love and the world of religion were always present in the world of John Donne, as was the world of poetry. His poetry was not written for financial gain, since it was rarely published, nor was it stimulated solely by the desire for notoriety, since Donne frequently expressed embarrassment about his writing. Rather, he wrote poetry because he had no choice but to write poetry. It was his way of confronting the worlds that he inhabited. Poetry enabled him to express the very turmoil and desires of his soul, and the soul does not exist in phases.

A reading of the poem

This sonnet in many ways condenses a number of the aspects of Donne's earlier poetry into a tight, fourteen-line structure and a rigorous rhyming scheme of *abba, abba, cdcdee.* It begins with the usual dramatic opening – indeed it is an opening that is spectacularly dramatic. The implied paradox of the 'three-personed God', the representation of the spiritual, being called upon to physically 'batter' Donne's heart, is both stunning and shocking. Before we can recover from it Donne launches us into a list of breathtaking verbs: 'knock, breathe, shine . . . rise, and stand, o'erthrow me . . . bend . . . break, blow, burn . . .' We are left gasping by this combination of action images, the conflict suggested in the paradox 'that I may rise, and stand, o'erthrow me,' and his clever use of the alliterative *'b'*. The first quatrain of this sonnet is a challenge not only to God but also to us, the readers.

In the second quatrain, Donne sustains this drama and intensity. He sweeps us into a wonderful conceit, comparing himself to a 'usurped town'. This combination of images to suggest Donne's dilemma enables us to understand intellectually and to empathise emotionally. It is the metaphysical conceit at its very best. Donne is betrayed by reason, God's 'viceroy', and without this support he is unable to surrender himself totally to God. He longs for God, the source of certainty, to dominate him, rather in the way that he hoped his lover might desire his domination in 'The Flea'.

The final six lines of the sonnet, the *sestet,* begin with a change in tone, though the content links to the previous quatrain. The city under siege was a common image in courtly love poetry for the woman who was reluctant to yield to her lover's advances. Violence and frenzied activity give way to courtly phrasing and language. Donne declares his intentions to God: 'Yet dearly I love you, and would be loved fain.' His confession that he is 'betrothed' to God's enemy is filled with the submissiveness and reluctance of the courtly lady; it is as if Donne has changed not only his religion but also his sex. He is trying to communicate his human vulnerability in the face of God's overwhelming power by drawing on the image of the female figure being overwhelmed by her lover's passion. It is a subtle and complex combination of images and ideas, a conceit that is both vivid and unsettling.

Donne develops the image in the following line, where he asks God to free him: 'Divorce me, untie, or break that knot again.' As his sense of fear and panic increases, so his imagery begins to intensify. He begs God to 'Take me to you, imprison me.' He concentrates all his desperation into the paradox: '. . . for I | Except you enthral me, never shall be free.'

Finally, driven to the very edge of his emotions, he grasps at a paradox that is profoundly shocking and deeply disturbing: 'Nor ever chaste, except you ravish me.' We are left reeling from this image and his total disregard for the conventional 'niceties' of expression. Does it represent Donne at his very best, or at his very worst? Only you can decide.

Alternatively

A. J. Smith commented on Donne's poetry: 'There is a calculated offence to decorum in the interests of truth.' Is this true for 'Batter My Heart'? Does Donne shock us in order to make us think? Or is it simply that his search for new and exciting combinations of ideas sometimes led him into lapses of good taste? Is there a place for decorum and good taste in the world of poetry? Or are they only restrictions imposed by those who are afraid to think?

At the round earth's imagined corners

Text of poem: New Explorations Anthology page 18

Background

See the notes on 'Batter my heart', pages 27–29.

Style

Donne's decision to write some of his poetry in *sonnet* form placed a number of restrictions on his writing. His poem had to consist of fourteen lines, as that is the required length of a sonnet. In addition, the Petrarchan form of the sonnet involved the creation of two parts to the poem, the *octet* and the *sestet*. The octet, which comes first, consists of eight lines, the sestet of six lines. A strict rhyming scheme is used to mark the two parts: for the octet *abba, abba,* for the sestet *cdcdee*. It is obvious that this rhyming scheme is quite complicated, and it requires a lot of effort to ensure that the sense and mood of the sonnet fit into the rhyming scheme successfully.

Generally, the octet describes a situation, while the sestet presents a meditation on or a reaction to the octet. The change in rhyme between the octet and the sestet is often mirrored by a similar change in the mood and tone of the poem. The final rhyming couplet, which forms part of the sestet, usually expresses the main theme of the sonnet.

A reading of the poem

Donne daringly uses a paradox to open this sonnet. His image of the 'round earth's imagined corners' is at once completely illogical, since something round has no corners, and wonderfully descriptive, in that it conveys a sense of boundless expanse. Indeed the quatrain creates a scene that is the poetic equivalent of 'Cinemascope'. Rather like the legendary director Cecil B. de Mille, Donne uses a cast of thousands to populate his magnificent backdrop. Angels fill the heavens, and 'numberless infinities' of souls go in search of their 'scattered bodies'. Behind all this activity, heavenly 'trumpets' ring out a clarion call of triumph. For this is a description of triumph: it represents the triumph over death of those saved by God. On the promised Day of Judgment, the souls who have inhabited Heaven may return to their bodies to embark on a life that will stretch to eternity.

The second quatrain expands this concept. Donne uses the device of the 'list' to communicate a feeling of multitudes and to emphasise just how total this triumph over death is. No matter what the cause of death is, whether 'flood', 'fire', 'war, dearth, age, agues, tyrannies,' or 'Despair, law, chance,' those who believe in God are guaranteed eternal life, while those who are alive on the Day of Judgment, provided they believe, can join in this transition to eternal existence 'and never taste death's woe.' This promise of eternal life was a powerful one in an age when death was a real presence in everyday life; but to attain it there had to be a complete act of faith, and it is this that Donne finds difficult.

In one sweeping movement, Donne shifts the focus of his sonnet away from the swarming Earth and the crowded heavens to himself. His concern for the dead – 'But let them sleep, Lord' – may sound compassionate, but it is founded on purely selfish reasons. Donne asks God to put off the Day of Judgment, quite simply because he is afraid. He is afraid that he has so many sins that he has not yet truly repented for them all. He is afraid that he is spiritually unprepared to face the Day of Judgment. Since he understands that ''tis late to ask abundance of thy grace' when he is facing God, he begs God to show him how to repent 'here on this lowly ground'.

Donne knows that the key to his salvation is repentance, and being Donne, he is equally aware of the fact that he is finding it difficult to repent sincerely, because he still doubts the certainty of God. He outlines his predicament with an unswerving honesty to God. If God can help him, Donne knows that he will be saved, just as surely as a condemned man will escape execution by the monarch placing his seal upon a document of pardon. But in Donne's case the seal is absolute, because it will be made not of wax but of blood, the blood of God. Perhaps at last Donne is beginning to grasp the ultimate certainty, or perhaps he is once again simply trying to persuade himself that there is a certainty.

Alternatively
'Donne elaborates and decorates at the expense of theme, sometimes so far that he displaces it altogether' (Michael Schmidt). Is this sonnet an uneasy combination of vivid description and confused intellectualisation? Does Donne become carried away by his own creativity to such an extent that he loses his theme completely? Is Donne claiming to be concerned with repentance and spiritual salvation when all the time he is really interested only in his own descriptive powers?

Thou hast made me

Text of poem: New Explorations Anthology page 20

Religious exploration seems to have played a continuing role in Donne's life. Long before his decision to change his religion he was concerned with forging a personal and independent religious philosophy. This was, perhaps, just another aspect of his quest for certainty that arose from his uncompromising intellectualisation of the experience of human existence. Izaak Walton, probably influenced by Donne himself, characterises Donne's religious struggle as the central force in his life. But this is really only a reflection of Donne's own desire to minimise the importance of his earlier, less religious work.

Whatever their motivation, Donne's religious poems convey the intense religious debate that raged not just within his mind, but also within his very soul. Some critics have suggested that Donne's approach to this debate was influenced by the spiritual exercises of Ignatius Loyola, the founder of the Jesuit order. Given Donne's early education and his family connections with the Jesuits, it is likely that he was familiar with Loyola's work. These exercises encouraged the individual to develop an intensely personal and emotional relationship with God through 'conversations' that were founded on inner debate and private reflection.

STYLE

Coleridge wrote of Donne's poetry: 'We find the most fantastic out-of-the-way thoughts, but in the most pure and genuine mother English . . . .' This sonnet is a wonderful illustration of this comment. Within the strict structural confines of the Petrarchan sonnet (fourteen lines, rhyming scheme, octet and sestet) Donne presents his complex spiritual struggle in a language that is both natural and simple. He is able to communicate the agonising dilemma he faces and the real terror in his soul in such a profound way that it comes as something of a shock to realise that he has written only fourteen lines.

A READING OF THE POEM

The dramatic opening that Donne has used so successfully in all his poetry, both secular and religious, becomes in this sonnet an expression of the essence of his emotional and spiritual turmoil. In one line he captures all the anguished questioning that haunts his soul: 'Thou hast made me, and shall thy work decay?' His lifelong quest for certainty is distilled into this one devastatingly simple question to God. He has left behind the intellectual gymnastics that occupied him in his youth. For Donne those bright, brittle days are past. Now his poetry has a personal intensity that is uncompromising and unaffected.

His description of the state of his life is stunning: 'mine end doth haste'. In an image that is both vivid and disturbing he conveys just what this 'haste' is like: 'I run to death, and death meets me as fast.' There is an inescapable inevitability about this line and a suggestion of a strange intimacy. Rather like two lovers irresistibly drawn together, Donne and Death move towards each other. Donne is completely focused on this inescapable meeting. All his previous life fades away in the face of this ultimate moment: 'all my pleasures are like yesterday'. It is no wonder that Donne's request to God, 'Repair me now,' vibrates with urgency. The time for clever intellectual tricks is over.

The second quatrain maintains this intensity. We see Donne poised, frozen with terror, between despair and death. The inner vision of his soul becomes, for him, a frail rope to cling to in his desperation: 'I dare not move my dim eyes any way.' But his horror increases as he realises that his 'feeble flesh doth waste', that the very hands that grasp this rope, the very eyes that focus on the safe horizon, are rotting away. His physical self, that body that in his youth had seemed to hold the certainty he craved, is now a dead weight, putrefying with sin, which drags him down 'towards hell'.

There is only one means of escape for Donne: his total faith in God. It is a terrible irony that the man who spent his life searching for certainty in the world outside himself should come to understand that the ultimate certainty could only be found within his own soul. The pure existence of God is not the answer; it is Donne's ability to believe in that pure existence that is the final solution. If he is empowered by God, given the strength to focus his 'dim eyes' so that he 'can look,' his state instantly alters. The dead weight melts away and he begins to 'rise again'. But he has to have the faith that God will empower him. Donne sways on the brink of this 'leap of faith'. Doubt, the weapon of their 'old subtle foe', the Devil, constantly tempts him. Doubt has for him such a terrible attraction that he cannot hold himself focused for even 'one hour'. In desperation, he pleads with God to help him escape. God's grace will release him from this terrible struggle, the weight dragging him down will fall away, and like a bird he will fly from the clutches of the Devil's art. God's grace will draw him onwards and upwards as smoothly and as irresistibly as a magnet attracts iron. It is an image of wonderful ease and beautiful certainty. Sadly for Donne, who had lived his life driven by the urge to intellectualise and rationalise, the action of a magnet can be scientifically proved, while the redeeming grace of God depends solely on an unscientific and profoundly irrational act of faith.

Alternatively
William Hazlitt commented on the metaphysical poets: 'The complaint so often made, and here repeated, is not of the want of power in these men, but of the waste of it; not of the absence of genius, but the abuse of it.' Is this the truth that lay behind John Donne? He frittered away his incisive intellect on glittering verses to entertain the crowd; he used his literary skills in a calculated attempt to grasp the trappings of wealth and power. For him, poetic genius was no more than a convenient tool of manipulation. It was a way to make life easier. He used his poetry for seduction, he used his poetry for self-glorification, and finally he used his poetry as a short cut to salvation.

Developing a personal reaction to John Donne

1. Why do you think John Donne wrote poetry?
2. Was his poetry based on the intellect, or on the emotions, or on a combination of the two?
3. What does the term 'metaphysical' stand for? Can John Donne be classed as a metaphysical poet?
4. What is a conceit? How is it used in Donne's poetry? Do you feel that the conceit is a successful poetic device?
5. What themes recur in Donne's poetry? What do they tell you about John Donne himself? Do you think he was a likeable man?
6. How did Donne use traditional poetic devices and structures in his work?
7. What is your reaction to the type of language and rhythms found in

Donne's poetry? Are they appealing to a modern reader?

8. Consider what aspects of Donne's poetry appeal to you and what aspects you find unappealing.

9. Has the work of John Donne anything to say to a twenty-first-century reader?

10. Do you think you will ever return to Donne's poetry, or will you be glad to leave it all behind?

Questions

1. Read 'The Flea', then answer the following questions.

   (*a*) (i) What impression of Donne's attitude to love emerges for you from your reading of this poem?

   (ii) Choose *two* phrases from the poem that especially convey that impression, and comment on your choices.

   (*b*) (i) Why does Donne introduce the flea into his poem?

   (ii) How does Donne's lover react to what he says? Support your answer by reference to the words of the poem.

   (*c*) Answer *one* of the following questions:

   (i) How would you describe Donne's tone in this poem? What words or phrases in the poem convey this tone?

   (ii) Would you write such a poem to a person you loved? Explain your view by reference to the words of the poem.

   (iii) Donne seems to have read a great many of his poems aloud to a small group. Choose *two lines or phrases* from this poem that you feel would have caused a reaction among the group, and explain what that reaction might have been in each case.

2. Read 'Song: Go Catch a Falling Star', then answer the following questions.

   (*a*) (i) What do you think is the point of this poem? (ii) Choose *two phrases* from the poem that especially convey this point to you, and comment on your choices.

   (*b*) What have all the strange tasks got to do with the theme of the poem? Illustrate your view by close reference to the text.

   (*c*) Answer *one* of the following questions:

   (i) How does the pattern of the lines in this poem emphasise what

Donne is saying? Support your view by referring to the words of the poem.

(ii) What is the mood of this poem? Refer closely to the text.

(iii) What part does rhyme play in this poem? Explain your answer by reference to the poem.

3. 'Donne's poetry represents an attempt to connect emotions with mental concepts.' Discuss this view, supporting your answer by quotation from or reference to the poems you have studied.

4. 'Donne's deliberate avoidance of poetic language gives his poetry a sense of realism.' In your reading of Donne's poetry, did you find this to be true? Support your answer by reference to or quotation from the poems on your course.

5. 'John Donne: A Personal Response.' Using this title, write an essay on the poetry of Donne, supporting your points by quotation from or reference to the poems on your course.

6. 'Underlying Donne's poetry is a unity of experience that is not immediately apparent.' Discuss this view, supporting your answer by quotation from or reference to the poems you have studied.

7. 'Donne's poetry is generally unpleasant and occasionally disgusting.' Give your response to this point of view, with supporting quotation from or reference to the poems on your course.

8. 'The poetry of Donne is a continuous commentary on the world and on himself.' In your reading of Donne's poetry, did you find this to be true? Support your answer by reference to or quotation from the poems you have studied.

9. 'Though Donne rejected the traditional poetry of his time, he was still greatly influenced by it.' Discuss this view, supporting your answer by quotation from or reference to the poetry on your course.

10. 'The tone of Donne's poetry is often unclear, and as a result the reactions it provokes can be confused.' Give your response to this point of view, with supporting quotation from or reference to the poems on your course.

Bibliography

Bennett, Joan, *Four Metaphysical Poets: Donne, Herbert, Vaughan, Crashaw* (second edition), Cambridge: Cambridge University Press 1953.

Carey, John, *John Donne: Life, Mind and Art,* London: Faber and Faber 1983.

Carey, John (editor), *John Donne: Selected Poetry,* Oxford: Oxford University Press 1998.

Everett, Barbara, *Donne: A London Poet,* London: Oxford University Press 1972.

Gardner, Helen (editor), *John Donne: A Collection of Critical Essays,* Englewood Cliffs (NJ): Prentice-Hall 1962.

Garrod, Heathcote William, *Poetry and Prose of John Donne,* London: Oxford University Press 1972.

Hamilton, Ian, *Keepers of the Flame,* London: Pimlico 1993.

Nutt, Joe, *John Donne: The Poems,* London: Macmillan 1999.

Schmidt, Michael, *Lives of the Poets,* London: Phoenix 1999.

Tamblin, Ronald, *A Preface to T. S. Eliot,* Harlow (Middx): Pearson Education 1988.

Walton, Izaak, *Walton's Lives,* London: Methuen 1895.

Wedgwood, C., *Seventeenth-Century English Literature* (second edition), London: Oxford University Press 1970.

2 *Robert* FROST

Marie Dunne

A literary life

Robert Lee Frost was born in San Francisco on 26 March 1874. He was a sickly child and received his early education at home. Though pampered by his protective mother, he was often harshly disciplined by his violent and drunken father. In 1885 his father died, following a long illness, leaving his family penniless. Robert moved with his younger sister, Jeannie, and his mother to Lawrence, Massachusetts, where his grandparents lived. His mother found employment in nearby schools, and the two children began their formal education in her class.

Robert entered Lawrence High School in 1888. He chose the classical curriculum: Latin, Greek, ancient and European history, and mathematics. During his final year he fell in love with a classmate, Elinor White. They married on 19 December 1895, when he was twenty-one and she was twenty-three. After finishing secondary school, Frost went to Dartmouth College, but he left in 1893, halfway through his first year. He taught his mother's senior class for several months until the term ended, then took a variety of low-paid jobs in a woollen mill, as a rural schoolteacher, and as a newspaper reporter. In September 1897 Frost entered Harvard University, but again left without a degree.

When he returned home he was encouraged by his doctor to become a farmer, in order to improve his health. At first in New Hampshire and later in Vermont he lived on small farms where the work – mowing, making hay, and apple-picking – was done by hand. He wrote his poems at night. Many years later he recalled his favourite activities as being 'mowing with a scythe, chopping with an axe, and writing with a pen'.

A WORKING LIFE

Neither farming nor poetry earned Frost enough money to support his wife and four children; so, at the age of thirty-two, he was forced to seek regular paid employment. A pastor of the First Congregational Church suggested to him that he should apply for a vacancy at Pinkerton Academy in Derry Village. A trustee of the academy told him he would be employed if one of his poems were read at the banquet of the Men's League of the Congregational Church. Frost submitted 'The Tuft of Flowers'. It was well received and secured him the position. He taught English, Latin, history and geometry, coached the debating team, advised the school newspaper and assisted with athletics. Exhausted by his workload, he moved from the academy in 1911 and became a lecturer in the teacher training college in New Hampshire.

A literary education

Frost devoted his free time to reading the major poets. He studied their diction, their imagery and their formal techniques in order to perfect his own writing. His work was heavily influenced by his classical education. The concise language, concentrated images and clarity of thought in his poems reflect this training, while his knowledge of strict classical metre allowed him to write with confidence in traditional forms. Biblical references reflect his early scripture studies.

Other influences on his work include Shakespeare, the English Romantics (Wordsworth, Keats and Shelley), and the Victorian poets (Hardy, Kipling and Browning). He followed the principles laid down in Wordsworth's 'Preface to the Lyrical Ballads' concerning the language, people, places and events appropriate to poetry. Like Wordsworth, he relied on incidents from 'common life' and discovered in them 'the primary laws of our nature'. He agreed with Wordsworth that these events should be described in 'language really used by men'. In his own poems he attempted to reproduce as accurately as possible the tone and modulations of the spoken word. 'Wordsworth was right,' he commented, 'in trying to reproduce in his poetry not only the words . . . actually used in common speech . . . but their sound.' He believed that rhymes should be unforced and natural, although, unlike many of his contemporaries, he refused to abandon the rules of poetry to achieve this effect. 'The most important thing about a poem . . . is how wilfully, gracefully, naturally, entertainingly and beautifully its rhymes are,' he wrote in 1939. He wanted the rhythm in his verse to spring from the tension that occurs when a strong rhythmic pattern based on iambic metre is played against the irregularity of ordinary speech. He repeatedly stressed the importance of the living voice, 'the rise and fall, the stressed pauses and little hurries, of spoken language', and insisted that the tone of voice added to the meaning of words in the poems.

Frost found modernist poetry unappealing and wrote instead about pre-industrial values, rural life, and nature. Yet there is nothing sentimental in his work: the world portrayed in his poetry can be bleak, lonely, chilled, blighted and deadly. Acknowledging this, Frost once said: 'There's plenty to be dark about, you know. It's full of darkness.'

First publications

For a long time Frost had difficulty finding a publisher. Partly as a result of this the Frost family decided to emigrate from America to England in 1912, and they settled at Beaconsfield, near London. Frost arranged his lyrical poems in book form and then sought a publisher. The collection called *A Boy's Will* appeared in April 1913; his second book, *North of Boston,* came out a year later. The books were widely praised, and Frost was quickly introduced into literary circles in London, where he met W. B. Yeats and Ezra Pound. He was very pleased when Yeats told Pound that *A Boy's Will* was 'the best thing that had come out of America for some time'.

A Boy's Will introduces the natural elements Frost would use in many future poems: stars, clouds, leaves, pools, brooks, flowers and birds. *North of Boston,* written between 1905 and 1913, saw a shift of emphasis from man as a solitary creature to man as a social being. Though he called it 'This Book of People', many characters in *North of Boston* experience a deep sense of loneliness. With his second publication Frost clearly indicated that, like the English poet Thomas Hardy, he would concentrate on the regional.

Frost is a New England poet. His previous experiences in low-paid jobs and on farms gave him an intimate knowledge of ordinary people living ordinary lives. His work expresses the value he placed on rural life, practical experience and the independence of the individual.

Return to America

Frost returned to America after the outbreak of the First World War; there he wrote his next book, *Mountain Interval,* which contains some of his best-known poems, including 'Birches', 'Out, Out –', and 'The Road Not Taken'. His characteristic themes of isolation, fear, sudden violence and death are all apparent here.

The favourable reviews *Mountain Interval* received strengthened Frost's reputation. He bought a farm in New Hampshire and supported his family by teaching, readings and lectures, as well as royalties from his books. In January 1917 he was made professor of English at Amherst College, Massachusetts. By 1920 he could afford to move to Vermont and devote himself to writing poetry and apple-farming. Following his fourth publication, *New Hampshire* (1923), Frost was awarded the Pulitzer Prize. He received the award four times in all: in 1924, 1931, 1937 and 1943. His fifth volume of poems, *West-Running Brook,* containing 'Spring Pools' and 'Acquainted with the Night', came out in 1928.

Sadly, Frost's personal life was as unhappy as his public life was successful. His sister Jeannie was committed to a mental hospital, where she remained until her death in 1929. His wife's health began to deteriorate rapidly. His eldest daughter, Lesley, who had dropped out of university and divorced her husband, angrily blamed her father for her problems. His favourite child, Marjorie, had a nervous breakdown and by 1930 developed tuberculosis; she died in 1934, aged twenty-nine, leaving a husband and baby girl. Irma, his third daughter, suffered from mental illness and, like Lesley, blamed all her problems on Frost.

Despite this turmoil, Frost produced *A Further Range* in 1936; it contains 'Provide, Provide' and 'Design'. Here he displayed his technical skills. Within this volume there is satire and comedy, the lyric, ballad, epigram, historical narrative and dramatic monologue.

Teaching, public appearances, interviews and readings kept him busy until tragedy struck again. On 20 March 1938 Elinor died from a heart attack. Unable to cope with her death, Frost left the funeral arrangements to Lesley; in a stormy scene she accused him of ruining her mother's life. Irma became permanently estranged from him, and his only surviving son, Carol, succumbed to deep depression. Frost was deeply upset. He turned to his friend, secretary and manager, Kay Morrison, for consolation. Disturbed by his mother's death and troubled by his father's relationship with Kay, worried by his wife's illness, a lack of money, and the belief that he was a failure, Carol committed suicide in 1940.

Frost looked to poetry to save him from despair. Many of his new poems were written for Kay, expressing his love for her. *A Witness Tree* (1942) won him his fourth Pulitzer Prize. His eighth volume, *Steeple Bush,* was published in May 1947 and is dedicated to his six grandchildren. Having held academic positions already in the University of Michigan, Harvard University and Dartmouth College, Frost returned to Amherst College from 1949 to 1963.

The final years

In his final years Frost enjoyed public acclaim. He travelled as a celebrated visitor to Brazil, Peru, England, Israel, Greece, Russia and Ireland. He had paid his first visit to Dublin in 1928, when he spent five pleasant days in the company of his friends, the writers Pádraic Colum and George Russell. Colum and Russell took him to a reception where he met Yeats once again. He returned to Ireland in June 1957 to receive an honorary degree from the National University of Ireland, presented by the Taoiseach, Éamon de Valera, who was chancellor of the university. In 1961 he was invited to recite 'The Gift Outright' at the inauguration of President John F. Kennedy, watched on television by sixty million people. On his eighty-eighth birthday, in 1962, he was awarded the Congressional Gold Medal; in the same year he published his final volume, *In the Clearing.* On 29 January 1963, two months before his eighty-ninth birthday, Frost died in a Boston hospital.

Principal volumes of poetry	**Poems for study**
A Boy's Will (1913)	'The Tuft of Flowers'
North of Boston (1914)	'Mending Wall'
	'After Apple-Picking'
Mountain Interval (1916)	'Birches'
	'Out, Out –'
	'The Road Not Taken'
New Hampshire (1923)	
West-Running Brook (1928)	'Spring Pools'
	'Acquainted with the Night'
A Further Range (1936)	'Design'
	'Provide, Provide'
A Witness Tree (1942)	
Steeple Bush (1947)	
In the Clearing (1962)	

The Tuft of Flowers

Text of poem: New Explorations Anthology page 90

A reading of the poem

'The Tuft of Flowers' introduces the themes that dominate much of Frost's poetry. These themes, developed as the narrative unfolds, include the passage of time, loneliness, communication, and the power of the imagination. The use of a first-person narrator makes the poem a more immediate and realistic experience; the reader is drawn into the poet's world and explores the themes 'as with his aid'.

The poem opens with the narrator setting out to turn the cut grass so that it will dry in the sun. In a scene reminiscent of the Romantic era, the speaker is depicted as a figure of isolation in the landscape. He searches in vain for the mower; 'But he had gone his way, the grass all mown.' The narrator concludes sadly that loneliness is intrinsic to the human condition, whether people work 'together or apart.' This marks the end of the first movement of the poem.

The second movement begins with the arrival of the butterfly who, like the speaker, is searching for something he cannot find. He flutters in confusion around the withered flowers on the ground and then returns to the poet, who prepares to continue with his work. The butterfly, however, draws his attention to the tuft of flowers beside the stream.

This leads us into the third movement. Unlike the other flowers, these have been spared by the mower, because he loved them. He left them to flourish on the bank 'from sheer morning gladness'.

In the final movement the poet examines the effect of this discovery. The flowers connect the mower and the narrator, who sees in them a 'message from the dawn'. Through the power of the imagination he is transported back through time to the early morning, when the birds sang as the scythe cut through the tall grasses. The speaker recognises in the mower 'a spirit kindred to my own' and can reach out across time and space to touch the thoughts of the absent labourer. This connection forces the speaker to revise his earlier opinion that humans are destined to be lonely and alone. Now he can confidently declare: 'Men work together – whether they work together or apart.'

The turning points in the poem are indicated by the use of the word 'but'. The speaker, who has eagerly sought the companionship of the mower, comes to the sad realisation

> But he had gone his way, the grass all mown,
> And I must be, as he had been, – alone.

Almost immediately he is joined by another creature.

> But as I said it, swift there passes me by
> On noiseless wings a bewildered butterfly.

He makes to turn away from the butterfly;

> But he turned first, and led my eye to look
> At a tall tuft of flowers beside a brook.

The narrator's mood undergoes a significant change as a result:

> But glad with him, I worked as with his aid.

A form of communication exists between the mower and the speaker; and the poem now ends with the consoling thought,

> Men work together – whether they work together or apart.

Imagery

The central image in the poem is the tuft of flowers called butterfly weed; Frost describes it as a 'leaping tongue of bloom'. The key word here is 'tongue', for the flowers 'speak' to him, bringing him a 'message from the dawn'. They enable him to hear the wakening birds and the whispering scythe. This message permits the speaker to commune imaginatively with the mower and hold 'brotherly speech' with him.

The mower with his long scythe is suggestive of the Grim Reaper. He cuts the grass, and possesses the power to kill the flowers or to spare them. He comes and goes silently and is never seen by mortal eyes. His power over life and death is contrasted with the helplessness of the butterfly on 'tremulous wing'. (Frost returned to the image of the flower, the moth and death in a later poem, 'Design'.) The mower should not be seen solely as a symbol of death: he is at the same time a farm labourer and a spiritual companion for the speaker, one with whom the speaker can communicate 'from the heart'.

Mending Wall

Text of poem: New Explorations Anthology page 94

This poem appeared in *North of Boston* (1914). During a reading, Frost explained that wall-mending was an occupation he used to follow. His neighbour was very particular every spring about repairing the boundary on their land. Frost never ceased to be amazed by the damage done to the wall during the winter; it reminded him of the line in St Matthew's gospel, 'There shall not be left here one stone upon another that shall not be thrown down.'

A READING OF THE POEM

In a note to the original edition of *North of Boston*, Frost stated that 'Mending Wall' considers the beliefs that separate men and takes up the theme where 'The Tuft of Flowers' laid it down. There are two characters in the poem, the narrator and his neighbour, who see the wall in very different ways. They are brought together to repair the damaged boundary in the spring. The poem opens on a mysterious note: some unidentified force exists that dislikes walls. The soft *'s'* sounds capture the sensation of the silently swelling ground that dislodges the stones. The broad vowels mimic the shape of the rounded boulders that roll off the wall, leaving *'o'* and *'u'*-shaped gaps behind.

Frost distinguishes between these unexplained gaps and those caused by the hunters. Of the gaps that he means, no-one 'has seen them made or heard them made . . .' In the spring the annual wall-repairing ritual occurs. Ironically, the narrator and his neighbour work together to maintain the boundary that separates them; they are unified by their divisions. It seems as if a magic formula is required to keep the stones in place. At first it is like a game. A more serious note is introduced when the need for the wall is questioned. Unable to provide a rational argument, the neighbour falls back on the proverb 'Good fences make good neighbours.' The narrator mischievously challenges this assumption. Borders wall things in, as well as blocking things out. They cause offence – a pun on the word 'fence'.

According to folklore, elves do not like walls or closed gates; but the speaker does not suggest this to his dourly practical neighbour. 'I'd rather he said it for himself.' The narrator wants the neighbour to reject the division, even imaginatively, for himself. He describes the man as 'an old-stone savage armed.' Not only is he working with stones but his attitudes are primitive, his beliefs have not evolved. He is as territorial as his Stone Age ancestors. He is armed not simply with stones but with dangerous, inflexible attitudes. His attitudes are unenlightened: 'he moves in darkness.' The neighbour, as dark and prickly as his pine trees, refuses to change sides. He sticks doggedly to 'his father's saying', repeating the proverb as proudly as if he had coined the phrase himself.

Balance

Frost always claimed he was not 'taking sides' in 'Mending Wall'. 'I've played exactly fair in it. Twice I say, "Good fences" and twice "Something there is" . . .' The tension between these two opposites is played out in the poem. With clear boundaries, each knows where his limits are, where he stands and what confines him; without a wall there is confusion and misunderstanding. Distance, like differences, can be good. This is one reason why the narrator informs the neighbour about the gaps, even though he later challenges him about the need to rebuild the wall.

The 'balancing act' Frost achieves between the arguments in the poem is mirrored in the image of the fallen stones:

> To each the boulders have fallen to each.
> . . . We have to use a spell to make them balance.

Frost presents strong arguments on both sides. However, it is slightly disingenuous for him to claim that there is complete impartiality in the poem. The 'something' that dislodges the boulders and swells the ground beneath the wall is, of course, frost heaving.

Themes

Frost explained that 'Mending Wall' is about boundaries. These boundaries can be physical, political, and psychological. The physical boundary in the poem is the stone wall. The two men repair the wall, working together to maintain their divisions.

We meet to walk the line
And set the wall between us once again.

Boundaries are often political in nature. In a discussion on 'Mending Wall' Frost once exclaimed: 'You can make it national or international.' Read in this way, the neighbours can be seen as representing different nationalities or cultures, separate yet coexisting peacefully, learning to respect their differences and co-operating to uphold them.

The psychological differences between the two men are perhaps the most striking. The narrator seems more open to change, willing to challenge accepted practices ('Why do they make good neighbours?'), humorous ('Spring is the mischief in me . . .'), more imaginative ('I could say "Elves" to him . . .') than his conservative neighbour. The narrator realises that sometimes 'we do not need a wall', but this notion meets with firm resistance: 'He will not go behind his father's saying.' His neighbour is a traditionalist and stands behind received wisdom with the same tenacity as he stands behind the stone wall.

Structure

The poem moves through three stages. The first phase is largely descriptive. Frost distinguishes between the gaps in the wall, those created by the unseen force and those made by hunters. In the second phase he introduces the neighbour and explains how the two men work to rebuild the wall. In the third and final phase he contrasts the attitudes of the men. The narrator is portrayed as mischievous, imaginative, progressive and questioning, while the neighbour is depicted as 'an old-stone savage armed,' conservative, lacking originality, staid, accepting and repetitive.

After Apple-Picking

Text of poem: New Explorations Anthology page 96

A reading of the poem

'After Apple-Picking' is a complex poem. At a surface level it can be read as a nature poem, like Keats's 'Ode to Autumn' – a celebration of the natural abundance of the harvest. At the same time it dwells on the languor of the weary harvester and can be compared to 'Ode to a Nightingale', with its lethargic mood and sensuous imagery. At a deeper level it can be read as a study of the creative process.

The orchard is described at the outset. The harvest is over. The air, heavy with the scent of mature apples, has a sensual, almost narcotic effect on the apple-picker. The long vowel sounds, the irregular rhyming scheme, the slow tempo and incantatory rhythm suggest that the repetitive work has lulled him into a semi-conscious state. (The word 'sleep' appears six times in the poem.) The speaker, like Keats in 'Ode to a Nightingale', sinks into a drowsy numbness. This suspension of consciousness releases his imagination. He enters a visionary state conducive to artistic creativity:

> I am drowsing off.
> I cannot rub the strangeness from my sight
> I got from looking through a pane of glass
> I skimmed this morning from the drinking trough.

In this dream-like state he evokes the sensuousness of the harvest. He can smell the 'scent of apples', see 'magnified apples appear and disappear,' feel 'the ladder sway' and hear the 'rumbling sound' of the fruit as it is loaded. The repeated sound patterns in the language used capture the sensuousness of the experience:

> There were ten thousand thousand fruit to touch,
> Cherish in hand, lift down, and not let fall.

Art cannot permanently transform life; the visionary state cannot be sustained for long. Frost accepts the transitory nature of the experience. Like the sheet of ice, 'it melted and I let it fall and break.' The creative effort has left him physically and mentally exhausted.

> I am overtired
> Of the great harvest I myself desired.

The creative mood disappears and he slips into sleep, long, dark and deep, as experienced by the hibernating woodchuck, or 'just some human sleep.' He has climbed down from the visionary heights, like the boy in 'Birches', and returned to earth.

Ways of seeing

Sight and insight are important issues in 'After Apple-Picking'. In the opening scene the speaker looks upwards towards Heaven and downwards to the barrel. This reflects the main movement in the poem, the ascent towards the visionary heights and the gradual descent to normality. The focus slips and becomes blurred when the speaker drowses off. He enters a semi-conscious state, neither awake nor asleep. Paradoxically, this releases his imagination and frees it from its sense-bound limitations. He now sees in a new way. The familiar becomes strange, transformed in a visionary world by his imagination. In this state his perspective changes, his perceptions intensify. The focus is sharpened and magnified. Even the smallest details on the apple are visible:

And every fleck of russet showing clear.

In his heightened state of consciousness he is doubly aware of every sensation.

My instep arch not only keeps the ache,
It keeps the pressure of a ladder-round.

This in turn leads to new insights and understanding.

One can see what will trouble this sleep of mine . . .

Finally, exhausted physically and mentally, he sinks into a long, natural sleep, his eyes closed, and he sees no more.

Mood

The poem describes the drift from consciousness to unconsciousness. The calm, peaceful mood in the opening lines is replaced by a sense of physical and mental exhaustion as the speaker becomes increasingly vague ('There may be,' 'upon some bough,' 'two or three'). The breakdown of the rhyming scheme and the repetition ('sleep' is mentioned six times, 'apple' or 'apples' seven times, 'I' sixteen times) reflect his weariness. It seems he is too tired to vary his vocabulary and maintain the discipline of a strict rhyming pattern.

The lethargic mood is reinforced through the use of long vowels and the slow, irregular rhythm. He enters a dream-like state, yet it is not without a feeling of unease. He is overtired and cannot escape the sensations of the day's work. There are moments of tension when he remembers the care required to prevent the fruit from falling:

For all
That struck the earth,
No matter if not bruised or spiked with stubble,
Went surely to the cider-apple heap
As of no worth.

The languid mood is re-established in the final lines, where the speaker approaches complete loss of consciousness.

The woodchuck could say whether it's like his
Long sleep, as I describe its coming on,
Or just some human sleep.

Birches

Text of poem: New Explorations Anthology page 99

A READING OF THE POEM

The poem begins with a description of the birches bending against a background of upright trees. Their movement inspires an imaginative response in the speaker: 'I like to think some boy's been swinging them.' These opening lines establish the tripartite structure of the poem: firstly there is the description of the trees, secondly there is the account of the young boy climbing the birches, and thirdly there is the speaker's response to this imagined scene.

The speaker describes the effect of the winter storms on the birches. He notes the noise they make as the ice-coated branches 'click', 'clack', and 'craze'. The hard *'cr'* sounds capture the tapping of the frozen twigs. The thaw causes them to shed their icy coverings. These 'crystal shells' litter the ground so thickly it seems that 'the inner dome of heaven had fallen.' This is a reference to mediaeval cosmology, which depicted the earth surrounded by crystal shells that held the sun, moon and stars in orbit. Shelley alluded to the same image in 'Adonais'. The great weight of ice bows down the trees. They never recover their original position but grow with their trunks arched and their branches trailing the ground. In a striking image, Frost compares them to girls, heads bent, drying their long hair in the sun.

The speaker departs from pure description to speculate about the cause of the trees' movement. He visualises a boy, alone in a natural setting, tempted from his chores by the trees. He imagines this boy to be independent and resourceful, someone who could 'play alone.' The boy challenges authority. He defiantly subdues his father's trees until 'not one was left I For him to conquer.' He flings outward, feet first, and rebelliously kicks his way to his destination. With practice, he combines caution with daring. Skilfully, like an artist, he learns the importance of maintaining his poise, until he reaches his point of departure; then he launches himself with carefree abandon through the air until he returns to earth. Similarly, a poet learns with practice 'over and over again' to take the 'stiffness' from his verse until he has mastered the poetic technique. A good poet, like a good climber, must not 'launch out too soon' but keep his poise and then, when the poem is completed, return to the prosaic world.

In the third section the speaker recalls that he was once a 'swinger of birches'. Now, when weary and troubled, he longs to recapture the freedom he knew in his youth. He would like to remove himself from the world for a short time and then return to begin afresh. This is not a death wish –

> May no fate wilfully misunderstand me . . .
> and snatch me away
> Not to return

– nor does he wish to escape from reality. 'Birches', Frost asserted, 'is not an escape poem. Anyone can see the difference between escape and retreat, and "Birches" is a retreat poem.' The speaker dreams of a temporary withdrawal from his worries. He describes this process as climbing towards, but never reaching, Heaven. He wishes to be set down gently again. Leaving and returning are both pleasant experiences. This leads him to conclude that 'One could do worse than be a swinger of birches.'

Balance

Frost's preoccupation with balance is evident from the opening line, where the birches 'bend to left and right'. The boy carefully climbs the trees until he is half-way between heaven and earth. He maintains his poise, 'not launching out too soon', and then at the right moment he kicks his way down through the air to the ground. Like the boy, the speaker in the poem wishes to get away and return. He believes in 'going and coming back'.

Frost balances the images in his poem: the sunlight and the ice, the straight trees and bent birches, the climbing boy and the 'girls on hands and knees', the black branches and snow-white trunk, heaven and earth, air and ground. The need to achieve a measure of balance or equilibrium is an underlying concern in much of Frost's poetry, including 'Mending Wall' and 'After Apple-Picking'.

Language

The language in the poem is, for the most part, simple and colloquial. Frost addresses the reader directly ('Often you must have seen them . . .', 'You'd think . . .', 'When your face burns.') The conversational tone creates an intimacy between the poet and the reader ('But I was going to say . . .', 'I'd like to get away'). Using the language of ordinary people is a hallmark of Frost's work. He contrasted this flat, almost prosaic speech with formal patterns such as:

> So was I once myself a swinger of birches.
> And so I dream of going back to be . . .

or the impersonal:

> One could do worse than be a swinger of birches.

'Out, Out –'

Text of poem: New Explorations Anthology page 102
[*Note: This poem is also prescribed for Ordinary Level 2008 exam*]

'Out, Out –' is based on an event that took place in Bethlehem, New Hampshire, in March 1910. Raymond Fitzgerald, the son of Frost's friend, was cutting wood with a chain-saw when he accidentally hit the loose pulley and lacerated his hand. A doctor was called, but the young man died of shock. The incident made a deep impression on Frost. He wrote the poem between 1915 and 1916.

A reading of the poem

The title of the poem is taken from Shakespeare's play *Macbeth*. When Macbeth is told of his wife's death he responds:

> Out, out, brief candle!
> Life's but a walking shadow, a poor player
> That struts and frets his hour upon the stage,
> And then is heard no more . . .

This poem, like Macbeth's speech, emphasises the brevity of human existence. The boy is depicted as a tragic hero, destined by forces beyond his control to meet an untimely and pointless death. The title may also refer to the blood flowing from the mutilated hand and the departure of life from the body.

The poem opens suddenly with the snarling machine cutting wood into sweet-smelling logs. The stove-length logs will be burnt for the life-supporting purposes of cooking and heating. However, the saw has the power to destroy as well as create. It reduces the wood to dust. The reader is reminded of the description of the body's decay after death: 'earth to earth, ashes to ashes, and dust to dust'. This image anticipates the fatal accident that will occur later in the poem. The mechanical noises, evocative of predatory animals and rattlesnakes, are suggestive of danger and death. The machine, a 'buzz-saw' (chain-saw), sounds like swarms of angry, stinging and biting insects.

These threatening images are contrasted immediately with the tranquil beauty of the natural world, as represented by the Vermont mountains. The effect is to heighten the menace of the saw. Significantly, the whole scene is enacted against the background of the setting sun. The fading light foreshadows the darkness that is shortly to fall upon the boy. As the sun sets, the brief candle of his existence will also be extinguished. His sister, homely in her apron, announces that supper is ready. Like the stove-logs, supper is life-sustaining. With cruel irony, the saw takes its cue, leaps to devour the boy's hand, and bites into the flesh.

The biblical overtones here of the Last Supper, flesh and blood, point towards the boy as an innocent victim, needlessly sacrificed, as the bystanders look on. In a double irony it appears as if he held out his hand to the saw:

> He must have given the hand. However it was,
> Neither refused the meeting.

The tragic hero always contributes to his own downfall. Betrayed by the embrace, he realises his fate.

> Don't let him cut my hand off –
> The doctor, when he comes.

The doctor, a figure traditionally associated with restoration and healing, unwittingly assists the malign forces operating against the young man, putting him in the 'dark of ether'. The boy dies. The final image of the living turning away from the corpse draws attention to the cold indifference operating in the universe that Frost frequently stressed in his work. Their attitude appears to concur with Shakespeare's conclusion that life is indeed a tale 'full of sound and fury, signifying nothing'.

Sentence structure

The opening lines are long, flowing and descriptive lines that set the scene. The lines shorten when the accident occurs; this quickens the pace of the poem and heightens the tension.

> And then – the watcher at his pulse took fright.
> No-one believed. They listened at his heart.

The use of pauses and exclamation marks adds to the drama and further increases the tension.

> Don't let him cut my hand off –
> The doctor, when he comes. Don't let him, sister!

The multiple caesuras at the end slow down the pace in order to echo with three little words the last three heartbeats as the boy's life ebbs away.

> Little – less – nothing! – and that ended it.

The full stop refuses to admit any continuation of life or hope. The brisk, matter-of-fact attitude is summed up in the brief line

> No more to build on there.

The return to normality is indicated in the full-length closing line.

Tone

There are many shifts of tone throughout the poem. The anger evident in the opening line subsides into calmness with the descriptions of the sweet-scented logs and the peaceful sunset over the Vermont mountains, only to return with double force as

> the saw snarled and rattled, snarled and rattled.

The narrator wistfully comments:

> Call it a day, I wish they might have said
> To please the boy.

Unfortunately he continues with the work, and when the accident happens his reaction, ironically, is to laugh with shock. Fear and horror succeed rapidly as the terror-stricken boy pleads pathetically with his sister not to allow the doctor to amputate his hand. The irony here is that the doctor can save neither his hand nor his life. The coldly factual statement 'and that ended it' prevents any suggestion of sentimentality entering the poem. 'Out, Out –' ends on a bitter note:

> And they, since they
> Were not the one dead, turned to their affairs.

The Road Not Taken

Text of poem: New Explorations Anthology page 104
[*Note: This poem is also prescribed for Ordinary Level 2008 exam*]

When asked to list his likes and dislikes, Frost included 'The Road Not Taken' as his favourite poem. It was written for his friend Edward Thomas, killed in the First World War. In the film *Voices and Visions,* Frost stated that the poem was in part a gentle satire on Thomas's inability to make decisions. 'No matter which way he went he was always sorry he didn't go the other way. And he could go on like that until eternity.' One day Frost said to Thomas: 'No matter which road you take, you'll always sigh, and wish you'd taken another.' It seemed to Frost that there was a fundamental human dilemma here that could provide material for a poem.

In May 1915, before the poem was published, Frost revealed that the dilemma was his own as well as that of his friend. He went on to acknowledge that he had always taken the less practical, more poetic way: 'Every time I have taken the way it almost seemed as if I ought not to take, I have been justified somehow by the result.'

The poem was also partly inspired by an unnerving experience Frost had in 1912. While walking towards two lonely crossroads after a winter snowstorm he met a figure approaching him who seemed to be his double – 'my own image'. The figure came up to him and passed silently by while Frost 'stood in wonderment' at 'this other self'.

'The Road Not Taken' was published in the *Atlantic Monthly* in 1915 and in *Mountain Interval.*

A reading of the poem

This poem suggests vast thematic issues through a simple narrative. The speaker stands in an autumnal wood at a point where two roads run off in different directions. Reluctantly he is forced to make a choice about which one he will take. Both roads seem 'about the same', so the focus is on the decision made and its consequences. The traveller cannot see where the first path will lead, as it bends in the undergrowth, so he chooses the other.

The grounds for his choice are unclear. While he states that this road had 'the better claim, | Because it was grassy and wanted wear', he goes on to admit that they were 'really about the same, | And both that morning equally lay' covered in leaves. He keeps the first for another day, knowing there is a finality inherent in his choice, and doubts he will ever return.

He conveys the sense of momentous, life-changing decisions in the final stanza when he predicts that in the future the speaker will look back on this moment 'with a sigh'. He knows he will regret losing the opportunity to investigate the other option. The choice he has made has serious consequences for him:

> I took the one less traveled by,
> And that has made all the difference.

Imagery

Frost uses imagery in an almost symbolic way to carry the meaning in the poem. The two roads in the yellow wood represent two different journeys through life. The narrator describes himself as a traveller who must choose which path to follow. One road bends in the undergrowth, making it impossible to see where it will lead, just as in life no one can foretell with certainty the outcome of a decision or what one's future will be like. Frost describes the woods as 'yellow' and the roads as covered 'in leaves no step had trodden black.' This suggests an autumn scene. Autumn is sometimes used in poetry to suggest maturity. The decision is being made at a time when the speaker is sufficiently experienced and wise to realise the implications of his choice; he knows 'how way leads on to way'. When he chooses, there is no turning back. He finally decides to take the road 'less traveled by,' and this changes his life completely.

Spring Pools

Text of poem: New Explorations Anthology page 106

This poem was written in 1925 in Ann Arbor, Michigan, where Frost lived while teaching at the university there. One spring evening, as he sat alone by a blazing fire, lonely and homesick, he thought of Vermont and New Hampshire, and the images that came into his mind prompted him to write 'Spring Pools'. The poem is influenced by the Romantic lyric 'To Jane: The Recollection' by Shelley and 'Ballad of Ladies of Olden Times' by Villons, which includes the line 'But where are the snows of yesteryear?'

A READING OF THE POEM

The title of this poem suggests fresh growth and renewal in the natural world when warm spring days return. The scene described in the first stanza, however, is bleak and wintry. The clear pools mirror the sky through the bare, leafless branches. In this icy-cold world the flowers and water 'chill and shiver' as if aware that their existence will be brief and they will soon perish. The pools will be absorbed by the roots of the trees, which will use the water to produce their dark leaves. The leaves will overshadow the flowers, denying them the sunlight they need to survive.

The second stanza emphasises the power of the great summer woods, whose immense strength can easily obliterate the still pools and the delicate flowers. Yet the dark trees are vulnerable, like the 'flowery waters and the watery flowers'. The pools were formed from the melted winter snows, only to be destroyed by the trees. The trees themselves will be destroyed by time.

IMAGERY

Frost uses nature images to elicit a range of responses in the reader. The scene itself generates conflicting emotions. The tranquil setting, the still pool mirroring the spring sky, the flowers and bare trees inspire awe at the beauty of the natural world. Yet it is a very cold scene, where the shivering flowers and chill water communicate a feeling of unease and fear.

The trees are a powerful and threatening presence in the poem. The warning that they should 'think twice' before they annihilate the pools and flowers reminds the reader that they are subject to an even more powerful force, which is time, the relentless destroyer.

The reversed adjectives and nouns in the 'flowery waters and watery flowers' evoke their frail beauty, yet the flowers feed on the pools and the pools were fed by the meltwaters from the snows destroyed 'only yesterday.' This final image of the brevity of existence does not permit a hopeful reading of the poem.

Rhyme and rhythms

A slow, steady pace is achieved through the use of long vowels, regular iambic pentameter, and a strict rhyming scheme, *aabcbc*. This suits the solemn tone of the poem:

> ˘ – ˘ – ˘ – ˘ – ˘ –
> These pools that, though in forests, still reflect
>
> ˘ – ˘ – ˘ – ˘ – ˘ –
> The total sky almost without defect . . .

The lines are long and sometimes run into each other in a conversational manner. Each of the stanzas is constructed around a single sentence. In the second stanza the lines flow almost without interruption, indicating the relentless processes operating in the natural world.

Themes

'Spring Pools' is more than a simple nature poem. It explores a number of themes found elsewhere in Frost's work.

Natural creation and destruction

The natural world destroys in order to create, and whatever is created is destined to be destroyed again. The snows melt into pools; pools water the flowers, and both are annihilated by the trees to produce foliage; the foliage will in its course be killed by the winter snows. The cycle of creation and destruction is incessant, inevitable and inescapable.

Indifference in the natural world

The natural world is an indifferent place. The seasons follow one another inexorably, producing and destroying: the winter snows, spring pools and summer woods. Nothing is spared, and existence is brief.

A bleak view of life

Time dominates creation. The massive trees, the small flowers, the deep snows and shallow pools are all doomed to destruction. The weak and strong alike will be swept away.

Natural beauty

The natural world is filled with beauty. This beauty should not blind us to the forces operating within it, nor shield us from the darkness that exists in nature.

Acquainted With the Night

Text of poem: New Explorations Anthology page 108

[*Note: This poem is also prescribed for Ordinary Level 2008 exam*]

Form

'Acquainted with the Night' is a meditative lyric composed in stanzas of *terza rima*. This form consists of linked groups of three rhymes following the pattern *aba, bcb, cdc, ded,* and so on. Frost was familiar with *terza rima* from his reading of Shelley's 'Ode to the West Wind'. Like Shelley's ode, this poem ends with a rhyming couplet.

A reading of the poem

This is one of Frost's darkest poems, where the mood is predominantly sombre, the tone unmistakably solemn. It expresses an overwhelming sense of anxiety, isolation and despair. The recurrence of the word 'acquainted' is an allusion to the passage in the Old Testament where the prophet Isaiah predicts the coming of one 'despised and rejected by men, a man of sorrows . . . acquainted with grief'. While the speaker is presented as a solitary figure walking at night through the city, the poem can be read as a psychological journey, where the townscape is coloured by the mental state of the speaker himself. The scenes portrayed are mental projections, reflecting the mood of the narrator. The world is covered in darkness and unrelieved gloom. The incessant rain is indicative of his depression as he travels through the blackness beyond hope and comfort, symbolised by the reassuring city lights.

In this 'saddest' of places he shuns human contact, refusing communication with any who might enquire. Jealously guarding his privacy, 'unwilling to explain', he retreats into his own silent world. The silence is punctured by a distant impersonal cry. The cry is 'interrupted', hinting at possible violence, repression, and suffering. The anonymity and impersonal nature of the incident deepens the fearful mood of the speaker. Yet he is not in immediate danger: the cry comes from far away, another street. These events occur beneath the 'luminary clock' – the moon, or perhaps a real clock – which marks the passage of time. This clock fails to offer guidance or comfort to those who look upon its face: it proclaims merely that 'the time was neither wrong nor right.'

In this short poem Frost explores his recurrent themes. He refers to darkness, isolation, the passage of time, sorrow, indifference, and an absence of communication between people. It is important to note, however, that the poem is set in the past. He writes that though he has 'walked . . . outwalked . . . looked . . . passed by . . . dropped his eyes . . . stood still and stopped the sound of feet', he has not escaped the night; instead he has undergone his ordeal alone ('I' is repeated seven times in fourteen lines), coped with it, and survived. 'I have been one acquainted with the night.'

Imagery

The poem is carefully crafted with images of darkness and rain overshadowing the first stanza, creating the bleak atmosphere that is sustained throughout. The images of light serve only to intensify the gloom. The city lights are distant, while the 'luminary clock' stands at an 'unearthly height . . . against the sky'. The second stanza is preoccupied with seeing and not seeing: 'looked', 'watchman', 'dropped my eyes'. The sounds accentuate the silences of the third stanza, reinforcing his isolation. The clock in the fourth stanza emphasises the impersonal nature of the world. The repetition of the opening line in the rhyming couplet is a reminder of the speaker's harrowing experience.

Design

Text of poem: New Explorations Anthology page 110

Form

'Design' is a perfectly executed sonnet composed of fourteen lines, divided into an *octet* and a *sestet*. The octet is largely descriptive, with little comment. The sestet poses a series of questions raised by the scene described in the octet. The rhyming scheme is *abba, abba, acaa, cc.*

A reading of the poem

The title refers to the idea that there is a design underlying the universe and that the one who created this design is a benign god. The concept, common in many religions, is supported by passages in the Bible. The poem challenges this belief, forcing the reader to face the dark side of the natural world and to confront the possibility that either evil is built into the universe as part of the design or there is no governing design in the first place.

In the poem, the normally blue flower and black spider have mutated into an unnatural colour for them: they are both white. White, the colour of innocence and purity, is here associated with treachery and death. The unsuspecting moth is lured by the heal-all, a medicinal flower, into the clutches of the predatory spider. The plump, well-fed spider is 'dimpled'; the coupling of this word with a spider creates a sense of evil triumphing over its hapless victim. The bloated, gloating spider has wrapped the moth in silken threads, thereby preserving the body so as to eat it later. The shroud-like case resembles a 'piece of rigid satin cloth'. Here the satin-like threads are woven into a sachet to cover the stiffened moth.

In the sestet Frost considers what malignant force corrupted the 'innocent' blue heal-all, making it white, what evil brought the albino spider to the very spot where it could ensnare the defenceless moth, what 'steered' the helpless creature to its ghastly end. One possible answer is that there is a 'design of darkness' woven into the very fabric of the universe. In the final line, however, a second possibility is proposed. The design, if one exists, may not affect 'things so small'; nature may be subject to a series of random incidents governed by chance.

The critic Lionel Trilling pointed out that Frost's poetry does not offer reassurances or affirmations of traditional beliefs; instead it presents the terrible actualities of life. Randall Jarrell also commented on the bleakness of Frost's vision, noting that his poems 'begin with a flat and terrible reproduction of evil in the world and end by saying: it's so, and there's nothing you can do about it.' If we accept and submit to the evil that befalls us, it should not be because of a religious acceptance that it is all for the best but simply because we, like the moth, are helpless to change the world. 'Design' offers little or no consolation to the reader.

Imagery

Frost presents the reader with two contrasting sets of images. The first consists of the spider, the blighted flower, the witches' broth, and death. The poet deliberately juxtaposes these images with beautiful and delicate objects – white satin, snowdrops, froth, and a paper kite – to contrast their innocent appearance with their deadly nature. The spider, plump and white, gorged, glutinous and murderous, has conspired with the blighted heal-all to kill the unsuspecting moth. The flower, moth and spider together form a horrific tableau representing death and disease. They appear to be the nauseating ingredients of a foul brew, prepared to begin the 'morning right' (a play on the word 'rite'). The scene, therefore, rehearses a daily ritual that casts an evil spell upon the universe. The effect is to 'appal' and to force the reader to examine the forces governing life and death.

Provide, Provide

Text of poem: New Explorations Anthology page 112

A reading of the poem

In this poem the old woman washing the steps was once a young and beautiful actor in Hollywood. She did not realise that she would age, so she failed to provide for the future. Fallen on hard times, she is now reduced to being a charwoman. According to Frost, the opening lines were inspired by a strike of cleaning women at Harvard College.

The poet suggests a number of ways of avoiding this woman's fate. One could die young, or, if destined to live a long time, become rich. He observes satirically:

If need be occupy a throne,
Where nobody can call you crone.

The rich and powerful always inspire respect, no matter how old. Some people rely on their intellectual abilities for security, others on fidelity and loyalty. To escape degrading poverty in later life it is better to buy friendship than to have no friends at all. Frost strongly urges the reader: 'Provide, provide'. At public readings he usually added, 'Or somebody else'll provide for you! And how'll you like that?' He urges readers to avoid hardship and the need to buy friends by providing for themselves.

Themes

This poem, written in seven triplets, deals with some of Frost's major themes.

The effect of time

Time destroys the 'picture pride of Hollywood', turning her into a 'witch . . . the withered hag'. It also impoverishes her; she must now 'wash the steps with pail and rag' to survive. Her fate is typical of many 'great and good'. Youthful success is soon eroded by time. The end is always hard, unless one learns to provide for old age.

The importance of independence

Frost admired those who could stand alone and fend for themselves. A central theme in the poem is that one should take control of one's own destiny, rather than be at the mercy of others. One should provide for oneself through accumulating wealth ('Make the stock exchange your own!'), power ('If need be occupy a throne'), knowledge ('Some have relied on what they knew'), or friendship.

Old age

Old age is seen as disfiguring, transforming beauty into ugliness. It is described as a descent, a going down into loneliness and misery. The old are subject to degrading poverty and derision. No memory of past successes can console them for their present plight or prevent 'the end from being hard.'

Imagery

The poem is structured around contrasting images of youth and old age, beauty and ugliness, wealth and poverty. These support the central theme: that youth and beauty eventually succumb to the ravages of time, and only those who provide for themselves will survive with dignity.

Frost uses images of witches, 'hags' and 'crones' to portray impoverished old age. These are contrasted with images of attractive, successful women. Frost chose Hollywood to represent a place where dreams and fantasies are brought to life. Dreams cannot survive in the real world; harsh reality explodes myths and fantasies. The screen goddess, the centre of attention, is now ignored as she scrubs the steps. But such hardships can be avoided. Political power and material wealth, symbolised by the throne and the stock exchange, are two ways of resisting the indignities of old age. Intellectual status, loyalty and 'boughten friendship' are means of surviving, ways of keeping the end from being hard.

An overview of Robert Frost

Background influences

Frost studied the classics, had a thorough knowledge of the Bible, and was well read in European and American literature. The Romantic and Victorian poets played an important role in shaping his poetic theory.

Romantic poetry (1798–1832)

Romantic poetry was written against a background of social, political, economic and religious change, not unlike the changes experienced by American society from the middle of the nineteenth century onwards. Frost was drawn towards aspects of their poetry when formulating his own distinctive poetic style.

- Wordsworth, Coleridge, Shelley and Keats, among other Romantic poets, believed that poetry should express the poet's own mind, imagination and feelings. His emotions, thoughts and experiences should form the central subject in his work.
- The lyric, written in the first person, became the preferred Romantic form. The 'I' is often the poet himself, not a persona created by the poet.
- The natural scene, accurately observed, is the primary poetic subject. Nature is not described for its own sake but as a thought-provoking stimulus for the poet, leading him to some insight or revelation.
- Romantic nature poems are usually meditative poems. The landscape is sometimes personified or imbued with human life. There is a reaction against a purely scientific view of nature. Humans are depicted as isolated figures in the landscape.
- The Romantics subscribed to Wordsworth's belief that poets should 'choose incidents and situations from common life' and write about them in 'language really spoken by men' who belong to 'humble and rustic life'.
- Wordsworth insisted the poet should use 'a certain colouring of imagination, whereby ordinary things should be presented to the mind in an unusual aspect.'
- The poet's visionary imagination rises above his limited, sense-bound

understanding and enables him to see things in a new way. The Romantics displayed a keen interest in visionary states of consciousness, dreams, nightmares and heightened or distorted perceptions.

• Romantic poetry is concerned with mystery and magic, folklore and superstition. The role of the imagination is related to the importance of instinct, intuition and the emotions or the 'heart' as the source of poetry, even though the 'heart' may be tempered by the 'head', the logical and rational faculty. According to Coleridge, 'Deep thinking is attainable only by a man of deep feeling.' The capacity to imagine permits the poet to enter a higher visionary state and regenerate the world.

Important romantic poets

William Blake (1757–1827)
William Wordsworth (1770–1850)
Samuel Taylor Coleridge (1772–1834)
George Byron (1788–1824)
Percy Bysshe Shelley (1792–1822)
John Keats (1795–1821)

VICTORIAN POETRY

Frost studied Victorian poetry in great detail. He cited Thomas Hardy and Robert Browning among his favourite poets. Three features of this poetry made a particular impression on him:

• the use of traditional forms, such as the sonnet
• the revival of the narrative poem, prosaic in style and casually colloquial in tone
• an abiding awareness of time and its effect on humans.

Robert Browning (1812–1889)

Browning turned the dramatic monologue into a major art form. Many of his best-known poems are dramatic monologues. Frost saw the potential of this form for his own work. Browning experimented with diction and syntax, creating a harshly discordant style in some poems. Frost was intrigued by the possibilities of playing discordant sounds off one another in a poem.

Thomas Hardy (1840–1928)

In his poetry, as in his novels, Hardy shows natural forces shaping human destiny. He portrays his characters at the mercy of indifferent forces, victims of fate in a world governed by chance. Like Frost, Hardy did not believe in a universe ruled by a benevolent god. Frost felt Hardy came closest to his own perception of life.

American writers

Frost was familiar with the works of such American writers as Ralph Waldo Emerson (1803–1882), Walt Whitman (1819–1892) and Henry David Thoreau (1817–1862).

Emerson was a philosopher and poet. He founded the Transcendentalist movement, which revered nature, and, like Frost, had been influenced by the Romantic movement. He encouraged writers and poets to make ordinary life the subject matter of their works.

Walt Whitman produced *Leaves of Grass* in 1855. This volume contained poems that were distinctly American in their setting and subject matter.

Thoreau wrote extensively about his experiments in self-sufficiency. The concept of the individual struggling to survive in rural America appealed to Frost.

Poetry and the historical tradition

Poets are part of a wider literary community, and their works belong to the historical tradition. Each poet can look back at the works of previous poets, while at the same time providing new material for the next generation. Frost believed the works of earlier poets provided a treasury of images and ideas available to all writers. He drew on the ideas and images, disguising and subtly altering his allusions, thereby enriching and deepening his poetry. The Bible, the classics, Shakespeare, metaphysical poetry, Romantic poetry, Emerson, Victorian poetry, popular ballads, even nursery rhymes, provided him with material for his poetry.

Some themes and issues

The natural world

Frost was a keen observer of the natural world. Plants, insects, geographical features and the seasons have their place in his poetry.

- Creatures: dimpled spiders, trapped moths, bewildered butterflies.
- Plants: butterfly weed, blue or white heal-all, yellow leaves, dark pines, apple trees, birches, russet apples, summer forests.
- The physical world: spring pools, winter snows, the sky, brooks, Vermont mountains.
- The seasons: autumn and winter are the dominant seasons, with falling leaves, bare trees, snow, ice, chill winds and rain.

The natural world is rarely described for its own sake or as a background against which the action of the poem takes place. Instead nature leads the poet to an insight or revelation. Often a comparison emerges between the natural scene and the psyche, what Frost called ‘inner and outer weather’.

Frost’s descriptions of nature are not sentimental. He describes a world that is bleak, empty and cold, where creatures suffer in silence and humans feel isolated. His natural world contains blight, darkness and death and therefore can be threatening, hostile or indifferent.

Isolation and communication

Humans are depicted as figures of isolation in the landscape. Not only are they isolated but they represent loneliness, and thereby acquire symbolic status. Loneliness can be seen as a human condition. Efforts to communicate effectively are at best difficult ('The Tuft of Flowers') and frequently fail ('Mending Wall'), are sometimes rebuffed ('Acquainted with the Night'), and can have unforeseen consequences ('Out, Out –').

Frost shared with Emerson and Thoreau the belief that individuality and the independence of the individual were very important. Frost in particular felt that people should stand alone and make their own choices. Note the repetition of 'I' in his poems.

The role of fate and chance

Frost is far less affirmative about the universe than the American Transcendentalists. Looking at nature, they discerned a benign creator, whereas he saw 'no expression, nothing to express'. In Frost's world, God is either hostile or indifferent to the plight of helpless creatures, who, like humans, are victims of fate or chance. His poetry records an ever-present, underlying darkness that erupts in a random manner with tragic consequences.

Mutability – the effect of time on people and nature

Time is perceived as being destructive:

- yesterday's flowers wither
- winter snows melt, spring pools are drained by trees, trees lose their leaves in autumn
- the boy dies at the end of the day
- time destroys beauty, impoverishes the elderly.

The effect of time can be overcome to some extent by the power of memories and the imagination ('The Tuft of Flowers').

The role of the imagination

The imagination enables the poet to see the world in a new way. In brief, intense moments he may enter a higher, visionary state. This allows him to regenerate his imaginative and creative capability and provides him with fresh insights and new inspiration for his poetry. This state cannot be sustained for long, however, and he must return to the real world.

STYLE AND TECHNIQUE: SOME POINTS

Language

From his study of Hardy's writing, Frost learnt how to achieve simplicity in poetry through the use of a few well-chosen words. He made a conscious effort to use ordinary language in his poems and captured the full range of human emotions, from joy to sorrow and from exaltation to fear, through the use of plain, monosyllabic speech. He stressed the importance of colloquial language, as it was appropriate to the subject matter in his verse and made his poetry accessible to a wide audience. Frost played the colloquial rhythms against the formal patterns of line and verse and constrained them within traditional forms, such as the sonnet or dramatic monologue. The plain diction, natural speech rhythms and simplicity of images contrive to make the poems seem natural and unplanned.

Frost used repetition for effect, to emphasise, and to add to the musical quality of his verse. He described sound in the poem as 'the gold in the ore', and added that 'the object in writing poetry is to make all poems sound as different as possible from each other.'

Rhyme

Unlike many American poets in the twentieth century, Frost upheld formal poetic values during the Modernist era, when formal practices were widely abandoned. He emphasised the importance of rhyme and metrical variety, observed traditional forms and developed his technical skills. He could claim without fear of contradiction that 'I am one of the notable craftsmen of my time.' His poetry is written so that the rhyming 'will not seem the tiniest bit strained'. He used *terza rima,* end-of-line rhymes, full and half rhyme. He also wrote in blank verse.

Verse forms

Frost used a wide variety of verse forms, including the sonnet, dramatic monologue, narrative and lyric. His preferred metre was based on the strict or loose *iambic,* as it echoed ordinary speech. The verse derives its energy from the tension that evolves when a rhythmic pattern based on strict or loose iambic metre is set against the irregular variations of colloquial speech.

Imagery

The imagery in Frost's poems is deceptively simple. There are images from the natural and the human worlds. Some are everyday and ordinary, some are grotesque and macabre. In a number of poems, such as 'Spring Pools', the imagery carries the meaning. Frost uses precise details to re-create the colour, texture and sounds of the world within the poem. This makes his poetry richly sensuous. Yet, using the same technique, he can paint a cold, bleak scene that is chillingly realistic.

His use of similes and metaphors creates layers of meaning in his poems. In 'Mending Walls', for example, the wall can be understood to be something that unites or divides, something that should be maintained or cast down. It can be physical, political, cultural or psychological.

Tone

The tone of voice used is vital to the meaning in Frost's poems. His poetry displays a great range of tone, and it may vary considerably within a particular poem. It can be precise and matter-of-fact, sympathetic, sad, relieved, strong and confident, despairing, humorous, dark and ironic, wistful or weary.

First-person narrative

Frost frequently used the first person for his narrative. The reader is permitted a glimpse into the speaker's life at a specific moment, often during a crisis. The use of the first person creates a feeling of reliability: the reader is given a first-hand account of an event, and trusts the accuracy of the narrator. The authenticity of the story is never doubted in 'Out, Out –', for example.

Dramatic stories

A strong narrative structure is apparent in many of Frost's poems. The narrator takes the reader through a series of events and actions, which lead to a dramatic conclusion. These events are often thought-provoking or provide an insight into life.

'The figure a poem makes'

(An essay by Frost published as an introduction to *The Collected Poems of Robert Frost,* 1939.)

Abstraction is an old story with the philosophers, but it has been like a new toy in the hands of the artists of our day. Why can't we have any one quality of poetry we choose by itself? We can have in thought. Then it will go hard if we can't in practice. Our lives for it.

Granted no-one but a humanist much cares how sound a poem is if it is only a sound. The sound is the gold in the ore. Then we will have the sound out alone and dispense with the inessential. We do till we make the discovery that the object in writing poetry is to make all poems sound as different as possible from each other, and the resources for that of vowels, consonants, punctuation, syntax, words, sentences, metre are not enough. We need the help of context – meaning – subject matter. That is the greatest help towards variety. All that can be done with words is soon told. So also with metres – particularly in our language where there are virtually but two, strict iambic and loose iambic. The ancients with many were still poor if they depended on metres for all tune. It is painful to watch our sprung-rhythmists straining at the point of omitting one short from a foot for relief from monotony. The possibilities for tune from the dramatic tones of meaning struck across the rigidity of a limited metre are endless. And we are back in poetry as merely one more art of having something to say, sound or unsound. Probably better if sound, because deeper and from wider experience.

Then there is this wildness whereof it is spoken. Granted again that it has an equal claim with sound to being a poem's better half. If it is a wild tune, it is a poem. Our problem then is, as modern abstractionists, to have the wildness pure; to be wild with nothing to be wild about. We bring up as aberrationists, giving way to undirected associations and kicking ourselves from one chance suggestion to another in all directions as of a hot afternoon in the life of a grasshopper. Theme alone can steady us down. Just as the first mystery was how a poem could have a tune in such a straightness as metre, so the second mystery is how a poem can have wildness and at the same time a subject that shall be fulfilled.

It should be of the pleasure of a poem itself to tell how it can. The figure a poem makes. It begins in delight and ends in wisdom. The figure is the same as for love. No one can really hold that the ecstasy should be static and stand still in one place. It begins in delight, it inclines to the impulse, it assumes direction with the first line laid down, it runs a course of lucky events, and ends in a clarification of life – not necessarily a great clarification, such as sects and cults are founded on, but in a momentary stay against confusion. It has denouement. It has an outcome that though unforeseen was predestined from the first image of the original mood – and indeed from the very mood. It is but a trick poem and no poem at all if the best of it was thought of first and saved for the last. It finds its own name as it goes and discovers the best waiting for it in some final phrase at once wise and sad – the happy-sad blend of the drinking song.

No tears in the writer, no tears in the reader. No surprise for the writer, no surprise for the reader. For me the initial delight is in the surprise of remembering something I didn't know I knew. I am in a place, in a situation, as if I had materialised from cloud or risen out of the ground. There is a glad recognition of the long lost and the rest follows. Step by step the wonder of unexpected supply keeps growing. The impressions most useful to my purpose seem always those I was unaware of and so made no note of at the time when taken, and the conclusion is come to that like giants we are always hurling experience ahead of us to pave the future with against the day when we may want to strike a line of purpose across it for somewhere. The line will have the more charm for not being mechanically straight. We enjoy the straight crookedness of a good walking stick. Modern instruments of precision are being used to make things crooked as if by eye and hand in the old days.

I tell how there may be a better wildness of logic than of inconsequence. But the logic is backward, in retrospect, after the act. It must be more felt than seen ahead like prophecy. It must be a revelation, or a series of revelations, as much for the poet as for the reader. For it to be that there must have been the greatest freedom of the material to move about in it and to establish relations in it regardless of time and space, previous relation, and everything but affinity. We prate of freedom. We call our schools free because we are not free to stay away from them till we are sixteen years of age. I have given up my democratic prejudices and now willingly set the lower classes free to be completely taken care of by the upper classes. Political freedom is nothing to me. I bestow it right and left. All I would keep for myself is the freedom of my material – the condition of body and mind now and then to summon aptly from the vast chaos of all I have lived through.

Scholars and artists thrown together are often annoyed at the puzzle of where they differ. Both work from knowledge; but I suspect they differ most importantly in the way their knowledge is come by. Scholars get theirs with conscientious thoroughness along projected lines of logic; poets theirs cavalierly and as it happens in and out of books. They stick to nothing deliberately, but let what will stick to them like burrs where they walk in the fields. No acquirement is on assignment, or even self-assignment. Knowledge of the second kind is much more available in the wild free ways of wit and art. A school boy may be defined as one who can tell you what he knows in the order in which he learned it. The artist must value himself as he snatches a thing from some previous order in time and space into a new order with not so much as a ligature clinging to it of the old place where it was organic.

More than once I should have lost my soul to radicalism if it had been the originality it was mistaken for by its young converts. Originality and initiative are what I ask for my country. For myself the originality need be no more than the freshness of a poem run in the way I have described: from delight to wisdom. The figure is the same as for love. Like a piece of ice on a hot stove the poem must ride on its own melting. A poem may be worked over once it is in being, but may not be worried into being. Its most precious quality will remain its having run itself and carried away the poet with it. Read it a hundred times: it will forever keep its freshness as a petal keeps its fragrance. It can never lose its sense of a meaning that once unfolded by surprise as it went.

Questions

1. 'The human being, lonely, helpless, and in crisis, is the main concern in much of Frost's poetry.' Discuss this statement with reference to three or more poems you have read.
2. 'Poetry begins in delight and ends in wisdom.' Consider Frost's poetry in the light of this statement.
3. 'Frost's poems are a celebration of the ordinary.' Discuss this opinion, with reference to three or more poems you have read.
4. 'The local and the universal are seamlessly woven together in the poetry of Robert Frost.' Is this statement justified? Explain your answer, referring to four poems by Frost.
5. 'Frost's poetry depicts the world as dark, dangerous, and ultimately indifferent.' Discuss this statement, with suitable reference to the poems on your course.
6. 'Natural images are used to convey human emotions and moods in the poems of Robert Frost.' Examine four poems by Frost in the light of this statement.
7. 'Frost takes a pessimistic view of life, unrelieved by any gleam of hope.' Discuss.
8. 'Frost's poems are deeply sensual.' Comment on Frost's use of language and imagery in the light of this statement, referring to at least four poems you have studied.
9. 'Universal truths plainly expressed are a feature of Frost's poetry.' Discuss.
10. 'Frost's poems are strangely beautiful, unbearably bleak.' Consider this statement, referring to at least four poems in your answer.
11. 'Sound is the gold in the ore.' Examine the importance of sound in Frost's poetry.
12. 'A wide range of tone and mood is found in Frost's poetry.' Discuss, referring to at least four poems in your answer.

Bibliography

Baym, Nina, et al. (editors), *The Norton Anthology of American Literature,* New York: Norton 1994.

Cook, Reginald, *Robert Frost: A Living Voice,* Amherst (Mass.): University of Massachusetts Press 1974.

Cook, Reginald, 'Robert Frost's asides on his poetry,' in *On Frost: The Best from American Literature* (E. Cady and Louis Budd, editors), Durham (NC): Duke University Press 1991.

Frost, Robert, 'The figure a poem makes,' in *The Collected Poems of Robert Frost,* Harcourt 1939.

Jarrell, Randall, 'The other Frost' and 'To the Laodiceans,' in *Poetry and the Age,* New York: Knopf 1955.

Meyers, Jeffrey, *Robert Frost: A Biography,* London: Constable 1996.

Pritchard, William H., *Frost: A Literary Life Reconsidered,* New York: Oxford University Press 1984.

Thompson, Lawrence (editor), *Robert Frost: Selected Letters,* New York: Holt, Rinehart and Winston 1964.

Thompson, Lawrence, *Robert Frost, vol. 1: The Early Years, 1874–1915,* New York: Holt, Rinehart and Winston 1966.

Thompson, Lawrence, *Robert Frost, vol. 2: The Years of Triumph, 1915–1938,* New York: Holt, Rinehart and Winston 1970.

van Doren, Mark, 'Robert Frost's America', in *Atlantic Monthly,* 1951.

Wordsworth, William, Preface to *Lyrical Ballads,* London: Arch 1802.

3 *Philip* LARKIN

John G. Fahy

Principal volumes of poetry

	Poems for study
The North Ship (1945)	
The Less Deceived (1955)	'Wedding-Wind' (September 1946)
	'At Grass' (January 1950)
	'Church Going' (July 1954)
The Whitsun Weddings (1964)	'An Arundel Tomb' (February 1956)
	'The Whitsun Weddings' (October 1958)
	'MCMXIV' (May 1960)
	'Ambulances' (January 1961)
High Windows (1974)	'The Trees' (June 1967)
	'The Explosion' (January 1970)
	'Cut Grass' (June 1971)

Wedding Wind

Text of poem: New Explorations Anthology page 203

GENESIS OF THE POEM

'Wedding-Wind' was completed on 26 September 1946, just after Larkin moved from Wellington to University College, Leicester. He was leaving behind a love affair with Ruth Bowman, which had become uncomfortable partly because of Larkin's feelings about marriage, which he viewed as a trap. Yet he was in love with her. 'Wedding-Wind' is one of a group of poems he wrote during September and October 1946 dealing with his confused feelings on leaving her. They include 'The Dedicated', 'Traumere', 'To a Very Slow Air', and 'And the Wave Sings Because it is Moving'.

'Wedding-Wind' was first printed in the privately published *XX Poems* in 1951 and was included in *The Less Deceived* in 1955.

VIEWPOINT

This dramatic monologue is spoken in the voice of a young woman on the morning after her wedding. This is an unusual stance for Larkin, as he rarely creates speakers who are not male and in the same social situation as himself.

Yet it is a fairly perceptive interpretation of that viewpoint. In the first stanza he explores the woman's uncertainty in her new situation, her feelings of being an outsider. She resents being left alone, however briefly ('he must go and shut it'). She is unsure of herself, feeling 'stupid in candlelight,' no longer certain of her identity ('Seeing my face in the twisted candlestick'), metaphorically blind in her new surroundings and role ('Yet seeing nothing'). This confusion is balanced by the romantic images of candlelight and wind, and any disgruntlement is dissipated by her obvious happiness at the end of the stanza and her need to share it with the rest of creation.

Her joyous mood continues in the second stanza, even in the context of the unromantic, mundane details of the countrywoman's working day: 'chipped pail to the chicken-run,' 'apron and the hanging cloths on the line.' The wind seems to embody her joy, carrying it forth on the wind's imaginary hunt 'through clouds and forests.' It is as if she is at one with the fulfilment of nature.

> Shall I be let to sleep
> Now this perpetual morning shares my bed?

Larkin is trying to find an image to carry the woman's feelings of sexual fulfilment, of happiness and joy, and he finds it in storm, wind and flooding. The passion of nature, its wild energy and the life-giving floods of 'all-generous waters' mediate the woman's emotions to the reader. But she is also aware of the fragile nature of her happiness ('like a thread | Carrying beads').

Larkin wrote many and varied poems to women. They are usually structured as addresses to the woman and written in a relaxed and familiar tone. But here, in this early poem, his strategy is different. He attempts to speak from the woman's point of view, 'boldly identifying himself with a female centre of consciousness', as James Booth says. Booth feels that the result is somewhat artificial. In particular, he feels that the second stanza is inadequate when the 'external images of nature are forced to do duty for internal emotional insights'.

Do you think Larkin's adoption of the female point of view is successful, that this dramatised empathy works? Examine the insights revealed, judge how well they are communicated, and evaluate their significance.

A positive view of love and marriage?

Is this one of those rare Larkin moments, offering an unqualified positive view of love and marriage? The ending does seem to suggest that love cannot be dried up, even by death.

> Can even death dry up
> These new delighted lakes . . .

But the very mention of death introduces the idea that all this joy is limited and finite. So, in spite of the exuberant romantic imagery, the wild energy of passionate nature, the unbridled joy and the sense of fulfilment, there are hints of love's fragile nature. We see this particularly in the image of 'a thread | Carrying beads'. As always with Larkin, the happiness is qualified. Andrew Motion, in his biography of Larkin, suggests that the rhetorical technique at the conclusion of the poem is camouflage: 'The final lines endeavour to annihilate his usual objections to happiness in a blaze of rhetorical questions.'

Themes

- Sexual fulfilment and happiness
- A woman's natural joy in her new love
- The empathy between the woman and nature: nature reflects her mood
- A hint of the fragile nature of human happiness.

At Grass

Text of poem: New Explorations Anthology page 205

[*Note: This poem is also prescribed for Ordinary Level 2008 exam*]

Background note

'At Grass', dated 3 January 1950, was printed in *XX Poems* (1951) and included in *The Less Deceived* (1955).

Andrew Motion traces the biographical background of the poem. The poet's father had died in 1948, and Larkin moved with his mother to Leicester. He found living with his mother very difficult, and though he and Ruth Bowman had become engaged in 1948, the relationship was going stale. In contrast, his friends, such as the Amises, seemed to be happy and prospering. The poem was written during the Christmas holiday, after he had seen a film about the retired years of a racehorse called Brown Jack.

From the evidence of Larkin's working notebook it seems that the idea of personal failure preoccupied him at this time. Perhaps the poem too can be seen to embody a statement about success and failure, albeit about outliving one's successes. Fame and glory are seen here from a different perspective.

Levels of meaning

At one level this is a naturalistic description of retired racehorses in a field at evening. The movements of these highly strung animals are realistically described, caught by the tense, uneasy rhythm of the language: 'one crops grass . . . moves about . . . the other . . . to look on . . . stands . . . again.' They are endowed with a certain pathos, because the poet wonders if, like humans, they remember their days of glory, the thrill of winning ('the long cry | Hanging unhushed', 'Do memories plague their ears like flies?') And, he goes on with a sense of humour, 'They shake their heads.' But of course it is also a naturalistic horse gesture from these beautifully evoked animals that 'stand at ease' or 'gallop for what must be joy' as they wait until 'the groom, and the groom's boy, | With bridles in the evening come.'

But this is not just a romantic chocolate-box scene. There are some ominous details that trouble this notion of bucolic bliss, even in the first stanza. Why are they sheltering in the 'cold shade'? And does that phrase carry its associations of death, as it does in classical mythology? The *s* sounds of 'shade', 'shelter' and 'distresses' create an uneasy effect. That the wind 'distresses' tail and mane further reinforces the notion that this is not an idyllically happy scene. The coldness and the dusk and these other details suggest the coming of death. And this becomes a poem about the end of life.

It is a retrospective look at life. Fame, competition, success and the moments of drama and glory are viewed in perspective from the point of view of the end. These successes are not downgraded because of approaching death: they are valued and celebrated ('their names live,' 'two dozen distances sufficed | To fable them,' etc.). But, as one critic assessed it, 'These worldly successes are put in the context of a full life and viewed somewhat hazily and dispassionately from the standpoint of the end.' So the poem portrays a controlled celebration of life. Achievements are celebrated but realistically seen in context. Note the irony of 'not a fieldglass sees them home'.

There is a sense too that the poet is trying, though not fully succeeding, to understand the meaning of it all – the meaning of life. The speaker seems to be always at a distance, either attempting to make out the scene or else attempting to attribute motive. There is the physical distance ('the eye can hardly pick them out', 'the cold shade'), the metaphysical or mental distance, where the poet does not quite understand but attempts to attribute motive ('the other seeming to look on', 'gallop for what must be joy'); and finally there is a time distance ('fifteen years ago, perhaps', 'faint afternoons'). The overall effect of this is to blur the focus a little, to introduce a note of hazy uncertainty, a slight bewilderment about the meaning of it all.

So the philosophy that underpins the poem is that life is to be enjoyed and success celebrated, but that the ultimate meaning or purpose is none too clear. Andrew Motion feels that '"At Grass" manages to suggest deep admiration for human lives well-lived and safely over.' He thinks that Larkin's feelings of regret and disappointment, which produced the poem, are transformed into appreciation: 'It is an envious poem which shows no trace of envy's corrosions.' Do you understand what he means by this statement, and would you agree with it?

Themes

- A celebration of life from the standpoint of the end
- The struggle to find significance and meaning in life
- The gentleness and naturalness of death.

Readings of the poem

It is a measure of the depth and richness of this poem that critics have interpreted it in widely divergent ways. Here are some of them; examine each in the light of your own reading of the poem.

- A traditional pastoral poem, nostalgic in tone, 'elegant and unpretentious and rather beautiful in its gentle way' (A. Alvarez). We have touched on this reading in 'Levels of meaning'
- A philosophical poem about life (see Andrew Motion's views in 'Levels of meaning')
- 'A post-imperial poem' (Blake Morrison). Morrison says the poem expresses feelings of loss and regret, such as might have been felt by the British people around 1950, when the poem was written. But can the horses be seen as symbols of empire?
- Tom Paulin says the poem shows Larkin's conservative approach to literature and his class prejudice: that (*a*) Larkin affects or attempts to take on a classical style – for instance in the use of 'cold shade', with its classical connotations, and in the description of the horses as retired generals, 'emblems of the heroic' – and that (*b*) the reference to grooms shows Larkin's support of the British class system. What is your reaction to this reading?
- James Booth says: 'If an ideological subtext could be detected in "At Grass" it would not be one of imperial nostalgia, but of animal welfare,' relating it to other poems in which Larkin shows an intense identification with the plight of animals, such as 'Myxomatosis' and 'Take One Home for the Kiddies'. Booth also points out that Larkin left a legacy to the Royal Society for the Prevention of Cruelty to Animals in his will.

  Do these readings provide some insight for your own interpretation of the poem?

Church Going

Text of poem: New Explorations Anthology page 208

Genesis of the poem

This poem was written in stages between 24 April and 28 July 1954. It was first published in the *Spectator* and attracted considerable notice for Larkin. It was included in the volume *The Less Deceived* (1955).

Development of thought in the poem

It follows a fairly common progress for a Larkin poem. The poet as speaker first describes in great detail an event he experienced. The description then gives way to a reflection or a philosophical analysis of the occurrence. So the poem proceeds from the particular to the general, from concrete details to abstract reflection.

It begins with the poet's casual visit to a church, where he describes the furnishing in some detail: matting, seats, stone, books, flowers, font, roof, lectern. For his narrative he cultivates a tone of studied superiority, more like the dismissive attitude of a pompous schoolboy: 'some brass and stuff | Up at the holy end.'

After his dismissive attitude and cynical actions of the first two stanzas ('I sign the book, donate an Irish sixpence'), he falls to thinking about the function of churches in our atheistic society. Perhaps a few will be selected as museums while the rest are allowed to fall into ruin ('a few cathedrals chronically on show'). Perhaps they will become places of superstition and dread ('after dark, will dubious women come | To make their children touch a particular stone'). Or will the places return to nature, to 'Grass, weedy pavement, brambles, buttress, sky'?

In the fifth stanza he speculates on the last user of this church. Will it be some architect with a specialist interest in churches ('and know what rood-lofts were'), or an antique dealer ('some ruin-bibber, randy for antique'), or a religious romantic searching for Christmas atmosphere ('or Christmas-addict . . .')? Perhaps it will be a committed unbeliever, like the poet ('bored, uninformed'), who nevertheless is drawn to this cross-shaped place because

> . . . it held unspilt
> So long and equably what since is found
> Only in separation – marriage, and birth,
> And death, and thoughts of these – for which was built
> This special shell.

Larkin, in an interview with Ian Hamilton, makes plain that what he values about the church is not religion but ritual, the marking of important stages or events in a life:

> Of course the poem is about going to church, not religion – I tried to suggest this by the title – and the union of the important stages of human life – birth, marriage and death – that going to church represents; and my own feeling that when they are dispersed into the registry office and the

crematorium, chapel life will become thinner in consequence.

He dismisses the church building as a vulgarly decorated barn ('accoutred frowsty barn'). Nevertheless he is pleased to be there, because it is a 'serious' place, where human compulsions are catered for and given form and recognition through religious doctrine and ceremony ('all our compulsions meet, | Are recognised, and robed as destinies. | And that much never can be obsolete'). So religious yearnings, immortal longings, awareness of the transcendent and such attitudes associated with a religious philosophy will become diluted into just being considered 'serious', rather than religious, for post-religious humankind.

> Since someone will forever be surprising
> A hunger in himself to be more serious.

Indeed, post-religious humanity will become so distant from a religious culture that the church will take on the insubstantiality and faintness of folklore: 'this ground, | Which, he once heard, was proper to grow wise in.' Religion will fade back into its primitive beginnings, where instead of a sophisticated theology it will just have some vague association with special places such as burial grounds, ground to grow wise in, 'If only that so many dead lie round.'

Voices and attitudes of the poet

This poem is communicated as a first-person narrative, yet this single voice of the poet adopts various tones throughout: flippant, cynical, dismissive, ironic and serious by turns.

The colloquial language used by the speaker in the first two stanzas ('there's nothing going on,' 'some brass and stuff | Up at the holy end,' 'God knows how long') suggests an ordinary fellow with a very dismissive attitude to all the trappings of religion. This is reinforced by the mocking self-image ('hatless, I take off | My cycle clips in awkward reverence') and by the writer's actions ('I sign the book, donate an Irish sixpence'). This is the flippant and dismissive voice of the unbeliever or the bored tourist. There are hints of a tougher, more cynical attitude in the ironic ambiguity of the title, which is hardly about church-going in the accepted sense. And what of the 'here endeth' response? Does he intend it to echo the demise of the church as well as the lesson?

But there are faint echoes too of a more serious attitude behind the dismissive mask. It is an 'unignorable' silence. Also, there is a slight hint of seriousness through the buffoonery of the hatless speaker taking off his bicycle clips 'in awkward reverence'. And it is this more serious tone that begins to predominate from the third stanza onwards as the style of the poem changes from narrative to reflective monologue. The cynical performing persona of the first two stanzas gives way to a slightly bewildered, lost speaker, out of touch with his surroundings ('yet stop I did . . . much at a loss like this, | Wondering what to look for; wondering . . .'). This less superior voice even invites the reader into his speculations ('when churches fall completely out of use | What we shall turn them into, if we . . . shall we avoid'). And it is this serious voice that speculates on the final end of post-religious society.

> But superstition, like belief, must die,
> And what remains when disbelief has gone?
> Grass, weedy pavement, brambles, buttress, sky.

Yet there are hints of the bored, cynical persona still in the 'cathedrals chronically on show'. The cynicism is emphasised by the alliteration. We can hear it too in the humour of 'let the rest rent-free to rain and sheep' and in the pun of 'dubious' women (it can mean 'disreputable' or 'inclined to doubt'), or in the 'Christmas-addict' image and the other final viewers of stanza 5. Following the serious consideration of the function of the church throughout history in stanza 6 ('held unspilt . . .'), the cynical voice snarls through again in the deflationary description that believers might find offensive: 'this accoutred frowsty barn'.

The final stanza is mainly in a serious voice, indeed a very forceful, confident voice that emphasises its points through the repeated alliterations: 'recognised . . . robed,' 'since someone . . . surprising,' 'hunger in himself'. So, in the main, there are alternating voices and tones – of the dismissive atheist and of the serious philosopher. The variety makes for a rich and complex poem.

A RELIGIOUS OR AN ATHEISTIC VIEW?

Perhaps it is the very complexity and variety of tone that has led to so many diametrically opposed readings of this poem. Some critics see it as a religious poem: 'The whole tone of the poem expresses doubts about the validity of atheism' (R. N. Parkinson).

- '. . . that religion offers explanations of the metaphysical elements surrounding physical life' (J. R. Watson).
- Andrew Motion views the poem as 'the speaker without faith, trying to recover the comfort it used to give'.
- James Booth talks about the 'unflinching scepticism' of 'Church Going'.
- Larkin himself said, in an interview with Ian Hamilton:

> It is of course an entirely secular poem. I was a bit irritated by an American who insisted to me it was a religious poem. It isn't religious at all. Religion surely means that the affairs of this world are under divine superveillance, and so on, and I go to some pains to point out that I don't bother about that kind of thing, that I'm deliberately ignorant of it – 'up at the holy end,' for instance. Ah no, it's a great religious poem: he knows better than me – trust the tale and not the teller, and all that stuff.

What do you think? What exactly is the speaker's attitude to religion? Could this be considered a religious poem in any sense? What exactly is Larkin looking for from the church? Is there any indication that people can fill up the gap left by God?

Do you think it could be argued that the speaker in this poem goes from an attitude of mocking 'half-belief' (agnosticism perhaps?) in the first stanza to regarding religion as mere superstition at the beginning of stanza 4? This superstition hardens into disbelief and strict secularism by the end of stanza 4, which in turn gives way to an acknowledgment in the last two stanzas that the church answers deep human needs, the hunger 'to be more serious'. Do you think he sees the church as fulfilling a social and psychological function, rather than a religious one?

Themes raised in the poem

- The function of churches in an age of unbelief
- A poem charting the stages in the breakdown of faith: scepticism (stanza 1), to superstition (stanza 4), to disbelief (stanza 4) and the return to nature.
- The human need to be 'serious' or philosophical at certain times in life
- The need for ritual and ceremony at certain watershed points in life: birth, marriage, death, etc.

Technical observations

Dramatic monologue

As befits a poem on this topic, it is structured as a debate with himself. It is a debate of much subtlety, as he changes tack and shifts the tone continuously.

Rhetorical questions

We get some indication of the persistent nature of this interior dialogue through the use of rhetorical questions, particularly in stanzas 3, 4, and 5: 'what . . . if . . . or . . . or . . . what . . . who . . . yet . . . but,' etc.

Humour

It is not without humour. Notice the irony of the title and of the 'here endeth' episode, and the pun of 'dubious women'. What other evidence of humour do you notice?

Setting

The setting is bleak, as befits the outlook, empty of people for the most part: empty church, barren ruin. People are either superstitious or eccentric, needy and unfulfilled in some way (the 'Christmas-addict', the antique-hunter).

Stanza form

For the stanza form he uses a weighty nine-line stanza with a reasonably regular rhyming scheme, sometimes with off-rhymes and half-rhymes (usually *ababcdece*).

An Arundel Tomb

Text of poem: New Explorations Anthology page 212

[*Note: This poem is also prescribed for Ordinary Level 2008 exam*]

BACKGROUND NOTE

Christmas 1955 was marked for Larkin by illness. First his mother fell ill with some unidentified problem, which worried Larkin. But as soon as she began to improve he himself fell ill with a suspected stomach ulcer. Tests showed nothing; but before going back to work in January 1956 Larkin and Monica Jones went for a short holiday to the south coast of England. They visited the cathedral at Chichester and viewed the 'pre-baroque' monument to the Earl and Countess of Arundel.

Because of health worries, Larkin had been brooding on death and mortality. In this poem, which he finished in February 1956, he is searching for some kind of permanence, exploring the possibility that love might survive death and time. But there is no easy answer to the problem of mutability. In the poem, while permanence of a sort is achieved by the couple (frozen in stone, holding hands), Larkin does not feel that the truth of their love survives (the detail of the hands was a later addition when the monument was being repaired). The poem shows Larkin's usual doubts about permanent relationships, about happiness, and about the survival of love.

'What will survive of us is love'

The poem displays Larkin's typically equivocal attitude to the possibility of permanent love and happiness.

From the first stanza we discover that 'side by side' they 'lie in stone,' frozen in their pose perhaps but nevertheless still persisting, despite the 'faces blurred' by time. This forms a fairly solid statement of permanence. The detail that affects Larkin most strongly – 'His hand withdrawn, holding her hand' – is a forceful image asserting the survival of romantic love over death.

But we are also aware, even in the first four stanzas, of many words and phrases that seem to qualify or undermine this assertion of permanence. The faces are 'blurred', the habits 'vaguely' shown, the hand detail has been 'commissioned' and perhaps doesn't reflect genuine emotion, the air 'would change'. Yet in spite of these hints of decay and change, Larkin still courageously insists, 'Rigidly they | Persisted, linked, through lengths and breadths | Of time' (stanzas 4 and 5). Their stone effigies have survived, after a fashion, and so, in a sense, they have transcended death.

At the level of intellect and in an almost metaphysically witty way, Larkin makes a fair attempt to convince himself and us. But at the level of image the whole weight of that fifth stanza emphasises the changing seasons:

> Snow fell, undated. Light
> Each summer thronged the glass. A bright
> Litter of birdcalls strewed the same
> Bone-riddled ground.

The synaesthetic imagery here (expressing something heard in visual terms – 'bright litter of birdcalls strewed') and the use of 'litter' to describe the music suggest the scattered richness of life, generously spread for the enjoyment of the living. These energetic sensations of life contrast poignantly with the 'bone-riddled ground' and the cold stone effigies. There are also the 'endless altered people', like a metaphorical tide, 'Washing at their identity'. All this nullifies the notion of permanence.

The lovers are even losing the dignity of their position in the sixth stanza, a situation emphasised by the alliteration of 'helpless in the hollow'. They are defenceless against the 'smoke in slow suspended skeins' (perhaps of war or pollution), their part in history dismissed as a mere 'scrap'. But, worse than all this, their truth is now questioned, or at least the truth of their effigy, the truth that survives in art. (Ironically, as Larkin discovered, the feature of the joined hands was not in the original monument but part of the restoration carried out in the eighteen-forties to repair damage to the tomb done during the Restoration and Civil War.) So this hand motif, not historically accurate, makes a public proclamation ('final blazon') they hardly meant. Where is the survival of true love here? Larkin is forced to acknowledge this as a mere pious hope, an impossible romantic ideal: 'prove our almost-instinct almost true'. The uncertainty is emphasised by the repeated use of the qualifier 'almost'.

So the pathetic assertion of the final line is not convincing in the context. The weight of this poem is towards the failure of love to transcend mortality, despite our hopes. It is yet another poem depicting the 'almost' aspect of human nature: what ought to be but what is not. Yet another poet is forced to accept the finality of death and the futility of our fervent hopes that love might transcend it.

Poems on a similar theme

Many well-known poems deal with the same theme. One of the early influences on Larkin was the poetry of Thomas Hardy. You might like to compare this poem with Hardy's 'During Wind and Rain' and decide if you find Larkin's tone softer than the bleak, uncompromising atheism of Hardy.

More closely connected in theme are Keats's 'Ode on a Grecian Urn' and Yeats's 'Sailing to Byzantium'. Keats explores the notion that the lovers' passion could survive in the pastoral scene depicted in the urn, frozen in art even more perfectly than in real life. Yeats's answer to mortality was to step out of nature into art and take the form of a golden bird on a bough in a Byzantine mosaic, and so sing on through the ages. But neither poet found adequate answers. Keats's lovers were cold and immobile, and, ironically, Yeats's bird sang about Time!

Themes

- **A poem about vain human hopes that love might transcend death** ('Rigidly they | Persisted, linked, through lengths and breadths | Of time,' 'our almost-instinct . . . is love')
- **Instead, what is borne in on us is the fragile nature of human effort, happiness and love** (they are 'helpless in the hollow', their contribution a mere 'scrap of history')
- **Even monuments cannot preserve the memory**
  - Here time erodes the effigies ('faces blurred', 'habits vaguely shown').
  - See Shakespeare on this theme.
  - Ironically, even the fading effigy is inaccurate ('The stone fidelity | They hardly meant').
- **The poem deals obliquely with various aspects of death**
  - the contradictory nature of thinking about it in terms of 'life after' – the 'supine stationary voyage'. The paradox here illustrates our confused thoughts on death and afterlife
  - the coldness of death, associated with the coldness of stone
  - the denial of expectations: this is what facing the unknown means ('They would not think to lie so long,' 'They would not guess')
  - the loss of identity in death ('up the paths . . . washing at their identity')
  - the lack of any control ('helpless in the hollow')
  - the final undignified scattering: death makes human debris ('the bone-riddled ground'). His treatment of death is quite personal. He deals honestly and intimately with what might be experienced by the Earl and Countess of Arundel. He does not employ the great rhetorical arguments we are accustomed to from Shakespeare's sonnets. The tone is fairly low-key – no great flights of rhetoric – and is all the more effective for that.
- **A bleak view of life**
  - Human beings are helpless in the face of death and time. Our vain hope that love might transcend this cycle is a mere 'almost-instinct almost

true'. Love can exist only inadequately in cold effigy. Truth is compromised. But we continue to make pathetic assertions, such as 'what will survive of us is love.'

Tone

In the opening verse the tone is that of a tourist, a neutral observer of some sort ('that faint hint of the absurd – | The little dogs under their feet')

- It becomes more personal at the end of the second stanza, with the introduction of the speaker's shocked reaction and the use of the word 'tender'. And it becomes the tone of a sympathetic neutral observer as he attempts to see their point of view ('They would not think,' 'They would not guess'). His sympathy becomes more pronounced in the penultimate stanza as he realises their helplessness and insignificance. He manages real pathos here. The personal involvement with this theme is signalled in the final stanza by the use of 'our' and 'us', as the truth of the Arundels is found to be a general human truth. There is a certain wistfulness, a 'wish it were otherwise' tone in the 'almost-instinct almost true' and in the pathetic final line.

Technique

Structure of the poem

It begins with description of an event and leads on to generalised reflection.

Structure of stanzas

For the most part, the stanzas are weighted towards the end, like a complex periodic sentence. They keep the main point to the end: see, for example, stanzas 1 and 2. This is a good narrative technique for building up a sense of drama.

Rhyming scheme

This follows a rigid pattern *abbcac,* which might lead to a certain jingly facileness, as in the first stanza, but for his use of off-rhymes to break it up, such as 'breadths – paths' in stanza 5 and 'prove – love' in the final stanza.

Metre

The metre is mostly iambic tetrameter. There is considerable use of enjambment to encourage flow. He even runs verses into each other: look at the enjambment of stanzas 5 and 6, which creates the sense of the ceaseless flow of time.

Imagery

The imagery is spare enough, yet effective. Imagery associated with death ranges from the expected 'monument' and 'bone-riddled ground' to the empathetic ‘helpless in the hollow’ and the paradoxical ‘supine stationary voyage’. The metaphor of the tide of history is not exactly original. The synaesthetic imagery of light and birdsong to evoke life is effective.

The Whitsun Wedding

Text of poem: New Explorations Anthology page 217

STRUCTURE

This poem is structured as a journey: indeed it recalls a real journey taken by the poet. The central metaphor is that of journey, and the loose narrative style, like that of a short story, is particularly appropriate to the subject of travel.

The poem communicates all the sensations, rhythms and impetus of a real journey. The sense of escape in the first stanza (‘all sense | Of being in a hurry gone’) gives way to the leisurely meandering of stanzas 2 and 3 (‘A slow and stopping curve southwards we kept’). This is followed by the more alert observations of stanzas 4 and 5 (‘Struck, I leant | More promptly out next time’). The sense of new urgency discovered in the latter half of stanza 6 (‘Free at last, | and loaded . . . We hurried’) builds up to that unexpected climax in the final stanza. This journey ends, as many do, with a feeling of release (‘somewhere becoming rain’). The romantic excitement and exhilaration of travel is well caught in the structure and movement of the stanzas (for more detail on this see page 87).

Larkin the observer: the tone of the poem

Larkin, as usual, is the detached, disinterested observer, only gradually becoming interested in the significance of the scene. Unconnected images of urban and rural England flash by (‘Wide farms went by’, ‘A hothouse flashed uniquely,’ ‘acres of dismantled cars’), which the poet hardly takes in (‘At first, I didn’t notice,’ ‘And went on reading’).

His attention is first caught by young women ‘grinning and pomaded’ ‘In parodies of fashion’ and then extended to others (fathers, mothers, uncles), described as caricatures for the most part: ‘fathers with broad belts’, ‘mothers loud and fat,’ ‘An uncle shouting smut’. The tone here is very disparaging; the eye is that of the cynical observer sneering at these pathetic, unsophisticated attempts at fashion (‘the perms, | The nylon gloves and jewellery-substitutes’). But the poet is lured closer, and by stanzas 5 and 6 he is tentatively identifying with characters and attempting to understand their thoughts (‘children frowned | At something dull,’ ‘fathers had never known | Success so huge and wholly farcical’).

The gradual lowering of his cynical guard, this drawing closer to and identifying with his subject matter, is noticeable too in the person of the speaking voice used. The early stanzas use the first person singular for the most part ('I was late,' 'I didn't notice,' 'I leant more promptly out'). The first person plural is then interspersed in the telling, until it has taken over completely by the final stanza ('There we were aimed', 'we raced', 'We slowed again'). The strident egocentric 'I' has given way to the more empathetic 'we'.

So this train journey carries significance for Larkin. This 'frail travelling coincidence' allows the poet to be linked temporarily with the rituals of common humanity, to share vicariously in the marriage celebrations and excitements, even to appreciate the power and attraction of marriage ('what it held I Stood ready to be loosed with all the power I That being changed can give').

But Larkin's enthusiasm for anything is rarely unqualified. He is aware that Cupid's arrow wounds as well as energises: one can fall in love or fall wounded. One senses that he is relieved at the end that the arrows have missed him, that the drama has moved on elsewhere ('Sent out of sight, somewhere becoming rain'). So the tone changes from that of disinterested and even cynical observer to one of empathy, understanding, even perhaps of admiration; yet he still maintains a sense of distance and a clear-headed awareness that marriage is not for him.

Themes

Larkin and marriage

This is probably the main theme that interested Larkin in the poem. We encounter a variety of ideas and attitudes on the subject of love and marriage. At first he found the weddings to be a somewhat grotesque spectacle: 'grinning and pomaded, girls I In parodies of fashion,' 'The fathers with broad belts under their suits', 'The lemons, mauves, and olive-ochres that I Marked off the girls unreally from the rest.' He is stressing the difference, the unreality, the out-of-placeness and the 'cringe-making' factors involved ('An uncle shouting smut').

The ceremonious aspect he definitely finds off-putting, better suited to mocking observation from behind a window than personal experience. Cleverly, he also presents it from the point of view of the guests, and their view of weddings is not unreservedly positive and is even sometimes paradoxical. Hints of possible disaster flow from 'Waving goodbye I To something that survived it.' It is betimes boring ('something dull') or awe-inspiringly dangerous ('girls . . . stared I At a religious wounding'), depending on the viewer.

But the most prominent attitude is one of conflicting feelings, found in the paradoxical simile 'The women . . . like a happy funeral' and in the final simile 'like an arrow-shower I Sent out of sight.' Some critics have felt that all the poet's paradoxical thoughts and feelings about love are gathered in that spectacular image (Cupid wounds as well as inspires: Larkin admires the couples but he will not join them), which Larkin himself said was inspired by the arrows fired by the English soldiers in the Laurence Olivier film of *Henry V.* They may be Cupid's arrows here, but they still cause suffering. Andrew Motion interprets as follows:

But while he admires the train-load of just married couples, he knows he cannot join them. Alone in his carriage, sealed behind his window, he is conscious of loss but appreciative of his singleness. As he prepares to watch them disappear, he reminds himself that the arrow-shower of love wounds as well as inspires.

In the final two stanzas Larkin has discarded his sneering, cynical mask. Does he envy their romantic closeness as they 'watched the landscape, sitting side by side'? He is aware of the preciousness of the moment, 'this hour', and of the power of that romantic journey. This is conveyed through the movement and energy of the last stanza ('we raced across', 'what it held | Stood ready to be loosed', 'we slowed again,' 'brakes took hold, there swelled'). There is a sense here of energy barely restrained, which finally bursts out 'like an arrow-shower . . .'

Larkin has recorded with admiration many aspects of the theme of love and marriage: the excitement and spectacle, the romantic journey, the dangers ('woundings'), and the sensual energy. His more cynical examination of the humdrum reality of marriage can be found in 'Self's the Man'; it is worth contrasting the two poems.

In 'The Whitsun Weddings' Larkin also touches on a broader aspect of marriage ritual. He considers it within the broad weave of human relationships – fathers, mothers, uncles, children, girl-friends, etc. – each seeing the wedding from a very personal perspective. Fathers enjoy the success but find it farcical, while women are more closely involved, sharing in the dangerous secret. Children are bored, uncles smutty, and girl-friends overawed ('stared at a religious wounding').

Larkin sees marriage against this background of disparate and often conflicting views. Is he marvelling that unity could come from such human fragmentation, or merely hinting that it is impossible? Certainly it is possible to see the weddings as a symbol of the unity of humanity. The coincidence of all of them on the same train, sharing this hour, speeding towards the same destination, is a powerful image of human harmony.

Larkin as chronicler of things English

Larkin in his time was considered by many as a spokesman for England, a sort of unofficial poet laureate of modern Englishness. The modern England he depicts in 'The Whitsun Weddings' is not exactly a Utopia. The sights and smells of industrial society ('smelt the fish-dock,' 'floatings of industrial froth,' 'reek of buttoned carriage-cloth', 'acres of dismantled cars') mingle uncomfortably with the traditional romantic, chocolate-box nature imagery ('where sky and Lincolnshire and water meet'). Perhaps the new multicultural society is best caught in that image seen by the newly-weds:

> – An Odeon went past, a cooling tower,
> And someone running up to bowl –

Here modern society, symbolised by the media and industry, is united with the traditional in a flashing train-window image, a new unity fused by coincidence.

Larkin chronicles customs, but they are disappearing customs for the most part: here the Whit weddings, in 'Church Going' the disappearance of religious practice. 'An Arundel Tomb' also depicts a vanished England. Is he seeking then to preserve what is vanishing? He certainly does not approach this in any nostalgic way, for he is always the unbeliever, the detached observer, the cynical tourist. But it must be remembered that the rituals and customs he writes about are those that give meaning and significance to ordinary events, and this he always comes to admit. And so it is with his chronicling of the Whit weddings.

Always what interests Larkin is the interpretation, the significance of these customs: religious practice in 'Church Going', marriage in 'The Whitsun Weddings'. The descriptive first sections of these poems are closely observed and humorously narrated, but his imagination really takes fire and the poems come alive when he begins to speculate on the significance of the customs.

Larkin usually chronicles from a safe vantage point: from behind the train window, from behind the mask of a 'yob' tourist ('Church Going'), from behind the historian's learning ('An Arundel Tomb'). There is often a medium of some sort between the poet and his subject, which gives us an interesting, ever-shifting perspective on this society he examines.

What do you think he is saying about modern society in these poems ('Church Going', 'An Arundel Tomb', and 'The Whitsun Weddings')?

Imagery

Larkin has a very accurate eye for detail, whether he is dealing with people ('girls, gripping their handbags tighter'), or things ('short-shadowed cattle', 'A hothouse flashed uniquely'). His technique is to saturate us with these disparate images. None is developed, no one is particularly significant on its own, but, taken together, the whole collage has meaning: the fusion in rural and urban England of modern industry and the traditional bucolic; the grotesque spectacle of weddings; and the new energy of the romantic journey. This technique gives a lively cinematic richness to the poem.

There are some startling and unexpected similes, as jarring at first as metaphysical conceits, such as the description of London's 'postal districts packed like squares of wheat'. And there is the central metaphor of journey, which holds the poem together and leads to that spectacular final simile: the arrow of love. This provides a unity, direction and impetus that carry the reader through at increasing speed and with growing excitement.

TECHNIQUE

How the structure of the stanzas and the rhythms of the language communicate meaning

Larkin uses great ten-line stanzas, like heavy railway carriages, to transport these poems. Large but not ungainly, they are streamlined by a very regular rhyming scheme: *abab cdecde*. The metre is often iambic pentameter, a good storytelling vehicle, matching the rhythm of the train.

> ˘ ‒ ˘ ‒ ˘ ‒ ‒ ˘ ˘ ‒
> A slow | and stopp|ing curve | southwards | we kept
>
> ˘ ‒ ˘ ‒ ˘ ‒ ˘ ‒ ˘‒
> A hot|house flashed | unique|ly: hedg|es dipped

But there is great variety. Notice the short, two-stress second line in each stanza; perhaps it recalls in metre the interrupted rhythm of the train, stopping frequently at all the stations.

The rhythm of the sentences within the stanzas is more important to the overall sense of the poem. He employs very long sentences, often spread sinuously over six or seven lines, and the result is that the reader is carried along at speed, as on a train journey. Not only is enjambment the norm within stanzas but, from stanza 3 onwards, each stanza runs into the following one, producing this effect of headlong movement.

If we examine a stanza or two in detail, we can see how the rhythms of his language help to communicate the meaning. After the conversational opening in the first stanza ('I was late getting away'), the structure of the next complex sentence – with its negative Latinate construction ('not till . . . did'), repeated long vowels ('all . . . all . . . all'), and the device of altering natural word order to hold 'gone' to the end of the sentence – suggests one long breath expelled with relief ('all . . . all . . . gone'). The sense of relief here is obvious in the rhythms of the sentence. The speaker is still conscious of the rushing train, communicated by the verbs 'ran' and 'crossed' and the short, staccato clauses: 'We ran | Behind the backs of houses, crossed a street . . . smelt the fish-dock'; but this headlong rush is slowed by the archaic word 'thence', strategically placed at the end of the line to slow us with its soft, sibilant sounds. We are then assuaged by the gentle *i* and *e* vowel sounds, the odd long *a*, and the regular iambic pentameter of the final two lines:

⏑ – ⏑ – ⏑ – ⏑ – ⏑ –

The riv|er's lev|el drift|ing breadth | began

⏑ – ⏑ – ⏑ – ⏑ – ⏑ –

Where sky | and Lin|colnshire | and wa|ter meet.

Through the rhymes and sounds of the language Larkin slowed us down, relaxed us for the journey. But he can also do the opposite: energise us, excite us, through the rhythms of language. Examine the final stanza. The sense of direction is established in the first image – 'There we were aimed' – which also prepares for the final arrow simile. The sensation of speed is conveyed through that long, breathless sentence stretched over seven lines. The lines run into each other (enjambment), preventing pauses at line end; any breaths come in the centre of the line. There is an awareness of barely contained energy, partly achieved by the strategic placing of the words 'held' and 'power' at the ends of lines 5 and 6, where they are weighted and emphasised.

This energy –'ready to be loosed' – is first reined back ('We slowed again . . . the tightened brakes took hold') but cannot be contained and finally erupts in the arrow image ('there swelled . . . like an arrow-shower'). The seesaw effect of energy and control and, finally, release is achieved through the rhythms of the language: structure of sentences, phrasing, placing of words in the line, etc. The structure of the stanza serves the meaning well for Larkin.

MCMXIV

Text of poem: New Explorations Anthology page 221

Background note

The poem was begun in November 1958 and finished on 17 May 1960. It was included in the volume *The Whitsun Weddings* (1964).

Themes

The preoccupying issues are difficult enough to pin down here. Is it a war poem with a difference, a poem of social comment about early twentieth-century society, or primarily a poem about the human spirit?

The poem features lines of volunteers, seen as in a faded photograph, enlisting for the First World War. But war is only an incidental backdrop here. Apart from a brief allusion to a sense of history and a possible hint of patriotic feeling ('fields I Shadowing Domesday lines'), it is not a conventional war poem. What it celebrates really is human idealism and the naïve innocence of people. With deep irony, the volunteers are shown

Standing as patiently
As if they were stretched outside
The Oval or Villa Park

and

Grinning as if it were all
An August Bank Holiday lark

and

Leaving the gardens tidy.

Their patience, good humour and sense of order contrast poignantly with the war backdrop.

Larkin expresses his theme overtly in the fourth stanza:

Never such innocence,
Never before or since.

He is conscious too of the vanity of human endeavour and the fragile beauty of human happiness ('marriages | Lasting a little while longer'). Even nature seems indifferent to humanity's struggle ('And the countryside . . . over').

It might also be read as a poem with a social theme. One critic read the poem as dealing with the leisurely and poetic sense of unity in Edwardian society. There is a feeling of leisure in the second stanza, with its 'shut shops', 'children at play | Called after kings and queens' and 'the pubs | Wide open all day.' But this is far from a nostalgic look at pre-war society. The archaic nature of this lifestyle is stressed in the details ('archaic faces', 'farthings and sovereigns'). The inequity of the social order is noticed ('differently-dressed servants | With tiny rooms in huge houses').

Against a backdrop of war, social inequity, and the indifference of nature, the idealism of humankind shines forth. But is this real or is it just a myth Larkin celebrates?

Technique

The poem is constructed as a collage of pictures and scenes, representative details creating a general impression and carrying the poet's theme.

Tone

There is a certain distance between the poet and his subject: the distance in contemplating an old, faded photograph; the barrier of long time. Also, the poet maintains his usual sense of irony ('Bank Holiday lark'); but he is not quite the detached observer. His admiration for their innocence shows through in the simplicity of the language:

Never such innocence,
Never before or since,

and he achieves a certain pathos in the last lines ('the men | Leaving the gardens tidy'). His sympathy for their fragile situation comes across.

Ambulances

Text of poem: New Explorations Anthology page 224

BACKGROUND NOTE

This poem was completed on 10 January 1961 and included in *The Whitsun Weddings* (1964). In one of life's little ironies, Larkin himself collapsed and was rushed to hospital by ambulance some five or six weeks afterwards. Despite numerous tests, the cause of his collapse remained undiagnosed; his biographer Andrew Motion feels the cause of his blackouts may have been psychological, that he was no longer able to deal with the complications of his relationships with Maeve Brennan and Monica Jones.

A READING OF THE POEM

This poem features Larkin's examination of death. He uses ambulances as a sort of symbol for it, a vehicle metaphor to carry the various ideas and nuances. In this way he can stress the very personal, private nature of death ('Closed like confessionals') and also the impersonal and mechanical aspect of it ('giving back | None of the glances they absorb'). It is everywhere ('All streets in time are visited'). The euphemism 'visited' makes it even more alarming. No one is safe ('children . . . women coming from the shops'). The ordinariness of the latter image is particularly chilling. Death is terrifying ('A wild white face') and has the power to alarm even the passers-by (*'Poor soul,* | They whisper at their own distress'). For Larkin it is the great truth ('So permanent and blank and true'), the answer to the question of the meaning of life ('the solving emptiness | That lies just under all we do'). It is an atheistic view of death and a particularly bleak view of existence.

The dying person is anonymous and sexless ('something', 'it'); death is a process of dissolution ('what cohered in it across | The years . . . At last begin to loosen') and final isolation ('Unreachable inside a room'). Larkin's view of death is unrelieved by any religious belief. It is chilling in its ordinariness, a modern, urban view of death, from the imagination of an isolated city-dweller.

IMAGERY

No tombs, funeral carriages or Grim Reapers are found here. Rather the imagery is taken from mundane urban living: ambulances, streets, traffic, children, women, rooms. Sparse, bare, colourless, these props create the perfect undistinguished stage setting for Larkin's death drama: the carrying away, the stowing, the loosening of all bonds, the dulling to distance all we are.

Tone

There is a certain light-heartedness about the witty first stanza ('giving back | None of the glances they absorb,' 'All streets in time are visited'). And there is an effort at a bleak pun in the fourth ('deadened air'). But mostly this is a very detached view of death. Notice the unemotional, impersonal tone of 'it is carried in and stowed,' 'sudden shut of loss | Round something nearly at an end'. 'The exchange of love' is a rather clinical style of reference for affection, friendship, and love. This clinically detached tone renders the poem even bleaker.

Rhyme and rhythms

The verse is constructed in fairly regular iambic tetrameters, with a strict rhyming scheme *abcbca*. There are some off-rhymes in the first and in the final stanzas, which give it an air of naturalness (absorb – kerb, room – come). Lines and even stanzas are run into each other; this helps the verse to sound more conversational.

In the final stanza Larkin manipulates the syntax, deliberately clouding the meaning to simulate the process of dissolution. Before the distortion it might have read: 'To lie far from the exchange of love, | unreachable inside a room | [Which] the traffic parts to let go by.' Once again the rhythms of language have been made to serve the meaning and overall effect.

The Trees

Text of poem: New Explorations Anthology page 226

Background note

This poem was dated 2 June 1967. It came during a period of relatively high productivity for Larkin, when he completed four poems in the next five months, all to be included in the volume *High Windows,* published in 1974.

A reading of the poem

This lyric describes the cyclical rebirth of nature and its effect on the poet. The emerging leaves stir uncertain emotions in the writer ('Like something almost being said'), in this case feelings more akin to melancholy than the expected joy ('Their greenness is a kind of grief').

Paradoxically, the emergence of new life sets the poet thinking of human mortality in the second stanza ('Is it that they are born again | And we grow old?'). Does he resent the trees' ability to re-emerge, dismissively described as a 'yearly trick'? Yet some enthusiasm for the fresh new life and energy has reasserted itself by the third stanza ('Begin afresh, afresh, afresh').

Imagery

Larkin sometimes uses nature images to convey human emotions and feelings. Here the spring trees call up conflicting emotions: enthusiasm for life and grief at the brevity of it.

The trees are almost personified in this poem. They are hesitant communicators ('Like something almost being said'), exhibiting melancholic emotions ('Their greenness is a kind of grief'), yet they put up a performance in public ('Their yearly trick of looking new'), and finally they are purveyors of hope ('Last year is dead . . . Begin afresh, afresh, afresh'). This positive note is reinforced by the 'unresting castles' metaphor, with its connotations of permanence and strength.

Tone

Larkin's usual gloom is evident in the first stanza. Is he the only poet who could find grief in greenness? Even spring stirs ambiguous emotions in his soul: 'a kind of grief'. Is there a hint of jealousy in his slightly sarcastic swipe at 'Their yearly trick of looking new'?

The third stanza is more positive in tone, with its repeated emphasis on a fresh start. But even this is qualified by the very ambiguity of the communication 'they seem to say'.

The Explosion

Text of poem: New Explorations Anthology page 228

[*Note: This poem is also prescribed for Ordinary Level 2008 exam*]

Background note

This poem, dated 5 January 1970, was probably inspired by a television documentary on the mining industry that Larkin watched with his mother during the Christmas holidays of 1969. The literary influence on it is most likely D. H. Lawrence, with his descriptions of mining villages. Larkin had read Lawrence avidly in earlier years. The poem is included in the volume *High Windows* (1974).

Themes explored

This is a narrative poem about an industrial catastrophe in a mining village, a pithead explosion resulting in the deaths of many men of all ages from that community. The catastrophe is dealt with obliquely: no details of the carnage, horror or pain are recorded; rather is it almost euphemistically described:

> At noon, there came a tremor; cows
> Stopped chewing for a second; sun,
> Scarfed as in a heat-haze, dimmed.

Indeed it is all the more powerful for that. Death is seen here as unexpected, coming literally out of the sun. Death is unfair, indiscriminate ('Fathers, brothers').

Larkin is recording how fragile humankind is in the face of blind fate. There is a heavy sense of foreboding about this poem ('Shadows pointed towards the pithead'). They seem impelled 'Through the tall gates standing open.' Is man a mere pawn of fate, innocently, happily trooping towards his destruction?

If not completely indifferent, nature seems at best to register the human disaster only for a moment ('cows | Stopped chewing for a second; sun, | Scarfed as in a heat-haze, dimmed'). Yet it is also nature that produces the hope in this poem, with that poignant image of the unbroken eggs. The human nest or community might be devastated, but the natural one survives. The wives too provide a continuity. Is woman a symbol of survival for Larkin? Certainly life goes on in this poem, and there is a powerful sense of continuity, as in 'The Trees'.

Imagery

There is a graphic evocation of the mining village, achieved through a wealth of realistic detail: pit boots, pipe smoke, beards and moleskins – all details of human accoutrements. Through this imagery, the living, breathing reality is conjured up.

Romanticised images of nature (rabbits, larks' eggs, etc.) suggest the innocent preoccupations of children. But nature's other face is also hinted at ('In the sun the slagheap slept'). The alliteration emphasises the ugly, amorphous mass, and there is a hint of possible threatening activity from the sleeping giant. But the image we are left with is that of the unbroken eggs, which become a symbol of survival and continuity at the end of the poem.

Religious imagery and scriptural allusions ('The dead . . . sitting in God's house', 'Plain as lettering in the chapels') give the poem a broader scope and a cosmic significance. We are made to see humankind against the broad tapestry of heaven and earth, and man becomes a heavenly being ('Gold as on a coin, or walking | Somehow from the sun').

TONE

On the surface it appears to be a neutrally descriptive poem, merely logging details. Indeed the pace of the rhythm rolling along somewhat monotonously would reinforce this impression. The speaker is at pains to keep his distance and remain uninvolved: 'it was said' and 'wives saw'. He avoids personal comment.

Yet that discipline seems to break down in the last line, where the pathos of that final image of the unbroken eggs and the ironic contrast with the shattered community releases all that held-back emotion. It is easy then to feel Larkin's empathy for that village. The emotion is all the more powerful for having been bottled up.

METRE

The metre is mainly non-rhyming trochaic tetrameter:

> – ◡ – ◡ – ◡ – –
> Shadows | pointed | towards the | pithead
>
> – – – ◡ – ◡ – ◡
> One chased | after | rabbits; | lost them
>
> – ◡ – ◡ – ◡ – ◡
> Fathers, | brothers, | nicknames, | laughter

Trochaic metre has been used to give an easy sing-song lilt to children's narrative poetry, for example by Longfellow in 'Hiawatha'. In 'The Explosion' the gently lulling monotony of this metre hides the awful reality of the subject. This is a further bleak irony in the poem, that it is a tragedy told in childish rhythms. Larkin claimed he was not aware he was using a metre similar to Longfellow's. Yet it is very effective and is maintained until the final line, which serves to further emphasise that line and so add to the emotion.

Cut Grass

Text of poem: New Explorations Anthology page 230

BACKGROUND NOTE

In the late nineteen-sixties Larkin became increasingly bitter, argumentative and right-wing in his social and political attitudes. He was particularly virulent in his views on the Labour Party government, trade unions, liberal prison regimes, immigration, and indeed the state of England generally. This gave rise to a good deal of bitter poetry; but this sourness does not seem to have pervaded his every waking moment, as he was capable of writing the elegant and delicate lyric 'Cut Grass' on 3 June 1971.

Theme

This graceful lyric deals with a common enough theme: the cycle of life in nature. But it approaches this topic with great immediacy and not a little drama. The poet marks how death can coexist with beauty in the freshness of a June day. Grass is cut to make hay, and 'long the death | It dies in the white hours | Of young-leafed June.' The poem emphasises the frailty of life, but this is more than balanced by the rich, abundant beauty of nature ('hedges snowlike strewn'), with its medicinal power ('Queen Anne's lace') and elegant energy ('high-builded cloud | Moving at summer's pace').

Imagery

The fairly obvious natural imagery of flowers, hedges and clouds has been freshened in a personal way by Larkin ('Lost lanes of Queen Anne's lace'). It is reinvigorated by a dramatic personification:

> Brief is the breath
> Mown stalks exhale.

Larkin himself felt that the imagery might be overdone. In a letter to Monica Jones after the poem was completed (1 August 1971) he wrote:

> Its trouble is that it's 'music', i.e. pointless crap . . . About line 6 I hear a kind of wonderful Elgar rhythm music take over, for which the words are just an excuse . . . Do you see what I mean? There is a point at which the logical sense of the poem ceases to be added to, and it continues only as a succession of images. I like it all right but for once I'm not a good judge.

Do you agree with his reservations about the imagery? Comment. Do you see what he means about the wonderful rhythm? Explain.

Rhythm and rhyme

Despite the short lines of irregular metre, a slow, elegant pace is achieved, mainly though the use of long vowels. For example:

> –   –   –
> Mown stalks exhale
> –   –
> Long, long . . .

He uses alliteration for musical effect: 'Brief is the breath', 'snowlike strewn,' 'Lost lanes of . . . lace.' This augments the music of the regular rhyme *abab* of each stanza.

Tone

Is there a certain wistfulness about the poet's contemplation of short-lived beauty? The grass is 'frail', the breath 'brief'. The inappropriateness of any notion of death in the 'white hours of young-leafed June' indicates some sadness. This wistfulness is carried on the sounds of the words, as we saw.

A brief overview of poetic preoccupations and themes

Suggestion

Consider these statements, then return to the individual poems for evidence to corroborate or rebut them. Make notes for yourself, together with quotations and references.

Larkin's awareness of modern society

When asked if writers should be concerned with political and social issues, Larkin said: 'The imagination is not the servant of the intellect and social conscience.' But while his poetry may not be directly motivated by specific social themes, Larkin was always alert to social behaviour, and many important aspects of modern society are reflected in his poems:

- Modern industrial society, with its human carnage and mechanical debris ('The Explosion' – on unsafe working conditions; also 'The Whitsun Weddings': 'industrial froth', 'acres of dismantled cars', recorded in all its grimy unloveliness)
- The bleakness of urban living: traffic, accidents, frightened people ('Ambulances')
- The random nature of social bonds: the 'random blend of families and fashions' ('Ambulances'); the juxtaposition of families with fashions serves to undermine and devalue the concept of family
- The vanity and empty glitter of our fashionable functions:

  Numbers and parasols: outside,
  Squadrons of empty cars, and heat,
  And littered grass ['At Grass']
- His vision of society encompasses both the industrial and the pastoral, the romantic and the modern: see 'The Whitsun Weddings', where the dismantled cars exist cheek by jowl with romantic England, 'Where sky and Lincolnshire and water meet.' This inclusive modern vision is summed up in the view from the train window:

  – An Odeon went past, a cooling tower,
  And someone running up to bowl . . .
- The society Larkin writes out of is a post-religious one (see 'Church

Going', which can be read as charting the stages in the breakdown of faith – from scepticism, to superstition, to disbelief)

- The function of churches in an age of unbelief is considered: they supply ceremonies that provide unity in our lives and mark significant points, places where 'all our compulsions meet, | Are recognised, and robed as destinies' ('Church Going')
- In place of the comfort of religion Larkin seeks consolation in rituals and social ceremony ('Church Going', 'The Whitsun Weddings', 'MCMXIV')
- Faith in the potential of the individual replaces religious faith (see 'Church Going': 'A hunger in himself to be more serious'; human idealism in 'MCMXIV')
- Conflicting qualities of humankind, destructiveness of war v. human idealism and naïveté: 'never such innocence', 'Grinning as if it were all | An August Bank Holiday lark' ('MCMXIV').

Love and marriage

- In general, Larkin yearns for the ideal of love as a solution to human isolation
- He toys with the vain hope that love might transcend death to prove

  Our almost-instinct almost true:
  What will survive of us is love ['An Arundel Tomb']
- Yet he is aware of the fragile nature of human happiness and love: 'helpless in the hollow', 'scrap of history' ('An Arundel Tomb'), and

  The thousands of marriages
  Lasting a little while longer ['MCMXIV']

  and also in 'Wedding-Wind', where the speaker is aware of how fragile her joy is – 'like a thread carrying beads'
- He deals with sexual fulfilment, happiness and joy from the woman's point of view: the naturalness of it, the animal satisfactions, 'Our kneeling as cattle by all-generous waters' ('Wedding-Wind')
- Admiration for the fresh love of newly married couples, appreciation of sexual energy:

  what it held
  Stood ready to be loosed with all the power
  That being changed can give ['The Whitsun Weddings']
- Yet marriage is not for him ('The Whitsun Weddings')
- Complete happiness in love is never achieved for Larkin: there is an untruth at the heart of the love statement in 'An Arundel Tomb'; love is qualified, as the speaker is still sad that she cannot share her happiness, in 'Wedding-Wind'.

Death

- Larkin is obsessed with the passage of time ('An Arundel Tomb', 'The Trees', 'Cut Grass')
- He neither makes a heroic attempt to defeat time, as Keats and Shakespeare do, nor takes refuge in stoical acceptance, like Hardy. He records the different faces of death and finds the odd crumb of comfort along the way
- Death is seen as the culmination of life ('At Grass')
- The naturalness and gentleness of death ('At Grass')
- Yet the essential aloneness of it: 'And not a fieldglass sees them home' ('At Grass')
- The bleaker side of death; note the capricious nature of death ('children strewn on steps or road, | Or women coming from the shops'); it is impersonal, alarming, the final loosening of all bonds, utterly comfortless ('so permanent and blank and true' – 'Ambulances')
- Death is wanton, and uncaringly decimates a community ('The Explosion')
- Larkin sees death as the meaning of life: 'the solving emptiness | That lies just under all we do' ('Ambulances')
- Nature somehow dilutes the bleakness of death; the cyclical nature of life and death in the seasons offers some hope ('Begin afresh, afresh, afresh') ('The Trees')
- Death in nature is beautiful, by contrast; death and beauty exist side by side:

  It dies in the white hours
  Of young-leafed June
  With chestnut flowers ['Cut Grass']

Nature

- Larkin is habitually conscious of nature in his poetry. In this selection is there any poem, apart from 'Ambulances', where nature does not provide the backdrop ('At Grass', 'An Arundel Tomb', etc.) or central imagery ('The Trees', etc.), if not the main theme itself?
- The restorative power of nature: see 'The Trees' and 'The Explosion'; nature provides a symbol of continuity and new life: 'Begin afresh, afresh, afresh' ('The Trees')
- Alternatively, nature can be indifferent to humankind: 'And the countryside not caring' ('MCMXIV'); the seasons roll on irrespective of humankind and its preoccupations:

  A bright
  Litter of birdcalls strewed the same
  Bone-riddled ground ['An Arundel Tomb']

- Nature is the only constant, the only survivor, outlasting many institutions, ideas, etc.
  And what remains when disbelief has gone?
  Grass, weedy pavement, brambles, buttress, sky ['Church Going']
- Nature exists side by side with industrial society, forming a new order, a new reality ('The Whitsun Weddings')
- Nature imagery is used by Larkin to express human emotion: 'perpetual morning shares my bed', 'all-generous waters' ('Wedding-Wind'). The critic Edna Longley draws attention to the pattern that all the richest moments 'of release and blossoming in Larkin's poetry . . . seem to demand natural imagery for their expression' (see 'Wedding-Wind', the end of 'The Whitsun Weddings').
- Death is acceptable, less threatening, natural in the context of the seasons ('At Grass', 'The Trees', 'Cut Grass').

THE POETIC PROCESS

- Larkin's own poetic process involved exploring an event or phenomenon through detailed description, which led on to reflection or analysis and finally revealed a truth or an insight ('Church Going', 'The Whitsun Weddings', 'The Trees').

Introspection and self-image

'Novels are about other people and poems are about yourself,' Larkin once said in a newspaper interview.

- Sometimes he indulges in direct introspection, as in the poem 'Toads', where he exhibits a deep sense of self-disgust and thinks of himself as 'a sack of meal upon two sticks'; and 'something sufficiently toad-like squats in me too.'
- But he shows a lighter, self-mocking attitude ('Church Going')
- Larkin as a loner, an isolate viewing life from a train window: see 'The Whitsun Weddings', where he appreciates love and marriage but decides that it is not for him. Is there a sense of relief at being a bystander?
- Yet he has a desperate need for love to survive ('An Arundel Tomb') and a desperate need for hope ('The Trees')
- Examine also other aspects of the poet's personality and attitude to life, as revealed in the poems, such as
  - his pessimistic outlook and constant sense of disillusionment
  - his agnosticism and lack of any religious comfort
  - the constant brooding on death, which limited his expectation of life
  - his interest in natural and social rituals, perhaps as an alternative to religion.

Larkin's philosophy

- Many critics find a sense of deep disillusionment and pessimism in Larkin's poetry:
  - 'the saddest heart in the post-war supermarket' (Eric Homberger)
  - 'a tenderly nursed sense of defeat' (Charles Tomlinson)
  - Andrew Motion says that Larkin has done a lot to create the image of himself as 'a Parnassian Ron Glum'.
- Examine the main areas of disillusionment in his life:
  - the lack of religious faith, which means that he has not got the comfort of that absolute in his life ('Church Going')
  - his atheistic view of the end of life is given full expression in all its bleakness in 'Ambulances' ('the solving emptiness that lies just under all we do')
  - the drudgery of work ('Toads'); the pointlessness of the struggle and the irony of all the effort ('not a fieldglass sees them home' – 'At Grass').
- We also find that his perpetual awareness of death colours all his attempts to celebrate life. For example, 'At Grass' celebrates the success of life, but it is a life that is over. Even the celebration of nature's beauty and abundant growth is qualified by the presence of death ('Cut Grass').
- Is there a reluctance on his part to ever acknowledge total happiness?
  - In 'Wedding-Wind', even here the woman has a little lingering sadness that she cannot share her happiness
  - In 'An Arundel Tomb', the manifestation of love that has, in a way, survived time is essentially flawed.
- Is there a somewhat cynical view of life that is fostered by the detached voice of the poet, by his remote stance and reluctance to be involved ('Church Going', 'The Whitsun Weddings')?
- Yet all is not unrelieved gloom:
  - The natural cycle brings hope of renewal – 'begin afresh, afresh, afresh' ('The Trees')
  - Human idealism and innocence is celebrated ('MCMXIV')
  - There is a yearning for hope ('An Arundel Tomb').
- Larkin himself denied that he was a completely pessimistic poet: 'The impulse for producing a poem is never negative; the most negative poem in the world is a very positive thing to have done.' From your reading of his poems, would you agree?

Some elements of Larkin's style

Dramatic monologue

Many of Larkin's poems (more than half of this selection) are cast in the dramatic monologue form. This results in a discussion, dialogue-type style of poem, albeit one conducted inside the poet's head. It produces an immediate, dramatic type of poem where we follow the ins and outs of the poet's thoughts as the argument develops.

This internal polemic is often obvious in the vocabulary and syntax of the poem. See 'Church Going', where all the hypotheses, possibilities and niggling doubts of the poet's thoughts are signalled by the use of 'what', 'if', 'or', 'or', 'what', 'who', 'yet', 'but', etc. These rhetorical questions are a common feature of Larkin's poetry (see the end of 'Wedding-Wind') and the means by which he arrives at truth in his poems.

Voice of the poet

Many of the poems are written in the first person. This would usually lend an openness and an intimacy to a poem, but Larkin protects himself from exposure by assuming a persona or cultivating a personality for this voice. He might assume the persona of a bored and sceptical tourist ('Church Going') or a knowledgeable historian ('An Arundel Tomb'), or that of a cynical traveller ('The Whitsun Weddings'). Usually the voice is disinterested, distant at first, only gradually assuming an interest. Some of the poems are written in the third person, where he can achieve an even greater sense of distance from his subject ('At Grass'). Quite different is the woman's voice he assumes in 'Wedding-Wind'.

Style of language

He employs a variety of styles of language. We find poetic language, metaphorical and descriptive, in many of the poems, for instance in 'An Arundel Tomb', 'MCMXIV', 'The Trees' and in 'Cut Grass' in particular, but it is employed in all the poems at times. But there are also many examples of ordinary colloquial language. This style is also used for moments of quiet immediacy: 'That Whitsun, I was late getting away' – or, for his cynical persona, 'some brass and stuff | Up at the holy end'.

Symbolism

He sometimes uses symbolism to express a truth, often at key moments (the end of 'At Grass', the end of 'The Whitsun Weddings'). Sometimes it is overused to carry interior feelings and complex emotions, as in 'Wedding-Wind'. Very often natural imagery is employed in this symbolism, as if only the power of nature can bring the thought, notion or feeling to birth and consciousness.

Settings

Natural settings feature in the poems: landscapes, fields, etc. ('At Grass', 'The Trees', 'Cut Grass'). These settings produce quite positive and uplifting poems, poems of some satisfaction and limited hope. Empty churches, ruined monuments and graveyards figure as settings for bleaker reflections on post-Christian society, on mutability, time and transience. Modern urban settings, such as ambulances and trains, give fleeting views of city people, scattered glimpses of life.

People in his poems

In general we encounter brief sketches or glimpses of people in his poetry, but rarely do we get any profound portraiture or exploration of an individual. We catch glimpses of old, frightened, stressed or threatened people ('Ambulances'). We meet caricatures to be sneered at: louts, 'ruin-bibber', 'Christmas addict', etc. ('Church Going'). There are generic lists of human beings: fathers, brothers, wives, men leaving the garden tidy, dark-clothed children at play ('MCMXIV', 'The Explosion'). Again, all are fleeting glimpses.

Larkin features quite a few lovers: the bride in 'Wedding-Wind', the many couples in 'The Whitsun Weddings', and the earl and countess in 'An Arundel Tomb'. But the treatment is rarely deep enough to create real people, though there is some attempt to get inside the thinking of the earl and countess (but they are safely dead!) and, more successfully, the bride in 'Wedding-Wind'. In general people are treated superficially, seen as generic examples, caricatured and sneered at or used as symbols. His most benign treatment of people occurs in 'MCMXIV' and 'The Explosion', and, ironically, both these communities are threatened with disintegration.

Technical variety

Explore the variety of stanza form he uses, from the heavy eight- to ten-line stanzas of 'Church Going' to the three-line stanzas of 'The Explosion'. Examine the variety of metres, such as the iambic tetrameter of 'An Arundel Tomb' and 'Ambulances' and the trochaic tetrameter of 'The Explosion', and study the different effects of each. Rhyme and sounds of words are employed for specific effects. (See the details in the critical commentaries on the individual poems.)

The Movement

In the nineteen-fifties Larkin was associated with a style of English poetry that came to be known as the 'Movement'. The group included Donald Davie, Kingsley Amis, John Wain, Thom Gunn, Robert Conquest, D. J.

Enright, and Elizabeth Jennings. Larkin became the most eminent poet of this group, if group it was. He himself doubted the existence of any coherent movement. This notion that there was a new style of poetry emerging was first launched in an article in the *Spectator* in October 1954 by J. D. Scott, who coined the term:

> The Movement as well as being anti-phoney is anti-wet; sceptical; robust; ironic; prepared to be as comfortable as possible in a wicked, commercial, threatened world, which doesn't look, anyway, as if it's going to be changed much by a couple of handfuls of young English writers.

For the most part their work was anti-romantic in style, plain-speaking and pragmatic. It was characterised by a tone of irony and self-doubt and a search for completely honest feelings. The ordinariness of the poet was central to their outlook, which was highly ironic, given the fact that many of them worked in universities.

Developing a personal reaction to the poetry of Philip Larkin

1. What common poetic issues does he deal with (i.e. themes you have met in other poets)?
2. What new issues does he deal with? Do you think these are important? Why? What insights into these issues did he give you?
3. What view of society and of the world do you get from a reading of Larkin's poetry? Does this accord in any way with your own view of the world? How is it different?
4. Do you find Larkin to be a forthright and honest voice? Explain.
5. In what senses would you consider Larkin to be a modern poet?
6. If you had to choose only one poem of his for an anthology, which poem would you select, and why?
7. Make a case for why we should or should not study Larkin in schools today.
8. What questions about his poetry or his philosophy would you like to ask the poet?
9. What do you like or dislike about the way he writes, the style of his poetry?
10. If you would like to read further, try *Philip Larkin: Collected Poems* (London: Faber and Faber 1988).

Questions

1. 'An awareness of mortality colours all the poems of Philip Larkin.' Consider this statement in the light of the poems you have read.
2. 'In Larkin's poetry the natural world is beautiful and restorative yet also vulnerable and transient' (Andrew Motion). Discuss this aspect of Larkin's poetry.
3. 'Despite inhabiting a bleak, post-Christian world, Larkin has a very positive view of mankind.' Discuss this statement with respect to the poems by Larkin that you have read.
4. 'Larkin finds it easier to contemplate the past than the future.' Discuss, with reference to the poems you have read.
5. 'Larkin's subject matter is largely his own inadequacy' (Charles Tomlinson). Discuss this reading of Larkin's poetry.
6. 'Larkin's poems feature a constant struggle between opposites, such as between sociability and solitariness, hope and hopelessness, fulfilment and disappointment.' Discuss.
7. 'Sadness is the dominant emotion in Philip Larkin's poetry.' Would you agree? Substantiate your opinions with reference to the poems.
8. 'We encounter a great variety of tone in the poetry of Philip Larkin, from the cynical and disillusioned to the wistful and nostalgic.' Examine the variety of tone you experience in his poetry.
9. 'The tone of Larkin's speaking voice is always that of the neutral observer.' Would you agree?
10. 'The image of the poet that comes across is that of a solitary soul on the fringes of society.' From your reading of his poems, would you agree with this perception?
11. 'Detailed observation of an event, place or phenomenon, followed by philosophical reflection that yields up the kernel of truth – this is a Larkin poem.' Examine the structure of at least two poems by Larkin to test the validity of this statement.
12. 'An effective use of symbolism is essential to the meaning of many a Larkin poem.' Explore any two poems from this point of view.

Bibliography

Alvarez, A. (editor), *The New Poetry,* London: Penguin 1962.

Booth, James, *Philip Larkin: Writer,* Brighton: Harvester-Wheatsheaf 1992.

Gibson, James (editor), *Let the Poet Choose,* London: Harrap 1973.

Hamilton, Ian, 'Four conversations', *London Magazine,* vol. 4, no. 6, November 1964.

Larkin, Philip, *Selected Letters of Philip Larkin, 1940–1985* (Anthony Twaite, editor), London: Faber and Faber 1992.

Morrison, Blake, *The Movement: English Poetry and Fiction of the 1950s,* London: Methuen 1986.

Motion, Andrew, *Philip Larkin: A Writer's Life,* London: Faber and Faber 1993.

Rossen, Janice, *Philip Larkin: His Life's Work,* London: Harvester Wheatsheaf 1989.

Swarbrick, Andrew, *Out of Reach: The Poetry of Philip Larkin,* Basingstoke: Macmillan 1995.

4 *John* MONTAGUE

Carole Scully

Praising the burden

Early Life

> 'Brooklyn born, Tyrone-reared, Dublin-educated, constituted a tangle, a turmoil of contradictory allegiance it would take a lifetime to unravel.'

This is how John Montague describes his own life and it is important for us to be aware of his life if we are to develop an understanding of his poetry, because Montague's life is the starting point for his writing. This is not to suggest that he writes a poetic diary. Rather, in his poetry he takes his own 'tangle' of experiences and observations and draws out of them lessons and Truths that are universally relevant. Thus, by reading Montague's poetry we may also begin to reflect on the 'tangle' that lies within each of us.

Montague has described his life as being 'a burden', and there is no doubt that his early life was a difficult one. He was born on 28 February 1929 in St Catherine's Hospital, Brooklyn. His parents had only recently been reunited after a separation lasting for three years. This separation had come about because of his father's political activities in Northern Ireland. Montague's father, James, had come from a comfortable Catholic family in Co. Tyrone; however, he had become actively involved in Nationalist activities after the Easter Rising in 1916. When Ireland was partitioned and Northern Ireland was established, James found it impossible to find employment. As a married man with two small sons, James decided that he had no choice but to travel to America, while his wife Molly and the children stayed behind in Co. Tyrone.

Unfortunately, when the family were reunited in New York life was still hard for them. John's mother found it difficult to bond with her new son, and this rejection proved to be a major issue in Montague's life and writing. When the American stock market collapsed in 1929 John's father, along with many others, lost his job. To make matters worse, his mother became ill with tuberculosis. The family lived in a 'speakeasy', an illegal drinking den, owned by John's uncle. But when John's uncle died the decision was made to send John and his two older brothers back to Northern Ireland, while James and Molly remained in New York.

For the two older boys it was a return to their 'home'. But for the four-year-old John it was an expedition into the unknown. Later he was to write, 'Losing a family and a country in one sweep must not have been easy, although for long I suppressed my earlier memories.' The effects of this early disruption on his environment are evident in Montague's search for a sense of identity in his writing, where he tries to work out who he is and where he belongs.

When the three boys arrived back in Co. Tyrone, John was separated from his two brothers. While they went to live with their maternal grandmother in Fintona, John was taken to live with his father's two unmarried sisters in the Montague family home in Garvaghey. The reasons behind this surprising decision were complicated. John's grandmother was an old lady who was reluctant to take on the rearing of a small child. Also, his father wanted one of his sons to grow up in the Montague environment.

So John lost his last remaining certainty, the presence of the two brothers that he had lived with constantly for the first four years of his young life. He found himself living with strangers, in an unknown house, set in an unknown landscape far away from the teeming streets of Brooklyn.

Education

John's aunts were two kind women, with his Aunt Brigid, in particular, providing great support for John. They made the sensitive decision to let John stay at home for a year before sending him to school. It was during this time that he began to explore the wide, open landscape of Co. Tyrone and to develop a love and appreciation of nature. This early interaction with the natural world was to have a positive influence on Montague: not only did it help him to begin to develop a sense of his own identity, but it also provided him with a wealth of experiences. As an adult poet, Montague frequently taps into this storehouse of childhood memories to produce the most wonderfully vivid pieces of writing, as in 'The Trout' and 'Killing the Pig'.

Montague has said that the 'few years from four to eleven' were 'a blessing and a healing'. He went to the local school and proved to be a bright pupil. However, this was not a completely happy time for him. When John was seven years old his mother returned home to Co. Tyrone, leaving his father in Brooklyn. However, she made no attempt to bring John to live with her. Perhaps she did not want to disrupt John's life by taking him from his aunts' home; or, perhaps, she had been so worn down by the disappointments of her life in America that she was unable to take on the responsibility of a young child. Whatever the reason, Molly went to live some eight miles away from her son, in her family home at Fintona, and they met only occasionally. The trauma of this second rejection was a major contributory factor to the little boy developing a stutter, as Montague suggests himself:

> 'I have no doubt that the separation from my mother, whatever the reasons for the decision, is at the center of my emotional life, affecting my relationships with women, shadowing my powers of speech . . .'.

In 'The Locket' Montague traces, with brutal honesty, his boyhood attempts to establish some type of relationship with his mother.

His mother was not the only female figure who exerted a negative influence on his development. The treatment that John received at the hands of a local teacher, who seemed to dislike the Montague family, may also have added to his speech difficulties. John was particularly good at reading, and one day he was sent to this teacher to read a passage aloud. Owing to the content of the passage, a description of a young, naked girl dancing under the moon, John became somewhat unsettled. In response, the teacher began to mock him and his accent, which still bore traces of his early years in Brooklyn. Indeed, Brooklyn continued to feature in young John's life, for his father was still living there and would do so until he returned to Northern Ireland in 1952, when John was in his twenties. In his poem 'The Cage' Montague confronts his relationship with his father, presenting an honest representation of their situation.

At the age of eleven Montague won a scholarship to St Patrick's College, Armagh. He found it an unhappy experience: 'Those five years in Armagh were the most cramped of my childhood.' His aunts were hopeful that he might discover a religious vocation. John, however, was less sure. Although he was impressed by the ceremony and rituals of the Catholic Church, he found something even more interesting – girls!

In 1946 Montague won a scholarship to attend University College Dublin, where he studied English and History. Initially he found it difficult to settle into college life. Then he noticed that the 'intellectuals', a group of students who controlled the English Literature Society and a literary magazine, were very popular with 'the brighter girls, who were often the more pretty'. John decided to become part of this group, and it was here that he discovered that he 'might possibly be able to write something like the kind of poetry I admired'. The connection between women and poetry persisted for Montague. In 'All Legendary Obstacles' Montague describes his feelings as he waits for his girlfriend to arrive on the train; while in 'The Same Gesture' he considers the nature of the love that he and his lover share.

Montague's involvement with the 'intellectuals' led him into the Dublin poetic scene, where he met such poets as Austin Clarke and Patrick Kavanagh. He was hopeful that engaging with this group might help him to develop his writing skills, so that he would be better able to understand and shoulder the burden of his life. Disappointingly, Montague found that, 'The poetic world of Dublin was acrimony and insult: a poem was to be kicked, not examined; the begrudgers ruled.'

However, his connection with this group did have two major effects on his development as a writer. He was horrified by the financial poverty and lack of recognition that both Clarke and Kavanagh endured, and he worked hard to gain recognition and financial support for the two men. As a result, Montague vowed that he would never rely on poetry for his income. He has stuck to this decision throughout his life and has worked in such areas as journalism and lecturing while continuing to write poetry. In addition, because of his negative experiences as a young poet, Montague has always been immensely supportive of other writers, commenting 'I would not wish anyone to go through what I endured as a young writer.'

The wider world

By the time Montague had completed his final exams in 1952, gaining a double First in English and History, he was very frustrated by his life in Ireland. Luckily, he received a scholarship to study in America. This not only gave him the opportunity to break away from the negativity of the Dublin poetic scene; it also offered him the chance to escape from the claustrophobic and inward-looking attitude that pervaded Ireland in the 1950s. He had long felt that Ireland was a country that existed on the fringes of the world. As a schoolboy during the Second World War he had followed the theatre of wartime actions, conscious that he was 'just a boy living on the edge of a giant historical drama'. In his poem 'A Welcoming Party', Montague expresses his sense of Ireland's peripheral position and the effects that it had on both himself and the Irish people.

He also developed the belief – one that he holds to this day – that for his writing to develop to its full potential he must engage with literary influences from all over the world. This is not to suggest that he is rejecting all that is Irish; on the contrary, he feels that 'The wider an Irishman's experience, the more likely he is to understand his native country.'

Montague landed in a very different world in America. He discovered the literary world that he had yearned for: 'a literary world filled with writers revelling in the creation of living, breathing poetry'. He embraced the opportunity to encounter new ideas and to develop deep friendships with other writers. His writing blossomed and he began to find some easiness in his shouldering of the burden of his life.

Having met his first wife in America, Montague returned to Ireland for some time before travelling to his wife's native country, France. There he met writers such as Samuel Beckett. Indeed, no matter where Montague has lived, be it in Ireland, America or France, he has always sought the company of other writers and artists because he sees the 'idea of a fertile community' as being of great benefit to the creative process. Furthermore, by being part of such groups, Montague developed a feeling of belonging that has contributed to his sense of identity. Finally, it was through these opportunities for open companionship and the enthusiastic pooling of ideas that Montague constructed and refined his view that writing in the twentieth century was a 'shared adventure': an adventure that both he and Northern Ireland had to become part of.

A modern form of Northern Irish poetry

In his evolution of a poetic style Montague has consistently had a double purpose: to develop a personal writing style, and to initiate a new form of writing for Northern Irish poetry. So, through his writing, he has acted as a kind of trailblazer, or as he describes himself, 'the missing link of Ulster poetry', because 'There had not been a poet of Ulster Catholic background since the Gaelic poets of the eighteenth century.'

This style rests on two foundations: first, Montague's awareness of the relationship between Ireland's past and the present; and second, his belief that for poetic progress to occur there must be an investigation and inclusion of influences from the international world of modern poetry.

Through his exploration of the connection between Ireland's past and present, Montague not only contributed to his writing style, but he also added to his own sense of identity. His awareness of his life being related to past lives gave him a sense of belonging to a living inheritance that was held within the Northern Irish countryside and further eased the burden of his living. The danger, as Montague sees it, is that modern life has taken the people away from their land and destroyed their sense of connection to the past:

> The whole landscape a manuscript
> We had lost the skill to read,

So in his poetry Montague frequently tries to highlight and emphasise this connection between the past and the present. In 'Like Dolmens Round my Childhood . . .' he examines his relationship with the past, as represented by the old people and the dolmens, and comes to an understanding that they are indeed very much a part of his own being and the present; while in 'The Wild Dog Rose' he uses the story of the attempted rape of one woman as a representation of the history of the political relationship between Ireland and England. For Montague's view of the past is no idealised vision: he confronts the violence, the harshness of the struggle and the determined endurance that lie within the past.

Allied to this emphasis on the relevance of the past is his drive to incorporate elements from modern writing, known as Modernism, into his own work and Northern Irish literature. From his earliest years in America Montague developed a close bond with writers who were at the forefront of poetic experimentation, such as Gary Snyder and William Carlos Williams, and he embraced and refined some features of Modernist writing in his poetry. In order to provide a stylistic context for our consideration of Montague's work we will briefly discuss four of these features: the Artist-centred View; Nature; Imagery; and Poetic Form and Language.

The Artist-centred View

Modernists emphasise the importance of the artist in the creative process. In poetry, this means that a poet examines experiences from his own life and the way in which he responds to his world, with a view to uncovering the universal Truths of life that have a relevance to all people. Therefore by reading a poem we, as readers, can come to a deeper understanding of the workings of our own lives and the world that we live in. This approach is closely connected to the Modernists' fondness for the Lyric poem. A Lyric poem is one in which the poet seeks to express an individual state of mind, mood or attitude. Poets usually write from a personal point of view, using the personal pronoun 'I' in their writing. Occasionally a poet might create an imaginary character, a persona, to express this personal point of view. Montague uses the Lyric form in many of his poems – for example in 'The Cage', 'All Legendary Obstacles' and 'A Welcoming Party' – and he has described how, as a young writer, he modified the form so that he would be able 'to express himself in a compressed, more direct, yet still clearly lyrical form'.

Nature

In Modernist writing, nature is used as a trigger to stimulate the imagination. Unlike Wordsworth and the Romantic poets, Modernists are not mainly concerned with trying to recreate the wonder of nature in words, although they do produce extremely vivid descriptions. Instead, Modernist writers place the emphasis on their imaginative responses to nature. For them, it is the way the individual processes what he/she experiences that is important. We can see this approach in Montague's poem 'Windharp'. As we noted previously, Montague developed his great love of nature when he was a child. For a time he felt a connection with the great Romantic poet William Wordsworth. However, Montague was uneasy with the way that Wordsworth tended to idealise nature. He developed a much more honest and uncompromising view of the natural world, evident in his imagery in 'Killing the Pig' and 'The Trout'.

Imagery

Modernists use imagery to achieve realisation. Realisation means that the poet conveys more than just the sensory realism of an object. Therefore it is not enough for them to do as the Romantics did and appeal to the reader's five senses. Modernist poets do use sensory-based images, but they also seek to create images that allow the reader to be fully 'there' with the object: to be completely aware of it and to understand clearly the nature of its being. In addition, because Modernist poetry frequently uses the artist-centred view, the images that are used in this realisation are connected together by 'a stream of consciousness'. This means that the poet tries to retain the immediacy and the energy of the way his thoughts and feelings blend and merge within him, rather like an internalised 'Lava Lamp'. This can prove to be both the pleasure and the pain of Modernist poetry. Sometimes the connections between the images mesh and we, as readers, experience an insightful understanding of the realisation that the poet seeks to convey. But there are occasions when, try as we might, the links remain unclear and all we are left with is a feeling of bewilderment. Although Modernists do accept bewilderment as a valid response, in such instances it is often helpful to simply allow the images to 'float' around 'inside your head' until the link reveals itself.

Poetic Form and Language

In an effort to give their realisations an undiluted vividness and accessibility for the reader, the Modernists firmly rejected traditional poetic forms and language. Rhyme was no longer considered essential, neither was the rigour of the fourteen-line sonnet. Instead blank or unrhymed verse, rhythm and short verse lines, sometimes consisting of only a few words, allowed the poet to grapple directly and intensely with the essential qualities of his topics and themes.

Such a method can be viewed as a kind of verbal paring back to the very core. In fact, one could compare this approach to the way in which 'text messaging' has caused the simplification of spellings and grammar so that we can communicate the essence of what we want to say as briefly as possible. Modernists use similar methods in their work, as they too alter the type of grammar and language used in poetic expression: make punctuation less rigid; do not have lines of poetry necessarily beginning with a capital letter; no longer cluster lines into stanzas; and replace obviously poetic words such as 'oft' and 'hence' with the everyday vocabulary of real life, as in the phrases 'the Clark Street I.R.T.' and 'work, phone, drive'. Montague summed up his approach to this abandonment of traditional poetic rules in a typically succinct phrase: 'I never strain a line to gain a rhyme.' This does not imply that any less work is put into the writing; rather that the work goes into different, and what could be regarded as more important, areas. Indeed, John Montague's work with words has an elegance and finesse that can be achieved only with a great deal of thought and effort.

The Modernist poets also took a new approach to the appearance of the printed poem on the page, and Montague urges a more experimental approach to layout, commenting:

> It is only a habit of mind which makes us expect a poem to march as docile as a herd of sheep between the fences of white margins.

Poems such as 'Killing the Pig' and 'The Wild Dog Rose' are good examples of his desire to break down the traditional methods of poetic presentation.

Praising the burden

There is a long distance to be travelled between Montague's discovering ways to ease his view of life as a burden and his developing the strength to praise that burden; and yet, it seems to me, that this is precisely the journey that he makes in his poetry.

We have seen how the young Montague's search for a sense of identity, to find out who he was and where he belonged, was impaired by a number of factors: the disruption of his childhood environment caused by his early move from America to Ireland; his father's absence; and, perhaps the most significant of all, his mother's rejection of him. Yet through his poetry Montague has found a way to come to terms with all of these life issues. He can now welcome the duality of his American/Irish background as a positive influence on his writing in that it provided him with a unique view. Of the many honours that he received in America he wrote:

> . . . destiny seems to have decided to give me back my lost childhood in America. . . . But . . . I am grateful to have explored Ireland so intimately.

He can even accept the damaged humanity of his parents, because of his muscular determination to view them in an honest and uncompromising way.

Indeed, it is evident from our consideration of John Montague's life and work that it is this same determined, uncompromising honesty that lies at the heart of his poetry. His exploration of Love confronts the reality rather than the dreams of romantic novels. His writing on Nature recognises and accepts the brutality of the survival instinct. His view of the past acknowledges the violence and harshness that are part of it and the influences, both positive and negative, that it can have on the present. He has questioned the accepted traditions of Irish poetry and turned to worldwide literary influences to develop his own style, which would reflect contemporary Ireland while at the same time initiating the rebirth of Northern Irish poetry.

John Montague has spent time travelling and living in France, America and Ireland, teaching in such universities as Berkeley, UCD and UCC. When he retired from teaching in 1988 he continued with his writing and now divides his time between France and Ireland. As the following passage suggests it seems that, finally, Montague has succeeded in finding the key to ease his sense of burden:

> . . . I approach my future with energy of gratitude: what were once obstacles are becoming miracles, and after years of ploughing rough ground I might be allowed a period of harvesting. For a rearing can be too drastic, despite Kavanagh's theory about all art being 'life squeezed through a repression'. . . . That dolorous discord, that forlorn note, still calls but something sustained me through those harsh, uncomprehending years. My amphibian position between North and South, my natural complicity in three cultures, American, Irish and French, with darts aside to Mexico, India, Italy or Canada, should seem natural enough in the late-twentieth century as man strives to reconcile local allegiances with the absolute necessity of developing a world consciousness to save us from the abyss. Earthed in Ireland, at ease in the world, weave the strands you are given.

It seems to me that this is why Montague's poetry is relevant and has something to offer to all those who read it. It tells of the recognition of what it is to feel lost and alone in a confusing world; the understanding that this is part of all human existence; the determination to accept the reality of one's own living, and from this to discover the strength to praise and celebrate the contribution that each one of us can make to the ebb and flow of humanity. He shows us the tangled strands of his life so that we may see our own tangled life strands and, with him, learn how to 'weave the strands you're given'.

Seamus Heaney once described John Montague as the 'whin bush of Irish Poetry'. Although I am most reluctant to disagree with Mr Heaney, I have to say that I find the image of a yellow gorse bush a little too fixed, too statically stoic for Montague. While I was writing this piece on Montague one image kept forcing its way into my mind. It was an image that I initially found surprising, yet one that steadily gained a relevance to my view of him. It was the image of a Gaelic footballer, managing the burden of the football with finesse and discipline as he powers towards his opponents, forging his way with an uncompromising strength and determination towards the goal. So it is with Montague. The refinement and elegance of his poetry are underpinned by a muscularity of focus and a determined and powerful honesty. Like Montague, the footballer is fully aware of the imminent presence of pain, suffering and defeat in what he is doing, and it is this awareness that makes the commitment of both breathtaking, their courage admirable, their engagement with life elemental. Montague once said, 'But though to understand, however dimly, is to begin to forgive, a writer should never forget.' It is Montague's unyielding resolve to understand, to forgive and most importantly of all, never to forget the 'human pain' involved in living, that enables him not merely to manage the burden of his life but to welcome it and, finally, to celebrate and praise it.

Killing the Pig

Text of poem: New Explorations Anthology page 234

The Appearance of the poem

Montague uses the layout of this poem to increase the impact of the content. By clustering connected lines together, by separating others and by a skilful use of punctuation, he controls the pace of reading. As a result, we are compelled to linger over certain descriptions, as with lines 5–10, while other lines interrupt the pace in an abrupt manner, as in lines 17–18.

A reading of the poem

Montague opens the poem with two words that are filled with such drama that they irresistibly attract attention, 'The noise.' The full stop that follows the two words forces the reader to a sudden stop, just as the real noise halts the farmyard activities. 'The noise' can penetrate walls and doors, so that even before the pig comes into view, it is the 'noise' that signals what is about to happen. The natural question that occurs in response to these two words is 'What noise?' So, Montague sets out to convey in vivid images the source and quality of the noise that has the power to stop the world in its tracks.

The image of the source of the noise, a pig being dragged to the slaughter, is brutally real. Montague does not shy away from the horror of the pig's situation, the 'iron cleek sunk in the roof | of his mouth.' Once again, a full stop forces the reader to pause, prevents a quick gliding over of this unpleasant description.

The parenthesis, the comment that occurs in the brackets in lines 5–10, has a disturbingly conversational tone about it. It is as if we are engaged in a chat about the weather. But the sense of horror is increased: not only is the pig suffering physically, with an iron hook through the roof of its mouth, it is also suffering mentally because it is aware of what the future holds: 'they know the hour has come'. The line 'they dig in their little trotters' emphasises the futility of the pig's resistance and has a kind of black comedy about it. We can visualise the large, fat pig pushing hard on four incongruously small trotters. It would be so much easier if the pig were cooperative, silently unaware, 'dumb', or even happily unaware, 'singing'. But this pig behaves in neither of these ways.

Suddenly, the 'noise' interrupts our 'cosy' conversation. Montague launches into a series of images in lines 13–16, to convey the nature of the 'noise', because 'no single sound could match it –'. Each of the four images has been condensed, reduced to its very essence, in order to vividly suggest the piercing, unsettling nature of the 'sound'. It has the qualities of a plane taking off; a lady opera singer hitting a high note; an electric saw cutting and scrap metal being crushed. All of these sounds are difficult to cope with because they push the human sense of hearing to its limits. There is also the suggestion that they are noises that occur as a result of great exertion. In a similar way, the pig's squeals represent his 'high pitched final effort' to resist his slaughter.

Once again, Montague reinforces the 'Piercing' quality of the sound. It is 'absolute' in that it is unconditional and unlimited. The pig puts his whole being into making this noise, so that his squeals fill the surroundings. Montague has worked very hard on his realisation of this sound, in the last eighteen lines, so that we comprehend both sensually and intellectually the qualities of the 'noise'. Then, without any warning, the noise stops.

With four words 'Then a full stop', he pivots the poem towards a completely different focus. The sound alters to a brief 'solid thump' and then the quietly squeamish squelches of knives at work. Unlike the persistent squealing, these noises occur 'swiftly', until the pig is hung up silently 'shining and eviscerated'. The image of the 'surgeon's coat', in line 27, at first appears clinical and sterile. But there is something deeply disturbing about the bloodied, shining, folded whiteness that it conveys. Both the pig's 'carcass' and the 'surgeon's coat' are inextricably linked with a detached attitude towards a living body. Mickey Boyle slaughters and butchers the pig with an unemotional efficiency. Similarly, the surgeon must remain independent from his patients' humanity while he works in order to operate as effectively as possible.

In the final five lines of the poem, Montague presents us with an immensely dramatic image that highlights the themes underlying the piece. The 'child', representing innocence and life, is given the pig's bladder and, in an unthinking acceptance of what has happened, happily plays with it. Yet surrounding this lively energy are 'the walls of the farmyard'. The walls that shelter the child and echo to his happy shouts are the same walls that were penetrated by the pig's death squeals. These walls have been built to house those who are engaged in the ending of life. The child in all his youthfulness lives in the moment, while the walls are suffused with past deaths. Thus Montague leads us to thoughts of the connections between Life and Death; Construction and Destruction; and the Present and the Past.

Structure

With this poem, Montague takes the Lyric form and gives it a leaner, more concentrated structure. The main concern of the lyric poem is to express an individual state of mind, mood or attitude in order to share the poet's feelings and thoughts with his reader. Montague certainly does this here, but his expression is trimmed of any niceties, so that it conveys the uncompromising reality of the situation. We encounter images such as 'an iron cleek sunk in the roof | of his mouth'.

In addition, Montague moves away from the standardised length for a line of poetry, instead adjusting the length of his line to reinforce meaning. For instance, when he describes the protracted sound of the electric saw he uses a long line: 'the brain-chilling persistence of an electric saw'; whereas when he writes of the sudden death blow inflicted on the pig, the lines are much shorter 'a solid thump of the mallet | flat between the ears.'

Language

It would be a mistake to think that because Montague uses language in a lean and condensed form his writing requires less effort. Similarly, because he uses the language of everyday conversational speech, one might fall into the trap of underestimating the amount of skill required to shape his writing. Consider the following lines:

> they dig in their little trotters,
> will not go dumb or singing
> to the slaughter.

The leanness and apparent simplicity of these lines is deceptive, since each word carries a wealth of suggestion and meaning.

Similarly, the use of everyday speech challenges the poet to initiate new word combinations and connections, as with the lines:

> But the walls of the farmyard
> still hold that scream,
> are built around it.

Here, Montague succeeds in conveying his theme by harnessing ordinary words in an extraordinary sequence.

Our appreciation of Montague's use of language becomes even greater when we notice his ability to incorporate such poetic devices as metaphor, assonance, alliteration and onomatopoeia into such a compact form of language. His use of the four metaphors in lines 13–16 is particularly disciplined, in that each makes a contribution to our understanding of the quality of the pig's squealing. Rather than losing the point in a cascade of metaphors, Montague ensures that there is a clear connection between the noise and the four metaphors.

Montague uses alliteration and assonance in an equally effective manner. Indeed, his use of such 'musical' poetic devices not only adds to the depth of sound in the poem, but it also increases the 'reality' of the images. Simply put, alliteration is where two or more words, close together, begin with the same letter. Thus the letter 's' in the following line suggests the sound of the knife slicing into the pig's flesh: 'Swiftly the knife seeks the throat'. Assonance is where two or more words, close together, have the same vowel sound. So the 'a' sound in 'a solid thump of the mallet | flat between the ears' conveys the force and action of the mallet hitting the pig's head. Onomatopoeia is also present in this quotation with the word 'thump', as this is a word that is made up of the sound that is created. By using 'thump', Montague recreates the hollow sound of the mallet hitting the pig's head. In this way, Montague appeals to the reader's sense of hearing as well as sight, in order to make the images seem more real and vivid.

Perhaps it is with his use of rhythm that Montague's consummate skill becomes particularly evident. As we have seen, he connects poetic line length to line meaning. This connection is reinforced by his mastery of rhythm. Montague is able to control line rhythm without disrupting the natural rhythm that suggests everyday speech, as can be seen in the following quotation:

> (Don't say they are not intelligent:
> they know the hour has come
> and they want none of it;
> they dig in their little trotters,

There is an obvious alteration in rhythm between the first three lines and the fourth line. The fourth line has a much quicker rhythm, in order to suggest the pig's determined resistance and the little steps that he is forced to make. This rhythm helps the reader to 'feel' the pig's legs stiffly stretched, locking his trotters into the ground.

The Trout

Text of poem: New Explorations Anthology page 236

A READING OF THE POEM

From the opening lines of this poem, Montague creates a vivid scene that involves his reader directly in the experience that is being described. So we are instantly lying on the bank with him, pushing back the rushes and sliding our hands gently into the river. His ability to convey this sense of immediacy is one of the key aspects that make Montague's poetry so accessible. This is largely due to his ability to construct images that appeal to a number of senses. Thus, in the first four lines we see and feel the solidity of the river-bank, the papery stalks of the rushes and the cool liquidity of the river water.

The image of the trout, in lines 5–6, is packed with sensory information. Not only can we see him suspended in a 'sensual dream', we can also feel the easy pulse of his relaxation. Montague's joining of the two words 'tendril' and 'light' creates a vivid image: 'tendril' suggests an almost erotic sensuality in that it calls up pictures of a slender, smooth shoot of a plant, like a fine shining curl of soft hair; while 'light' suggests a feeling of weightlessness, a brightness and a warmth. Montague's realisation of the trout enables us to become one with him; we too are held in the 'fluid sensual dream.'

In the second stanza, Montague sweeps us out of the water and back onto the bank. We are there with the 'I', poised above the trout, suspended not in water this time, but in a kind of all-powerful, airy expectation. The hunter watches, while his prey has no knowledge of the hunter's existence. But the hunter–prey relationship is deeper than this in that the hunter almost becomes part of the prey, so focused is his attention. The hunter feels his identity vanish and is left 'Savouring my own absence'. Again, there is an erotic element in this deep-level connection, where the hunter feels his 'Senses expanding'.

The third stanza plunges us back into the river again, but this time the focus is on the hunter stealthily moving to capture the trout. The slight disturbance caused in the water strokes the trout pleasurably. Again, the hunter is totally focused on the prey: 'I could count every stipple'. But this fascination does change the hunter's objective. He wants to trap the fish, and so he is very careful to 'cast no shadow', since this would alert the fish to his presence.

This lack of sympathy on the hunter's part continues into the final stanza, where we feel the hunter close his hands around the trout, still unsuspectingly motionless apart from his erotically 'lightly pulsing gills'. Suddenly, Montague quickens the pace of the poem and the moment of capture happens with the shock of 'I gripped.' It is at this point that Montague's accomplishment as a poet becomes evident. In the final lines of the poem he completely reverses the balance of power. Up until now, the hunter has been portrayed as powerful and in control, determined to catch the fish irrespective of the effect that this will have on the creature. But in lines 23–24 the hunter understands what his actions mean for the trout. The trout's 'terror' is communicated so vividly that the hunter can actually taste it. This tasting reference is extremely effective, since the hunter will eat the fish, but it also suggests his gut-wrenching response to the fish's panic. The hunter's unshakeable desire to trap the fish has unleashed responses that he never expected, not only in the fish, but also in himself.

Themes

Once again with Montague, apparent simplicity dissolves to reveal a complexity of thinking. Initially 'The Trout' seems to be an extremely vivid description of the capture of a fish; a masterly use of words to 'paint' a stunning picture.

Gradually, however, the compacted density of Montague's imagery creates intellectual connections that go far beyond the scene at the centre of the poem.

The relationship between the hunter and prey is explored. We feel the hunter's obsessive attentiveness and his sense of power. Similarly, we experience the trout's oblivious relaxation. Montague conveys the intense intimacy that the two share. Then he alters the poem's perspective, so that we confront another aspect of this relationship; the hunter's loss of control in the face of the shock of his prey's terrified response.

There is a sensual aspect to this relationship. Indeed, it is no accident that human pairings are often seen in hunter-and-prey terms. This balance of control, desire, fascination and fear are all present in male-and-female relationships. Indeed, there is a heightened level of sensuality in the poem, with a physical intensity in his use of the senses of sight, touch and taste that is suggestive of eroticism.

John Montague has frequently used the image of fishing to illustrate his view of the act of writing poetry. Thus, this poem could also be seen as an examination of the creative process. The effort to capture something that is 'slippery' and difficult to hold; the feeling of being 'lord of creation'; the obsessive fascination; and the shock of finally trapping something that is not quite what was expected, could all be applied to an artist's struggle to create.

Structure

In appearance 'The Trout' seems to have a more traditional format than 'Killing the Pig', having four stanzas of six lines with each line beginning with a capital letter. However, the lines do not end in a definite rhyme scheme, although there are occasional subtle end rhymes:

> And tilt them slowly down**stream**
> To where he lay, tendril-light,
> In his fluid sensual **dream**.

Montague makes other adjustments to the traditional format in order to create a more effective vehicle for his thoughts. His use of punctuation departs from the usual end-of-line method. Instead he uses punctuation sparingly, to control the rhythm of his lines and to reflect the actual meaning and movement expressed in his writing. So the first stanza has no punctuation until the fifth line, where commas initiate a brief pause before moving on to a full stop at the end of the sixth line. This absence of punctuation serves to reinforce the smooth continuity of movement in the parting of the rushes, the hands sliding into the river and moving under water. The commas cause the reader to pause over the brilliant pairing of the words 'tendril-light', so that the image is absorbed and our sense of the trout is heightened. If we compare this first stanza with the final one of the poem, the differing effects of his use of punctuation become evident. In the fourth stanza the increased punctuation serves to reflect the breathless mixture of excitement and fear, the sudden movements and the shock of the moment.

Language

Montague skilfully uses assonance, alliteration and rhythm to cause his reader to feel a part of the experience. Assonance, where two or more words close together have the same vowel sound, appears in the very first line, 'Flat on the bank I parted'. This repetition of the 'a' sound conveys the sensation of lying stretched at full length, totally grounded, on the river bank. Alliteration, where two or more words close together begin with the same letter, is used in an equally effective way, as for instance in the final line of the poem, 'Taste his terror on my hands.' The 't' sounds make the reader move his tongue as if to spit out something unpleasant, thereby reinforcing the sensory appreciation of the moment.

In addition, Montague's use of 's' and 'l' sounds is particularly successful, as with the papery, dry whispering of the 'Rushes to ease my hands' and the smooth liquidity of 'And tilt them slowly downstream'.

Montague controls the rhythm of this piece with the skill of a composer. In lines 13–14, for example, he uses assonance and rhythm to convey the hunter's actions:

> As the curve of my hands
> Swung under his body

Similarly, his use of assonance and 'l' sounds in 'Under the lightly pulsing gills' initiates a rhythm that reflects the fish's movements.

In his use of such poetic devices, Montague is continuing the work that was begun in early Irish poetry and rediscovered by Austin Clarke. His appreciation of the musicality of language and his ability to marry sound, rhythm and meaning enable Montague to realise scenes and experiences vibrating with life and reality.

The Locket

Text of poem: New Explorations Anthology page 240

A reading of the poem

The first two lines of this poem have a nursery-rhyme or songlike quality about them: 'Sing a last song | for the lady who has gone'. The sing-song rhythm of these lines reinforces this impression. Interestingly, Montague has commented that one particular folk-song, 'The Tri-coloured Ribbon', was in his head when he wrote this poem. However, it quickly becomes clear that this is no nursery rhyme, no light-hearted ballad. Rather than being a queen or a maid, this lady is in fact a much darker character, a 'fertile source of guilt and pain.' The following lines are filled with palpable distress and, at the same time, a deliberate attempt to be rather dismissive about that distress:

> *The worst birth in the annals of Brooklyn,*
> that was my cue to come on
> my first claim to fame.

The line in italics is the phrase that Montague's mother frequently repeated in connection with his birth. His use of italics may be simply to indicate that this is, indeed, a quotation. But the change in the type-face has additional effects: it serves to emphasise the phrase in that it stands out visually from the rest of the poem; it also calls up inscriptions on tombstones or memorials, as if to indicate that Montague, despite all his adult achievements, feels that this will always sum up his role in life. Finally, it acts as a kind of emotional distancing mechanism because, unlike the rest of the poem, it highlights the fact that these are not Montague's words, neither are they his feelings.

There is a definite attempt to create an emotional distance between Montague and what he is describing, as with his use of the word 'cue', which conjures up images of actors and plays; and also in the apparently throwaway remark, 'my first claim to fame.' Montague seems to be trying very hard to minimise his reaction to his mother's comment. Nevertheless, despite all his effort, it is his 'pain' that comes through.

This brittle veneer of glibness continues into the second stanza and hangs on the word 'Naturally', as Montague tries desperately to accept and justify his mother's treatment of him as natural. His mother's longing for a girl is presented as a valid reason for her behaviour. Yet once again the veneer cracks, and we see the damage that lies beneath it. The image of the 'infant curls of brown' is very moving. It conveys the vulnerability of the baby and is suggestive of the young Montague's efforts to win his mother's affection by being an attractive baby with a head of brown hair. But it was all in vain, for he had made the 'double blunder': the lumbering heaviness of these two words emphasises the weight of the 'awful sins' that this small, attractive, vulnerable baby had committed by 'coming out, both the wrong sex, | and the wrong way around.' These, then, were the 'sins' that Montague had committed in his mother's eyes: he was not a girl and he was a breech birth, that is he came bottom first rather than head first.

Clearly the baby had absolutely no control over either of these situations, and yet he feels 'guilt' and justifies his mother's reaction with the phrase 'Not readily forgiven'.

As the brittle veneer of glibness hung on the word 'Naturally' in the second stanza, it pivots on the word 'So' in the third stanza. 'So' suggests a logical, cause-and-effect relationship, that all his previous explanations make his mother's rejection of him perfectly understandable: 'So you never nursed me'. It is a simple line, but the heartbreak is clear in his change of address from 'she' to 'you' for his mother. Montague sweeps on to another of his mother's phrases, notably not in italics this time: '"when poverty comes through the door | love flies up the chimney"'. Thus we encounter another excuse offered as a justification for her behaviour: being poor had destroyed her capacity to love. This may well have a degree of truth about it, but it seems immensely sad that the two quotations that Montague remembers from his mother are so negative.

In the fourth stanza, Montague maintains this cause-and-effect connection by beginning it with the word 'Then'. However, this poem is not outlining a scientific procedure, it is the description of a profoundly affecting series of actions that culminate in the horribly simple line, 'Then you gave me away'. So, we can see that with the first lines of the second, third and fourth stanzas Montague works hard to clothe an emotionally charged situation in a quasi-logical sequence. But despite his efforts it is evident that, try as he might, Montague knows that this logic is only apparent and not real at all.

Montague's reaction to his mother's 'giving away' of him is deeply moving. Rather than withdrawing entirely from her and meeting her rejection with one of his own, he goes to great lengths to try to establish some form of relationship with her. He cycles the eight miles to see his mother, knowing full well that if he did not she 'might never have known' him. Once there, he cannot expect to be treated as a son, to be fussed over, asked all those 'irritating' questions that mothers ask their children because they love them dearly. Instead, Montague has to 'court' his mother 'like a young man'. His use of the word 'court' links back to his use of the word 'lady' in line 2 of the poem: these words are suggestive of Courtly Love, that is, the type of love that features in the stories about King Arthur and his Knights of the Round Table. Films such as 'A Knight's Tale' and 'First Knight' give some idea about the way that Courtly Love worked. The knight was expected to woo, or try to win, the lady by giving her gifts or performing heroic deeds. All his efforts were designed to prove his loyalty and devotion to her. Frequently the knight went through all of this without any real hope of the lady returning his devotion. Clearly, this idea of love tells us a great deal about Montague's approach to his mother. He 'teasingly' unties her apron and persuades her to sit 'drinking by the fire'. But the focus of their conversation is very definitely on the mother and the 'wild, young days' of her youth.

Montague's genuine sympathy for his mother is revealed in his recognition of the brief time that she lived a happy and carefree life. Her life quickly deteriorated, until she 'landed up mournful and chill'. His sympathy is particularly evident in his use of the word 'wound' in line 30, where he deliberately plays upon the two ways in which this word can be read: wound as in 'to wind,' meaning 'to wrap', and wound as in 'to injure'. By doing this, Montague increases the layers of suggestion in his writing in order to convey the depth of his mother's emotional injuries.

The fifth stanza captures the moment of his departure, to cycle the eight miles back to his home with his aunts. It is a dramatic snapshot that vibrates with lost opportunities and damaged souls. Despite all Montague's wooing there is no sense of positive warmth from his mother. Instead, she can only signal her emotional response in her customary negative terms: '"Don't come again," you say, roughly, | "I start to get fond of you, John,"'. Once again, the young Montague responds with a generosity of spirit to yet another rejection, understanding that these words are simply 'the harsh logic of a forlorn woman'.

At this point in the poem, the reader could be forgiven for believing that Montague has reached the heart of what he is trying to reconcile within himself. He has been brutally honest in confronting the nature of his relationship with his mother, and seems to have arrived at a point where he can make allowances for her. But Montague's writing has a muscularity about it that prevents him from avoiding the true reality of a situation. He cannot complete the poem until he has expressed all the aspects of this problematic relationship. Thus in the final stanza he tells us how, after his mother's death, he discovered that she wore 'an oval locket'. Heartbreakingly, enclosed within this locket, like a precious moment frozen in time, was 'an old picture', not of her husband, nor a lost love from her carefree youth, but 'of a child in Brooklyn', Montague himself.

So how can Montague call this a 'mysterious blessing'? Surely it is no more than the ultimate lost opportunity, the final rejection out of so many? Yet, it seems to me that if we relate the locket back to the Courtly Love imagery that he used previously, his attitude begins to make sense. His mother wore the locket 'always', in the secret gesture of a woman who wants to cherish and to protect, to hold close and to nurture. For him, it represents the unspoken words of love that the lady gives to her knight when she presents him with her colours before he enters the tournament. It holds the promise that the love that Montague offered was, finally and wondrously, returned. While the lady of the Courtly Love stories is prevented from openly responding by the customs of the time, Montague's mother is trapped within the 'cocoon of pain' that life has wound around her. Thus, for Montague, the locket is indeed a 'mysterious blessing'.

Depiction of character

Montague has the remarkable ability to convey character vividly by using a series of condensed phrases that highlight key personality traits. So, in this poem, he does not give us any physical description of his mother. The most we learn about her appearance is that she used an apron, she was pretty when she was young and she wore a locket. What Montague does instead is to concentrate on her words and actions. He tells us some of her comments:

> *The worst birth in the annals of Brooklyn,*
> 'when poverty comes through the door
> love flies up the chimney',
> 'Don't come again,'. . .
> 'I start to get fond of you, John,
> and then you are up and gone';

All these words carry a terrible feeling of negativity. They express the lost hopes of a woman who was deeply wounded by a life that she found disappointing and painful; who was afraid to unwind her protective but imprisoning 'cocoon of pain' because she expected more wounds and was 'resigned to being alone.'

Her actions largely reinforce this 'harsh logic'. She longs for a girl baby and then cannot accept the baby boy who arrives after a difficult birth. Nowadays, such behaviour would be seen as being indicative of post-natal depression, but in the 1920s this condition was unknown. She avoids the emotional and physical contact of nursing her baby. Finally, she gives him away. Then, in later years, when he is no longer a baby and cycles some eight miles to see her, she has to be teased and persuaded to spend some time with him. There is the suggestion that in allowing Montague to untie her apron she is permitting him some small level of closeness and intimacy. But in the final analysis she is utterly unable to allow him or herself to untie her 'cocoon of pain'. She speaks to him 'roughly' and all her behaviour is indicative of 'a forlorn woman'. The only positive action is, of course, her constant wearing of the locket. Her tragedy was that the 'cocoon of pain' would not allow her to wear her locket openly, nor to display what was in her poor, battered heart.

Themes

On a first reading the theme of this poem seems to be Montague's relationship with his mother. He tells of her rejection of him, his attempts to win her round, her inability to respond in any major way, and then her death. Finally, after her death, he discovers the locket and he takes this to be a sign that she did, indeed, love him.

Although this is the main theme of the poem, there are other themes that lie alongside it. Montague's writing often begins with his individual experience of life and then expands outwards to embrace wider issues. Thus, a second theme in this poem is that of Life having the potential to be a negative force. It can destroy human hopes and batter human hearts into a condition in which love and positive human feelings cannot be expressed openly. Through this poem, Montague finds it possible to face and acknowledge this possibility.

Allied to this is the third theme – that of the dehumanising and brutalising effects that have arisen out of the political situation in Northern Ireland. His parents were forced by this turmoil to move to poverty and disappointment in America, which led to the break-up of the Montague family. Thus the dysfunctional nature of his family reflects the dysfunctional nature of the society of Northern Ireland.

Language

Montague's management of rhythm and tone is extremely successful in 'The Locket'. As we have seen, Montague had the song 'The Tri-coloured Ribbon' in mind when he wrote this poem and the opening stanza has a strong sing-song rhythm and tone. Try reading the highlighted words louder than the others in the following two lines:

> **Sing** a **last** song,
> **For** the **la**dy **who** has **gone**,

This not only produces the sing-song effect, it also sounds rather like a church bell tolling at the funeral of Montague's mother.

Rhythm and tone are part of everyday speech. We each have a particular rhythm in our way of talking: some may have a fast rhythm, while others are much slower. Our tone changes to match the feeling behind our words. When Montague quotes his mother's comments, he does not try to shape them into a poetic form; instead he leaves them with her own distinct rhythm and tone:

> 'when poverty comes through the door
> love flies up the chimney',
> 'Don't come again,'. . .
> I start to get fond of you, John,
> And then you are up and gone';

If we listen to these words, we can hear something of what Montague's mother was really like, just as we heard the bell tolling in the first two lines of the poem. The rhythm of these lines is neither as regular nor as smooth as in lines 1–2. It is as if his mother's unhappiness is strangling the words that she speaks, so that they come out in a staccato, broken-up manner. There is a roughness about their tone that hints at a woman who has become tougher because of her hard life: a woman who is afraid to be gentle or loving because she has been deeply hurt.

This is in marked contrast to the rhythm and tone of the final stanza. Here, Montague discovers that his mother always wore his picture in a locket. The rhythm is much slower than that of his mother's speech. Montague achieves this effect by using commas to introduce pauses in the way that we read the lines. Similarly, the tone is much gentler. The overall impression is of Montague speaking quietly because he is amazed by what he has discovered, and because he realises that his mother was not as tough as her speech had suggested.

The Cage

Text of poem: New Explorations Anthology page 244

[*Note: This poem is also prescribed for Ordinary Level 2008 exam*]

A READING OF THE POEM

'My father, the least happy man I have known.' The opening sentence of this poem is a perfect example of Montague's ability to condense a lot of information into a few significant words fastened together in a taut structure. By using simple, straightforward words, Montague makes the poem accessible and easily understood. But it is the way that he connects the words together that lifts them into the realm of poetry. So, we meet the first two words 'My father' followed by a comma. We have seen previously how Montague uses punctuation to control the rhythm of the poem and the impact of his words. Here, his use of the comma forces the reader to pause, to linger on the idea of Montague's father. It is as if we are in conversation with Montague and he has said 'My father', then stopped. We have to wait for him to go on, to choose the words that will sum up this man in an appropriate manner. The wait is worthwhile, because Montague comes out with a character summary that is stunningly descriptive despite its brevity: 'the least happy | man I have known.' The phrase says it all, paints a picture of a man who lived life largely in the absence of joy and humour, whose main impact on his son's existence was that he was 'the least happy man' that Montague had ever encountered. Interestingly, unlike Montague's poem on his relationship with his mother, 'The Locket', where he constantly refers to himself, using words such as 'I', 'my' and 'me', there is no further use of 'I' until the final stanza of 'The Cage'.

From this point, the poem takes flight into a series of vivid images that put flesh on this 'least happy man'. Again, it is Montague's use of conversational language that draws us into the poem. It is so easy to read, yet the emotion conveyed by the words makes it a very moving piece. This is not only because the man himself led such an unfulfilling life, but also because of the way in which his son, Montague, was affected. So we read of a man drained of colour by his years working underground. There is the suggestion that the physical paleness of his face represents the sucking out of his life force. He is only a white, half-alive creature, rather like the victim of a vampire. The narrowness and the pointlessness of his life are conveyed in the following three lines with tightly packed phrases like 'the lost years' and 'listening to a subway'. What a way to live!

The tone of the second stanza lifts slightly with Montague's use of the word 'But' and the rest of the opening line, 'But a traditional Irishman'. There seems to be some comfort here. The implication of the 'traditional Irishman' is of a cheerful, social individual who likes a 'drink'. And, as we read down through the second and third stanzas, it seems that Montague's father fits this preconception. He drinks 'neat whiskey' and smiles at his neighbours. However, certain words and phrases used in these stanzas suggest that all is not quite as positive as it seems. Montague's father does not simply leave his work; he is 'released'. This use of the word 'released' is brilliant in that it suggests his father's feelings of being trapped, of being imprisoned by the metal mesh in his ticket-box. Like an animal in a zoo he escapes from his cage, but, sadly, he still carries the effects of his captivity with him into freedom. So, his drinking is not simply for social purposes; it is driven by the determination to forget, to blot out the memories. The terrible and tragic aim of his drinking is described by Montague's pairing of two words, 'brute oblivion'. There is an immense feeling of waste in the fact that this reasonless, unthinking forgetfulness is the only condition that Montague's father 'felt at home in'.

Against this background, the father's 'march down the street' has the brittle quality of pretence about it. Before going out this man has 'picked himself | up', suggesting not only that he had physically fallen down in a drunken condition, but also that he had been 'down' mentally and emotionally. The father's feelings of a rather pathetic pride are conveyed by the fact that his neighbourhood is 'all-white'. It is clearly one of the few things that he can hang on to: he and his neighbourhood are better than those that are non-white.

When Montague's father finally returned to Tyrone in 1952, the poet was in his twenties. The fourth and fifth stanzas describe a walk that the pair took. Montague's father is at home in this place that he has not seen for over twenty years; he remembers the route; it is 'as though | he had never left'. Sadly, his relationship with his son is not so comfortable. There is no sense of companionship between the two men. In fact Montague likens them to the ancient Greek father and son, Odysseus and Telemachus. Odysseus left his wife, Penelope, and his young son, Telemachus, to fight in the Trojan War. You may have seen this war portrayed in the film 'Troy'. After Troy had fallen, Odysseus had many adventures and did not return home for twenty years, by which time

Telemachus was a young man. When he got home Odysseus sent Telemachus into exile, because he had been warned that he should not trust his son. Unfortunately the warning referred to another of Odysseus' sons, who later accidentally killed Odysseus. Montague had just won a scholarship to the USA and was soon to leave Ireland, so his comparison calls up the idea of the father returning as the son leaves. There is also the suggestion that the two men, like Odysseus and Telemachus, are somehow destined by Fate never to live in the same place. In addition, just as Montague uses images from Courtly Love in 'The Locket' to provide an emotional distance from the situation, here he employs images from Ancient Greek mythology for the same reason.

Yet in the final stanza we see that, once again, Montague's unyielding determination to confront reality has enabled him to develop a feeling of sympathy for, and acceptance of, his father as a human being. This acceptance gives Montague the strength to remember his father as he really was: a vulnerable, ageing man with a 'bald head' caged 'behind | the bars of the small booth' where he worked. His father had, indeed, been scarred by injuries that he had received in a car accident. But more than that, Montague clearly believes that he was a man whose life had been irreparably damaged, lastingly marked, by forces outside of his control, the political situation in Northern Ireland. It was this 'car crash' with Destiny that made his father into a 'ghostly' shadow of himself and 'the least happy | man' that Montague had ever known.

Themes

Once again we see Montague beginning with the details of his own particular life, and then expanding into wider issues. So the main theme of this poem is the nature of Montague's relationship with his father.

Montague's second theme deals with the negative effects of the political situation in Northern Ireland. His father, and his relationship with his father, are representative of the damage that was caused by the Northern difficulties. His father, like so many other Irishmen, was forced to leave his homeland. These men lived lives that that did not make him happy; they lived lives filled with 'lost years'. They were frequently separated from their families for long periods of time and this meant that the effects of the Northern political situation were carried through to the next generation.

Depiction of character

Montague makes his father just as real as his mother, but he uses different methods to describe him. He gave very few physical details about his mother, but he tells us quite a lot about how his father looked: a pale, bald man who had a scar on his forehead. Also, Montague directly quoted a number of the things that his mother used to say, but we never hear his father's voice at all. He seems to be a man who was beaten into silence by the life that he led.

However, Montague does use actions to highlight key personality traits. His father spent years trapped underground 'listening to a subway'. He 'drank neat whiskey' and then 'picked himself | up'. Then he would 'march down the street | extending his smile'. His life in Brooklyn was clearly very unhappy, but he disguised his unhappiness in front of his neighbours. Once back in Ireland, he seemed to be much more at home and more relaxed. He could walk 'across fields'. It was as if 'he had never left'.

A SENSE OF PLACE

We have already seen how Montague is able to create vivid images that not only make us see what he is describing, but also enable us to experience them emotionally and intellectually. This ability is particularly evident in 'The Cage', with his contrasting descriptions of Brooklyn and Garvaghey. Because Montague uses lean and condensed language his descriptions create a strong impression. First we encounter Brooklyn's underground world, where the darkness and artificial lights make the workers pale and the subway trains cause the ground to 'shudder'. Then we come up into the light of the 'all-white' neighbourhood, filled with the sound of the bells of St Teresa's church. Montague appeals to the senses of sight and hearing to make us 'feel' that Brooklyn is a hard world filled with noises, metal and people.

Garvaghey, on the other hand, is a much softer, calmer place. There are fields edged with 'hawthorn on the summer | hedges' and 'a bend of the road | which still sheltered | primroses'. Montague's father can 'walk' rather than 'march' here, and he does not have to pretend to smile any more. Again, Montague appeals to the sense of sight; we can 'see' the green fields, the white hawthorn blossom and the yellow of the primroses. As for sounds, in marked contrast to Brooklyn, there are none: just the quiet of the summer countryside.

Windharp

Text of poem: New Explorations Anthology page 248

THE APPEARANCE OF THE POEM

As with 'Killing the Pig', it is worthwhile taking a moment to consider the way that this poem appears on the page. It is essentially one long sentence that is broken up into lines of three or four words. The result is that the shape of the poem reflects the continuous movement of the wind, rising and falling in gusts. In this way, Montague uses the appearance of 'Windharp' to contribute to his realisation of the wind.

A reading of the poem

Montague's writing in this poem is marvellously taut and condensed. Using lines of only three or four words, he evokes the many aspects of the wind, so that we do not merely see, hear and feel the wind, but we also understand the essence of its force and energy. 'Windharp' is like an Impressionist painting, in that it does not seek to represent the wind in a factual sense; instead, Montague drives his writing onwards by his use of a 'stream of consciousness' approach to the images that he creates. As we considered previously, Modernist writers try to reproduce the way in which thoughts develop and connect in a continuous internal processing of life's experiences. This approach enables Montague to create his own personal realisation of the wind. In order to communicate this realisation, Montague presents a series of analogous images that, within his mind, have a similarity to aspects of the wind that he considers essential. Thus if we look at the first line of the poem, 'The sounds of Ireland,' it is clear that Montague is highlighting what he considers to be an essential aspect of the wind: the way in which 'that restless whispering' of the wind acts on the whole countryside of Ireland and produces a variety of sounds. His 'stream of consciousness' then goes on to consider some of these sounds, and Montague portrays them in a series of images: 'seeping out of | low bushes and grass'; 'wrinkling bog pools' and 'scraping tree branches'.

So far, the connections that he makes are pretty understandable. However, Montague begins to move his realisation of the wind onto a deeper, more personal level with the images that he calls up from line 9: 'light hunting cloud, | sound hounding sight'. Here he seems to be using images from fox-hunting to illustrate an aspect of the wind. Montague may be trying to convey the rough-and-tumble connection between light and cloud, sound and sight that exist when the wind blows across the Irish landscape. Remember, the images that the poet uses may have only a partial and personally based correspondence with the original object, and my interpretation need not necessarily be the correct one. Again, he pushes his realisation to even greater personal depths with the next image, of 'a hand ceaselessly | combing and stroking | the landscape'. Montague's linking of the wind to a hand may seem rather puzzling at first, nevertheless, if we allow the two images to float around inside our heads for a while, the connection begins to reveal itself. The wind acts like a hand on the landscape in that it suggests a close and intimate form of physical contact. The wind moves on the countryside like a hand involved in combing and stroking but, instead of hair, the hand combs through trees and fields of grain and it strokes grass on the hillsides or water in a mountain lake. Again, coming from this combing and stroking imagery, the 'stream of consciousness' moves on to the final analogous image: that of a mountain pony. With this image Montague seems to be suggesting that the wind has a positive effect on the countryside, in that it makes the landscape gleam just like the glossy coat of the pony. This could mean that the rippling trees, the waving grass and the water all sparkle with light. Equally, he could be suggesting that the movement caused by the wind brings the countryside to life. It seems to be filled with an energy that is absent when the wind is not blowing. There is the feeling that the landscape of Ireland, like the pony, willingly submits to the wind's actions because they both realise that these actions will be pleasurable, and will make them better than they would have been had the 'combing and stroking' not taken place.

Themes

The most obvious theme in this poem could be simply the realisation of the wind in a vivid and emotionally affective word-painting. However, there is another theme interwoven with the condensed, yet vibrant images that Montague creates. If we look at these images, we can see that they are all centred on the idea that the wind possesses an energy that has a significant and positive effect on the Irish countryside. If we relate this concept back to the title of the poem, 'Windharp', there is the implication that Montague sees Ireland's countryside as being like a windharp: just as the wind blowing across the windharp's strings creates beautiful notes, notes that would not exist without the intimate interaction between the two, so the wind acting on the landscape of Ireland creates a beauty that would not exist without the intimate interaction between land and moving air. This beauty is not only the concrete beauty of a world in movement it is also the beauty found in the creativity present in this intimate interaction. So, a second, less obvious theme is that of Montague considering the Creative Impulse and the part that the Irish environment plays in this Creative Impulse.

Language

As we noted previously, during his college days in Dublin Montague became involved in the Dublin poetic scene. There he met the poet Austin Clarke and was immensely impressed with Clarke's efforts to incorporate many of the old Gaelic poetic devices into his poetry. Old Irish poetry was performed out loud by bards and so it was extremely 'musical' to the ear. This musicality came from the use of such devices as internal rhyme, assonance and rhythm. In 'Windharp', we can see Montague carefully utilising these effects to add to his realisation of the wind. For example, he avoids using the end-of-line rhyme in favour of the much more subtle approach of internal rhyme: '**sound hound**ing sight'. The unexpected appearance of this internal rhyme contributes to the words rolling easily off the tongue, because the human brain likes and finds pleasure in rhyming words. Of course, there is also assonance here, in that both words have the same vowel sound of 'ou'. The echoing effect created by Montague's use of these devices is suggestive of repeated gusts of wind blowing over the Irish landscape.

Similarly, Montague handles the rhythm of this poem very skilfully indeed. The rhythm is grounded in the fact that the poem is one long sentence, interspersed with commas. This creates a continuous, flowing rhythm that captures the wind's movement. Within this rhythm Montague introduces other brief rhythms that reflect the imagery, as in 'that restless whispering', where the 's' sounds and the building up of syllables from 1 (that) to 3 (whispering) create a feeling of air moving.

This elegance in Montague's writing is particularly evident if we make a comparison between the different rhythms used in two lines from this poem:

> wrinkling bog pools,
>
> combing and stroking

Both lines consist of only three words, yet the first line has a jagged, edgy rhythm conjuring up ripples on water; while the second line has a soothing rhythm created by the balancing of the two syllable words, 'combing' and 'stroking', on either side of the monosyllabic 'and'.

All Legendary Obstacles

Text of poem: New Explorations Anthology page 251

A READING OF THE POEM

This poem has a marvellously cinematic opening. It is as though we are sitting in front of a wide cinema screen, watching a camera pan from the east coast to the west coast of America. Once again Montague uses his condensed style of writing to create a real sense of place. We can 'see' the 'long imaginary plain' spread out before our eyes; we 'climb over' the hugely 'monstrous ruck of mountains'; and we 'feel' the drenching coldness of 'The hissing drift of winter rain.'

However, in spite of the 'reality' of this scene, there are indications in the first stanza that the poem is not simply about two lovers separated by bad weather and a difficult and arduous train journey. Montague inserts two words, 'legendary' and 'imaginary', into his vivid descriptions that hint at the complexity underlying this poem. The word 'legendary' establishes a connection between the poem and the world of myths and legends, where gods and heroes encounter challenges and 'monstrous' ordeals that are far greater than those of the ordinary, human world. Similarly, 'imaginary' evokes a world that is not restricted by what we know and expect – a world where anything can happen, and usually does.

In the second stanza Montague moves the focus of the poem down onto an individual figure: himself. He has spoken about the circumstances in his life that led to this experience: he was waiting to meet his girlfriend, who was later to become his first wife, after a period of separation when they were based in different colleges in America. Montague's anxiety and uncertainty, evident in his restless 'shifting | . . . from station to bar' contrast with the assurance and the certainty of the trains that 'sail | By', unhindered by the heavy rain.

Finally, in the third stanza, the train that he has been waiting for 'All day' arrives at the station. The time is significant: 'midnight' conjures up images of intense darkness, a time when the supernatural world is very close to our everyday world. We can imagine his girlfriend's face 'pale | Above the negro porter's lamp', glowing in a ghostly manner against the wet blackness of the night. Montague's reaction to her arrival is unexpected. He clearly loves this woman deeply, as he has waited for a whole day for her arrival; however, he is 'too blind with rain | And doubt to speak'. He can only stretch forward 'Until our chilled hands met.' The word 'chilled' implies more than simply the coldness of a wet winter's night. It conveys a sense of emotional tension and apprehensiveness. Montague feels 'doubt' about the situation. But it is not only his hands that are 'chilled'. The implication is that his girlfriend's hands are also cold – perhaps from exhaustion as a result of her arduous journey, or perhaps because she too feels a certain anxiety. The image of Montague reaching up to clasp her hands is suggestive of his trying to draw his girlfriend from one world into another. They are both in an incapacitated state: he is 'blind' and cannot speak; while she is 'pale'. The meeting of their 'chilled hands' suggests the triumph of their hope and their faith in each other because they have bridged the distance that separated them, represented by the gap between the platform and the train.

In the final stanza the focus moves onto his girlfriend, with Montague using 'You' rather than 'I'. We learn that she has also had a difficult time, but it is clear that Montague does not know or understand all that she has endured. This highlights the fact that, no matter how much the two love each other, they will always be two separate people and this unchangeable individuality places a limitation on their love. Her difficulties are summed up in the lines, 'You had been travelling for days | With an old lady'. As we have seen in 'The Locket' and 'The Cage', Montague is very adept at using behaviour to reveal character. Here, the 'old lady' seems to be rather correct and proper in her attitude: like a true lady, she wears gloves and she rubs a 'neat circle' on the window. She watches the two lovers 'Move into the wet darkness'. There is some feeling of optimism about the lovers' relationship when we read that they are 'Kissing', indicating that they are gradually becoming more intimate, that the degree of separation between them is slowly being reduced. However, it is not a totally optimistic ending because the final words of the poem tell us that the two lovers are 'still unable to speak'.

Theme

It is evident that Montague is writing about the theme of love in this poem. However, this is no sugary-sweet consideration of a romantic, idealised love. With the same uncompromising honesty that he used to view his mother and his father, Montague describes the true reality of his love. And again he clothes this strength of vision with an elegance of expression and a finesse of language. In an interview with Dennis O'Driscoll, Montague said of this poem:

> It's a complicated poem: there's a lot of water in it, railway trains in it (I lived close to the old 'El' when I was a boy in Brooklyn). But I don't really want to explicate it, except that the Orpheus myth comes in . . .

If we take each of the points that Montague mentions, we may well arrive at some better understanding of this 'complicated poem'. However, as was discussed previously, we do need to remember that the connections established by the imagery of Modernist poetry can be quite subtle, since they arise out of the poet's personal 'stream of consciousness'.

There is, indeed, 'a lot of water' in 'All Legendary Obstacles'. From the very first stanza the poem vibrates with watery images, and echoes to the sounds of water in lines 4–6, 10–12, 15–16 and 22–24. The connection between love and all this water is not immediately clear. In the first stanza the 'hissing drift of winter rain' could be seen as one of the 'legendary obstacles' that the lovers have to overcome before they can be reunited. Yet if we look at the way that this rain causes the huge rivers, the Sacramento and the San Joaquin, to flood, there is the suggestion of 'Flooding' in an emotional sense. Rather like early Hollywood films used crashing waves to imply intensity and intimacy, the rain-filled rivers rushing through the land could be seen as images of the way in which love sweeps through the human heart and soul. Thus, as he waits at the station, Montague's anxious anticipation and his awareness of all that is making the lovers' reunion difficult are underpinned by the overwhelming nature of his love for this woman.

The image of the 'water dripping | From great flanged wheels' has something of tears being shed about it. The trains that 'sail | By' represent disappointment for Montague because they are not the trains that will deliver his girlfriend to him. We have all waited to meet someone, so we can easily imagine the way in which Montague's excitement increases with the sight of each train coming towards the station and then the crashing distress when each train continues by. The 'great flanged wheels' shed the water as carelessly as they crush Montague's hopes and expectations of love.

'I was too blind with rain' is a clearer representation of the connection between water and love. Montague is in such a heightened emotional state by the time that his girlfriend finally arrives that he is simply unable to function in the normal, expected way: he cannot see properly and he cannot speak. He is almost paralysed by the power of his feelings.

In the final stanza we see the two lovers move away 'into the wet darkness'. There is a positive indication in this movement, in that the water was one of the 'legendary obstacles' facing the lovers and they have now triumphed over it by being reunited. There is a feeling of the 'wet darkness' embracing the two, implying that they willingly surrender themselves to their love. It also hides them from the watching old lady, who seems to be waiting for some act of failure. So, it allows their loving intimacy to be shared in privacy. But there is also a sense of entering into an unknown state. The 'darkness' prevents others from watching the two lovers, but equally it prevents the lovers from seeing where they are going. In this moment they are happy to focus purely on each other and on their love, but there is the implication that there could be something lurking out there in the 'wet darkness' that might threaten their love.

The connection between the images of the trains and the poem's theme of love is somewhat less ambiguous. On the one hand the trains symbolise hope and expectation, because it will be a train that will help the two lovers to overcome the 'legendary obstacles' that face their love. Montague knows that his lover will step down to him from a train, and so each train is greeted with a surge of his love. However, the trains that do not stop cause him to feel an intense disappointment. In this way they too become another obstacle that has to be overcome.

Finally, we must consider the poem's framework of the Classical myth of 'Orpheus and Eurydice'. Orpheus was able to sing so sweetly that savage beasts would follow him, the trees would bow down to him and wild men would become gentle. He fell in love with Eurydice and they were married. But one day, while she was trying to escape from the advances of an unwelcome lover, Eurydice stepped on a snake that bit her and she died. Orpheus went down into the Underworld to try to recover his wife. He played such beautiful music on his lyre and was so brave that Hades, the god of the dead, agreed to release Eurydice back up to the world of the living. Hades set one condition, however, he told Orpheus that he must walk towards daylight without looking back to make sure that his wife was following him. Orpheus managed to do this until he had almost reached daylight: but then he looked back at Eurydice. Instantly, Eurydice died again and was taken back down to the Underworld, while Orpheus returned to the land of the living alone.

Why, then, should Montague feel that this mythical story was relevant to his situation: waiting for his girlfriend at a train station during bad weather? There is the connection that both Montague and Orpheus are creative individuals. There is also the similarity that both couples are in love and separated by formidable obstacles. But Montague may have chosen to locate his poem within the framework of the Orpheus and Eurydice story because it is Orpheus who fails Eurydice, and the incident that leads to their love being put under threat – the snake bite – is caused by a force outside of the lovers' control. Montague seems to feel anxious about his ability to truly love his girlfriend without letting her down: 'I was too blind with rain I And doubt to speak'. There is also the suggestion that he is anxious that something outside of their control may happen that will lead to the destruction of their perfect love: 'Move into the wet darkness I Kissing, still unable to speak.'

What does Montague communicate about the theme of love in this poem? First, he recognises that being in love is not an easy experience. Frequently there are obstacles to that love that have to be overcome, and there are forces that may seek to damage or destroy that love. Second, he understands that love has no guarantees about it, no matter how much we might wish that it had. He is anxious that he will somehow fail his girlfriend and the love that they share. On the one hand he is enthralled by and celebrates the perfect love that they share, but on the other hand he fears that this perfection will not last. This is an ambiguity that we probably all share about love.

Interestingly, it seems to me that there are similarities between the focus of this poem and U2's song 'I still haven't found what I'm looking for'. Perhaps you might like to listen to it and decide for yourself.

The Same Gesture

Text of poem: New Explorations Anthology page 254

A reading of the poem

We have already seen the way in which Montague's poetry possesses an elegance of expression that is underpinned by a muscularity of focus. This poem is a particularly good example of both of these qualities. The short, poetic line; the sense of order imposed by the five-line stanzas; the condensed, everyday language; the exacting honesty of imagery: all combine to create a masterly piece of writing.

The elegance of the first stanza is evident from the opening words: 'There is a secret room I of golden light'. The simple refinement of these words belies the strength of emotion that underpins them. The image of this wonderful 'secret room' filled with 'golden light' inspires us all to remember a place where we, too, felt safe and warm. But it is at this point that Montague's muscularity of focus kicks in. He is not content to leave us wallowing in our nostalgic memories; instead, he tells us what happens in this apparently idyllic place: 'everything – love, violence, | hatred is possible'. There is something distinctly shocking about these lines. The 'secret room' is not a haven of calm and tranquillity at all, but somewhere that is filled with the unrestrained passion of 'love, violence, | hatred'. However, with the final line of this stanza, consisting of the three simple words 'and, again, love', Montague skilfully reinstates a feeling of peaceful orderliness.

Montague maintains this feeling of orderliness in the following six lines, where he describes their love making as having the elegant ritual of a religious 'rite', or the formalised pattern of movements of 'court music'. Yet, in spite of the apparent detachment of these descriptions, the emotional impact of the lines is inescapable. The couple achieve an 'intimacy of hand | and mind' that produces a 'healing'. What the lovers share is more than a purely physical release; rather, their physical actions, 'the shifting of | hands', enable them to connect in a truly meaningful way.

The level of their intimacy is expressed in lines 12–15. Montague's repetition of words connected with nakedness in these lines communicates the depth and honesty of their relationship. Their nakedness is not simply physical, but also emotional and spiritual. They are each truly themselves and they are each truly of the other, because of the complete honesty that lies at the heart of their meetings in this 'secret room'.

Yet, wonderful as such nakedness is, it cannot last for ever, and in the fourth and fifth stanzas Montague presents us with a series of vivid and dramatic images that represent the lovers coming out of the 'secret room', with its passionate honesty, and back into the humdrum routine of ordinary life. The lovers find themselves obliged to function in the everyday world. They may no longer share that intense and passionate intimacy, but they do still have the memories that they 'must remember'. These memories are so distinct that they ripple through the lovers' everyday actions. So the simple act of changing the gears in a car becomes a reminder of the loving movements and the emotional warmth that they shared. There is an elegant sense of closure in the final three lines of the poem, arising out of the beautiful connection that Montague establishes between them and the opening two lines:

> There is a secret room
> Of golden light . . .
>
> the same gesture as
> eased your snowbound
> heart and flesh.

The 'golden light' of the 'secret room' has succeeded in thawing out the 'snowbound | heart and flesh', just as the sun melts away the ice at midday. In the face of such a magical experience, is it any wonder that the two lovers carry the memories of it with them always?

Theme

Within this poem Montague explores the theme of love, but it is a very specific type of love. It is the love shared by two people in a very particular environment, a secret room. The implication is that their relationship has to be conducted in secret. It cannot be allowed to expand into the whole of their lives and worlds. Perhaps because of the secret and restricted nature of their love, it is very intense. This intensity reveals itself both in the emotions that they experience within the room, 'love, violence, | hatred', and in the way that they view their intimacy as 'a rite | like court music' that eases the 'snowbound | heart and flesh.' It is this balance between raw, passionate emotions and an almost religious, ritualised respect for what they share that gives this poem a greater impact. It is interesting to note that even though this is a deeply personal piece of writing, Montague never uses 'I'. His use of 'we' is indicative of the shared closeness of their connection.

Rhythm and punctuation

We have already noted that there is a skilled elegance about Montague's writing here, in the sense that he uses words in a simple yet graceful manner. His use of rhythm and punctuation play a major part in the creation of this elegance. If we highlight the stressed words in the opening lines of the poem, and read the highlights slightly louder, it is clear that they have a very measured and regular rhythm:

> There **is** a **secret** **room**
> Of **gol**den **light** . . .

Thus, the meaning of these words is underpinned by the rhythm to create an image of a tranquil, calm environment. This is further reinforced by the lack of punctuation, so that the words run smoothly. But, Montague suddenly destroys this impression in the following lines:

> . . . where
> everything – love, violence,
> hatred is possible;

These words deal with passionate, unrestrained emotions, and as a result Montague deliberately uses a much more irregular rhythm, further broken up by his use of punctuation.

Like dolmens round my childhood . . .

Text of poem: New Explorations Anthology page 257

[*Note: This poem is also prescribed for Ordinary Level 2008 exam*]

A READING OF THE POEM

In the very first line of this poem, Montague establishes the fundamental partnership of images that lies at its heart, the 'dolmens' and 'the old people'. He then goes on to give a series of vivid and realistic 'pen pictures' of some of the old people that he remembers. In 'The Locket' and 'The Cage' we saw how Montague used a variety of methods to suggest character, including physical description, references to actions and behaviour and quoting favourite sayings. He uses a number of these methods once again in 'Like Dolmens Round My Childhood'.

The first stanza describes Jamie MacCrystal by means of his behaviour and actions. His habit of singing to himself suggests a gentle eccentricity, while his kindness and generosity are shown by his regular gift of a penny to the young Montague and his feeding of the birds in winter. Jamie MacCrystal was a nice old man. This makes the description of the terrible incidents that happened after his death all the more shocking, when robbers tore his cottage apart looking for money. The only slightly positive note is the fact that the robbers did not touch poor Jamie MacCrystal's dead body.

In the second stanza we meet Maggie Owens. We learn that she 'was surrounded by animals'. This would seem to indicate that she, too, was a kindly and caring old person. But then Montague tells us that she 'was a well of gossip defiled' and he calls her a 'Fanged chronicler'. Montague's choice of words such as 'defiled' – meaning 'polluted' – and 'Fanged' make it clear that Maggie is not quite as nice as we thought. She liked to gossip, but not just the harmless chit-chat that we all enjoy. Maggie's gossip had a nasty and vindictive quality to it because she liked to 'deride', or make fun of people. However, just as we come to the conclusion that Maggie Owens was a rather unpleasant person, Montague tells us that her 'need to deride' came from the fact that she was 'lonely'. Maggie Owens obviously had a caring side, shown by her concern for animals, but her ability to be caring towards other people had been twisted and destroyed by her terrible loneliness.

The Nialls are the subject of the third stanza. We never learn who the Nialls were, whether they were male or female, brothers or sisters. They lived in a beautiful place with 'heather bells' and 'clumps of foxglove.' Tragically, the Nialls were unable to appreciate this beauty, as they were blind. All they had to make up for their lack of sight is a 'Blind Pension and Wireless'. Montague's description of their 'Dead eyes' that 'serpent-flickered' sounds like a child's view of these old, blind people. The implication is that as a child he was slightly afraid of them, because of their disability. Nevertheless, he was happy to shelter in their cottage and listen to the crickets chirping until the rain passed. We get the feeling that the Nialls never moved far away from their home: their blindness trapped them in a narrow and largely isolated world. Yet, there is a feeling of warmth about the open door, which allowed the young Montague to shelter, and the crickets chirping.

Mary Moore, in the fourth stanza, was a much more active person. She was always out and about tending to her cattle. It is obvious from Montague's description that Mary was fighting a losing battle to maintain her farm. She lived in a 'crumbling gatehouse', her cattle were 'lean' and lived in a 'miry stable'. Her life was one of unending hard work and, because of this, Mary Moore became a hard woman filled with 'fierceness'. However, once again Montague shows us that people are not always as they appear. This fierce, hard-working lady who constantly wore a 'Bag-apron and boots' loved romantic novels. All her longing for love was revealed in her dreams of 'gypsy love-rites'. Sadly, Montague makes it clear that Mary Moore never got to fulfil any of these wonderful dreams.

Finally we encounter Billy Eagleson. At first, Billy seems to be quite a heroic, independent chap. He is 'wild' and this wildness led to him going against the rules of Northern society by marrying a Catholic servant girl. True, he did wait until all his family were dead, so perhaps he was not quite so independent as we first thought. Perhaps he was nothing more than a lonely old man craving some sort of companionship. Nevertheless, because of his marriage, he was rejected by his own religion and his wife's religion. He became an outcast who could be teased and ridiculed by the local gangs of children. His feeble attempts to hit the boys with his 'flailing blackthorn' stick make him seem a rather pathetic figure. But, in spite of enduring rejection by both Protestants and Catholics, Billy still felt moved when the 'Orange drums banged' and the Loyalist men marched in 'bowler and sash' declaring their loyalty to the sovereign.

In the sixth stanza, Montague shifts the focus of the poem onto the 'Curate and doctor': the only two people who seem to show any interest in the old men and women. Whether out of a sense of duty, or a genuine concern for the old, these two are willing 'to attend them'. We see them struggling to reach the isolated homes 'gulping mountain air'. However, the doctor and the curate are not simply calling to visit the old people; they are going to deal with their dead bodies. Here Montague once again describes the true reality of the situation with uncompromising honesty. As the old people largely lived alone, isolated from love and care, so they died alone, without love and care. Occasionally, their bodies are 'found by neighbours', but the 'smokeless hearth' and the phrase 'cast in the mould of death' suggest that the old people were dead for a long time before anyone came to check on them.

It is this uncompromising honesty in describing the harshness of the old people's lives that Montague carries forward into the final stanza. His comment 'Ancient Ireland, indeed!' is written with the strength and contempt of a man who wants to destroy the idealised view of 'Ancient Ireland' being a perfect world. Instead, Montague wants us to recognise and understand the negative aspects of 'Ancient Ireland'. It was a society where superstition was widespread, where feuds were pursued with 'fierceness', where old people were left to live and die in loneliness and isolation. Once Montague realises this, his attitude towards the old people changes: they no longer haunt him in his dreams, because he understands that 'the old people' have a 'permanence' about them. Like the dolmens, the old men and women have a lasting quality in that they are part of Montague's heritage: they are part of the past world that made him what he is.

THEME

Montague uses the individual life-stories of the old people to illustrate the harsh and divided nature of the Northern Ireland society that he grew up in. He feels that we must recognise that Northern Irish society has its foundations in the past, in superstition and feuding. It is only by doing this that we can move on to creating a new and more caring community.

THE TONE OF THE POEM

The tone, that is the emotion or attitude expressed in the poet's words, tends to change quite a lot in this poem. In his descriptions of the old people there is often a mixture of a tone of affection and sympathy with a tone of anger and contempt. Jamie MacCrystal is written about with affection: ' He tipped me a penny every pension day'. With Maggie Owens and Mary Moore, Montague uses a sympathetic tone as he comes to understand the reasons for their behaviour. Although he is angry and contemptuous about Maggie's love of 'gossip defiled', he understands that it comes from 'her lonely need to deride'. Similarly, Mary's 'fierceness' is only a pretence to hide her longing for the romance of 'gypsy love-rites'. In the final stanza he sees the old people as 'figures of fear and friendliness' because as a child he may have found some of them frightening, but as an adult he came to regard them as friends because he saw them as lonely and isolated human beings.

At times, Montague's tone echoes with his childhood voice. So when he remembers that Maggie Owens was 'reputed a witch', we hear the voice of a small boy who believes that witches really exist. Similarly, his tone is one of giddy excitement as he describes how the boys 'danced around' Billy Eagleson shouting 'To hell with King Billy'. Clearly, most adults would not feel like this about such behaviour, so this tone is the voice of the young boy Montague, who enjoyed youngsters getting away with making fun of an adult.

In the final stanza his tone is filled with anger and contempt for the superstition and harshness of the society of 'Ancient Ireland'. However, it becomes much calmer and more affectionate when he speaks of 'the old people', because he understands the part that they played in his development:

> I felt their shadows pass
>
> Into that dark permanence of ancient forms.

The Wild Dog Rose

Text of poem: New Explorations Anthology page 262

A READING OF THE POEM

Section 1

Montague immediately draws his readers into this poem by vividly describing the journey he makes to visit the 'cailleach', an old woman. His attention to detail really makes his descriptions come alive. We can see the cottage, the misshapen trees and the 'rank thistles'. We can hear the 'savage whingeing cries' of the old woman's dogs.

As with the old people in 'Like dolmens round my childhood . . .' Montague places his childhood attitude to the old woman,' that terrible figure who haunted my childhood', alongside his adult understanding of her as 'a human being | merely, hurt by event.' Indeed, his use of the Irish word 'cailleach' sums up his mixed feelings about her as it can mean 'an old woman' or 'a Witch'. When he first sees the old woman he reverts back to 'the terror of a child'. Indeed, she has a rather witchlike appearance, appearing as 'a moving nest | of shawls and rags' with a 'great hooked nose', 'the staring blue | of the sunken eyes', and 'mottled claws' instead of hands. However, his adult reaction takes over and he is able 'to greet her . . . in friendliness.'

Montague stands and listens to the old woman speaking. It is clear that she goes on at length about her past. Montague listens patiently because he understands that the old woman does not have anyone to talk to, and that it is her loneliness that makes her drone on 'rehearsing the small events of her life.'

Section 2

Montague introduces the important image of 'the dog rose' at the beginning of this section. This flower is very different from the other plants that we have encountered previously in the poem: the trees twisted 'by the mountain winds' and 'the rank thistles | and leathery bracken'. There is something special about the Dog-rose because it 'shines in the hedge'. This could well be because the flowers of the Dog-Rose are either white or pink, with a pale yellow centre: colours that would stand out against the greens and browns of the other plants.

Suddenly, the tone of the poem changes to one of terror and fear as we hear the old woman's story of her attempted rape by 'a drunk'. As she struggles with her attacker, the old woman calls on 'the Blessed Virgin herself | for help' and finally she does manage to escape from the man.

Section 3

The image of the 'dog rose' occurs once again. It still 'shines in the hedge', but here Montague supplies more details about its appearance. The Dog-Rose may seem to be a delicate flower with 'Petals beaten wide by rain' and its 'slender, tangled, arching branch'. Indeed, it even 'sways slightly'. However, for the old woman, the Dog-Rose symbolises 'the Holy Mother of God and | all she suffered.' This capacity for endurance is represented by the fact that the Dog-Rose 'is the only rose without thorns'. Thus, the Dog-Rose is incapable of wounding or causing suffering; it simply persists and withstands. Montague realises that it is these qualities that give the Dog-Rose a strength, a strength that is suggested by the scent of the flower: ' the air is strong with the smell | of that weak flower'. So, although the flower of the Dog-Rose may have a 'crumbling yellow cup' and 'pale bleeding lips | fading to white' and petals that are 'bruised', he understands what the old woman recognises: that this flower has a power, a power that resides in each of its 'heart- | shaped' petals, a power that resides in the figure of the Blessed Virgin, a power that 'shines in the hedge', a power that fills a lonely, frightened old woman with courage to endure in the face of brutality.

Themes

Montague explains the political aspect to this poem as follows:

> 'Ireland has often been seen as feminine, . . . and her colonisation has aspects of rape – becoming even more complicated when colonial England became Protestant and Ireland remained Roman Catholic, attached to the medieval ethos of the Virgin Mary.'

If we consider the image of the Dog-Rose and the old woman's endurance and strength within this context, they become symbols of the survival of Ireland. Indeed, in the past, the rose was frequently used as a secret code-name for Ireland.

In addition, there is a strong religious element to the poem in the connection that is made between the Dog-Rose and 'the Blessed Virgin'. The old woman's faith in the Blessed Virgin gives her the strength to resist her attacker. Furthermore, in Section 3 the Dog-Rose is described as a 'yellow cup', conjuring up an image of a golden chalice. Both the Blessed Virgin and the chalice symbolise the healing power of faith, the healing power that the old woman has experienced. However, the power that is suggested by the Dog-Rose and the Blessed Virgin may not be totally triumphant, as Montague has pointed out:

> In 'The Wild Dog Rose', as she is being almost raped the woman prays to the Blessed Virgin. The Blessed Virgin is symbolised for her by the wild dog rose, but the end of the poem describes that as a 'weak flower'. This is her comfort. The poem doesn't say that it accepts that comfort, just that she has been able to draw strength from it as people do from whatever they can manage to believe in.

A Welcoming Party

Text of poem: New Explorations Anthology page 268

A READING OF THE POEM

Montague's decision to open this poem with a quotation in German serves to create a context for his writing. The use of the German language signals that this piece is somehow connected to a world beyond Montague's home in Garvaghey. The nature of the question asked provides a further clue, 'Wie war das möglich?', 'How did this happen?' This is the same question that many used after the attack on the World Trade Center in New York. It is a question that expresses the inability of the human mind and heart to understand something terrible.

So, Montague's first stanza begins to describe the 'something terrible' that he encountered. He conveys the setting for his boyhood experience in two brief phrases, 'That final newsreel' and 'at the cinema door'. Once again, Montague's ability to condense the essences of a life experience into a few brief words is evident. He moves on to vividly portray the horror of the scene that is shown in the 'final newsreel of the war'. At this point we do not need to ask 'Which war?'; the German question has made it clear that Montague writes of the brutality of World War II.

The phrase 'Met us at the cinema door' does more than simply tell us that Montague was in a cinema. It also conveys a feeling of these horrible images, not only filling the darkness of the cinema but also the minds of those who were watching them. Montague, with his customary uncompromising honesty, likens these half-alive 'shades' of human beings to insects in a series of deeply disturbing images. They make 'Clicking' noises with 'what remained of their heels' and out of 'nests of bodies like hatching eggs' break 'insectlike hands and legs'. This is the stuff of nightmares, made all the more dreadful by the inhuman wailing, the 'ululation' filling the air. But this is not a nightmare; it is the reality of a Nazi concentration camp.

In the third stanza Montague echoes the movements of a film camera by shifting the focus of his descriptions away from panning across the enormity of the horror to pictures of individual suffering. We see 'a mouth like a burnt glove' ragged and blackened by brutality, and 'upheld hands' that seek some small, kindly response to their suffering, 'the small change' of the souls of the watchers.

Such images overwhelm both the young Montague and his companions. They simply cannot believe that human life can exist in such dehumanised forms and so they ask 'Can those bones live?' He realises that, up until now, he has lived in a world that is on the edge of experience. His world is localised and narrow in its outlook and restricted in its vision; it is 'parochial', a small parish far away from real life.

However, in spite of the shock of this realisation, Montague simply cannot absorb the impact of what he has seen. The 'doves of mercy' are unable to soar, not through any hardness or lack of humanity on the part of Montague, but simply because the scenes that he witnesses are so completely outside his experience, his 'parochial brand of innocence', that he cannot respond to them. Just as we all watched in shock as the Twin Towers collapsed, so Montague is stunned by what he has seen.

The final stanza of the poem may seem to be rather unfeeling in the light of the descriptions that Montague has so vividly portrayed. Yet it is filled with his muscular honesty, his determination to represent things as they are, not things as we would like them to be. The young Montague understands that he has witnessed 'one meaning of total war'. He realises that war is much more than coloured flags on a map, or heroic deeds and shared victories. He has seen a glimpse of the wide world that lies beyond his 'parochial' one. But, once he leaves the cinema, he returns to his own world of the 'Christian school', where he runs to 'belt a football through the air'. He does this because it is all that he can do. He is a young boy, who has little experience of life and, rather like a small child running to his parents for comfort, Montague seeks out the safe normality of his small world. And there is a kind of triumph in this. Just as we went back to the normality of our lives after '9/11', so Montague's return represents the indomitable strength of the human spirit. We know that we will never be quite the same, Montague knows that he will never be quite the same; but what will continue is the human will to live.

Themes

On one level, this poem can be seen as a consideration of the horrors of war: the dehumanised 'insectlike' figures represent man's inhumanity to man, his capacity for brutality. It traces Montague's boyhood realisation of the true implications of war: 'I learnt one meaning of total war'.

However, Montague also addresses the position of 1940s Ireland on the world stage. As a society struggling to redefine its identity after a shattering War of Independence and civil war, Ireland was economically impoverished and deeply inward-looking. Out of his encounter with the 'newsreel of the war', Montague comes to an understanding of Ireland's position at the outer regions of world events: 'To be always at the periphery of incident'. He also recognises that this isolationism disables the Irish people in that they do not feel part of the greater world.

Tone

Montague uses the conversational language of everyday speech to great effect in this poem, because each familiar word and phrase vibrates with a profound intensity of tone. The opening stanza conveys the setting for the poem, but then we encounter the line 'Clicking what remained of their heels.' The impact of the words 'what remained' is tremendous. Despite the matter-of-fact simplicity of the language, the tone is one of shocked horror.

There is a similar effect with the question, 'Can those bones live?' in the fourth stanza. These four deceptively simple words capture the utter incredulity with which Montague watches the nightmare images. He cannot believe that human life can persist in such dehumanised forms.

There is a tone of frustration in the lines 'To be always at the periphery of incident | Gave my childhood its Irish dimension; drama of unevent'. As he grew older Montague became increasingly resentful of the intellectual isolationism that ruled Ireland, and in 1952 he left Ireland with great relief to study in America.

When Montague remembers his boyhood reaction to what he had seen, in the final six lines of the poem, his tone changes to one of regret, but it is regret tinged with understanding. He knows that his actions of going back to his 'Christian school' in order to 'belt a football through the air' were totally inadequate and represented a failure on his part. In this way, he allowed the 'doves of mercy 'to 'falter'. But the adult Montague can understand that as a young boy, reared in the 'parochial' world of 1940s Ireland, he simply did not have the capacity to respond to such images.

So the various tones that resonate through this poem reveal it to be the adult Montague's acknowledgment of the wide-ranging and lasting effects that the 'newsreel of the war' had on him. As a young boy he was unable to make this acknowledgment; but now, through his adult acknowledgment, he is able to set 'the doves of mercy' flying again.

Developing a personal reaction to John Montague

1. What is the relationship between Montague's poetry and his life? How does his poetry influence his attitude to his life experiences?
2. What themes occur in Montague's poetry? Are they all relevant to your life or are some more relevant than others?
3. How would you describe the language that Montague uses in his poetry? What is your reaction to the type of language that he uses?
4. In your own words, describe the process of 'realisation'. Did you encounter any realisations in your reading of Montague that you found particularly successful?
5. How do you feel about the 'stream of consciousness' approach to imagery? Did it help or hinder your understanding of what Montague was communicating in his poetry?
6. Does Montague's approach to the layout and organisation of his poetry excite your interest, or would you rather he used more traditional formats?
7. Select four words that you feel describe John Montague's poetry. In each case, use references from his work to justify your choice.
8. Consider what aspects of Montague's poetry appeal to you and what aspects you find unappealing.
9. John Montague was born in 1929 in America. What can his poetry say to young adults living in twenty-first-century Ireland?
10. What will you remember from your work on John Montague after you have completed the Leaving Certificate examination?

Questions

1. Read 'The Locket', then answer the following questions:

1. (a) How did this poem make you feel?
   (b) Describe the kind of relationship that Montague had with his mother. Refer to the poem in your response.
   (c) What picture do you get of John Montague's mother from the poem?
2. Answer **ONE** of the following:
   (a) Do you think that 'The Locket' is a good title for this poem? Explain your answer.

   OR

   (b) Imagine that you are making a short film based on this poem. Choose **two scenes** and describe the images and music that you would use.

   OR

   (c) 'And still, mysterious blessing,

I never knew, until you were gone,'
What does Montague discover after his mother has died? Why do you think he calls this discovery a 'mysterious blessing'?

2. Read 'Like dolmens round my childhood . . .', then answer the following questions:
   1. (a) Which **one** of the old people in the poem do you feel the most sympathy for? Explain the reasons for your choice.
      (b) 'Sometimes they were found by neighbours,
      Silent keepers of a smokeless hearth,
      Suddenly cast in the mould of death.'
      From these lines, what do you understand about the way that the old people died?
      (c) How does Montague's attitude to the old people change in the last four lines of the poem?
   2. Answer **ONE** of the following:
      (a) The following list of phrases suggests some of the poet's attitudes to the old people:
      - *He likes them.*
      - *He feels sorry for them.*
      - *He is afraid of them.*

      Choose the phrase from the above list that is closest to your own reading of the poem. Explain your choice, supporting your view by reference to the words of the poem.

      OR

      (b) Imagine that you are the curate **or** the doctor in the poem. Describe how you feel about visiting the old people.

      OR

      (c) 'Like dolmens round my childhood, the old people.'
      Can you explain the connection between the old people and the dolmens? Do you think that the poem helps you to understand this connection? Give reasons for your answer.

3. 'Introducing John Montague.' Write out the text of a short presentation that you would make to your class group under the above title. Support your point of view by reference to, or quotation from, the poetry of John Montague that you have studied.
4. '*Dear John Montague . . .*'
Write a letter to John Montague telling him how you responded to some of his poems on your course. Support the points you make by detailed reference to your chosen poems.
5. 'The poetry of John Montague appeals to his readers because we do not simply read it, we feel it physically and emotionally. Write an essay in which

you discuss this statement, quoting from or referring to his poems to support your discussion.

6. 'Poetry never deals with the problems of real life.'
   Imagine that one of your friends has made this comment to you. Respond to the comment, referring to the poems by John Montague on your course.
7. 'The unforgettable John Montague'. You have been asked to submit an article with this title for your school's poetry magazine. Write out your article, supporting your points by quotations from or references to your chosen poems.
8. John Montague looks at life with honesty and understanding. Discuss. Support the points you make by reference to the poetry of Montague that you have studied.
9. 'John Montague: a poet for the twenty-first century.' In response to the above statement, write an essay on the poetry of Montague. Support your points by detailed reference to the poems on your course.
10. What impact did the poetry of John Montague make on you as a reader? In your answer you might like to consider some of the following:
    - *Montague's outlook on life*
    - *his use of language and imagery*
    - *the themes of his poems.*

Bibliography

Brown, Terence, *Northern Voices: Poets from Ulster*, Dublin: Gill and Macmillan 1975.

Corcoran, Neil (editor), *The Chosen Ground: Essays on the Contemporary Poetry of Northern Ireland*, Bridgend, Mid Glamorgan: Seren Books 1992.

Deane, Seamus, *Celtic Revivals: Essays in Modern Irish Literature 1880–1980*, London: Faber 1985.

Dunn, Douglas (compiled by), *Two Decades of Irish Writing: A Critical Survey*, Cheadle: Carcanet Press 1975.

Garratt, Robert F., *Modern Irish Poetry*, Berkeley: University of California Press 1986.

Harmon, Maurice (editor), *Irish Poetry after Yeats*, Dublin: Wolfhound Press 1979.

Johnston, Dillon, *Irish Poetry after Joyce* (second edition), Syracuse: Syracuse University Press 1997.

Lampe, David (editor), *Born in Brooklyn: John Montague's America*, New York: White Wine Press 1991.

Lucy, Sean (editor), *Irish Poets in English*, Cork: The Mercier Press 1973.

Kernowski, Frank, *John Montague*, New Jersey: Associated University Presses Inc. 1975.

Montague, John, *Company: A Chosen Life*, London: Duckworth 2001.

Murrray, Christopher (editor), *Irish University Review: Special John Montague Number*, 19.1 Spring 1989.

The Arts Show: *John Montague*, R.T.É. 7 November 1995.

Quinn, Antoinette (editor), *The Figure in the Cave and Other Essays*, Dublin: Lilliput 1989.

Welch, Robert, *The Structure of Process: John Montague's Poetry*, Coleraine: Cranagh Press 1999.

5 *Adrienne* RICH

Carole Scully

The poetry of power and revolution

EARLY LIFE

> My own luck was being born white and middle-class into a house full of books, with a father who encouraged me to read and write.
>
> (Adrienne Rich, *When We Dead Awaken: Writing a Re-Vision*)

This brief description by Adrienne Rich of her childhood suggests that her formative years were spent in a secure and solid home where she was intellectually stimulated by a supportive parent. Indeed, there is a truth in this interpretation, but equally truthful is the fact that, in later years, Rich had to struggle to come to terms with certain features of her early life.

Adrienne Rich was born in Baltimore, USA, on 16 May 1929, in the hospital where her father, Arnold, worked as a doctor. He was also a teacher and a researcher in the Department of Pathology in Johns Hopkins Medical School. It was only as she grew older that Rich fully appreciated just how unique her father was in the academic world of Baltimore. Arnold was one of a very small number of Jews who taught in the Medical School and, as such, he had to endure a lengthy delay in his appointment to the Professorship of Pathology at Johns Hopkins simply because no Jew had ever held the chair before.

Arnold's attitude to his Jewish heritage was a complex one that proved to be one aspect of her childhood that Rich struggled to reconcile in later years. Arnold did not hide the fact that he was a Jew, once commenting to Adrienne, ' You know that I have never denied that I am a Jew . . . I am a scientist . . . I have no use for organized religion . . . I am a person, not simply a Jew.' (Adrienne Rich, *Split at the Root*). Ironically, according to Rich, Arnold's appearance very definitely revealed his ethnic roots because he had dark hair and eyes and a large, hooked nose.

However, it is clear that Arnold deliberately created a family and social environment where Jewishness, although not denied, was certainly avoided in favour of Christian values. He married a Protestant woman and his two daughters were sent to an Episcopalian school. He and his family mixed with people who considered it impolite to mention such words as 'Negro' and 'Jew'.

Arnold expected his wife and daughters to behave 'correctly' at all times in the belief that, as Rich put it, 'With enough excellence, you could presumably make it stop mattering you were Jewish. . . .' (Adrienne Rich, *Split at the Root*).

Rich's mother, Helen, was ideally suited to such a lifestyle. From a once-wealthy southern family, Helen had been reared in a world where the Christian ethos was the foundation of good social behaviour and where the old-fashioned, genteel values of white, middle-class good breeding were prized above all else. To be seen as 'common' was the greatest sin of all for any woman. Rich's mother diligently attempted to pass on these values to Adrienne and her sister, advising them, that in relationships with men, 'It was in the woman's interest to cultivate "mystery", conceal her actual feelings.' (Adrienne Rich, *Split at the Root*). This was another aspect of her early years that Adrienne Rich would later struggle to reconcile.

Yet, Helen was more than simply a 'southern belle'. Prior to her wedding, she had been a gifted pianist and composer. At one point, she had even considered becoming a concert pianist, but had decided against it because of the predominantly male nature of the classical-music world at that time. Once she met Arnold Rich, Helen gave up any career ambitions and devoted herself to caring for her husband and daughters. She did continue to play the piano and taught both of her children to play, but her exceptional musical talent was only ever expressed in private. Rich's experience of the way in which marriage had forced her mother to abandon the open expression of her ability proved to be another feature of her childhood that would affect her adult life.

Adrienne's parents instilled a respect for education in their daughters. Indeed, both girls were educated at home for some time before joining the school system. Adrienne was particularly close to her father. He gave her access to his large library of books and continually encouraged her to develop her intellect and to write poetry. Adrienne was a bright child who enjoyed such pursuits. She worked hard to impress her father and to produce the type of views and the style of poetry that would gain his approval. However, Arnold's approval was not gained easily. In later years, Rich vividly described the rigours that he put her through as a young girl: 'He prowled and pounced over my school papers, insisting I use "grown-up" sources; he criticized my poems for faulty techniques. . . .' (Adrienne Rich, *Split at the Root*).

Adrienne more than fulfilled her father's hopes with her brilliant academic career. In 1947, she went from high school to the all-female Radcliffe College, part of the prestigious Harvard University. Yet, ironically, it was here that she began to encounter ideas that would challenge her to reassess her childhood experiences, ideas that would ultimately lead her to a prolonged and bitter break from her parents.

RICH'S JEWISH HERITAGE

At Radcliffe, Rich met with young Jewish women who were not only her equals intellectually and academically, but who were also fiercely proud of their Jewish culture and religion. In Rich's own words, ' They took me on.' They taught her 'the names of holidays and foods, which surnames are Jewish and which are "changed names"; about girls who had their noses fixed. . . .' Although she knew that she would be unacceptable as a Jew to strict Jewish families because her mother was non-Jewish, Rich found something within her that responded to these revelations. She knew that she was 'testing a forbidden current', because she was deliberately going against her father's wishes. But even more dangerously, Rich was aware that she 'was flirting with identity' (Adrienne Rich, *Split at the Root)* .

Up until this point in Rich's life, because of the efforts of her father and mother, her Jewish heritage had not really impinged on her existence. During her childhood, she had the view that 'Jews were in the Bible and mentioned in English literature . . . but they seemed not to exist in everyday life.' (Adrienne Rich, *Split at the Root*). In 1946, at the age of sixteen, she had gone to a cinema to watch films showing the Allied liberation of the Nazi concentration camps, but when she had told her parents what she had seen they were 'not pleased. I felt accused of being morbidly curious, not healthy, sniffing around death for the thrill of it.' (Adrienne Rich, *Split at the Root)*. The confusion and guilt that Rich felt as a result of this experience restrained her from engaging in any such similar incidents for a long time.

Now, however, the more independent Rich would not be so easily diverted. She did struggle to reconcile her own desires with her wish to please her parents but, finally, she decided to address the unresolved issue of Jewishness that had lingered from her childhood years. Gradually, she came to see her father's lack of concern for his Jewish heritage as a veneer that covered an ambivalent mixture of 'self-hatred' and 'Jewish pride'. He 'lived in an increasingly withdrawn world, in his house up on a hill in a neighbourhood where Jews were not supposed to buy property.' (Adrienne Rich, *Split at the Root*). Her determination to embrace her Jewish roots marked the beginning of her separation from her parents and from the social and cultural mores and conventions that they had worked so hard to instil in her. In 1953, she married Alfred H. Conrad, a Jewish economist who was teaching at Harvard. Her parents did not attend the wedding. It was to be several years before she would communicate with them again.

DOMESTICITY AND RICH'S POETRY

This separation, particularly from her father, caused Rich not only to reassess her relationship with him but also his influence on her writing. It is undeniable that Arnold Rich had a profound effect on his daughter's early intellectual and creative development. As we have seen, he pushed her to achieve academically and he drove her to refine her writing skills. He had given her books dealing with the technical aspects of poetry, such as metre and rhyme, in order to guide her writing towards a style that he regarded as being 'correct'. In Arnold Rich's view, 'correct' poetry was poetry that demonstrated a knowledge and mastery of traditionally accepted poetic forms.

Indeed, when Rich's first book of poetry was published in 1951, in her final year at Radcliffe, it was widely praised for its technical quality. The poet W. H. Auden, who chose the book for the Yale Younger Poets Award, wrote of it :

> Craftsmanship includes, of course, not only a talent for versification, but also . . . an intuitive grasp of much subtler and more difficult matters like proportion, consistency of diction and tone, and the matching of these with the subject at hand; Miss Rich's poems rarely fail on any of those counts.

In later years, Rich was to view such poems as 'Storm Warnings', 'Aunt Jennifer's Tigers' and 'The Uncle Speaks in the Drawing Room' as having a 'conscious craft' about them. Each of them was 'an arrangement of ideas and feelings, pre-determined, and it said what I had already decided it would say.' (Adrienne Rich, *Poetry and Experience: Statement at a Poetry Reading*). Indeed, there is an undeniable elegance of form and a gracefulness of expression about such lines as:

> And set a match to candles sheathed in glass
>
> ('Storm Warnings')

> When Aunt is dead, her terrified hands will lie
> Still ringed with ordeals she was mastered by.
>
> ('Aunt Jennifer's Tigers')

> Some have talked in bitter tones,
> Some have held and fingered stones.
>
> ('The Uncle Speaks in the Drawing Room')

However, the radical alterations that took place in Rich's life following the publication of her first anthology began to change her approach to her writing. After the acrimonious and bitter split from her parents, she struggled to escape from her intense desire to please her father both in her life and her writing. Freed from the constraints and preconceptions of her father's view of poetry, Rich began to explore other ways of expressing her thoughts and feelings, so that she was not simply recreating a 'male' style of poetry, but finding a way of expressing her own 'female' experience in poetic terms.

In addition, she began to think about the way that her relationship with her father had been influenced by the fact that he was male and she female:

> In my separation from him, in my realization at what price that once-intoxicating approval had been bought, I was learning in concrete ways a great deal about patriarchy, in particular how the 'special' woman, the favoured daughter, is controlled and rewarded.
>
> (Adrienne Rich, *Split at the Root*)

Thus, once again, her early childhood experiences – in particular her relationship with her father – affected her later development. She began to examine the patriarchal nature of her society where, she believed, the hierarchical form of relations between men and women ensured that men were allocated the dominant, powerful role in family and society, while women were kept in a subservient and powerless position.

However, it was not only Rich's childhood experiences that influenced her at this point in her life. Her marriage to Alfred opened up a new world to her, one that would profoundly change not only her writing but also her whole way of living. As with many modern poets, Adrienne Rich has coupled her writing of poetry with extensive prose writings describing her intellectual and emotional development, thereby enabling her readers to directly connect her poetic development to her life. Consequently, she has written openly and honestly about the early years of her marriage, tracing the emotional confusion and the ambivalence that she felt about her role as a wife and mother.

From her childhood experiences, Rich already had some doubts about the effects that becoming a wife had on a woman's position in the world. She had witnessed her mother's surrendering of her career as a pianist and her submission to the role of dutiful wife. It is clear from her writing that Rich did love her husband, Alfred, but there was a very deliberate aspect to her decision to marry him. She saw it as a way of enabling her to participate in the Jewish culture of home and family, that culture that had been denied to her by her parents: ' I longed to embrace that family, that new and mysterious Jewish world.' Furthermore, she regarded her marriage as a statement about her position as a female poet:

> Because I was determined to prove that as a woman poet I could have what was then defined as a 'full' woman's life, I plunged in my early twenties into marriage and had three children before I was thirty.
>
> (Adrienne Rich, *Split at the Root*)

It may seem a rather confusing choice for her to make, given her growing questioning of the patriarchal nature of society, but, at that point in her life, marriage seemed to answer many of the questions that Rich was facing. Yet there was still a sense of uneasiness about her situation that haunted Rich, an uneasiness that she felt unable to express openly in her writing:

> In those years, formalism . . . like asbestos gloves . . . allowed me to handle materials I couldn't pick up barehanded.
> (Adrienne Rich, *Poetry and Experience: Statement at a Poetry Reading*)

Thus, the image of the storm in her poem 'Storm Warnings' and the disenchantment felt by the female character in 'Living in Sin' are Rich's veiled references to the increasing turmoil that she felt within herself. Another device that Rich used to mask her expression of her confusion was the use of a male character, as in 'The Roofwalker'.

She considered this uneasiness as somehow unnatural, an act of disloyalty to her husband and, as her family grew, to her three sons. She struggled on with her writing in the context of her roles of wife and mother. Her second book of poetry was published in the same month that she gave birth to her first son. Again, it was received positively, and her poetry was judged to have a 'gracefulness' about it. Rich, however, was not satisfied with these poems. On the one hand, she recognised the positives in her life: a well-received second book of poems; a loving husband and a new son. On the other, she had times when she felt ' doubts', 'mild depression' and 'active despairing'.

By the time that her third son was born, Rich's writing had almost ground to a halt. She experienced a terrible weariness, 'that female fatigue of suppressed anger and loss of contact with my own being'. She found that her daily routine of housewifely and motherly duties left her little or no time to actually write. Above all, she felt a terrible sense of failure: failure as a wife and mother, and failure as a poet. She came to the conclusion that she either had to accept 'failure' as her lot in life and continue on with the way things were, or to find some way of making sense of what she was experiencing and what she was feeling. She decided that she would have to find 'some synthesis by which to understand what was happening to me'. (Adrienne Rich, *When We Dead Awaken: Writing a Re-Vision*).

Finding a synthesis

The 1950s and 1960s were a time of great political upheaval in America. As you may have learned from your CSPE course, during this time a number of movements developed with the aim of bringing about greater freedom for particular sections of American society. Along with many other academics and intellectuals, Adrienne Rich and her husband became actively involved in Civil Rights groups. Later in her life, Rich expressed the view that the impetus for this involvement grew out of her early experiences of 'a social and familial world in which there was a great deal of splitting'. (Adrienne Rich: *An Interview with David Montenegro*). In other words, she felt that she had lived her formative years in a family split between Jewish and Gentile (non-Jewish) cultural roots and in a society split between Black and White. For her, the Civil Rights-based movements seemed to offer some way of uniting all of the split parts of her identity.

One such movement was founded to coordinate the struggle of American blacks to bring about an end to segregation and to achieve full rights of citizenship. For a time, Dr Martin Luther King was its leader.

The film entitled *The Rosa Parks Story* shows the types of social restriction that black people endured at the time and the methods that they used to change their position in American society. It tells of Rosa Parks' refusal to give up her bus seat to a white passenger in 1955 in Alabama. At the time, such an action was considered to be a violation of the segregation laws. Rosa Parks was arrested and, as a protest against this action, Dr Martin Luther King led a boycott of the bus system. Finally, in 1956, the buses were desegregated.

Rich found herself responding to this movement because it gave black people the opportunity to voice how they felt about their position in American society. It was this development of a language to express a sense of oppression that struck a chord with Rich. As she said in her interview with David Montenegro, 'That was the first place where I heard a language to name oppression. And it was an enormous relief. . . .' For Rich, this marked the beginnings of her open acknowledgement of her own sense of oppression and her awareness that language and power are inextricably linked.

At the same time, the Anti-War movement was steadily growing following the involvement of United States troops in Vietnam. Many American universities, such as Berkeley, witnessed large student demonstrations where intellectuals and musicians expressed the deep dissatisfaction that a large number of Americans felt at the time. One such musician was Joan Baez, whose rendition of the song 'We shall not be moved' became a popular anthem. Here again, we can experience something of the atmosphere of these times in the film *Born on the Fourth of July*. In this film, Tom Cruise portrays the life of Ron Kovic, who was paralysed fighting in Vietnam and subsequently became an Anti-War activist.

As with the black Civil Rights movement, Rich found that the Anti-War movement also challenged accepted forms of expression, because they were seen as conveying only the views of the pro-war political establishment. Consequently, a new language gradually arose out of Anti-War protests, one that expressed a rejection of America's position in Vietnam and questioned the balance of political power in the world.

However, it was Rich's involvement with one group in particular that was to have the most profound effect on her life and her work: that of the Women's Liberation Movement. The concept of Women's Liberation, or Feminism, developed in the United States alongside the other Civil Rights movements. It challenged the traditional roles allowed to women in American society. As the film *Mona Lisa Smile* with Julia Roberts illustrates, in 1950s America a college education for women was available only to well-off, white women. However, even among these women, the roles of wife and mother were generally considered to be far more important that any career. Consequently, as had happened with Rich's own mother, marriage usually meant that a woman focused on supporting her husband, running her home and caring for her children, abandoned any career aspirations.

Until she encountered the Women's Liberation Movement, Adrienne Rich had thought of herself as isolated and alone in her feelings of frustration and dissatisfaction. Now, she met women who felt the same as she did. She threw herself into the movement. She revelled in the debates and the conversations with women who, like her, had experienced a profound despair arising out of the boundaries and expectations that society placed upon them because they were women. She found that not only did she relate to women on an intellectual level, but she also responded to them physically and sexually:

> ' The suppressed lesbian I had been carrying in me since adolescence began to stretch her limbs. . . .' (Adrienne Rich: *An Interview with David Montenegro*).

After seventeen years of marriage, Rich left her husband and then fell in love with a Jewish woman. At last, she had found the connection, that synthesis, that which would reconcile and unite all the 'split' elements that she had absorbed in her childhood.

Language and power

As we have seen, Rich's involvement with Civil Rrights movements had awakened her to the intimate relationship that exists between language and power. She realised that the language that we use in everyday life is more than simply a means of communication enabling each one of us to survive and function.

Humans are, in general, social animals who live with other human beings. Clearly then, on one level language is used to ensure that our individual basic survival needs are met within a group situation: we each communicate in order to obtain the food, clothing, shelter and any other objects that are needed for day-to-day living. But there is more to human life than this. We are highly complex creatures, both emotionally and psychologically. To live fully we need to be able to express our thoughts and our feelings successfully and satisfactorily.

However, it has long been recognised that individual expression is potentially a disruptive element to the continuing good order of the group or society in which humans live. Therefore, human societies have tended to institute some form of social hierarchy where there is an ultimate governing power whose role is to ensure that the society continues to function successfully, even if this means that the needs of individuals or groups within that society are not always met. In practice this means that those who hold the governing power in a society decide what is socially acceptable, that is, what is good for the continuance of that society; and what is socially unacceptable, that is, what is damaging to the continuance of that society.

The language that is used by the people who govern and the people who live in a society reflects and supports what is socially acceptable in that society, while also expressing rejection and disapproval for that which is deemed to be unacceptable. The governing power will frequently take steps to suppress or eliminate language that expresses views running counter to acceptable thinking, since this represents a threat. This suppression or elimination can be conducted subtly or overtly. History provides us with many examples of such overt actions, for instance, the book burnings conducted by the Nazis.

Indeed, our own recent Irish history is a perfect illustration of the connection between language and power, since English control of Ireland meant that a social situation was constructed where the ability to speak English was considered to be an advantage. In 1831, the Irish National School System was established, with English as the only acceptable 'school' language even in totally Irish-speaking areas. Conversely, when it came to constructing a Constitution for the new Irish Free State, one of its very first articles, Article 4, emphasised the connection between language and power when it stated: 'The national language of the Irish Free State (Saorstat Eireann) is the Irish language. . . .'

For the Civil Rights movements in America, the language that was used in their society did not reflect either their beliefs or values; rather, it embodied the beliefs and values of those in power. In this way, each word that they spoke in their everyday lives served to emphasise their lack of power and to represent their submission to those governing. At that time, those who were governing were stereotypically and overwhelmingly white, financially secure, heterosexual males. Thus non-white people, poor people, workers, pacifists, homosexuals and women decided that part of their movement towards gaining power had to be the development of a language that did truly reflect what they regarded as important.

Adrienne Rich's participation in Feminism, and her lesbianism, led her to view the very language that she had used so 'gracefully' and with such 'craftsmanship' as representing both the chains that held women in captivity in a male-controlled, patriarchal society, and the rope that they could use to climb to power and liberty. She understood 'how our language has trapped as well as liberated us, how the very act of naming has been till now a male prerogative, and how we can begin to see and name – and therefore start afresh.' (Adrienne Rich, *When We Dead Awaken: Writing a Re-Vision*). Together with other feminist writers, Rich set about finding words to express their new identities; to dismantle a language that they felt echoed with the message that men held all the power in society; to allow women to access power and to revolutionise the very structures of society:

> Women are speaking to and of women in these poems, out of a newly released courage to name, to love each other, to share risk and grief and celebration. . . . The creative energy of patriarchy is fast running out. . . .
> (Adrienne Rich, *When We Dead Awaken: Writing a Re-Vision*)

Thus, from the late 1950s on, Rich began to recognise that not only should her writing have a political dimension to it, but also that her very life should embrace a political stance. For her, politics was 'not something "out there", but something "in here" and of the essence of my condition'. Rich believed that the time had come for women to focus on the role that they had played in previous societies, their role in the present society, and the role that they could play in the society of the future.

Nor was this going to be an easy task, either for women or men. On the one hand, women had no models on which to base their vision of a new 'woman-driven' world. So, there were bound to be feelings of fear and confusion in some women, when faced with the sufferings of women in the past and the uncertainty surrounding women's roles in the future. Thus in 'Power', about Marie Curie's denial of the cause of her dreadful physical condition, can be seen a representation of the reluctance of some women to acknowledge the truth of the female/male relationship. On the other hand, men would also experience fear and confusion, as they had to confront this challenge to the traditional, patriarchal society that had served them so well for so many centuries.

Most difficult of all, however, was the fact that women and men were now beginning to speak a different language, because women were no longer content to use the words that had been formed by and for a male-centred society. Her later poems, such as 'Our Whole Life', 'Trying to Talk with a Man' and 'Diving into the Wreck' express many of those concerns.

RICH'S LATER LIFE AND POETRY

Although Rich had finally found the 'synthesis' that she had been looking for to draw together the 'split' elements of her life into an understandable whole, she still had to endure some very difficult times. In 1968 her father died, and in 1970 her husband Alfred committed suicide. Rich was deeply upset and her poem 'From a Survivor' communicates her profound sense of loss with an uncompromising honesty. In addition, she has had to undergo a series of operations for arthritis and in 1992 she had spinal surgery.

However, Rich has also had happier times. In 1976, she began living with another writer, Michelle Cliff. She has continued to write both poetry and prose while lecturing in a number of American universities, including Columbia, Cornell and Stanford. The quality of her work has been frequently acknowledged, ranging from the National Book Award in 1974, through two Guggenheim Fellowships and the Brandeis Creative Arts Medal in Poetry, to the Lannan Foundation Lifetime Achievement Award in 2000. In 1997 her principles led her to decline a National Medal for the Arts from the then President of the United States, Bill Clinton, commenting, 'I do know that art . . . means nothing if it simply decorates the dinner table of the power that holds it hostage. The radical disparities of wealth and power in America are widening at a devastating rate. A president cannot meaningfully honour certain token artists while the people at large are so dishonoured.'

Rich's later poetry is clearly very different from her earlier work in appearance, structure, expression and content. The tight elegance of 'Aunt Jennifer's Tigers' is strikingly opposed to the cluster of words and spaces used in 'Power'. The refined clarity of language in 'The Uncle Speaks in the Drawing Room' contrasts with the challenging connection of words found in 'Trying to Talk with a Man'. The hesitant, careful expression of uneasiness in 'Storm Warning' gives way to the confident heroism of 'Diving into the Wreck'.

The manner in which Rich has continually and uncompromisingly wrestled with the poetic form reflects the way in which she has wrestled with the experiences of her life. Initially, she learned her poetic craft from men: her father and the male poets that she studied. She strove to write in a way that had 'occasional surprises . . . but control, technical mastery and intellectual clarity were the real goals' (Adrienne Rich, *Poetry and Experience: Statement at a Poetry Reading*). In doing so, she received great praise for her ability from such distinguished male writers as W. H. Auden, but she also had to suppress aspects of her identity, of her womanhood.

It was this act of suppression that caused Rich to feel a terrible sense of confusion and, for a time, the ordered formality of her poems provided her with a comforting means of escape from this confusion. Inevitably, she was driven to face the reality of the conflict inherent in her life and the lie of the order that she had so frantically tried to make a truth. As her life experiences expanded, so too did her poetry. She began to re-form her writing, so that there was still that refinement in her choice of words and phrases but there was also an openness to 'let the unconscious offer its materials', to allow her imagination to work on experience. She no longer hid behind her writing; instead she used it to engage directly with her life. Thus her poems became 'experiences, that contribute to my knowledge and my emotional life' (Adrienne Rich, *Poetry and Experience: Statement at a Poetry Reading*). It is notable that she characteristically writes in the present tense, so that her poems appear as processes in action.

With immense bravery and an unbroken determination to be truthful, Adrienne Rich opens up the process of her act of living to us, her readers – not to provide answers, nor to supply solutions, but simply to share and acknowledge the value of a life experience, in the hope that we too will move towards a greater sharing and acknowledgment of the value of all life experiences:

> '. . . in the more recent poems something is happening, something has happened to me and, if I have been a good parent to the poem, something will happen to you who read it.'
> (Adrienne Rich, *Poetry and Experience: Statement at a Poetry Reading*)

There is, indeed, a heroic quality about the role that she has assigned for herself and the task that she has undertaken, but there is also an underlying sense of unremitting solitariness. For like Aunt Jennifer, like the woman 'Living in Sin', like the 'naked man fleeing' and like 'the Algerian', Rich writes as a figure on her own. Although occasionally she may, like the diver in 'Diving into the Wreck', feel a sense of wholeness or she may celebrate the fact that she is a 'Survivor', the wholeness and the celebration never totally nullify the image of Rich standing alone with her fists raised against the society that surrounds her. And yet she fights on, encouraging her readers to witness her struggle to find a language that will have the power to change the world that she inhabits. She is driven to do this in the hope that each of us will be impelled to seek words for our worlds and, in so doing, empower ourselves to revolutionise society so that humanity can enter into a new age, where all have the power to speak and the right to be heard.

Aunt Jennifer's Tigers

Text of poem: New Explorations Anthology page 272

[*Note: This poem is also prescribed for Ordinary Level 2008 exam*]

BACKGROUND NOTE

Along with 'The Uncle Speaks in the Drawing Room' and 'Storm Warnings', 'Aunt Jennifer's Tigers' comes from Rich's first collection of poetry, published in 1951 while she was in her final year at Radcliffe College. At this time, Rich was writing in a way that was influenced by her father's opinions on poetry and the work of the male poets that she had studied. These poems are notable for their ordered appearance on the page, their tight structure, their elegance of expression and their management of tone.

In later years, Rich saw this mastery of the technical aspects of writing poetry as providing her with a way of subtly expressing her sense of unease about the world that she inhabited because, at that time in her life, she felt unable to declare it openly. Thus, her poems should be seen as multi-layered. They often appear on the page as vivid descriptions of a dramatic moment or situation. However, a careful reading of these descriptions reveals the intricate connections that Rich has built into her images, so that the reader gradually comes to understand the issues and themes that lie at the heart of her pieces. Thus, in spite of the control that she exerted on the poems, they do have an emotional resonance that vibrates within each word, so that the feelings expressed in these pieces linger hauntingly.

TECHNICAL QUALITY

'Aunt Jennifer's Tigers' is made up of three stanzas, each of four lines. The rhyme scheme is tight and regular: *aabb ccdd eeff.* However, Rich has mastered these structural elements to such a degree that they do not interfere with either the reading or the meaning of the poem. Rather they control the pace, so that the reader is encouraged to take time over reading the poem. Indeed, Rich's skilful use of her vocabulary merits careful reading, as she invests a considerable depth of meaning and implication into her use of colour, nouns and verbs. Rich also uses the sounds of her words most effectively, to reinforce the images that she creates. So, the alliteration (where two or more words close together begin with the same letter) in the words 'fingers fluttering' (line 5) emphasises the nervous anxiety of Aunt Jennifer. Similarly, the alliteration of 'prancing, proud' (line 12) conveys the assured certainty of the tigers.

A READING OF THE POEM

The opening image of this poem bursts off the page, filled with colour and excitement. Rich describes an embroidered scene of golden tigers moving confidently through their natural environment. They gleam like gems against the lush, green vegetation. There is a wonderful feeling of life and energy about this opening image: the strong, beautiful animals surrounded by the growing, flourishing jungle. The verbs that Rich uses to describe the tigers, 'prance' and 'pace', indicate that these creatures are totally free in their surroundings. They are masters of their territory who fear nothing, and because of this freedom and power, they have a dignity and confidence that is in marked contrast to the behaviour of the men, who huddle under a tree.

Thus, in the four lines of her opening stanza, Rich has effectively established a number of key elements that will reappear again in the poem: the colour gold, the concepts of freedom and power and the image of the male figure.

In the second stanza, Rich shifts the focus of the poem away from the wonderful tigers and the cowering men, and onto the hands of the person who created them, Aunt Jennifer. It quickly becomes clear that Aunt Jennifer is very different from the tigers. Her movements suggest anxiety and nervousness. Her hands 'flutter' like panic-stricken little birds. They are so delicate, so lacking in physical strength, that her fingers have difficulty with the ivory needle that she is using to embroider the picture. Unlike the tigers, Aunt Jennifer is struggling to cope with her environment. The creamy white of the ivory conjures up an image of the pale, almost bloodless, skin of Aunt Jennifer's fingers, as if her struggle is sucking all life out of her. The fact that the needle is made of ivory is significant, since man obtains ivory by killing elephants. So, the ivory of the needle represents man's triumph over the strength and freedom of the elephant and the power of life and death that he holds over this wild animal.

But, the ivory needle is not the only object that is causing difficulties for Aunt Jennifer's hands. What is really weighing them down is her golden wedding ring. In the first stanza, gold was associated with the beautiful, powerful, free tigers; in the second stanza, gold is linked with a cold, heavy piece of metal that drags down the light, agitated movements of Aunt Jennifer's fingers. Interestingly, the Latin word 'oppressare', meaning 'to weigh down', gave rise to the word oppression. For although Aunt Jennifer wears it, this is very definitely 'Uncle's' ring – a means of oppression. Like a harness or a yoke, the ring symbolises the control and power that Uncle obtained over Aunt Jennifer by marrying her. Just as the ivory needle indicated the subjection of the elephant, so the ring testifies to the enslavement of Aunt Jennifer by a male figure. The fearful male figures in the first stanza are no more. The male figure in the second stanza brings death, uses creatures for his own ends and exerts a powerful control over his female partner. It is notable that the Uncle has no name. It is his oppressive bulk and presence that loom not only over fragile Aunt Jennifer, but also over the second and third stanzas.

The image of the golden wedding ring reappears again in the first line of the third stanza, along with Aunt Jennifer's fingers. In direct contrast to the first stanza, where energy and life filled every word, the third stanza evokes death. Aunt Jennifer is motionless, her creamy-white fingers, now finally drained of the blood of life, have been stilled by death – but the ring is still upon them. So, even in death, Aunt Jennifer still carries the emblem that signifies her lack of power and freedom. Rich's use of the words 'ordeals' and 'mastered', in connection with the ring, link back to the image of the ring in the second stanza. In Rich's view, Aunt Jennifer's marriage to the 'Uncle' committed her to a life of oppression and subjection to the power of her husband. For Aunt Jennifer, marriage forced her to yield up her own power, to surrender her control of her life and to suppress her own feelings and wishes. For Rich, the wedding ring is not a symbol of love or mutual commitment, but of male oppression and female repression.

In the final two lines of the poem, Rich returns again to the tigers that Aunt Jennifer struggled in life to embroider. They are still free and powerful. They are everything that Aunt Jennifer gave up once she entered into marriage with the Uncle. They celebrate their living, while Aunt Jennifer simply endured hers. Yet what we must not forget is the fact that it was Aunt Jennifer who created the tigers. It was she who chose the coloured wool and worked it through the screen. Do the tigers represent a small act of rebellion by Aunt Jennifer against the control and mastery of her husband? Are they the symbols of a tiny flame of freedom and power that endured deep within this anxious, delicate, birdlike woman? Could the small and rather cowardly male figures in the first stanza represent the apparently submissive Aunt Jennifer's real opinion about her husband? It would be wonderful to think that Aunt Jennifer was, indeed, a rebel with a needle, that her embroidered screen was a gesture of her defiance.

But perhaps there is not such a positive ending to the poem. Aunt Jennifer's tigers are splendid in their freedom and power. However, they are not truly alive. They are creatures woven in thread and fabric, stretched within the frame of a screen; like captured and preserved butterflies they are stuck on a panel. Perhaps this is the true tragedy that Rich sees in Aunt Jennifer's life: marriage to the domineering, male Uncle broke her spirit to such an extent that even if some small flame of freedom and power did survive within her, it was neither flickering nor active but static and unmoving, frozen and fixed by her own powerlessness in the face of the Uncle's all-consuming, all-powerful oppression.

Imagery and themes

The following are simply suggested relationships between images and themes in this poem; you may find others in your reading:

Aunt Jennifer:	Female
	An oppressed figure

	Unable to express herself openly Timid and lacking in confidence
The Tigers:	Free Powerful Confident figures
Uncle:	Male The oppressor
The Wedding Ring:	An instrument of oppression

The Uncle Speaks in the Drawing Room

Text of poem: New Explorations Anthology page 275

BACKGROUND NOTE

See Background Note on 'Aunt Jennifer's Tigers' (page 164).

TECHNICAL QUALITY

This poem exhibits the same skilful mastery of the technical features of poetry as is displayed in 'Aunt Jennifer's Tigers'. It is made up of four stanzas, each consisting of six lines. The rhyme scheme of *abbacc* provides an ordered substructure to the poem, while not interrupting the natural arrangement or the sense of the everyday language. Therefore, the piece reads naturally, as if we are simply engaged in a conversation. However, this simplicity and naturalness should not be mistaken for a lack of craft on Rich's part. A closer analysis indicates that she has combined everyday words into a series of stunningly dramatic images reinforced by appropriate musical phrases. So, in the first stanza, she brings the mob to life with their 'sullen stare', their 'bitter tones' and, most disturbingly of all, their 'stones'. Rich uses alliteration to strengthen the vividness of this image. Her use of 's' sounds and repetition in the phrases 'Standing sullen' and 'sullen stare' evoke the rebellious whispering and murmuring of the hostile crowd. Similarly, the assonance (where two or more words close together have the same vowel sound) and rhyme in lines 17–18 'ruby/thunder' and 'bowl/roll' effectively convey the vibrations that threaten the grandfather's precious bowl.

A READING OF THE POEM

The title of this poem, ' The Uncle Speaks in the Drawing Room', establishes the tone of the piece. Rich's use of a nameless persona (an assumed character), known only by his title of Uncle, makes this male character seem distant and unapproachable, someone who is aware of his position and proud of his status. Similarly, the setting of the 'Drawing Room' gives the whole scene a formal, rather ceremonial quality, since this room was traditionally reserved for entertaining guests to the house. Consider how different our expectations would be if the title read 'Uncle John Speaks in the Kitchen'. This title is an excellent example of the way in which Rich uses apparently simple, everyday words to imply a multitude of suggestions to her readers. That is why, with Rich's poetry, we should read and reread in order to capture and appreciate the fullness of her work.

In the first stanza we hear the Uncle speaking about the 'mob'. He describes their simmering discontent in a calm, rather detached manner. It is clear that, as befits his venerable position as 'Uncle', he is determined to maintain a 'stiff upper lip', to provide a steadying influence over the rest of the family. He is a man who lives in a comfortable world where houses are arranged around squares and have the architectural luxuries of windows, balconies and gates. He recognises that it is this world that the mob resents and, given the courage, would like to destroy. However, he remains steadfastly unperturbed, even in the face of their stones.

His dismissive attitude continues into the second stanza, where he describes the behaviour of the mob as 'follies that subside'. He deliberately reduces their concerns and actions down to nothing more than foolishness that will soon pass away. Up until this point, Rich has managed the tone of the Uncle's speech very skilfully, so that it is consistently controlled and steadily dignified. However, in line 8, the Uncle's confident assurance seems to slip a little. He begins to undercut his speech with phrases that suggest some doubt on his part, as with 'none the less'. His use of 'us' indicates that he still regards himself as a leading figure in a particular group, but there is a growing disquiet in the tone of his voice. He even uses the word 'fear' in line 11. But the 'fear' that he feels does not arise out of a concern for himself or the others who belong to his group; rather, he is fearful for the elegant objects that fill his prosperous world: the delicate, glass vases and chandeliers. The threat of the mob's stones to such breakable items cannot be ignored.

Hastily, the Uncle recovers himself in the first two lines of the third stanza. He seeks to reassure his listeners that nothing will be thrown, no violent acts will occur. However, once again, his underlying disquiet seeps through his words. Almost in spite of himself, he is drawn to remember an incident where the 'grandsire' of the group 'stood aghast'. Clearly, Rich's use of 'grandsire' is a deliberate one on her part, conveying a male person who is both respected and held in high esteem. The image of such a figure standing transfixed by dismay must be a disturbing one both for the Uncle and for those others who have descended from such a man. Once again, it is an object that has led to such a shocking reaction – a red glass bowl vibrating in a thunderstorm. This is a particularly effective image that conveys the depth of the Uncle's anxiety. The ruby-red colour of the bowl conjures up images of blood; while a thunderstorm is an unstoppable, uncontrollable force that sweeps away man's power in an instant. In spite of all his efforts, the Uncle's 'stiff upper lip' is quivering and he reveals his worst fears.

With the fourth stanza, the Uncle tries to recover his position. He gives up his attempts to dismiss the potential threat of the mob and, instead, seeks to urge his listeners to stand together in the face of the threat. Rather like a military leader in wartime, such as Sir Winston Churchill during World War II, the Uncle exhorts his group to remember the ties that bind them. He reminds them of the special 'treasures' that they have inherited from their shared past: a past when mobs did not gather and murmur threateningly against the order of society. These 'treasures' which surround them are not only the beautiful objects from a 'calmer age', but also their genetic inheritance from their ancestors who lived in the 'calmer age' that enables them to appreciate fully the beauty and worth of these objects. For they, along with the Uncle, are of a 'kind' that is better than the mob, because they value the elegance of objects such as the balconies and gates, glass bowls and chandeliers.

The final two lines of the poem vibrate with a confusion of emotions. We could interpret the Uncle's image of his 'kind' positioning themselves between the beautiful glass objects and the mob as a positive and inspirational one, revealing his supreme confidence that his 'kind' will survive. Indeed, his attitude has validity in that many feel that beautiful works of art should be above political upheaval and ought to be protected no matter who is in power. However, his confidence does seem to be rather brittle. In line 13, the Uncle had categorically stated that the mob would not throw 'missiles'. Tellingly, in the final line of the poem he describes the mob as 'missile-throwers'. Could these lines be simply the hysterical ravings of a man who knows that, in spite of all the bravado of his 'stiff upper lip', the end has come for his 'kind'?

Imagery and themes

The following are simply suggested relationships between images and themes in this poem; you may find others in your reading:

The Uncle:	Male The oppressor A member of the ruling section of society At the top of the hierarchy Has the power to express views/opinions Desires to maintain the status quo

The Mob:	The oppressed At the bottom of the hierarchy No power to express views/opinions Violence the only means of expression Figures of revolution A threat to the established social order Desires to change the status quo
Windows Balcony Gate Crystal vase Chandelier Ruby bowl	Objects that represent the values of the dominant, oppressive section of society

Storm Warnings

Text of poem: New Exploratins Anthology page 278

[*Note: This poem is also prescribed for Ordinary Level exam in 2008*]

BACKGROUND NOTE

See Background Note on 'Aunt Jennifer's Tigers'.

TECHNICAL QUALITY

Initially this poem appears to be very similar to 'Aunt Jennifer's Tigers' and 'The Uncle Speaks in the Drawing Room'. It has the same regularity of appearance, with four stanzas, each made up of seven lines. However, on closer inspection we begin to notice an important structural difference: rhyme is not a feature of this poem. Whereas 'Aunt Jennifer's Tigers' and 'The Uncle Speaks in the Drawing Room' both had strong, regular rhyme schemes, this poem has not. Instead, Rich relies on metre and rhythm, along with assonance and alliteration, to give her writing a technical elegance and grace.

An excellent example of her technical mastery of these elements is line 6: 'And walk from window to closed window, watching'. To appreciate the metre of the line read the following highlighted letters slightly louder: 'And **walk** from **win**dow **to** closed **win**dow, **watch**ing'. There are five stressed syllables (the highlighted letters). This gives the line a rhythm that conjures up the sound of the wind buffeting against the windows. Her use of alliteration, with the repeated 'w', creates a similar effect of wind blowing in gusts: 'And **w**alk from **w**indow to closed **w**indow, **w**atching'. Rich employs assonance to further reinforce the impact of this line. She interweaves 'a', 'o' and 'i' sounds to convey the impression of the ever-changing cadence of the gusts: '**A**nd w**a**lk fr**o**m window to closed window, watching'.

You might like to compare and contrast Rich's approach to conveying the movement of the wind with that of John Montague in his poem 'Windharp', also in this anthology.

The dramatic lyric

This poem is written as a dramatic lyric. A lyric poem has a strong personal element in that it communicates the feelings or state of mind of an individual. The individual who is speaking can be either the poet, engaging in a direct communication with the reader, or an imaginary individual, a persona created by the poet who expresses certain thoughts or feelings. A lyric poem is not concerned with telling a story. However, some poets do create a context or setting for the individual, as Rich does in this poem, and this approach is known as a dramatic lyric.

A reading of the poem

The first stanza of the poem creates an image that sweeps from an instrument that measures pressure, a barometer, held inside the windows and walls of the house, out into a sky filled with 'gray unrest' and 'walking winds' hauling at the trees. The effect of this image is to convey the smallness of the house that is protecting the barometer and the speaker, and the uncontrollable vastness of the sky and wind. The apparent tranquillity that is contained within the house, where the speaker is reading a book while sitting on 'a pillowed chair', seems to be very vulnerable and fragile. The walls and windows offer some protection against the violence of the wind. Unlike the trees, the speaker, her book and her chair are not being physically pulled about by the wind. Nevertheless, the wind does have an effect on them in that the speaker abandons the book and the chair and is drawn, it seems irresistibly, to look out at the turmoil.

The second stanza is an important one. Up until this point, it seems as if Rich is simply writing a description of an approaching storm. However, as we know from her other poems, Rich uses dramatic situations and concrete images to give expression to abstract and complex thoughts, feelings and beliefs. Thus, in the second stanza, the focus of the piece shifts away from the weather elements signalling change in the physical world, and on to the idea that emotions are also subject to such changes. Just as a calm, blue sky can become a turbulent grey, so a calm heart can become troubled. In both cases, we humans are largely unable to foretell exactly when this alteration will occur. In the first stanza, the barometer had indicated a fall in pressure 'all the afternoon', but it did not give a precise time for the storm's arrival. The air currents that carry the weather move invisibly, uncontrollably and unpredictably in the skies above us, swirling into calm areas. So it is with emotions. They too move invisibly, uncontrollably and unpredictably into hearts that were once quiet. Yet, there is a suggestion that the speaker's heart may not have been completely calm. Rich establishes a connection between the image of the 'silent core of waiting', in line 9, and the heart, in line 13. Is she suggesting that this heart too was a 'silent core of waiting'?

In the third stanza, Rich again returns to the image of the barometer used in the first stanza. She links it to the image of a clock. Both are man-made instruments that seek to give us some feeling of control in the world. A clock indicates how time is passing; a barometer indicates how the weather is altering. But they can only indicate. Neither of them has any control over the elements that they are linked to: the clock cannot stop time passing; the barometer cannot stop the weather changing, nor stop the wind from shattering it into fragments. In the final image of the third stanza Rich creates an image of futility in the face of inevitability. The closing of window shutters, nothing more than strips of wood joined together, is essentially a pointless action when set against the uncontrollable, destructive power of the wind. Clearly, she is suggesting that it is the same with emotions. We may run around closing our emotional 'shutters', attempting to suppress emotional alterations, but we are simply wasting our time. The emotional change will occur inevitably.

The fourth and final stanza of the poem returns to where the poem began: inside the house with the wind raging outside. The speaker sets about shutting out the storm as it increases in its intensity. She pulls the curtains and lights a candle. Again we have frailty set against overwhelming power, futility set against inevitability. The curtains are nothing more than thin fabric; the candle, despite apparently being protected by glass, can be extinguished in an instant. These instruments of 'sole defense' are pathetic. Despite all the speaker's actions, the turbulent wind still manages to penetrate into the tranquillity of the house. It squeezes in through the gaps that exist in this seemingly solid structure: the 'keyhole' and 'the unsealed aperture'.

The final two lines of the poem are stunning. The simplicity of the words contains a wealth of expression that is breathtaking. The 'I' of the speaker becomes 'we', releasing the poem from the limitations of individual expression into the communication of a political position. Rich swings the impact of the poem away from the single 'heart' and onto the concepts of power and powerlessness. The speaker stands with others who have had to learn to suppress their desire for change, to reject their awareness that change is necessary. This suppression and rejection may well have come partly from their own fear as well as from external forces, but they indicate a powerlessness about the group. However, for all the power of the factors that force this group to put up a 'sole defense against the season', there is an ominous inevitability about the phrase 'troubled regions'. The calm that the learned defensive actions bring about is a limited one. The actions do not calm the 'troubled regions'; they simply temporarily resist the trouble. The clear implication is that just as the wind infiltrates its way into a house, just as emotional change creeps into the heart, so groups who behave in a 'learned' way finally, and inevitably, break free to gain the power to behave as they want to behave.

Imagery and themes

The following are simply suggested relationships between images and themes in this poem; you may find others in your reading:

The Storm:	Change/alteration Emotional change Social
The Wind:	The force of change
The House:	A construction that appears to contain calm tranquillity It appears to offer protection against the turbulence of change.
Weatherglasses Clocks Curtains	Objects within the house that appear to offer control and power, but in reality offer only an illusion of control and power.

Living in Sin

Text of poem: New Explorations Anthology page 282

Background note

During the 1950s Adrienne Rich began to change the way that she wrote poetry. She moved away from the more formal style evident in 'Aunt Jennifer's Tigers', 'The Uncle Speaks in the Drawing Room' and 'Storm Warnings'. Rich saw this progression as developing out of her growing understanding that her poetry and her life experiences were intimately bound together. She felt that the demands of formal poetry restricted her expression, noting in later years, 'Experience itself had become too much for that.' (Adrienne Rich: *An Interview with David Montenegro*).

Thus, she began to write poetry where she allowed her readers to witness the ways in which her imagination acted on her life experiences. Rich has characterised her early poems, as represented by 'Aunt Jennifer's Tigers', 'The Uncle Speaks in the Drawing Room' and 'Storm Warnings', as poems that were written with precision '*about* experiences' (Adrienne Rich, *Poetry and Experience: Statement at a Poetry Reading*); while her later poems, as represented by the remaining seven poems in this selection, were actual experiences, written in the present tense, where a process was happening.

Structure

It is immediately evident that the structure of this poem is radically different from Rich's earlier pieces. The ordered appearance created by regular stanzas has been abandoned in favour of 26 uninterrupted lines of varying lengths. Similarly, rhyme is no longer a feature of her writing. The punctuation is much looser, with sentences spilling over a number of lines and the use of dashes and dots. This approach gives the piece an unresolved, open quality and a sense of immediacy. Whereas her earlier poems sought to put some sort of form on experience, Rich is now comfortable simply allowing experience to stand on its own. It is important to note, however, that this does not imply less effort on Rich's part. In many ways the abandonment of the rules of formal poetic writing demands more effort from the writer, since the language used must be shaped, not according to a series of accepted rules, but by a sense of honesty and integrity.

A reading of the poem

Rich again uses the device of situating her poem within a dramatic situation. We are introduced to 'She' in the opening line of the poem. 'She' is clearly a woman who has decided to rebel against the accepted norms of social behaviour in 1950s America, as is indicated by the title of the poem, 'Living in Sin'. This phrase was used to describe a couple cohabiting without being married. The couple live in a 'studio'. There are suggestions of an unconventional, artistic lifestyle about the word 'studio'. It is just the sort of place where two people would 'live in sin'. But the second line of the poem introduces a note of emotional conflict. There is the rather romantic reference to 'the furniture of love', but 'She' no longer sees the romance: her main concern is with the dust that covers 'the furniture of love'. Her emotional conflict continues into lines 3 and 4, where we learn that dust is not the only difficulty that 'She' faces: the taps in the 'studio' are noisy and the windows are dirty. 'She' feels guilty about her disenchantment. After all, the decision to 'live in sin' was a brave one at that time, and required great faith that the love that was shared would conquer all. In this way, her irritation at these less-than-perfect objects seems to her to be an act of disbelief in their love.

Lines 4–7 present the reader with a description of how 'She' imagined 'Living in Sin'. It is a vision of perfection, with perfect pears on a perfect plate, a perfect piano draped in an exotically perfect shawl, and a perfect cat chasing a perfectly 'amusing' mouse.

The contrast between this idealised perfection and the grubby reality of the 'studio' is evident in lines 8–14. It echoes to the heavy footsteps of the milkman in the early morning; it is chilly and it is untidy, with bits of cheese and empty bottles left lying around. Rich's use of the word 'sepulchral' conveys the gloominess that 'She' feels. As if all of this were not depressing enough, we encounter a beetle on one of the kitchen shelves, evidently only one of many that scuttle around the flat. The three dots convey a sense that 'She' is plunging downwards on a waterfall of depression.

However, line 15 interrupts these gloomy thoughts: 'he' is getting up. This is the 'he' with whom 'She' chose to 'live in sin'. Unfortunately, the reality of the situation that 'She' finds herself in is embodied in the description of 'her man'. He does not look at her and smile, nor enfold her in a loving embrace. On the contrary, he does not even seem to notice her. He yawns, fiddles about on the piano, scratches his chin and goes out to buy cigarettes. This is hardly the stuff of a great Romantic Love.

Unable to withstand the irritation of the untidiness of the flat, 'She' embarks on a frenzy of housework: making the bed and dusting. Unfortunately, the objects in the flat seem determined to thwart her efforts to impose something of the perfection that she imagined onto them. Annoyingly, she is so intent on her cleaning that she forgets to watch the coffee-pot and it boils over, causing more mess for her to clean up. Perfection seems to be slipping further and further away.

In line 23, the tone becomes slightly more hopeful, as we learn that during the day 'She' regains her love. Perhaps 'he' brought her back some flowers, or wrote a song for her on the piano, or held her close. Whatever happened, 'She' manages to escape from the harshness of the reality of their situation and to immerse herself once more in their love. But, sadly, this escape is only temporary. Her feelings of disenchantment never really go away. Although the darkness of the night hides the grubbiness of their flat, her sleep is disturbed by her awareness that the light of day will once more reveal it in all its depressing untidiness.

The Theme

By simply referring to the couple as 'She' and 'he' Rich enables the theme of the poem to develop from a single situation into the expression of her political viewpoint. Thus, the theme of this poem addresses the fundamental differences that Rich sees as existing between men and women because of the radically different roles that they are allocated by the social structure of the traditional, patriarchal society. Love may draw them together, but these profound differences prevent them from communicating on a meaningful level and, consequently, prevent the couple from developing their love.

Coupled with this, Rich acknowledges that women are in many ways their own worst enemies when it comes to breaking free from the traditional roles allowed to them by a patriarchal society. Rich takes the view that women are programmed from birth to behave in certain ways that reinforce their own subservience and the dominance of males in society. So, the 'he' in the poem is totally unmoved by the condition of the flat, because his traditional training does not involve anything to do with housekeeping. On the other hand, the 'She' cannot resist her learned responsibility for housekeeping and she succumbs to the urge to clean the flat. However, it is significant that these actions do not provide her with any lasting sense of fulfilment. Nor, indeed, does the love that drew her to the man. The final image of the poem conveys the recurring disquiet and disenchantment that she feels about her role.

Perhaps within the context of Rich's political viewpoint, the title of the poem 'Living in Sin' might be more concerned with the endless compromises and disappointments that she feels women are forced to endure in a male-dominated society, rather than the sexual connotation that this phrase normally suggests.

The Roofwalker

Text of poem: New Explorations Anthology page 286

Background note

See Background Note on ' Living in Sin' (pages 173–4).

Style and structure

With 'The Roofwalker, Rich continues to push back the poetic, intellectual and emotional boundaries that she had struggled with for so long.

In poetic terms, 'The Roofwalker' is significant for two main reasons. Firstly, there is a further loosening of punctuation. In this respect, Rich was influenced by the work of Emily Dickinson. Here, she uses dashes in lines 16–21 and in line 32. Whereas full stops and commas give a sense of definite structure and composition, the use of dashes conveys the immediacy and openness of developing thoughts. Rich writes in a 'stream of consciousness'. This means that the poet tries to retain the immediacy and the energy of the way that personal thoughts and feelings blend and merge, rather like an intellectual 'Lava Lamp'. Rich's dedication of this poem to the poet Denise Levertov is significant, since Levertov focused on the development of such a style where the thinking process was reflected in line and image.

Secondly, Rich's use of the ' stream of consciousness' technique is connected to her belief that poetry should be a process, in that it empowers both the poet and the reader to engage in the act of becoming, to be changed. The dashes reinforce the sense of process that underlies the poem, since they appear to be more open, more transitional, than the closure and finality of full stops.

Despite this loosening of style, Rich maintains a strong sense of coherence in the poem. Much of this coherence stems from the comparison she establishes between herself and the builders. This metaphor acts most successfully as a structural support for the piece.

A reading of the poem

Although this poem is significantly different from Rich's earlier poems, it does contain familiar features. It is a dramatic lyric, so we have the piece located in a dramatic context, with an individual figure expressing thoughts and feelings. In this respect Rich's poems often seem to be like condensed plays, or scenes extracted from a film.

Lines 1–12 are a masterpiece of descriptive writing. As readers, we see the gathering gloom of night with the last streaks of daylight silhouetting the figures of the builders and illuminating the roof. We hear the stillness now that their work is finished: the hammers lie still and the pulleys rest. Rich's comparison of the builders on the roof to sailors on board a ship effectively communicates her emotional response to these men. She is impressed by them, as they move about high above the ground with the same confident balance that experienced sailors have on board ship. She sees them as 'Giants' in that they seem to be greater, more heroic, than normal human men. A 'wave' hovers above their heads; they walk on a 'burning deck', but they do not panic. For these men, danger is to be embraced and conquered, rather than feared and avoided. And yet, the presence of the 'wave' and the 'burning deck' could be indicative of a threat to the builders and their world. They may not be aware of it – indeed, they may be 'indifferent' to it – but the threat is still there.

The space that is placed at this point, between the first and second section, is important, since it acts as a bridge drawing the reader across from one context to another. Lines 13–15 mark a movement away from the external setting of the poem to the internal world of thought and emotion. Rich establishes a connection between herself and the builders in that she, too, is exposing herself to danger. Like the builders, she is 'up there', but, unlike them, there is a feeling of isolation and vulnerability about Rich's position.

The second space, between the second and third sections, again acts as a bridge to the final section of the poem. We are drawn further into Rich's 'stream of consciousness' as she reflects on the reality of her position. Continuing to make references to the 'builder' metaphor, Rich sees her life as being one of great effort that has achieved very little. Having struggled to make a 'roof' she finds that she 'can't live under' it, unlike the builders who stride about confidently on top of it. The 'roof' is seen as an object that oppresses Rich, while, conversely, it supports the male builders in all their assured confidence. Furthermore, her hard work of calculating and adjusting to create a good, strong structure appears to have been fruitless. For the problem lies not with her effort, nor indeed with what she was attempting to construct, but with her lack of choice.

Rich regarded the ability to choose as being an essential aspect of living as a human being with power. To be denied choice is to have the rights of one's humanity denied. Therefore, the fact that 'A life' chose the speaker in this poem, rather than her choosing it, doomed her efforts to failure. Rather like an electrician being forced to fix a burst water-pipe, Rich recognises that she has skills, she has abilities, but she is being obliged to use them in a situation where they are not suitable. Unlike the builders on the roof, who are perfectly 'at home' in their situation, Rich feels exposed and terrified.

Her use of the 'naked man fleeing' image to express her feelings may seem rather surprising in view of the way that she portrays male figures in her earlier poems. Indeed, her use of this image is open to a variety of interpretations. At times in her writing, Rich employs a male character to mask her expression of her own confusion. Thus, the 'naked man fleeing' is a 'safe' way for her to write about her innermost thoughts and feelings, because they are linked to a male figure who is clearly very different from the female Adrienne Rich. At other times, the male figure is a way of representing her intellectual experimentation with alternative ways of being. So, she presents us with the image of the 'naked man fleeing', who could be engaged in the alternative existence of sitting in a peaceful room reading. The implication is that it could be just so with Rich's own life, if things were very slightly different. Such a slight difference would mean that instead of experiencing deep unhappiness with her life, she could be happy with it.

Rich establishes a pointed connection between the words 'difference' (line 29) and 'indifference' (line 32). Difference is suggestive of the recognition of the need for, and the ability to initiate, change. Indifference suggests unwillingness and a lack of the ability to change. Rich is aware of the need for change in her life, the need for things to be different in the world. But, as yet, she is unable to initiate this change. She is powerless and panicking, trapped within a way of living that she has tried so hard to make successful. Rich may long for the calm quietness of being comfortable with her life, but the fact that she once again returns to the image of the 'naked man fleeing' in the final two lines of the poem is significant. Her final use of the 'naked man fleeing' image suggests that Rich knows, only too well, that such comfort will never be found in her present way of living.

Imagery and themes

The following are simply suggested relationships between images and themes in this poem; you may find others in your reading:

The Builders:	Male

	Powerful Confident In control
The Roof:	An object that oppresses and represses Rich An object that supports and empowers the builders
The 'naked man fleeing':	Male Powerless Vulnerable Afraid Representing Adrienne Rich?

Our Whole Life

Text of poem: New Explorations Anthology page 289

BACKGROUND NOTE

By the early 1970s Adrienne Rich was very much involved in Civil Rights movements. She felt increasingly drawn to groups who, because of the social structures at the time, were powerless to give expression to their beliefs and values. Such groups as non-white people, pacifists, homosexuals and women joined together in order to challenge the dominance of white, financially secure, heterosexual males.

As a result of her experiences with these groups, Rich developed the view that language and power are inextricably linked. She felt that as most human societies are traditionally male-dominated, with men holding power, then the words that are developed and accepted into everyday use by all those who live in those societies must also be male-dominated, in that they reflect male-centred values and beliefs. Rich saw this male-dominated language as a method of preventing other groups both from injecting their values and beliefs into the language of their society, and from having access to power. Therefore, she advocated that for disempowered groups to gain access to power, so that they could bring about a societal acknowledgment of their rights and needs, they had to develop an alternative language that was not male-dominated.

STRUCTURE AND STYLE

The appearance of this poem is very different from the ordered compactness of, for example, 'Aunt Jennifer's Tigers'. Instead there is an apparently loose grouping of phrases, sometimes with 3 or 2 or even just 1 line.

The absence of punctuation gives the passage a continuous, unbroken feeling that effectively creates the 'stream of consciousness' technique. This, along with her use of conversational language, gives the impression that we, as readers, are actually inside Rich's head, witnessing her thoughts connecting and interconnecting. However, this connecting and interconnecting does not take place in a haphazard or disordered manner. In spite of the rather loose appearance of the poem, Rich creates a strong sense of coherence by carefully placing words in a sequence of meaning, as with 'translations', 'fibs' and 'lies', and by using an intricate web of echoed images based on 'eating' and 'burning'.

A reading of the poem

The main thrust of this poem is evident from the first four lines, where Rich connects three words that are of fundamental importance to her theme: 'translation', 'fibs' and 'lies'. There is a deliberate and significant progression in the meanings of these words. Translation means that a word in one language is interpreted into another language. A fib is a trivial or unimportant lie. Lies, however, are deliberately untrue statements. Thus we move from a straightforward act of changing one word into another language without any alteration in its 'truth' of meaning, through a slight adjustment to its 'truth' of meaning: until, finally, the word loses all of its 'truth' of meaning. Rich's imagery of the 'knot' of lies, self-destructing in its attempted 'eating' through its own tangle, indicates that when a word loses its truth, when it becomes a lie, it becomes fossilised, because it is no longer able to communicate meaningfully. Clearly, for Rich, the lifeblood of a word lies in its 'truth' and honesty of expression. Indeed, Rich's revulsion for words that are lies is effectively conveyed by the rather nightmarish image of something 'eating' itself.

The image of 'eating' is carried forward into line 5, where we have the word 'bitten'. Here Rich suggests a tremendous feeling of tense repression, where words are not spoken through an open mouth but come out through clenched teeth. Her use of the 'blowtorch' image introduces the concept of 'burning', suggesting that words may form inside the mind and the mouth, but somewhere between this and actually saying them aloud, some force burns off their original meaning and shapes them into completely different words with completely different meanings. Thus the words, like 'dead letters', never get to deliver their original meaning. Instead, they are burned and remoulded into words that are lies, words that express the values and beliefs of those who hold power: of the oppressors.

The group represented by Rich's use of the term 'Our' may struggle to resist such a force. But, irresistibly, they will find themselves lured by it: initially by the apparently innocent act of 'translation'; then by the seemingly harmless use of 'fibs', until they find that they are engaged in telling lies, using the ‘oppressor’s language’. In this way the group has no language of its own, and therefore it has no power.

In lines 10–15 Rich introduces an image that is both vivid and disturbing: that of ‘the Algerian’. This unfortunate man is ‘burning’ with pain. Yet he is powerless to express his incredible suffering because he cannot use the language of the man in power, the doctor. The ‘Algerian’ can do no more than simply stand wordless, displaying his terrible wounds. In these five lines and with this final image, Rich draws together the sequence of meaning and webs of imagery that hold this poem together. Thus the progression from ‘translation’, to ‘fib’, to ‘lies’ that cause injury leads to ‘a cloud of pain’; the ‘eating’ and biting become the guttural sounds emanating from the dried mouth of the ‘Algerian’ and the burning of paint mutates into the burning of a human body.

Most horrifying of all, Rich links the mutilated body of the ‘Algerian’ with those whom she writes for, the ‘Our’ in the opening line of the poem. Her message is clear: both she and this group have spent their collective life trying to communicate what they honestly thought and felt to their oppressors. Their lack of success has not only increased their powerlessness, but it has also caused them to suffer intensely. They stand alongside the ‘Algerian’, mute with pain.

Imagery and themes

The following are simply suggested relationships between images and themes in this poem; you may find others in your reading:

Translation Fibs Lies }	A sequence representing the steady erosion of the ‘true’meaning of a word so that it loses its ‘honesty’ of expression
The Algerian:	Male Trying to communicate but unable to be understood Powerless Suffering Representing a powerless social group
The Doctor:	Male Unable to understand Powerful – can heal and banish pain Representing a powerful social group

Trying to Talk with a Man

Text of poem: New Explorations Anthology page 292

BACKGROUND NOTE

Between 1939 and 1945, the United States of America spent some $2 billion on developing the atomic bomb, in a project known as 'The Manhattan Project'. This research was carried out in a laboratory specially constructed by the government in the geographically isolated Los Alamos, New Mexico. Scientists engaged in the project, along with their families, were obliged to move close to the laboratory and to live in temporary housing. Their work culminated with the explosion of an atomic bomb on the morning of 16 July, 1945.

STRUCTURE AND STYLE

Rich employs a rather loose clustering of lines, a conversational style of language and the lyric form to give this poem a wonderful sense of immediacy.

Her arrangement of the lines of this poem into groups of varying lengths might at first appear to be almost accidental. However, on closer reading it becomes evident that each group pivots around a central concept that contributes to developing the theme of the poem.

Similarly, her use of conversational language is deceptively natural. This natural quality is underpinned by Rich's masterful use of punctuation. It is significant that some groups of lines in the poem have little or no punctuation, while others are peppered with a variety of punctuation marks. In this way, Rich successfully captures the variety of pace that is evident in everyday speech, while at the same time skilfully using punctuation to control the speed at which theis poem is read, so that key words are emphasised as in the line 'they reflect lights that spell out: EXIT'.

Finally, this poem is written as a dramatic lyric. For a discussion of this literary technique, read the note on 'The Dramatic Lyric' attached to the analysis of ' Storm Warnings'.

A READING OF THE POEM

The opening two lines of this poem create a dramatic environment that immediately captures the reader's interest. Rich seems to be writing about scientists experimenting with bombs out in the desert. The references to the United States' development of the atomic bomb are evident.

Initially, the second group of lines, 3–7, seem to be no more than a description of the geography of the desert with 'an underground river' moving around 'deformed cliffs'. Rich suggests the free-flowing nature of the river by her omission of punctuation, resulting in this section being read without interruption. Significantly, Rich shifts the overall meaning slightly by introducing the concept of 'understanding' in line 5. This linking of the river with 'understanding' presents the reader with a challenge, since at this point in the poem the connection between the two is not clear.

Lines 8–14 do little to help the reader to resolve this challenge. Instead, we encounter a list of apparently unconnected items. However, on closer examination we see that this list is a collection of snapshots, images that express aspects of the type of society left behind by those who came to the desert. So, there are 'LP collections' alongside 'the language of love-letters'. The insertion of the 'suicide notes' in the middle of the list creates a jarring effect, rather like a wrong note in the middle of a phrase of music. It carries an unsettling implication: this society may not have been quite as pleasant as the other items on the list suggest.

The fourth section, lines 15–19, is also undercut with a sense of unease. The image of the 'ghost town' and the sound of the 'silence' give the desert an overwhelming feeling of desolation. There is no sign of growth or development here. The 'dull green succulents' appear as jagged forms that simply endure. The once busy town is empty and silent. In spite of the speaker's declaration that they intended to 'change the face' of the desert, it is evident that change will never come about in such a place as this.

Disturbing as the expansive silence of the desert is, Rich introduces an even more frightening type of silence in lines 20–25. The speaker reveals that the vast silence that filled lines 15–19 did not actually come from the desert, but from within the speaker and her companion. This silence exists between them. Try as the couple might to cover up this silence by talking, it remains ever-present: a continual reminder of how they are unable to communicate in any honest, true or meaningful sense.

It is at this point that the reader solves the challenge that Rich had presented with her use of 'understanding' in line 5 of the poem. The setting for this poem may appear to be two people, who have moved to the area to test bombs, out walking in the silent desert. However, it now becomes clear that the silent desert is simply an image, a metaphor, to express the terrible lack of communication that lies between the couple.

The implication of the poem's title becomes clear: the couple are a woman, – the speaker – and a man. At times, these two people may almost arrive at a point of understanding, just like the underground river forces its way around cliffs. At times, they have each given up aspects of their lives in an effort to be united as a couple. But in the present moment of the poem, this woman and man are caught in incomprehension: like the cactuses, they simply endure. There is nothing flourishing or developing between them. Their relationship is nothing more than a 'ghost' of what it might have been.

For this is the tragedy that Rich explores in the final two sections of this poem: the possibilities, the potential of their relationship that the woman and man are unable to seize. In lines 26–36 we learn how their inability to communicate denies them the joy of being a 'true' couple. There is no mutual support, no shared caring. Instead, they say words that speak of support and caring, but mean nothing. The speaker notes her companion's uneasiness. Like a caged animal he paces about restlessly and his eyes are haunted by the desire for escape, to find the 'EXIT'. He is simply unable, or even perhaps unwilling, to respond to her.

In the final three lines of the poem, Rich draws the piece together. As she had opened it with the concept of testing, she now returns to this concept again. In line 1, the speaker had referred to 'testing bombs'. In line 39, the testing is now of 'ourselves'. The speaker watches and listens helplessly as the man talks of the 'danger' in a frantic attempt to avoid confronting it. In the face of his avoidance, her use of 'we' in the final line has a hollow ring to it. For this couple 'we' is a lost possibility. They are each doomed by their inability to communicate with the other on any meaningful level. In a brilliantly damning phrase, we learn that the woman feels 'more helpless' when she is with her male partner than when she is apart from him. Equally, he regards her with panic as a bringer of danger. Try as she might to 'Talk with a Man' the speaker is, most definitely, not with the man, and nor is he with her.

The theme

Rich deliberately avoids personalising the characters in this poem. We learn very little about them other than that one is female and the other male. In this way, the two become representatives for all women and all men. In a similar way, her list of aspects of the world that they had left behind stands for society as a whole rather than one local society.

Thus, she uses the confrontation between the two to represent the political confrontation that she sees as existing between all women and all men. As her woman speaker seeks to talk on a meaningful level to the man, so Rich regards this as reflecting the efforts of feminists to engage with men, the holders of power in society. Equally, the man's reluctance, and indeed panic, when faced with what he sees as the 'danger' inherent in the woman's attempts to talk with him meaningfully, represents the reluctance of men in power to consider an alternative social structure to the traditional patriarchal hierarchy.

Diving into the Wreck

Text of poem: New Explorations Anthology page 296

Background note

See Background Note on ' Living in Sin' (pages 173–4).

Structure and style

This poem is surprising because of its length, and there is no doubt that, initially, the 94 lines can be quite off-putting for the reader. However, Rich's mastery of the technical aspects of writing poetry enable her to provide a strong sense of sequence and coherence that serve to maintain the focus of the piece throughout the 94 lines.

The sense of sequence partially arises out of her moving the action of the poem in a logical and natural manner from the solid deck of the schooner, above water, down to the fantastical depths of the wreck under water. Thus, the narrative element in the poem, the story that it tells of diving into the sea, adds to the establishment of a sense of sequence.

Rich's careful arrangement of the different sections of the poem also contributes to the sense of sequence. The first five sections begin with a capital letter and end with a full stop. This reflects the way in which each of these sections deals with a specific action and experience. Although Rich loosens this capital letter – full stop arrangement in the sixth to the tenth sections, where it is extended over two and three sections, the sense of sequence is successfully maintained.

The coherence is established by Rich's linking and repetition of images and words. For example, the first section of the poem describes the preparations that the diver makes. Once again, there is a logical link between the items that she puts on (the wet-suit, the flippers, the face-mask) that gives this section a coherence, a sense of unity. Similarly, her repetition of the words 'came' and 'wreck', in the opening lines of the sixth and seventh stanzas, forms a clear connection between the two, as does her use of the image of the wreck as a body with the linked parts of a 'flank', a 'face' and 'ribs'.

It is this careful attention to such technical details on Rich's part that enables her to maintain the focus of this extended piece. She never allows her reader to forget that we are indeed 'Diving into the Wreck'. However, this poem is more than simply the story of a dive under the sea. It is far more complex, in that the story of the dive tries to represent, or illustrate in a concrete way, the process of Rich's search for alternatives to the hierarchical society that will enable her to more fully understand the true nature of its traditionally accepted social and political rules.

A reading of the poem

In an effort to unravel the complexity of this poem we will look first at the narrative, concrete aspect of each section in the poem. In each case, that will be followed by a consideration, in italics, of what political messages are represented by the narrative.

Adrienne Rich has frequently observed that her later poems are concerned with 'process' and 'Diving into the Wreck' is a wonderful illustration of this, since it focuses on the process of an exploratory dive into the sea. The connection that Rich establishes in the first line between this dive and myth is a significant one, in that it alerts her readers to the fact that this poem is more than simply a narrative telling a story of a diver diving down to a wreck.

In section 1, lines 1–12, Rich outlines the preparations that the diver has made for the dive. She has done her reading; put film into her camera; made sure that her knife is sharp. All these preparations have taken her some time. She then 'dresses' herself for her journey into an alien environment. With all the deliberate care of a warrior preparing to go into battle, the diver puts on her wet-suit, flippers and mask. Again, this all takes time. As readers, we can't help but wonder what it is that drives the diver to go through all this. We then learn that she must undertake this exploratory dive alone. One of the main rules in sub-aqua diving is that, for safety reasons, divers should never dive alone. The fact that the diver is unable to adhere to this rule introduces an unmistakeable feeling of danger into this section. If we look again at all the diver's preparations we see that there are hints of danger there, too. Worryingly, we learn that the book that the diver read is a 'book of myths' and myths have a large element of fiction about them. Surely the diver should be reading books filled with facts. The images of the knife and the 'body-armour' also suggest that there is some threat to her safety.

Section 1 can be interpreted as illustrating the way in which Rich felt compelled to undertake the task of exploring alternatives to our traditional social structures, in order to see more clearly the true nature of our society. Careful preparations were necessary before this task because it was potentially dangerous, not so much physically but psychologically and emotionally, since it would lead to the destruction of what had long been accepted as the 'right' way for human beings to live as a group. Bravely, Rich undertakes this task alone. This section conveys her determination even in the face of the loneliness of her role.

The second section, lines 13–21, begins innocently enough with the image of a ladder. This ladder seems to be something that will help the diver to enter the water as safely as possible, and in this way it appears as a positive object. However, Rich makes the point that the ladder is useful only if the user knows how it should be used: without that knowledge, the ladder becomes no more than a gathering of rope and wood. Rather like ' the book of myths' in the first section, the ladder offers a form of help to the diver that is not entirely reliable or trustworthy.

Section 2 introduces the 'ladder' in order to represent Rich's awareness that there are ways to investigate alternative social and political structures to the one that we use. There is a sense of confidence and assurance arising out of the knowledge acquired by those who have set about such an investigation.

The third section, lines 22–33, is an excellent example of the technical mastery in Rich's writing. Her repetition of the short phrase 'I go down' conveys not only the depth, but also the distance of the diver's journey down the ladder. Her progress is slow and difficult: her fingers become disabled and she is reduced to crawling. These vivid images capture the tremendous effort that the diver has to make, and the suffering that she has to endure, in order to go into this other environment. Once again, the loneliness of her exploration is emphasised in lines 31–33. The diver forces herself onwards, not knowing when she will break through from her familiar environment into the new one. It is a dangerous situation for her as she is clearly tiring, and yet she is unwilling to give up.

Section 3 illustrates the tremendous effort required to explore these social and political alternatives to the traditional, hierarchical society. The 'ladder' that had appeared to offer help is not really of any help at all: this process of exploration is still hard and difficult. Again, Rich feels that she is undertaking this task on her own. This section expresses feelings of exhaustion, frustration and loneliness, balanced by the determination and courage to continue with the task.

At first the opening lines of the fourth section, lines 34–43, seem to suggest that the danger has vanished, as the diver finally enters the water. She is enveloped by a wonderful mixture of blue and green far more vivid than the air that she has left behind. But suddenly, the feeling of danger returns when the diver begins to black out. Her body is finding it hard to cope with this watery environment. Still, rather than giving up, the diver reassures herself about the safety of her equipment and decides that she will learn how to deal with this new world.

Section 4 depicts the way in which Rich initially feels overwhelmed by her engagement with social and political alternatives to her society. Her feeling of panic and her near-blacking out represent the challenge that she faces when she decides to abandon the traditionally accepted social and political rules of living. Nevertheless, this section once again ends on a note of determination: she will learn to cope.

In fact, her efforts to learn how to cope are so successful that in the fifth section, lines 44–51, she admits that she has almost forgotten the reason why she is diving. She is filled with such wonder by the beauty around her that her determination to engage in a process of exploration weakens.

Section 5 once again portrays the difficulties Rich faces in her task. She is so fascinated by these alternative ways of living, and those who actually live according to them, that she begins to lose her determination to explore the true nature of our traditional society.

In the sixth section, lines 52–70, the diver forces herself to put into words the purpose that drives her: 'I came to explore the wreck.' This sentence is more than a simple collection of words: it expresses both the reason for her process of exploration and the aim that she hopes to achieve. In this way, the six words 'I came to explore the wreck' are indeed 'purposes' and 'maps' that both drive and direct her. The diver tells us that she wants to see the truth of the wreck, both bad and good, the 'damage' that it has suffered, and 'the treasures'. She is no longer satisfied by 'the book of myths'; she wants to see the 'real' thing. Rich very carefully employs a series of images to suggest the ambivalent feelings that the diver has towards the wreck. On the one hand, she feels respect for it and is careful to 'stroke' it with her torchlight. Similarly, she feels sympathy for it trapped beneath the water, separated from the warmth of the sunlight. She regards it as having a 'threadbare beauty'. On the other hand, she recognises that the wreck was a 'disaster'.

Section 6 introduces the problematic image of the wreck, which has been interpreted in a number of ways. However, if we set it within the context of our overall interpretation of the political messages that lie behind this poem then the wreck, logically, stands for our traditional form of society. Although Rich feels some affection for this traditional society, since she is familiar with it, her determination to confront the true nature of this society returns.

The final section of the poem, lines 71–94, begins on a note of triumph: 'This is the place'. The diver has achieved her goal of exploring the wreck. She has survived the dangers that faced her and she has done so alone. It is at this point that Rich introduces the rather perplexing image of the androgynous, male/female figure. This image seems to suggest that, because of her success, the diver is transformed into an alternative way of existing, one that is not restricted by narrow definitions, one that banishes her sense of being alone. She is no longer 'I' or 'she' or 'he', but 'we'. In this androgynous body the diver is empowered to explore and analyse the true nature of the wreck, in order to work past the glittering surface and confront the 'rot' that lies underneath. Suddenly, the realisation is grasped: the diver, and all of those others who are like her, are connected to the wreck because it has played a part in their formation, and they have played a part in its 'course'. Although they may reject and abandon the wreck, they will return to it frequently, carrying the same objects that featured in the first section of the poem: a knife, a camera and a book of myths. Thus the poem does not really end by offering a definite alternative to the traditional social structure. Instead it emphasises the importance of the process of exploration of those alternatives, in order to understand fully the true nature of our existing society.

Section 7 brings together the representations that we have encountered earlier in the poem. The arrival at the wreck and the exploration of it suggest the success of Feminists and other Civil Rights' movements in highlighting the terrible inadequacies and the unjust distribution of power that lie at the base of the traditional, male-dominated, patriarchal society. This section also expresses one of the major difficulties facing all those who reject the traditional society. Try as they might, they will never fully erase the influence of that traditional society. Rich proposes that there are two ways to view this indestructible link to a despised society: it could be born out of 'cowardice', a reluctance to totally sever all connections; or, alternatively, it might indicate 'courage', a willingness to confront the past.

The androgynous figure is the direct opposite to the lonely diver in the earlier six sections: 'I' has become 'we'; restrictive definitions such as 'she' and 'he' do not apply to it. The underlying sense of danger and the need to learn how to cope with this alternative environment have been transformed into feelings of empowerment and understanding.

THE THEMES

The themes addressed in this poem are open to a variety of interpretations. The following is one of the more widely accepted interpretations. However, you may wish to consider alternatives:

- The diver is determined to dive into an alternative environment, indicating that Rich considers the exploration of alternative social structures as being politically vital.
- The dive itself is a dangerous undertaking, suggesting that this social exploration is also difficult and dangerous, because it threatens the stability of the existing, traditional social structure.
- The diver manages to conquer fear and becomes transformed into a different form of being, an androgynous figure. This implies that Rich believes that if this social exploration is undertaken with courage and determination, then it will open up new ways of living where there are greater freedom and power for all.
- The wreck has a superficial beauty but underneath, in the ship's hold, there is decay. Rich uses this image to convey her political stance regarding the society that she lives in: on the surface it appears to be good and fair but, in reality, this traditional social structure keeps power in the hands of a few and denies power to groups who disagree with aspects of the society.
- The poem ends with an image of the wreck being revisited time and time again by those whose 'names do not appear' in the 'book of myths'. This illustrates Rich's awareness that, although she and others like her may seek to abandon this traditional social structure and to create an alternative one, they will never be able to escape completely from its influences. Nevertheless, it is politically vital that the exploration of alternative social structures continues.

- Rich does not offer any concrete alternative to the wreck, implying that once again it is the exploration process that is of political importance. She believes that we should not be diverted from this simply because we are uncertain about the exact form of these alternatives to the existing, traditional social structures, since such an exploration will lead to a better understanding of our existing society.

From a Survivor

Text of poem: New Explorations Anthology page 301

Background note

In 1953, Adrienne Rich married Alfred H. Conran, a Jewish economist who was teaching at Harvard. The couple went on to have three sons. Along with Adrienne, Alfred became actively involved in many of the Civil Rights movements that emerged in America in the 1960s. After seventeen years of marriage, Rich separated from her husband. Soon after, Alfred committed suicide. This poem is a reflection on their marriage and Rich's feelings for her late husband.

Style and structure

The poignancy of this poem lies in Rich's use of straightforward, everyday, conversational language to express her reaction to her husband's suicide. She makes no attempt to soften the emotional impact by the use of such technical devices as clever rhymes, beautiful imagery or musical language. Instead, she simply uses ' the 'stream of consciousness' technique, allowing her thoughts to develop and connect on the page. (For an explanation of 'the 'stream of consciousness' technique, see the notes 'Style and structure' for 'The Roofwalker'.)

The appearance of the poem, with one, two, three and more lines interrupted by spaces, reinforces the sense that we are reading her thoughts and experiencing her feelings as they are actually occurring. However, this approach to structure does not represent a lack of effort on Rich's part. Her careful use of highly significant words to communicate a wealth of implications and suggestions indicates that a considerable amount of time and thought went into this piece.

A reading of the poem

Rich opens the poem with a reference to their marriage, calling it an 'ordinary pact'. Her use of the word 'pact' is significant since it suggests that, in Rich's view, the ceremony of marriage is like a treaty between two opposing forces. The two opposing forces are, of course, a man and a woman.

In an incredibly immediate and natural style of writing in lines 3–5, she expresses her amazement at the fact that when they married, both she and Alfred actually believed that they could make a success of it. However, Rich does not suggest that any lack, or fault, on their parts caused the failure of their marriage. Instead, she states that the marriage was doomed because of 'the failures of the race'. In other words, their marriage failed because of the society in which they lived. As we have seen previously, Rich came to see the traditional, male-dominated, patriarchal society as an oppressive one that sought to eliminate and reject any person or group who did not believe in the values of that society.

In lines 6–9, we learn that both she and Alfred simply did not know that their marriage would be destroyed by the social structure within which they lived. Her comment that this ignorance on their part could be seen as either 'Lucky or unlucky' indicates the ambivalence of her feelings about her marriage. It could have been 'lucky' in the sense that if they had known that their marriage would be destroyed by their society, then they would never have married. Clearly, Rich feels that there was something of value in the time that they spent together. On the other hand, their lack of knowledge could be seen as being 'unlucky', because when their marriage ended they had the dreadful emotional upset and heartbreak that occurs with the failure of a relationship.

With the benefit of hindsight, Rich looks back at her young self and the young Alfred and is amazed at their innocent and naïve belief that they were 'special', that they were different from all the other men and women who also tried to make a 'pact' and were equally unsuccessful.

Line 10 marks a change in the tone of the writing. Up until this point, the tone has been one of slightly puzzled amazement that she and Alfred could have actually believed that a marriage between a man and woman might be successful. With line 10 the tone becomes much more intense. The shorter lines indicate the strength of Rich's feelings. She remembers her husband's body and the way that her feelings towards both him and his physical presence changed over the years. Initially, she accepted the traditional male/female roles dictated by the patriarchal society. Thus Alfred was the dominant figure, 'a god' who had 'power' over Rich's life. But as time passed she began to see that both the body and the man were, in fact, limited and vulnerable. Indeed, it is fair to say that we all have the tendency to idealise our partner in the first exciting days of a new love affair. It is only as the excitement and novelty wears off that we begin to see that this person is just as human as we are.

Rich uses simple words and phrases, in lines 17–20, to give a vivid and moving description of her relationship with Alfred. Their lives had been connected for almost twenty years. The fact that Rich remembers the exact number of years indicates the level of importance that she attaches to their time together. We can almost hear the sob in her voice when she talks of Alfred being 'wastefully dead'. Once again her use of one word, 'wastefully', proves to be deeply significant. It is evident that Rich valued her late husband's existence. His death represents the 'waste' of the contribution that she clearly believes he would have made to the development of a new and better way for all men and all women to live together. The closeness of their relationship is revealed in her reference to the conversations that they had about making a 'leap' into this other way of living.

The final four lines introduce a more positive tone into the poem. Rich still feels a sense of loss because Alfred is dead, but she can acknowledge the fact that she, herself, has succeeded in embarking on the process of finding a new way of living. This process is much slower and happens in 'brief, amazing moments' rather than in the dramatic and sudden 'leap' that she and Alfred had spoken about. Nevertheless, the process is still immensely valuable and worthwhile because it is ongoing. It is these lines that reveal the reason why Rich entitled this poem 'From a Survivor' – for she is the survivor. Unlike Alfred and unlike their marriage, both regarded by Rich as casualties of the repressive and destructive forces of the traditional, patriarchal society, Rich has managed to survive. Even more importantly, her survival is not based not on her resigned acceptance of that traditional, patriarchal society. Instead, her survival is driven by the determination to explore alternative social structures that will fill the lives of both women and men with 'amazing moments' that promise the freedom of endless possibilities.

Punctuation and meaning

Rich's use of punctuation plays a very important part in the successful communication of meaning in this poem. It is noticeable that she uses very little punctuation in the piece, in order to reflect her use of 'the stream of consciousness' technique. Here Rich's thoughts and feelings, largely uninterrupted by punctuation, have such immediacy and honesty that her words are filled with a great depth and intensity of meaning. As readers, we know that she is speaking to us from the heart.

It is highly significant that this poem, ending as it does with a celebration of the joy and freedom that comes from living a life filled with 'amazing moments' of possibilities, does not have a full stop after the final word. In this way, Rich reinforces the sense of endless possibilities that lead on in a never-ending and empowering process.

Power

Text of poem: New Explorations Anthology page 305

[*Note: This poem is also prescribed for Ordinary Level exam in 2008*]

BACKGROUND NOTE

Adrienne Rich frequently writes about individual successful women from history, such as the poet Emily Dickinson. However, although these women did achieve success, it was often accompanied by a lonely lifestyle. This poem deals with one such woman: Marie Curie.

Marie Curie (1867–1934), along with her husband Pierre, worked on isolating radioactive elements from a type of uranium ore known as pitchblende. At the time, it was most unusual for a woman to be a scientist and to engage in scientific research. The Curies isolated two radioactive elements from the pitchblende: polonium and radium. The couple were awarded the Nobel Prize for Physics in 1903. Later, in 1911, Marie was awarded the Nobel Prize for Chemistry, making her the first person ever to win two Nobel Prizes. Unfortunately, owing to her constant exposure to high levels of radiation, Marie developed leukaemia and died in 1934.

STRUCTURE

The structure of this poem makes it a rather challenging one to get to grips with on a first reading. Rich again uses the 'stream of consciousness' technique. Therefore, we see a varied arrangement of the lines of poetry, ranging from a single line to clusters of lines and images that do not immediately appear to be connected.

However, there is a further structural development evident in this poem. Rich not only surrounds her lines with space, but she also inserts space into the very lines of poetry themselves. In this way, she deconstructs the traditional compact poetic line as used in 'Aunt Jennifer's Tigers', for example, and turns it into a loosely connected grouping of phrases. This, allied with her minimal use of punctuation can make it difficult to understand, on a first reading, what Rich is expressing.

A READING OF THE POEM

Rich's reference to history in the first line suggests that the present and the past are very closely linked. It seems as if there is only a thin skin of soil that separates them from each other. Rich sees the soil as a kind of storage space for our past history. This image calls up pictures of archaeologists digging down and finding artefacts that have survived from previous ages. It is interesting to note that Rich has conveyed all of this meaning in just eight words.

The next image, of the digger digging up an old bottle, follows on from the first line in that the bottle is an example of one such item that has been stored in the soil. However, it is not an archaeologist who finds it but a large, mechanical digger. Rich's use of the word 'flank' to describe the bank of earth where the discovery takes place connects back to the first word of the poem, 'Living'. She sees the mound of soil as a living thing, like a huge figure lying on its side. The present and past meet, as the modern mechanical digger lifts the old medicine bottle out of the earth. In doing so, the digger has punctured the thin skin that separates the present from the past. The bottle is still intact, even after one hundred years, and contains a liquid that promises to cure everything from a high temperature to depression. It is clearly not possible to develop a medicine that could do all those things: therefore the bottle obviously came from one of the many 'quack doctors', unqualified medical practitioners or con-men, who used to travel around America in the nineteenth and early twentieth centuries selling fake medicines.

There is a sudden shift of focus in the next section of the poem, lines 6–17, where Rich explains that she has been reading about Marie Curie. Along with her husband, Curie worked extensively with radioactive substances. As a result of her exposure to these radioactive elements she began to suffer physically. Rich refers to Curie's 'radiation sickness' causing her eyes to be blinded by cataracts and the skin on her hands to crack and ooze pus.

However, the main focus of Rich's attention does not fall on Curie's wonderful discoveries that earned her two Nobel Prizes, nor on the fact that Marie Curie was one of the few female scientists in the late nineteenth and early twentieth centuries and, as such, was treated with suspicion by the predominantly male world of Science. Rich is much more concerned with Curie's reaction to her 'radiation sickness': her denial that it was the radioactive substances that had made her sick. Rich is amazed by Curie's refusal to acknowledge the truth and is certain that Curie 'must have known' that it was 'radiation sickness'.

The final four lines of the poem, lines 14–17, can be interpreted in a number of ways. This ambiguity arises out of Rich's use of spaces between the words and her lack of punctuation.

One interpretation sees these lines as a reference to Marie Curie's steadfast denial, right up to her death from leukaemia, that the radioactive substances that had made her famous had also doomed her to death. In this way, she refused to accept that her physical injuries were caused by 'the same source as her power': that is, by her position of fame in society.

An alternative interpretation sees these lines as being related to Rich's belief that women have long been prevented from gaining any meaningful power by the traditional, patriarchal society that has been dominant for much of history. The image of the bottle containing the fake medicine that helps with 'living on this earth' refers to the way that this traditional social structure has fooled women into thinking that they do have some power. Thus, the final four lines can be seen as expressing Rich's view that Curie, as a woman, was unable to cope with the power that she gained because she came from a gender unused to dealing with 'real' power and, as a result, she was destroyed by it.

A third interpretation suggests that the emphasis should be placed on the act of denial. For women to gain 'real' power, they have to deny the identity that has been forced on them by the traditional, patriarchal society. In other words, they have to stop behaving according to the male view of how a woman should behave, and they have to stop using words about themselves that have been formed by men. In Rich's opinion, this behaviour and language have done nothing for women but cause them to feel wounded and damaged because they have been imposed on them by a completely different gender. So women have to sacrifice this identity, this selfhood, and struggle to find their own behaviour and words. In this context, Curie's denial that her 'wounds' were caused by 'the same source as her power' means that Curie refused to accept that she, as a woman, had been deeply injured, and ultimately would be destroyed, by the same male-dominated world that had also made her famous by giving her awards.

The final interpretation to be considered here rests on Rich's ongoing analysis of the differences between men and women. In 'Power' the female figure on the one hand, Marie Curie, gains power through hard work and the sacrifice of her health. On the other hand the male figure, represented by the bottle containing the fake medicine developed by 'quack doctors', tries to gain power through deception and trickery.

In the final analysis, it is up to you, as the reader, to choose whether you agree or disagree with these interpretations. Indeed, you may choose to develop an interpretation of your own for this poem. Adrienne Rich sees the power of choice as a fundamental element in becoming an empowered human being. The power of choice is also part of the pleasure that comes from being a reader of poetry.

An overview of selected themes and aspects of Adrienne Rich's poetry

RICH'S PORTRAYAL OF THE FEMALE ROLE IN SOCIETY

- Aunt Jennifer's Tigers
- Living in Sin
- The Roofwalker
- Our Whole Life
- Trying to Talk with a Man
- Diving into the Wreck
- From a Survivor

Power

Rich's portrayal of the male role in society

Aunt Jennifer's Tigers
The Uncle Speaks in the Drawing Room
Living in Sin
The Roofwalker
Our Whole Life
Trying to Talk with a Man
From a Survivor

Rich's portrayal of the relationship between men and women

Aunt Jennifer's Tigers
Living in Sin
Our Whole Life
Trying to Talk with a Man
Diving into the Wreck
From a Survivor

Power and language

The Uncle Speaks in the Drawing Room
Our Whole Life
Trying to Talk with a Man

Power and women

Aunt Jennifer's Tigers
Living in Sin
Our Whole Life
Trying to Talk with a Man
Diving into the Wreck
From a Survivor
Power

Impending revolution and change

Aunt Jennifer's Tigers
The Uncle Speaks in the Drawing Room
Storm Warnings
Diving into the Wreck
From a Survivor

Rich's use of the dramatic lyric form

Storm Warnings
The Roofwalker
Trying to Talk with a Man
Diving into the Wreck
From a Survivor
Power

RICH'S USE OF THE 'STREAM OF CONSCIOUSNESS' TECHNIQUE
The Roofwalker
Our Whole Life
Trying to Talk with a Man
Diving into the Wreck
From a Survivor
Power

RICH'S EARLY 'MALE-INFLUENCED' POEMS 'ABOUT EXPERIENCES'
Aunt Jennifer's Tigers
The Uncle Speaks in the Drawing Room
Storm Warnings

RICH'S LATER 'FEMALE-CENTRED' POEMS THAT 'ARE EXPERIENCES'
Living in Sin
The Roofwalker
Our Whole Life
Trying to Talk with a Man
Diving into the Wreck
From a Survivor
Power

Questions

1. Read 'Aunt Jennifer's Tigers' and answer the following questions:
   1. (a) What picture do you get of Aunt Jennifer from the poem?
      (b) 'Aunt Jennifer's tigers prance across a screen'.
      Describe in your own words how you imagine the screen that Aunt Jennifer embroidered.
      (c) Based on your reading of the poem, what impression do you get of the nature of Aunt Jennifer's relationship with Uncle?
   2. Answer **ONE** of the following:
      (a) Why do you think Aunt Jennifer embroidered the screen?
      Refer to the poem in your answer.

OR

(b) Imagine that you have been asked to make a short film of this poem. Outline the overall atmosphere that you would like to achieve and the images, sound effects and music that you would use to create this atmosphere.

OR

(c) 'The tigers in the panel that she made
Will go on prancing, proud and unafraid.'

What do you understand these last two lines of the poem to mean?

2. Read 'Storm Warnings' and answer the following questions:

1. (a) How, in the first stanza of the poem, does Rich help us to imagine the stormy weather? Refer to the poem in your answer.

   (b) How does the person in the poem react to the oncoming storm?

   (c) '... Weather abroad
   And weather in the heart alike come on
   Regardless of prediction.'
   What is Rich saying about emotions in these lines?

2. Answer **ONE** of the following:

   (a) What does this poem tell you about Rich's state of mind? Refer to the poem in your answer.

   OR

   (b) 'I draw the curtains as the sky goes black.'
   Do you think that the person in the poem will be successful in her attempts to keep the storm out of the house? Give reasons for your answer.

   OR

   (c) Can you suggest another title for this poem? Support your suggestion by reference to the poem.

3. Read 'Power' and answer the following questions:

1. Which **ONE** of the following phrases do you feel best suggests Rich's reaction to the digging up of the old bottle:?
   – She is not interested in it
   – She is fascinated by it
   – She is frightened by it.

   Support your choice by reference to the poem.

2. What impression do you get of Marie Curie's life from your reading of the poem?

3. Answer **ONE** of the following:
   (a) What does this poem tell you about Rich's attitude to Marie Curie? Refer to the poem in your answer.

   OR

   (b) 'her wounds came from the same source as her power'
   What do you understand this last line of the poem to mean?

   OR

   (c) Write a paragraph in which you outline the similarities **and/or** differences between 'Power' and 'Aunt Jennifer's Tigers'.

4. With reference to **at least six** poems by Adrienne Rich that you have studied:
   (a) Outline her portrayal of the position in society held by **either** women **or** men.
   (b) Do you agree or disagree with this portrayal?

5. 'Power is a central concept in the poetry of Adrienne Rich.' Respond to this statement, referring to the poetry by Rich on your course.

6. 'Adrienne Rich's poetry consistently reveals her mastery of the technical aspects of writing poetry.' Discuss this statement, with reference to **at least six** poems by Rich.

7. 'Rich's view of the world is firmly based in 1960s' America, and has little to say to present-day Irish readers.' Write an essay in response to this statement, quoting from or referring to the poems on your course.

8. 'An Introduction to Adrienne Rich.'
Write out the text of a public talk that you might give on the poetry of Adrienne Rich. Your talk should make reference to the poetry on your course.

9. *Dear Adrienne Rich . . .*
Write a letter to Adrienne Rich, telling her how you responded to some of her poems on your course. Support the points you make by detailed reference to the poems you choose to write about.

10. 'Why read the poetry of Adrienne Rich?'
Write out the text of an article that you would submit to a journal in response to the above title. Support your response by quoting from, or referring to, the poetry on your course.

A short bibliography

Cooper, Jane Roberta (editor), *Reading Adrienne Rich: Reviews and Revisions, 1951--81,* Michigan: The University of Michigan Press 1984.

DeShazer, Mary K., *Inspiring Women: Reimagining the Muse,* New York: Pergamon Press 1986.

Dickie, Margaret, *Stein, Bishop and Rich: Lyrics of Love, War and Place,* North Carolina: The University of North Carolina Press 1987.

Erkkila, Betsy, *The Wicked Sisters: Women Poets, Literary History and Discord,* Oxford: Oxford University Press 1992.

Gamble, Sarah (editor), *Feminism and Postfeminism,* London: Routledge 2001.

Gelpi, Barbara Charlesworth and Gelpi, Albert (editors), *Adrienne Rich's Poetry and Prose,* New York: W. W. Norton 1993.

Keyes, Claire, *The Aesthetics of Power: The Poetry of Adrienne Rich,* Athens and London: The University of Georgia Press 1986.

Kolmar, Wendy K. and Frances Bartkowski, *Feminist Theory: A Reader,* Boston: McGraw Hill 2005.

Rich, Adrienne, *On Lies, Secrets and Silence: Selected Prose 1966–1978,* New York: W.W. Norton 1979.

Rich, Adrienne, *What is Found There: Notebooks on Poetry and Politics*, New York: W. W. Norton 1993.

Roberts, Neil (editor), *A Companion to Twentieth Century Poetry,* Oxford: Blackwell 2003.

Sunstein, Cass R. (editor), *Feminism and Political Theory*, Chicago: The University of Chicago Press 1990.

6 *Sylvia* PLATH

Ann Hyland

Introduction

Sylvia Plath was born in Boston, Massachusetts, on 27 October 1932 to Aurelia Schober Plath and Otto Plath. Shortly after his son Warren's birth in 1935, Otto Plath fell ill. His condition was treatable, but he refused to consult a doctor. In 1940, following an operation, he died. Neither of the children attended the funeral.

These events had a huge effect on Sylvia's life. Her father's illness deprived her of both parents' attention for much of her early life. His death, which she sometimes saw as suicide because of his refusal to seek medical help, left her feeling bereft. She never came to terms with her grief and anger at his loss, and these feelings resurfaced in her last poems.

Sylvia's childhood taught her the value of being a 'good girl'. Her mother's approval was gained by being quiet, not disturbing her invalid father, reading and writing, and also doing well in school. This she achieved with little difficulty: remarkably intelligent and very ambitious, she always earned high grades. Her writing life began early, and her first poem was published when she was only eight.

She was a brilliant pupil in secondary school, consistently earning A grades. Attractive, vivacious, and active in school clubs, she led a busy social life. She worked hard but loved clothes, dancing, music and dating.

One problem that she refers to in her letters to her mother and in her journals was her anxiety to conceal her academic ability from the boys she dated: she felt (probably rightly) that her popularity would suffer if she upstaged them academically. In the conservative 1940s and 50s girls were meant to be 'nice': that is, genteel, polite, and above all feminine – certainly not ambitious and intellectual, publicly questioning the status quo. There was an all-pervasive pressure to conform to society's expectations.

By the end of her secondary school career she had achieved some success as a writer and artist. A number of her stories had appeared in *Seventeen*, a popular teenage magazine, while some poems and drawings were published in the *Christian Science Monitor.* She had also been introduced to the works of authors who were important influences on her writing: D. H. Lawrence, Virginia Woolf, Emily Dickinson, Dylan Thomas and W.B. Yeats. In 1950 she entered

Smith College, Massachusetts, a prestigious women's university, where her academic and writing success continued. At the end of her third year, in June 1953, she won a guest editorship with a young women's magazine, *Mademoiselle.* This involved living in New York for the month. Her work schedule there was demanding, and she was also expected to fulfil endless social engagements. The whole experience was exhausting.

On her return home to Wellesley she became severely depressed. She was treated with electro-convulsive shock therapy, which seems to have been disastrous: far from curing her, it propelled her into a serious suicide attempt. Her life was saved only because her brother discovered her hidden in the cellar three days after she disappeared. She entered a psychiatric hospital, where she recovered with the help of a sympathetic psychiatrist. This experience formed the basis for her novel *The Bell Jar,* published in 1963.

She resumed her studies in Smith College in January 1954, graduating with first-class honours the following year. She won a Fulbright Scholarship to study literature in Cambridge, England, where she met Ted Hughes, a young English poet ('that big, dark, hunky boy, the only one there huge enough for me'). They fell in love, and they married in June 1956.

On completing her studies in Cambridge she accepted a teaching job in her old university, Smith College, and moved to America with her husband for two years. 'Black Rook in Rainy Weather' and 'The Times are Tidy' date from this period.

Shortly after the couple returned to London, in December 1959, her first collection, *The Colossus and Other Poems,* was published. Their daughter, Frieda, was born in April. The following year they moved to Devon, a move that increased her work load. She devoted much energy to turning their old manor-house into a home and to working the extensive garden that surrounded it, in addition to acting as her own and her husband's literary agent and caring for Frieda.

Her son, Nicholas, was born in January 1962. During this time, despite her many domestic tasks and the work involved in looking after two small children, she was writing. Poems from this period include 'Morning Song', 'Finisterre', 'Mirror', 'Pheasant', 'Elm' and 'Poppies in July'. She also completed *The Bell Jar.*

For some time Sylvia and Ted's relationship had been growing troubled, and they separated in August 1962. She remained in Devon, caring for the children and writing, but suffered poor health and recurring depression. Yet this period saw the flood of creativity that produced the poems that made up her second book, *Ariel,* including 'The Arrival of the Bee Box'. She herself was amazed at what she was writing: ' I am . . . writing like mad – have managed a poem a day before breakfast. All book poems. Terrific stuff, as if domesticity had choked me' (*Letters Home,* 12 October 1962).

In December she moved to London with her children. To her great joy she succeeded in renting a flat where W. B. Yeats had once lived. The winter of 1962/63 was one of the coldest on record in England, which added to the trauma of setting up a new home alone. She had problems with heating, power failures, and getting a telephone. She and the children suffered from severe colds, and she had trouble finding a reliable child-minder. These difficulties exacerbated her depression. Despite this, she continued writing; 'Child' dates from January 1963.

However, her difficult circumstances eventually overwhelmed her. Early on the morning of 11 February she left some milk and food by their beds for the children and sealed the door to their room to ensure their safety. She then took an overdose of sleeping pills, sealed herself in the kitchen and gassed herself.

Sylvia Plath's fame has grown steadily since her death. At first this was mainly because of the dramatic circumstances of her suicide: the fame she had always longed for became hers for the wrong reasons. However, the publication of *Ariel* and the *Complete Poems* showed that she was indeed a poet of genius, whose work deserved recognition for its own sake.

The facts of Sylvia Plath's life are easily told. Less simple to assess is the mass of material that has been written about her since (and because of) her suicide. She is variously seen as

- a brilliant but fragile genius
- an ungrateful daughter who hated her mother
- a loving daughter whose loyalty and affection are reflected in her letters home
- an over-ambitious manic depressive
- a controlling and jealous wife who pushed her husband into a love affair
- a loving wife and mother whose life was destroyed by her husband's betrayal
- a virulent feminist whose marriage break-up and suicide expressed her outrage at the ties of domesticity.

In fact it seems that those who write about Sylvia Plath can use her life story to prove almost anything. One reason for this is that she was married to, and just separated from, a famous poet who went on to become Poet Laureate. Another is the quantity of material she wrote. Apart from the poems there are many short stories, essays, and articles for magazines. She also did radio broadcasts and was the subject of a number of interviews. But perhaps most widely quoted – to support points of view that can be utterly contradictory – are the journals she kept from her earliest days almost to the time of her death, and her thousands of letters to family and friends. And indeed these *Letters Home* (published in 1975) and the *Journals* (1982) tell a lot about her. They reflect her 'exaggerated, high-voltage, bigger-than-life personality and imagination'. They show a young woman who thought about everything, and longed to live life to its fullest. Here is a tiny sample of her opinions:

• On writing: 'It is as necessary for the survival of my haughty sanity as bread is to my flesh.'
• 'And by the way, everything in life is writable about if you have the outgoing guts to do it, and the imagination to improvise. The worst enemy to creativity is self-doubt.'
• On herself: 'I want, I think, to be omniscient . . . I think I would like to call myself "the girl who wanted to be God".'
• On life: 'God is this all it is, the ricocheting down the corridor of laughter and tears? of self-worship and self-loathing? of glory and disgust?'
• On depression: 'I have been and am battling depression. It is as if my life were magically run by two electric currents: joyous positive and despairing negative – whichever is running at the moment dominates my life, floods it.'
• On children: 'Graduate school and travel abroad are not going to be stymied by any squealing, breast-fed brats.'
• On being a woman: 'Learning of the limitations of a woman's sphere is no fun at all.'
• On marriage: 'I plan not to step into a part on marrying – but to go on living as an intelligent mature human being, growing and learning as I always have.'
• 'I am afraid of getting married. Spare me from cooking three meals a day – spare me from the relentless cage of routine and rote. I want to be free.'
• On having children: 'Children might humanise me. But I must rely on them for nothing. Fable of children changing existence and character as absurd as fable of marriage doing it.'
• On poetry: 'A poem can't take the place of a plum or an apple. But just as painting can re-create, by illusion . . . so a poem, by its own system of illusions, can set up a rich and apparently living world within its particular limits.'
• 'Technically I like it to be extremely musical and lyrical, with a singing sound.'
• On the issues that mattered to her: 'The hurt and wonder of loving; making in all its forms – children, loaves of bread, paintings, buildings; and the conservation of life of all people in all places.'
• On politics: 'I do believe I can counteract McCarthy . . . by living a life of honesty and love . . . it is in a way serving my religion, which is that of humanism, and a belief in the potential of each man to learn and love and grow.'

Regardless of where people stand on her personality and life, all are agreed on Sylvia Plath's unique and distinctive voice, and on the impact she has had on the poetry of the end of the twentieth century. The inscription on her headstone could be read as a metaphor for her life: *Even in the midst of fierce flames, the golden lotus may be planted.*

Black Rook in Rainy Weather

Text of poem: New Explorations Anthology page 350

> 'If only something would happen!' Something being the revelation that transfigures existence; works a miraculous presto-chango upon the mundane mortal world – turning the toads and cockroaches back into handsome fairy princes. (*Journals,* April 1953)

Sylvia Plath was always aware of the need for inspiration to trigger her creative impulse: she hoped for a moment of insight, a 'miracle', to work a change on the 'mundane mortal world', enabling her to create. She wrote 'Black Rook in Rainy Weather' at a time when she was finding it a struggle to write, despite her conviction that writing was her life's work.

A READING OF THE POEM

The growing acceptance of identity as a writer is one theme. The year is at the 'stubborn season of fatigue' – late autumn or winter. The speaker is warily walking, 'trekking' in the rain, when her eye is caught by a black rook hunched above her on a twig. Everything around is dull and low-key: bird, rain, 'spotted leaves', 'mute sky', 'ruinous landscape'. Despite this, the speaker is vaguely expectant: a miracle may occur, a trick of light may 'hallow' (make sacred) something as ordinary as a kitchen table or chair, causing it to glow with heavenly radiance. The muse or inspiration may appear as a 'miracle', a 'celestial burning', transforming what might otherwise be an uneventful life, giving

> A brief respite from fear
> Of total neutrality.

She doesn't know what inspiration may surprise her, or

> . . . flare
> Suddenly at my elbow.

The black rook in the rain may even shine and force her to give it her full attention – 'seize my senses'. Therefore she is watchful: such a miracle has happened before.

One such miracle would be the inspiration to create something extraordinary from her dull surroundings, to

> Patch together a content
> Of sorts.

She might write, create something wonderful. The 'mute sky' may not grant the desired 'backtalk', but the speaker knows that 'miracles occur'. Waiting for the muse is like

> The long wait for the angel,
> For that rare, random descent.

She is prepared to wait.

Landscape

Plath's poetry is often highly subjective, focusing on her inner self, her feelings and thoughts – even when she appears to be writing about the outside world. She uses her immediate surroundings as a metaphor for her feelings and ideas.

This is evident in her treatment of landscape. One critic has described how her poetic landscapes embody associations between scene and mood; she calls them 'psychic landscapes'. She notes Plath's 'ability to transform realistic objects and scenes into consistent sets of metaphors for her thoughts and emotions'. These concrete objects, however, are clearly realised – made real – by Plath's skilful use of language and imagery.

'Black Rook in Rainy Weather' creates a clear picture: the speaker is out walking doggedly on a wet day when she sees a black rook hunched on a bare tree. Everything around is dull and lifeless: sodden fallen leaves, the dark, rainy day, the 'ruinous landscape'. Having set the scene, the speaker quickly moves to her own fears and limited expectations. She is hopeful that (with luck, maybe, perhaps . . .) even such a dull scene may be transformed. The cause of this transformation – miracle, descent of an angel – would seem to be something that might fire her imagination.

Essentially, the bleak place is a metaphor for the speaker's own bleakness. Her mood, like the scene, might be suddenly transformed by a sudden radiance, a miracle, a flash of inspiration. The mute sky may grant her the 'backtalk' she desires.

Themes

- Hope – the expectation of a sudden change for the better
- Despondency – the grim dullness of 'neutrality'
- Creativity – the miracle of a sudden inspiration
- Miracles – the rareness and randomness of life-enhancing moments of brilliance.

TECHNIQUE

Use of contrast

There is a strong contrast between the dullness of the landscape and the radiant miracle that may occur. The speaker knows that the most 'obtuse object' – black rook, bleak day, dullness, kitchen chair – can be transformed by a miracle, a 'celestial burning', the 'descent of an angel'.

The difference between actual dullness and possible radiance is strongly marked. Plath underlines the blackness by her choice of adjectives: wet, black, desultory, mute, sceptical, minor, obtuse, wary, dull, ruinous. The verbs too convey dispiritedness: hunches, fall, complain, trek, haul, wait. The repetition of the sound 'rain' in line 3 adds to the general bleakness. In complete contrast to this, the hoped-for change is conveyed in terms of brightness: light, fire, incandescence, radiance, flare, shine. It is linked with the divine: miracle, hallowed, angel.

Language

The language of 'Black Rook in Rainy Weather' includes a mixture of the colloquial and the formal. Almost slangy expressions are used side by side with archaic words (words that have fallen out of use). Particularly striking are the semi-Biblical words: 'hallowed', 'bestowing largesse', 'portent'. These contrast strongly with the everyday sound of 'I can't honestly complain,' 'with luck', 'of sorts'. In your opinion, what is the effect of this?

How convincing do you find the possibility of this miracle? Do you feel that the speaker has already experienced such a moment? Look at her description of the moment – the words used to describe it. Be aware also of the many parenthetical statements: 'although', 'I admit', 'may', 'it could happen', 'with luck', 'of sorts', 'if you care to call' . . . . There is certainly no doubt of her wariness.

Rhyme and rhythm

Throughout Plath's career she worked painstakingly on technique, rewriting and reworking her poems until they were as close to perfect as she could make them. In earlier poems her attention to technique is sometimes too obvious, almost overshadowing the subject matter, the theme.

'Black Rook in Rainy Weather', one of her earlier poems, is carefully crafted. Before reading the comments below, reread it, paying attention to rhyme (end-rhyme, half-rhyme), consonance (rhyming consonants), assonance, alliteration and rhythm. Note down any patterns you observe.

Perhaps the most striking feature of this poem is the carefully patterned rhyming scheme. There are five end-rhymes, repeated in each stanza: in other words, the rhyming scheme is *abcde, abcde, abcde*. In every stanza there is also internal rhyme: stiff twig; arranging – rearranging – rain; desultory – design; table – chair.

The rhythm is also skilfully worked out. Mostly the poet uses three-beat lines, but in each stanza this is broken by a four-beat or (occasionally) a five-beat line. The variation avoids monotony, and also gives some interesting effects. Look at the opening lines and notice the effect of the pattern: the grouping of stresses –

> ˘ ˘ – – ˘ –
> On the stiff twig up there
>
> ˘ ˘ ˘ – – –
> Hunches a wet black rook
>
> ˘ – ˘ ˘ – ˘ – ˘ ˘ – ˘ ˘ ˘ –
> Arranging and rearranging its feathers in the rain

– slows down the voice, drawing attention to the rigidity of the bird, emphasising the bleakness of the scene.

Commenting on 'Black Rook in Rainy Weather' in a letter to her mother, Plath criticised its 'glassy brittleness'. What do you think she might mean?

The Times Are Tidy

Text of poem: New Explorations Anthology page 354

'The Times Are Tidy' was written in 1958, at the height of the socially, politically and materially self-satisfied era of President Eisenhower. It was a time of complacency, when any challenge to the status quo – the way things were – was quickly silenced. The 'establishment' – the powerful elite – viewed change as unnecessary and as a threat to its survival. The smug satisfaction of this decade in the United States was all-pervasive. Artists in general suffered under the oppression of a culture that saw anything that differed from the norm as a threat. This was the McCarthy decade, when those suspected of socialist or communist sympathies were blacklisted. According to one commentator,

> in 'The Times Are Tidy', Plath uses irony and humour to deflate . . . behaviour she finds questionable. The poem focuses on the collapse of moral standards and the all-pervasive addiction to comfort and conformity which so strongly characterised the 1950s.

Some ideas

The 1950s – the 'tidy times' – are contrasted with the very 'untidy' times of the world of legend, an era when heroes fought dragons, and witches cast spells and brewed magic potions, risking burning at the stake for their practices.

The 'stuck record' of stanza 1 suggests the tendency of the needle on a worn record to go 'ruh-ruh-ruh' when it sticks. It may symbolise the social boredom and monotony of the time.

The 'watchful cooks' were probably the critics of corrupt political values, who were often dismissed and blacklisted. The corruption or (at best) damaging inactivity of politicians could therefore continue without being too closely observed, allowing the 'mayor's rôtisserie' to turn around 'of its own accord': there was no interference in the continuous political graft and favour-giving.

Humour and irony

Plath used humour in all her writings, sometimes light and amusing, bringing a smile to the reader's face; more often black and biting. She particularly ridiculed what she found self-important or pompous. Her humour is seen in her use of wordplay, entertaining images, and sound effects that sometimes echo nursery rhymes or popular jingles. Very often her humour underlined a serious message.

In 'The Times are Tidy' the decade of smug comfort ('cream an inch thick') and boredom ('stuck record') in which she lived is described ironically. No self-respecting hero would want to live in it: there is 'no career' in adventure; dragons have 'withered to leaf-size'. Witches, with their magic herbs, love potions and talking cats, have been burnt up. Plath sets the present age against the world of legend, of fabulous creatures and mythical heroes.

The final lines are deeply ironic: the very elements that have thrilled children of all ages have disappeared or been forced out. But yet they 'are better for it'. Life may be flat, boring, uneventful, 'a stuck record' – but it is suggested that the 'cream an inch thick' is more than compensation for the lost excitement. The imagination is starved, adventure is dead; but life is rich and comfortable, predictable and safe. Plath seems to suggest the ironic question: what else could children (or even adults) want?

Think of the connotations of 'cream'; note down some of the phrases in which it is used. What point is the poet making here? Do you consider it an apt image with which to conclude this poem?

Themes

- The political corruption of an era that sees material gain as all that counts
- The collapse of moral standards in public life, where self-seeking, greed and corruption dominate
- Self-righteousness – the justification of the status quo because it benefits the elite
- The death of the spirit of adventure, the failure to challenge the 'dragon' of political smugness and corruption, which threaten to suffocate society.

Morning Song

Text of poem: New Explorations Anthology page 356

Plath wrote 'Morning Song' ten months after the birth of her first child, Frieda, on 1 April 1960. She intended it to be the opening poem of a new collection entitled *Ariel.* The first word of the poem, and therefore of the book, is 'Love', setting a warm, positive tone for the collection. It is one of a number of poems she wrote to or about children and motherhood.

Her attitude towards performing the duties of motherhood was often ambivalent. She was aware of the repetitiveness of the work involved in caring for babies, and the inroads it would make on her time; however, this was the negative side of being a mother: it did not cloud her deep love for her children, which is always clear and unequivocal.

A reading of the poem

The opening image creates a warm, loving mood. The speaker addresses the child directly, affirming that she was conceived in love, set in motion 'like a fat gold watch'. The tone is tender and humorous. The mother then recalls the infant's birth, her first cry establishing her place 'among the elements'.

The new parents talk of her arrival, magnifying it; but they also feel threatened by it. The world is a 'draughty museum' and this 'statue' in its 'nakedness' is vulnerable – making them aware of their own vulnerability – 'shadows our safety'.

The 'bald cry' brings a change of scene, from the intimacy of lines 1 and 2 to the chilly world – the 'museum' – where the parents feel their safety is shadowed. The mother feels displaced, unimportant. Even though her love helped to create this child, she now feels that she is no longer necessary. She compares herself to the cloud that brings rain, creating a pool of water: the cloud is momentarily reflected in the pool before the wind slowly blows it on:

> . . . slow
> Effacement at the wind's hand.

This seems to suggest that she is briefly reflected in her child but is then displaced, effaced. It is as if the mother has nothing more to give: the child is autonomous.

However, this troubling idea gives way to the present reality of the child's need of its mother, the mother's attentiveness to the child. The child's 'moth-breath' is almost imperceptible, but the mother hears it. At the first cry she 'stumbles' from bed, heavy and cow-like in her flowery pink nightdress – a note of self-mockery here. She moves towards the child, whose open mouth is 'clean as a cat's.' This startling image suggests the delicate pinkness of the child's mouth.

As morning breaks, the single cry changes to a 'handful of notes' – echoing the 'bald cry' of stanza 1. The image of the 'vowels [rising] like balloons' suggests the beauty of the sounds, and adds a note of playfulness.

Imagery

Plath's images are remarkable for their clarity and unexpectedness. Highly concrete, often drawn from ordinary, everyday things, they catch the reader unawares. The 'fat gold watch' of stanza 1 is simple but vivid, witty and unusual. Its marked rhythm is emphatic:

> – ˘ – – –
> like a fat gold watch.

The description of the world as a 'drafty museum' and new babies as 'naked statues' is a most unusual image, one that makes the reader think. It is an image she has used before: it suggests a world that has held on to its past, storing events, people, everything that makes up our life – not a very comfortable place, but perhaps not unsafe for the new 'statue'.

Imagery is effective in contrasting the infant's lightness and delicacy and the mother's clumsiness and heaviness: the baby's 'moth-breath | Flickers' (notice the lightness of the sounds as well as the delicacy of the image), her 'clear vowels rise like balloons'. The mother, however, is portrayed as homely and a little clumsy: she stumbles 'cow-heavy', swathed in a 'floral . . . Victorian nightgown.'

Imagery is also central to the contrast between the first three stanzas and the last three. There is a conscious development in animation: watch, statue, walls, mirror and even cloud are inanimate objects, just things, incapable of independent activity; moth, cat, singer (child) and cow (mother) are living creatures, capable of acting alone. Can you suggest a reason for the change from inanimate to animate? What is the effect on the reader?

Feelings

'Morning Song' evokes a number of moods. There seems to be a placid acceptance in stanza 1 ('fat gold watch', the midwife's matter-of-fact action, the 'bald cry [taking] its place among the elements'). However, this changes in stanza 2: the world is now cold – 'a drafty museum' – and the adults seem dwarfed by the place. Their 'voices echo', they are 'blank as walls', and their safety is threatened. Why? Does the baby's nakedness make them feel more vulnerable? Or perhaps the new arrival reminds them that they are now an older generation, facing death?

The sense of unease becomes even stronger in stanza 3. The speaker seems to feel that she has nothing to offer the infant: she is mirrored in the child for a while, before being slowly effaced by the passage of time.

These feelings of dislocation, unimportance and impermanence are quickly dispelled by the present moment, evoked vividly in stanza 4. The baby's gentle breath, the rose-patterned room and the watchful mother in her old-fashioned nightdress create a scene of warmth and intimacy.

The remaining stanzas reflect the growing feeling of connectedness between mother and child: one cry brings her to the child, whose mouth is wide open. The dawn breaks to the baby's clear 'handful of notes'. Intimacy, love, joy and pleasure dominate these stanzas. What do you think Plath may be saying here about motherhood?

What is your final impression of this morning song?

Finisterre

Text of poem: New Explorations Anthology page 358

'Finisterre' (Finistère) is the French name for a region in the west of Brittany. It means 'land's end' – the point where land gives way to sea.

Plath and nature

Plath wrote many poems that describe a scene or a place – landscape poems. In these she creates a vivid picture of the place described, conveying a strong sense of the atmosphere and mood of the place at a particular time. Also, she frequently uses the scene described to draw the reader into the mood of the speaker. A number of critics have used the term 'psychic landscapes' to describe such poems.

In 'Finisterre' a seemingly ordinary – though wild and remote – place is described in graphic terms that reflect fear, hopelessness and death. The scene actually becomes secondary to the feelings, despite the speaker's detailed, realistic descriptions. The rugged black cliffs extend into the sea, which pounds them with explosive force. The comparison with 'knuckled and rheumatic' hands 'cramped on nothing' is striking. This is quickly followed by a series of unusual metaphors for the rocks: 'faces of the drowned', 'old soldiers', 'messy wars', 'hidden grudges'. The poet personifies them, creating a powerful metaphor for anger, destruction, and death. The mood evoked is sinister and grim.

Stanza 2 opens with a lovely picture of the small, delicate flowers – trefoils, stars, and bells – edging the cliff, almost like embroidery. But the lightness is quickly dispelled: such flowers might have been embroidered by 'fingers . . . close to death'. And this strikes the note for the remainder of the stanza: death is omnipresent. The mists are described as

Souls, rolled in the doom-noise of the sea.
They bruise the rocks out of existence, then resurrect them.
They go up without hope, like sighs.

The speaker walks through them, and they almost suffocate her: 'They stuff my mouth with cotton,' and leave her 'beaded with tears.'

In 'Black Rook in Rainy Weather' Plath also used nature as a vehicle for feelings. What is the impact of this approach?

THE MONUMENT

Our Lady of the Shipwrecked, as described in stanza 3, would certainly be one reason why the souls of stanza 2 go up without hope! She is aloof, self-important, and self-absorbed,

. . . three times life size,
Her lips sweet with divinity.

She strides towards the horizon, in love with the sea. Far from ignoring those at her feet, she doesn't even appear to know of their presence. The marble sailor is distraught, but gets no attention; the black-clad peasant woman appears to feel that directing her prayers to the praying sailor may be more effective than trying to establish contact with Our Lady of the Shipwrecked.

The monument described here is of a kind not uncommon in Brittany, once a deeply religious region: a kneeling figure looking up to an upright figure, which is looking up to heaven. (Think of the popular statues of Our Lady of Lourdes.) What impression do you form of Plath's response to this monument?

IRONY

There is considerable irony in the description of Our Lady of the Shipwrecked. The statue to whom people pray understands nothing. Her love is for the 'beautiful formlessness of the sea', the source of the shipwrecks she was erected to protect against. She dominates the scene, taking the narrator's – and therefore the reader's – attention away from the underlying horrors of the earlier stanzas. Her pink-tipped cloak, her sweet appearance and her love for the sea seem wildly inappropriate when compared with the doom-laden bay. And how can she love something that has such hideous secrets, hides grudges?

Plath is setting up an ironic contrast here. How effective do you think this is?

There is humorous irony in the final stanza also: in the contrast between the chatty peasants, with their commercial stalls, and the ancient grudging rocks of stanza 1. The only reference the stallholders make to the headland is rather off-hand: 'The Bay of the Dead down there'. The name, however, alerts the reader to one possible explanation for the gloom of the opening stanzas. It also conveys how ordinary it is to those who make their living from tourists. The trinkets on the stall – flapping laces, postcards, necklaces, toy ladies – add to the feeling of ordinariness. It almost seems that, in creating such a homely picture, the narrator is mocking her own over-reaction to the scene in stanza 1.

Another ironic – and humorous – contrast is that between the 'toy ladies' and Our Lady of the Shipwrecked. They are miniature ladies, made from fragile shells – 'trinkets the sea hides' – with no claim to anything other than prettiness. She, on the other hand, is gigantic, made from marble, and is associated with God – 'lips sweet with divinity.' However, she offers no comfort to those who pray to her; whereas the shell ladies are pretty – and available to those who wish to buy them.

The conclusion seems to be deliberately jaunty: 'These are our crêpes. Eat them before they blow cold.' What is the impact of the tone here?

Imagery

The strong visual imagery that is a feature of Plath's poetry is evident in 'Finisterre'. Her ability to create 'startling, beautiful phrases and lines' (Ted Hughes) is rightly celebrated. Here the promontories of rock are

> . . . the last fingers, knuckled and rheumatic,
> Cramped on nothing. Black
> Admonitory cliffs

Dark underwater rocks 'hide their grudges under the water.' The notion that mists 'bruise rocks out of existence, then resurrect them' is a remarkable description of the effect of fog.

Can you identify images that you find particularly striking? What is their impact?

Sound effects

The poem is written in nine-line stanzas, a heavy, formal structure that is particularly appropriate for conveying the weighty terrors of the opening stanzas.

The language too is heavy and forceful, with harsh sounds: 'admonitory', 'knuckled', 'gloomy', 'dump of rocks', 'sea cannons', 'budge', 'grudge'. Harsh '*k*' and '*g*' sounds echo through it, as do long vowel sounds: 'exploding', 'faces', 'drowned', 'gloomy', 'old'. The pounding rhythm of these lines echoes the pounding of the cannoning sea.

Contrast this with the lightness of stanza 4. The same nine-line stanza is used, but the effect is quite different. How does the writer achieve this? Look at colour, sound effects, rhythm, line length, use of dialogue.

Themes
- A rather grim seascape
- The failure of formal religion to answer people's needs
- Hidden unhappiness and hopelessness
- Fear of the unknown.

Concluding note
In general, 'Finisterre' is a remarkable re-creation of a scene and of a mood. The narrator's progress through the place is reflected in what she sees, hears and feels: sea, sounds, weather, rocks, flowers, monument, stallholders. All of it is coloured by Plath's unique imagination.

Mirror

Text of poem: New Explorations Anthology page 362

Commentaries on 'Mirror' are immensely varied. At one extreme it has been described as 'silly adolescent scribbling which simply informs the reader that Plath is like everyone else, searching the reaches for what she really is' – an unusually dismissive attitude. At the other extreme it is considered to be a wonderfully complex meditation on the conflict between woman as creative writer and woman in the socially acceptable role of wife, homemaker and mother. In between there is a wealth of opinions.

The variety of interpretations shows how 'Mirror' touches the life experience of many people. Ironically, the poem has become a mirror in which each reader sees his or her concerns reflected – making one wonder if this was Plath's intention.

Before you read the following notes it would help you if you were to arrive at your own understanding of what Plath is saying. It might be useful to make notes about your response to the poem as a whole, or to individual images or ideas.

Background note
In her personal life, Sylvia Plath frequently questioned who she was. Expectations for a young woman in the late 1950s were limiting: appearance was important, as was marrying suitably and being a good wife, homemaker and mother. For Plath, with her fierce ambition to be a successful writer, such a world was deeply threatening. She certainly loved to look well, enjoyed dating, wanted to marry, have a home and have children – but not at the cost of her writing.

From early in her life she returns frequently in her *Journals* to her fear that marriage would oblige her to bury her creative genius in order to attend to the daily round of housework and baby-minding, which was the lot of most married women in that era.

> Will I be a secretary – a self-rationalising housewife, secretly jealous of my husband's ability to grow intellectually & professionally while I am impeded – will I submerge my embarrassing desires & aspirations, refuse to face myself, and go either mad or become neurotic?

Women writers had an even harder struggle than most: their work was often seen as 'nice', a neat accomplishment – but not necessary. These concerns may have helped to inspire this poem.

A reading of the poem

The 'I' persona of stanza 1 is identified as a mirror only through the title and the named functions. Without the title, this stanza would read like a children's riddle poem. The reader, however, has little difficulty in guessing the identity of 'I'. How much of the poem would you need to read to identify it?

Having identified itself as a mirror, it then informs the reader in stanza 2 that it is a lake. The shift in meaning forces the reader to question the other elements of the poem. This *duality* (doubleness) is echoed in many places and adds to the difficulty of giving a definitive reading.

Stanza 1 seems clear and unambiguous at first reading. Short, simple statements set out the precision, truthfulness and objectivity of 'I'. However, these statements raise many questions when examined closely. Why does a mirror need to explain that it is without preconceptions? 'unmisted by dislike'? 'not cruel, only truthful'? If it is as objective and exact as it claims, why does it 'think' (an inexact statement) that a wall could be part of its heart? Can a mirror have a heart? How does this fit in with its own notion that it is exact?

Perhaps because of these contradictions and the almost childlike certainties, the tone of this stanza is light and breezy. The wittiness of the riddle format, the precise details, the simplicity and the fast rhythm all add a humorous note. Even the self-importance of the mirror – a little god – is amusing, as is the wordplay on 'I' and 'eye'.

The opening statement of the second stanza – 'Now I am a lake' – adds a new dimension, causing the reader to revise the first reading of stanza 1. Is the mirror choosing an image to describe itself as it is in the mind of the woman 'who bends over me'? This woman is not just looking at the superficial reflection: she is 'searching my reaches for what she really is.' A silver, exact, four-square mirror has no reaches: it is flat, two-dimensional. It can only reflect back the surface image: there is no depth, no murkiness, no darkness. Yet the woman sees there something that makes her turn away, escape what she sees or suspects by looking 'to those liars, the candles or the moon.'

The 'truth' follows her – 'I see her back and reflect it faithfully' – and her tears and agitation are the mirror's reward. Despite this she returns: the truth she finds in the mirror is important to her. 'Each morning' in the mirror she sees her face, sees that

> she has drowned a young girl, and in me an old woman
> Rises towards her, like a terrible fish.

One simple interpretation of this is that she sees her youth 'drowning', and watches with horror the approach of old age – which she views as monstrous, a terrible fish.

This raises other questions. Why 'drowning'? This implies suffocation, sudden loss, not the gradual fading of youth. The old woman and the terrible fish are terrifying – and certainly don't come from the mirror. They rise up from the murky depths of the lake, the darkness, the reaches of the woman's subconscious.

The frightening truths that rise from the depths are what the woman meets when she searches for 'what she really is' – her true identity. This is not the pretty, docile, smiling, youthful woman that society admires: it is something frightening, dark, ugly, terrible – and true.

Themes

- Knowing oneself
- Ageing
- Identity: the double self
- Fear
- The human condition.

Two-sidedness

A poem is not necessarily part of the life story of the poet, nor of those around her; the 'I' persona is not the poet narrating her life experiences. However, those experiences inform the poet's work; they are the raw material from which she shapes her poetry.

You may find it helpful, therefore, when studying this poem to look back at Plath's life. Of particular relevance to 'Mirror' is the fact that she spent long years striving to achieve high ambitions: a consistent 'alpha' (A grade) pupil through school and university, she always strove to give of her best. It often appears, though, that she judged her best not just by her own very high standard but also by the far more unpredictable standard of winning the recognition and approval of others. This was true of her work and of her life: she seemed to need constant affirmation of her worth. One consequence of this was a pleasant, smiling appearance, the 'all-American girl' image – 'a maddening docility', according to Robert Lowell, whose writing class she attended – which often concealed so-called negative emotions such as anger, disappointment, resentment, jealousy and hatred.

In several of Plath's poems she presents a double image, two sides of a person: in 'In Plaster' (1961), for example, the speaker – the body encased in plaster, a metaphor here for the inner self – talks about the plaster cast that she has had to wear and recognises its whiteness, its coldness, and its utter dependence on what it encases. When the clean white plaster is removed this ugly, hairy, old, yellow person within will be revealed; but the speaker is determined to 'manage without' the plaster. In this way what appears clean, bright and pleasant is in fact only cheap plaster; the true self may be ugly – but it is the real self.

> I used to think we might make a go of it together –
> After all it was a kind of marriage, being so close.
> Now I see it must be one or the other of us.
> She may be a saint and I may be ugly and hairy,
> But she'll soon find out that doesn't matter a bit.

What similarities do you see between this and 'Mirror'?

Revealing one's true identity

A committed poet, Plath knew the importance of speaking from the heart. But speaking from the heart means saying things others might not approve of, expressing socially unacceptable feelings. It means revealing one's true identity, and risking rejection. 'Mirror' could be read as an expression of this conflict. At this time in her life Plath's style and subject matter were undergoing a change, which eventually gave birth to her most powerful and controversial poems, many of which voice sentiments that a lot of people experience but don't talk about.

The mirror could be seen as a metaphor for her 'golden girl' image – silver, exact, reflecting back what others projected, not creating any controversy. But the lake has hidden depths, and when these are searched, murkiness, darkness, terror and ugliness are revealed – and the demure young lady is drowned. This mirror therefore has a bright side and a dark side, like Plath herself – like all who share the human condition.

Pheasant

Text of poem: New Explorations Anthology page 364

'Pheasant' is a wonderful evocation of the beauty and vitality of a bird that is under threat of death. Read it through a few times just for enjoyment.

Get a sense of the speaker's attitude to the bird (note how this is conveyed). Her relationship with 'you' also colours the poem; the tension generated by the opening lines is sustained to the end, and underlined by the closing plea. Pay particular attention to her use of clear images, precise detail, language, colour and contrast to paint a picture of what she sees now, and remembers from last winter.

A READING OF THE POEM

The opening line is the narrator's heartfelt plea to 'you' not to kill the pheasant this morning, as he had said he would.

The pheasant is pictured in strong, visual language: the narrator is startled by

> The jut of that odd, dark head, pacing
> Through the uncut grass on the elm's hill.

She values it for its sheer beauty, its vitality. The bird seems to her to be at home on the hill – 'simply in its element.' It is kingly – visiting 'our court' (possibly a play on the name of Plath's home, Green Court). Last winter it had also visited during snowy weather, leaving its tail-track and its large footprint, which differed from the 'crosshatch' of smaller birds.

Returning to the present, she captures its appearance in a few graphic words – 'green and red', 'a good shape', 'so vivid', 'a little cornucopia', 'brown as a leaf' – as it 'unclaps' its wings and flies up into the elm, where 'it is easy.'

The narrator feels that she is the trespasser: she disturbed the pheasant as it sunned itself in the narcissi. She turns again to 'you', pleading once again for its life: 'Let be, let be.'

VOICE

One strength of this poem lies in the personal voice of the narrator. It is as if the reader is looking in on a moment of her life – eavesdropping on her words to 'you'. The tone is intimate, immediate. Her plea is clear and unambiguous: 'Do not kill it.'

Her response to the pheasant is equally immediate: it rings absolutely true; there is no doubting the sincerity of her admiration. Can you pinpoint how this effect is achieved?

The pheasant is described in a concrete, detailed manner. There is indeed nothing 'mystical' about it: it is so vivid, so alive that this alone should be reason enough to let it be. Plath captures the vividness in a few well-chosen details: movement (jut, pacing, unclaps), colour (dark, green, red, brown), and shape (print of its big foot, tail-track). Its very sense of being at home here gives it a kingliness: it paces the hill, 'in its element', 'visits us', settles in the elm where it 'is easy', making the narrator feel she trespasses 'stupidly.'

Her statement that

> . . . it isn't
> As if I thought it had a spirit

suggests the idea that it has indeed a spirit, that she feels some mystical connection with it. Everything she says gives the impression that it has a superior claim to this place, and a right to live.

Mood

The pleas that open and close the poem suggest tension between 'I' and 'you'. Her spirited defence of the pheasant is sparked by her recollection that 'you said you would kill it this morning.' The abruptness makes the statement sound like an accusation.

These words, and her defensiveness, suggest another scene, not described here. Why has 'you' threatened to kill the bird? Why are they in conflict about it? Do the final words suggest defeat or victory? While there are no answers to these questions in the poem, looking at the possibilities can help you to determine the tone of the poem.

Themes

- Tension
- The rights of wild creatures
- The mystery of beauty.

Technique

Verse form

The verse form of this poem is *terza rima,* a form that Plath used frequently. This is an Italian term meaning 'third rhyme', and it is based on three-line stanzas, where the first and third lines rhyme. Often the end-sound of the second line becomes the rhyme of lines 1 and 3 in the next stanza, and so on, creating the sound-pattern *aba, bcb, cdc* . . . The stanzas are therefore interlaced.

This verse form is an effective one for building a narrative: it creates a series of short, interlaced vignettes. In this poem each stanza traces some aspect of the pheasant's appearance or its actions, with the grammatical sentence often carrying the thought through the break into the next stanza. This creates an almost casual flow, despite the formal structure of the poem.

Rhyme

A glance through the poem will show that *terza rima* is used consistently, though the rhymes often depend on *consonance* (rhyming final consonants) rather than on the more traditional and more obvious end-rhyme.

The effect of this muted rhyming pattern is a subtle music, an effect Plath strove to achieve in all her poetry. The singing quality of the poem is helped by her use of assonance and repetition. Again a quick look at any stanza reveals examples. In stanza 1, for example, there is

> . . . kill it this morning.
> . . . kill it. It startles . . . still.

Can you find other examples?

Rhythm

Pay attention also to the 'voice-rhythm' of the lines, the way many lines echo the rhythm of normal speech. While this creates an impression of ease and simplicity, it is in fact a highly skilful achievement, requiring mastery of technique.

Style

While Plath's attention to technique is evident when one studies 'Pheasant' closely, it does not stand out or impose itself on the reader. Form here serves the content: it draws attention to what the poet is saying, or adds to the beauty of the poem. It is not simply an end in itself.

Compare this with her technique in earlier poems, such as 'Black Rook in Rainy Weather'. Can you explain the difference? A look at the poet's level of engagement with her topic might be a good starting-point.

Elm

Text of poem: New Explorations Anthology page 366

Sylvia Plath dedicated 'Elm' to her friend Ruth Fainlight, an American poet. This is one of the first poems in which the distinctive voice of Plath's later poetry is heard. She always drew on her own experiences for material for her poems; but these late poems reflect a level of intensity not found in 'Finisterre' or 'Black Rook in Rainy Weather'. They also have a freedom, a lack of constraint and natural flow quite unlike the careful patterning of her earlier poems.

Some critics have linked the deep fear and rage expressed in 'Elm' with the growing tensions in Plath's marriage at the time of writing. These possibly triggered a renewal of the unresolved grief caused by the loss of her father at the age of eight, and of the depression that had caused her to have a nervous breakdown at the age of twenty. Part of the treatment for depression at that time was electric shock treatment, most probably the source of the image of scorching burning filaments used here and in other poems.

But it is important to emphasise that while these factors clearly influenced Plath's choice of theme and style, she is not writing about her life. A poem is an artistic creation, a work of art, which may be inspired by external events but is not a documentary about those events.

'Elm' is a complex poem. It is best perhaps to listen attentively to it several times to tune in to its deeply felt emotions, its energy. Try not to concentrate too much on understanding or interpreting individual lines or stanzas: respond rather to the general effect, the rich images, the sounds, the rhythm and, above all, the feelings that infuse it.

A reading of the poem

The speaker seems to be quoting the words she imagines the elm is directing to her. The elm – speaking as 'I' throughout – taunts 'you', the speaker, the source of the fear released in the poem, for her fear of the unknown. 'I know the bottom . . . I do not fear it,' she claims – unlike 'you', who fears it. 'You' hear the sea – or perhaps the voice of nothingness, a voice she is familiar with since her madness.

'You' foolishly seeks love – a 'shadow' that has galloped away. The elm will mimic that galloping sound all night, driving you to near-death: 'Till your head is a stone, your pillow a little turf'.

The taunting voice of the elm then describes some of the nightmarish horrors she knows, horrors that suggest a nervy, exhausted state:

- the sound of poisons, rain, 'this big hush', and its fruit, 'tin-white like arsenic'
- sunsets – atrocities that 'scorch to the root', making its 'filaments burn and stand'
- the wind, a destructively violent force that leaves nothing unharmed, will 'tolerate no bystanding', causing the elm to shriek
- the merciless moon, a symbol of barrenness, whose cruel radiance burns; when freed from the elm, this moon is flat – like a woman who has had radical surgery.

The frenzied violence of the verbs – scorch, burn, stand, break up, fly, shriek, drag, scathe – eases off in the next stanzas. The elm challenges 'you' for releasing the bad dreams that now 'possess and endow me.' The distinction between 'you' and the elm – so clear at first – is blurred. 'You' now seems to inhabit the elm – perhaps it is the dark, fearful side of the elm.

The elm turns from external violence to inner terror – a 'cry' that

> . . . flaps out
> Looking, with its hooks, for something to love.

She feels a terrifying 'dark thing', with its 'soft, feathery turnings', that sleeps in her, something that is also wicked, malignant. These 'soft feathery turnings' sound even more sinister than the wild violence of the earlier stanzas.

Silent inward terror gives way to a less claustrophobic tone. Looking outwards again, the elm watches 'clouds pass and disperse.' They may be the 'faces of love', and – like the love that went off like a horse in stanza 2 – they are irretrievable, gone for ever. The taunting voice that earlier mocked 'you' for her need for love has changed. The elm too seems to feel bereft (or possibly angry?): '. . . I agitate my heart'.

She now changes from the confident, knowing, fearless voice of the early stanzas to a fearful, petrified being, 'incapable of more knowledge.' This sounds as if she knows at some level what she could learn (does in fact 'know the bottom') but does not want to truly understand.

The cry, the dark thing, is now a face, 'so murderous in its strangle of branches', a creature whose 'snaky acids hiss' and freeze the will. The elm is now struggling with 'slow, isolate faults', which are self-destructive, potentially fatal, 'that kill, that kill, that kill.'

Language

Plath's language in this poem is extraordinarily rich. The opening is simple and direct. 'I know the bottom, she says. I know it with my great tap-root'. Indeed many lines in the poem are written in the same simple, unvarnished style:

> 'Love is a shadow'.
> 'I let her go. I let her go'
> 'This is rain now, this big hush.'
> 'I am terrified by this dark thing | That sleeps in me;'
> 'Its snaky acids hiss.'

It is this directness that strikes the reader most forcibly on a first reading.

The tactile quality that is so often noted in Plath's poetry is evident here: words like 'stone', 'turf', 'arsenic', 'burn and stand', 'scathes', 'soft, feathery turnings' evoke things we can feel or hear or touch or taste. Every line of the poem contains concrete language – words, phrases and images that pile up to create a vibrant and powerful effect. It is as if each sensation, each feeling, each moment described is etched out. This has a powerful impact on the reader; the effect is cumulative until the final

> . . . isolate, slow faults
> That kill, that kill, that kill.

Imagery

While her experience is conveyed through metaphors, these are not used for their cleverness. The images used are powerful, conveying depth of feeling in richly evocative terms.

Re-examine the images that you find most striking. Notice the sparseness of the language: many of the statements are simple and clear, depending on strong verbs and nouns for their impact.

The central metaphor, the elm, is drawn from her immediate surroundings. 'The house in Devon was overshadowed by a giant wych-elm, flanked by two others in a single mass, growing on the shoulder of a moated prehistoric mound' (Ted Hughes). It features in a number of her poems, including 'Pheasant'; the bird settled in it, 'easy'. In 'Elm', however, there is no ease. Indeed the first draft of this poem opened with the lines 'She is not easy, she is not peaceful.'

Many of the images used here recur in other Plath poems: sea, horse, moon, scorching, clouds, acid, colours. By reusing the same images throughout her work she has created a series of symbols that echo and link up with each other, gaining an additional force from repeated use.

THEMES

Like 'Mirror', 'Elm' has been read and interpreted in innumerable ways. Some themes are:

- the 'stigma of selfhood' (Plath wrote these words at the top of the first draft of this poem) – the awful fear of being oneself
- despair and frustration
- the paralysis of fear
- the loss of love
- jealousy
- dissatisfaction
- the threat of madness
- exhaustion.

TECHNIQUE

Form

The close observance of writing rules – technique or form – sometimes made Plath's poems seem over-controlled. As her work developed she moved away from such tight control towards a freer style. 'Elm' is a good example of her success in overcoming what she herself called a 'clever, too brittle and glassy tone', a move that enabled her 'to speak straight out, and of real experience, not just in metaphorical conceits'. It is remarkably open and intense, reflecting feelings that come from the deepest self.

Rhythm and rhyme

Written in *tercets* (three-line stanzas), this poem flows with the poet's feelings. There is no attempt at a rhyming scheme. What difference do you think this makes? The lines are free-flowing and varied in length. Can you suggest why this is?

There is, however, consistent use of internal rhyme: assonance, alliteration, repetition. Even in its wildest moments, this poem sings. Commenting on her later poems, Plath said: 'I speak them to myself . . . I say them aloud.' Can you find any evidence of this attention to sound effects in 'Elm'? Listen to it again, and pay close attention to the impact of sound effects, sentence length, one-liners and direct speech.

NOTE

This poem benefits from repeated readings. Trying to make sense of each individual line or stanza will only confuse you. Listening to it and re-reading it several times will enable you to tap into the energy and the powerful emotions that infuse it.

Poppies in July

Text of poem: New Explorations Anthology page 370

A READING OF THE POEM

The first part of 'Poppies in July' presents the physical appearance of the poppies: their intense red colour, the wrinkly petals, their light, flickering movement in the wind, their 'little bloody skirts!' However, the metaphors used go well beyond simple description: the poet is indirectly telling a 'story', rather than merely describing flowers.

Firstly, the poppies are associated with fire – usually a metaphor for vitality or life force in Plath's poetry. Here the fire is like 'hell flames', normally connected with intense pain. However, the speaker does not know whether they hurt her: 'Do you do no harm?' They do not burn the speaker – or if they do, she doesn't feel the pain. This suggests a state beyond pain, a sense of numbness.

She is exhausted; this may be caused by the sheer vividness of the poppies. They are fully alive, but she is apparently unable to experience life. They seem to plunge her into despair at something that is happening to her in her life. Her pain is underlined by the references to blood: they look like

> . . . the skin of a mouth.
> A mouth just bloodied.

or 'little bloody skirts'. The flowers are personified, given human characteristics.

The 'I' persona can't be like the poppies, it seems: she can't feel their burning, share their vitality. She is not fired by any life force or vitality. She can't bleed: 'If my mouth could marry a hurt like that!' Even her state of not feeling pain seems to distress her. It's not that she is not in pain: she just can't feel it, which brings its own anguish.

She turns from the appearance to the hidden properties of the poppies in the second part of the poem – their 'fumes', their 'opiates' (opium is extracted from the seeds of the white poppy), which can cause sleep, oblivion. She longs for the 'dulling and stilling' state they could induce in her.

The red poppies, a symbol of life, colourful and vivid, could help the speaker to escape into the dull, colourless world of oblivion, away from the exhaustion caused by the intensity of life, by the agony of just being. She longs for non-being.

Tone

There is a strong contrast between the vividness and vitality of the poppies and the dull, lacklustre mood of the speaker. She watches them, sees their 'flames', but 'cannot touch' them; even though she puts her 'hands among the flames', 'nothing burns.' She feels exhausted simply watching them: her mood seems directly opposite to the mood she attributes to the poppies.

She gives the impression that she can't participate in life – can't bleed, can't sleep, can't 'marry a hurt'. These lines suggest the feeling of desperation that leads her to yearn for oblivion:

> Dulling and stilling.
> But colorless. Colorless.

Background

'Poppies in July' is one of a series of poems where the 'I' persona turns in on herself, dealing with some deep-seated grief; she does not disclose the source and nature of this, but the feeling is strongly conveyed. She longs for oblivion, but does not explain why. However, on reading the poem we get the sense that life itself is too much for her.

A companion poem to this one, called 'Poppies in October', written some months later, is quite different in tone. Here the blazing red of the poppies – 'brighter than sunrise' – is

> a gift
> A love gift
> Utterly unasked for.

This underlines the sense that it is not the poppies that generate the sense of grief and hopelessness, the desire for oblivion: it comes from within the speaker; but it is only temporary.

Comparing three poems

'Pheasant', 'Elm' and 'Poppies in July' were written around the same time (in April and July 1962). In each poem the speaker is engaging in a struggle with some threatening force beyond herself. Each seems to re-create or suggest a scene in the drama of tensions within her life – a scene involving suspicion, hurt, jealousy and anger.

Reread the three of them together, and note how the mood of the speaker seems to progress. In 'Pheasant' she is quite rational, though fearful for the pheasant. Her plea is logical and ordered and based on very ordinary claims: the beauty of the pheasant, its kingliness, colours, right to be in this place. At the same time the reader is aware of her tension right through the poem, and of the note of possible surrender in the final line: 'Let be, let be.'

In 'Elm' the speaker has lost love; it has galloped away and is irretrievable. The anguish experienced is expressed in a series of harsh, brilliant metaphors, conveying deep feelings of rage, terror, anguish and finally exhaustion.

'Poppies in July' reflects that same exhaustion: the vividness and movement of the flowers make the speaker feel exhausted. There is a sense of deep pain: 'hell flames', 'mouth just bloodied', 'bloody skirts'. She longs for oblivion, for non-being.

The Arrival of the Bee Box

Text of poem: New Explorations Anthology page 372

[*Note: This poem is also prescribed for Ordinary Level 2008 exam*]

The bee poems

Over one week, in October 1962, Sylvia Plath wrote a cycle of five poems, generally called the 'bee poems', set in the world of bee-keeping. All five are written in five-line stanzas, and they form a unit in that they move logically through the various phases of bee-keeping.

These poems grew from her own experience. Her father's speciality was bees: he studied them throughout his life, and wrote two highly regarded books on the subject. Given her lifelong obsession with her father, it is not surprising that Plath should have found it an interesting topic. Indeed, one of her earlier poems was entitled 'The Bee-Keeper's Daughter'.

After the birth of her son Plath decided to keep bees, and she turned to the local bee-keepers' society for help in setting up her hives. Each of the poems in the cycle deals with a practical element of bee-keeping, drawing on the poet's initiation into this skill. But each one is also a metaphor for something in life: it is as if through these poems she found a way of defining her identity, coming to terms with elements of life.

The story of the poem

The story of 'The Arrival of the Bee Box' is straightforward: the narrator has taken delivery of a bee box ordered some time before. She describes its appearance, and also the appalling noise that comes from it. This she finds threatening, but also fascinating: she 'can't keep away from it.' Looking through the little grid, she sees only 'swarmy' darkness. She considers sending them back, or possibly even starving them. These considerations don't sound very convincing, however; she quickly goes on to wonder how hungry they are, and whether they will attack her when she unlocks the box. There are flowers in the garden that should attract them away from her when they fly out. She concludes by apparently deciding to free them tomorrow: 'The box is only temporary.'

Themes

- Freedom and repression
- Self-expression
- Being oneself
- Control.

Metaphor

Metaphor is the use of a word or phrase that describes one thing with the purpose of explaining or giving an understanding of something else. In describing the arrival of the bee box and her reactions, Plath explores a number of themes through a series of rich metaphors.

The bee box

The bee box itself is presented as something solid, ordinary: a 'clean wood box', 'square as a chair' and very heavy. The language here is direct and wholesome: even the rhyme of 'square' and 'chair' seems to underline its homely quality. However, this ordinariness quickly changes. The next line brings in a sinister note – or possibly it is merely humorous: this could be the coffin of a midget or a square baby were it not for the noise coming from it.

The box clearly means more to the speaker than a practical way of transporting bees. It immediately suggests death ('coffin') and threat ('dangerous'). Discovering that a familiar object is sinister and threatening is truly frightening: it seems to remove the feeling of safety one has around everyday things. She is fascinated and frightened. It contains, locks in, something she wants to keep in but also wants to release.

The bee box can be seen as a metaphor for containment, imprisonment or repression; this repression could come from concern for outward appearances, form, doing the right thing, trying to be what others expect, to behave in an acceptable way, saying the correct words, not being yourself, denying your true self. This is a form of repression, of boxing in something so that others will accept what they think you are. Remembering Plath's concerns about her life and her art, can you see why this seems an apt interpretation?

The bees

The sense of something sinister is heightened in stanza 2. The threat comes from the contents of the box – the bees, their noise, their clamour, their apparent anger.

Plath uses three metaphors to describe the hidden bees, each of them an image of power and oppression:

- They are like tiny shrunken African hands, packed for export: black, clambering – like slaves in a slave-ship. She has power over them: she could free them, but wonders how.
- They are like a Roman mob, safe individually but 'my god, together!' The exclamation mark (unusual in Plath's poems) suggests many possibilities. Not being an autocrat, a Caesar, she feels she can't control them.
- They are just maniacs – thus also locked away, mad, a threat to others unless controlled by someone else.

Some critics see these as metaphors for the narrator's voice. If the box is external appearances, the bees may be seen as the speaker's inner life, feelings, real self or core of identity. This true self, her authentic voice, is locked in by convention. Her repressed words are 'a din', 'a noise that appals', 'unintelligible syllables', 'furious Latin.' Suppressed by rigid outer form or convention, they are unintelligible, formless and fearsome.

Her dread of releasing these words and ideas is so great that she wonders about getting rid of them, starving them: 'I need feed them nothing'; but the idea is half-hearted. Can you see anything in the structure of this statement that might imply that she doesn't fully mean it?

She fears that she herself may suffer if she releases the bees (or words):

> 'It is the noise that appals me . . .'
> 'I have simply ordered a box of maniacs.'
> 'I wonder if they would forget me'
> 'They might ignore me immediately'

In what way do you think she would be hurt by her own words? by her own poetry? by releasing her imaginative powers?

Tree

The narrator then imagines herself turning into a tree to avoid their anger. The reference to Daphne connects her (the speaker) with other women – she is not alone in her fear. The references to the 'blond' flowers of the laburnum and the 'petticoats of the cherry' also connect her with women.

How might her silence, her repression of her real self be echoed in the lives of other women at that time?

INTERPRETING THE POEM

This is only one interpretation of this rich metaphorical poem. There are others: look back at 'Mirror' and 'Elm'. Do you see anything that connects with them? Note the resemblances and the differences. As with many poems, 'reading in' one meaning can be simplistic, blocking the way to other possible interpretations and ideas.

TECHNIQUE

Wordplay and sound effects

There are several examples of Plath's clever wordplay and witty sound effects in this poem: the short '*i*' sound of 'din in it' combined with the repeated '*n*' seems to mimic the bees' buzzing; the almost unpronounceable 'unintelligible syllables' echoes the meaning of the words.

She also uses internal rhyme (square – chair – square – there), and also repetition (grid . . . grid – dark . . . dark – black . . . black). These are effective: sometimes they underline a point or highlight a word; always they make the poem sing.

The five-line stanza used in 'The Arrival of the Bee Box' is similar to that used in all five bee poems. There is, however, one difference in this poem: there is an additional single line at the end of the poem:

> The box is only temporary.

It is almost as if it has escaped – has been freed – from the form of the poem.

NOTE

This is a complex and rich poem, one that will benefit from several readings. As it is part of a cycle of five poems, reading it together with the other four may add to your understanding.

Child

Text of poem: New Explorations Anthology page 375

[*Note: This poem is also prescribed for Ordinary Level 2008 exam*]

A READING OF THE POEM

This simple poem is almost like a lullaby. The mother addresses her child, wanting to fill his eye,

> the one absolutely beautiful thing

with wonders.

The tone at first is clear and bright. She longs to fill his vision with colour, ducks, newness and flowers. He is like a flower-stalk without wrinkle, or a pool that reflects the beauty of the world. However, the tone changes in the final stanza; the narrator turns away from the child and his world to

> this troublous
> Wringing of hands.

She sees another world that is the direct opposite of the light and flower-filled world of the child,

> . . . this dark
> Ceiling without a star.

This could perhaps be a reflection of her fears for the child in a world that is often antagonistic to beauty and dangerous for the helpless. It might also refer to her own feelings of unhappiness and depression. There is a marked contrast between the joyful, limpid quality of the first three stanzas and the dark, unlit, enclosed space of the last line. What effect has this on the reader? What is your response to the poem?

Plath and children

'Child' is one of a number of poems that Plath wrote about children, in particular her own children and her relationship with them. It is an eloquent love poem, reflecting a strong connection with them and with the world she would like to show to them. However, in most of these poems the poet turns from the tender joy and lightness of her child's world to anxiety; the conclusion here creates a strong sense of darkness, chilliness. There is a suggestion that she fears threatening forces that may hurt the child.

Style

'Child' is written in the three-line stanza form, one that Plath used often in her later poems. Here it seems particularly appropriate. The sort stanzas are clear and uncluttered, the rhythm quick and light. Most lines have two or three beats, giving the poem an easy, flowing movement.

The theme is simple: love, childhood joys, motherhood, and also fear and anxiety about the bleakness that may threaten the child, the 'troublous wringing of hands'.

The language is concrete: the narrator lists simple objects that bring joy to children: colours and ducks, the zoo of the new, flowers and water. Her fear too is worded in concrete terms: 'wringing of hands', 'dark ceiling without a star.'

Compare this poem in tone, theme and style with 'Morning Song'.

Overview of the poems

This is a brief look at the selection of poems by Sylvia Plath that you have studied. The points made here represent one interpretation of her work. It is important that you develop your own response to each poem; where this differs from the suggestions given here, trust your own judgment. Reread the poem, and validate your opinion.

Background

Plath wrote incessantly during her short life: poetry, short stories, articles, essays and one semi-autobiographical novel. Her writings were first published in magazines on both sides of the Atlantic; later they appeared in book form.

She considered poems written before 1956 as 'juvenilia'. Her first published book, *The Colossus,* includes only poems written after this date, among them two of the poems you have studied, 'Black Rook in Rainy Weather' and 'The Times are Tidy'. Her remaining poems were published after her death in three collections: *Ariel and Other Poems, Crossing the Water* and *Winter Trees.*

Her last poems are generally seen as Plath's outstanding achievement. Here she truly found her voice, expressing herself in a distinctive, unique style. She was aware of this herself: while writing them, she informed her mother:

> I am a writer . . . I am a genius of a writer; I have it in me. I am writing the best poems of my life; they will make my name . . . (*Letters Home,* 16 October 1962).

Her husband describes these poems equally glowingly:

> Her real self showed itself in her writing. . . . When a real self finds language and manages to speak, it is surely a dazzling event. (Ted Hughes, foreword to *The Journals of Sylvia Plath,* 1982)

Reading Plath's poems

There is a widespread tendency to interpret Plath's work as autobiographical, to read her poems as if they tell her life story. While it is quite obvious – and probably inevitable – that a writer's life will influence what she writes, it is important to understand that poetry is art. Writing about this issue, Ted Hughes pointed out that the reader must learn 'to distinguish between a subjective work that was trying to reach an artistic form using a real event as its basis, and a documentary of some event that did happen'.

Some critics read her later poems exclusively in the light of her suicide. They argue that she signals her suicide (intentionally or otherwise) in a number of her last poems, through various references to despair, rage, loss, separation or death.

That is by no means as obvious as these critics claim. Many of these poems are the work of a woman who is coming into her own, recognising her own needs, using her own voice, finding her true self. Look back, for example, at 'The Arrival of the Bee Box'. This is about facing and releasing the fears that are hidden beneath the surface – not about a woman who is contemplating death.

It is important to read the poems as they stand. Looking for signs of what was to happen afterwards in her life is to predetermine how the poems should be read, not actually attending to the poem itself.

THEMES AND ISSUES IN THE PRESCRIBED POEMS

The writer's identity

In 'Black Rook in Rainy Weather' (1956), one theme is the poet's identity as a writer. The speaker, surrounded by wintry bleakness, longs for the miracle that will transform this into something radiant. That miracle is the creative impulse, the imagination that will change an otherwise uneventful period. For the speaker, this miracle was of vital importance.

Motherhood

Plath wrote many poems dealing with all aspects of pregnancy, childbirth and motherhood, at a time when writers, especially poets, rarely touched on such topics. Her best-known work on the theme, 'Poem for Three Voices', evokes powerfully the variety of emotions experienced by women around pregnancy, miscarriage, motherhood and adoption. Her poems on this theme are remarkable for their lyricism (song-like quality), depth of feeling, and tenderness.

> What did my fingers do before they held him?
> What did my heart do, with its love?

However, being a realist, she also reflected the other side of being a mother: the drudgery, the anxieties, and the level to which a mother is bound to her child.

> I have never seen a thing so clear . . .
> It is a terrible thing to be so open: it is as if my heart
> Put on a face and walked into the world.

Both attitudes are seen in 'Morning Song'. The mother's life is shadowed by the child's arrival, but is enriched by the joy of love. 'Child' also reflects the simple pleasure she derives from her child; his eye is the one absolutely beautiful thing that she longs to fill with the beauty of the world. But there is also an underlying threat to the child's safety, which distresses her.

Identity

Plath frequently returned to the issue of double identity in her writing. The subject of her undergraduate dissertation in Smith College was 'The Magic Mirror: A Study of the Double in Dostoevsky Novels'. Her interest in what appears on the surface and what is hidden is reflected in 'Mirror'. Here, the depths hide something frightening and sinister, something the woman would prefer to avoid but cannot escape.

'Elm' also deals with doubleness: the apparent calm of the elm in the opening stanzas, and the hidden terrors that surface as she talks.

A similar preoccupation is at the heart of 'The Arrival of the Bee Box'. The practical, square box is a simple container: apparently there are no mysteries here. However, it conceals something sinister, but also fascinating.

Nature

Plath's abiding interest in the world around her, her interest in nature, is reflected in many poems. Her descriptions are remarkable for their concrete, precise detail.

'Finisterre' paints a graphic picture of the scene before her eyes, conveying the harshness of the sea, the bleakness of the rocks, the delicacy of the flowers on the cliff and the effect of the mist.

'Black Rook in Rainy Weather' is strong in visual details, accurately portraying a scene on a wet, wintry day.

Her painterly style creates graphic images in 'Pheasant': the bird itself, the flowers, the hill and elm in the background, the earlier scene where the snow was marked with the 'crosshatch' footprints of various birds.

Through unusual images, 'Poppies in July' captures the vivid colour and fluid movement of the poppies' petals.

'Pheasant' reflects her stance against the destruction of nature, a concern that features in many of her poems.

Psychic landscapes

While Plath's descriptions of landscapes and seascapes are striking, the scene is at times simply the backdrop to the mood of the speaker.

'Black Rook in Rainy Weather' is strong in visual detail, but the place does not really matter. What comes across as significant is the mood of the speaker, the sense of tentative expectancy. The landscape is almost a backdrop.

In 'Finisterre', the place is identified by the title. The landscape is captured in a series of wonderful images. Many of these are personified: cliffs are 'admonitory', rocks hide their grudges, the sea wages war and mists are without hope. The place assumes an atmosphere that is oddly human.

TECHNIQUE

Style

Plath's style changed considerably during her career, but there are certain features that mark all her work:

- remarkable use of language
- unusual and striking imagery
- humour.

Language

Plath's 'crackling verbal energy' is apparent in her poems' biting precision of word and image. Her writing has been variously praised for its tactile quality, power, incisiveness, control, taut originality and luminosity. Joyce Carol Oates observed that 'the final memorable poems ['Elm', 'Poppies in July' and 'The Arrival of the Bee Box', among others] . . . read as if they've been chiselled with a fine surgical implement out of arctic ice.' In her *Journals,* Plath constantly urges herself to develop a 'diamond-edged', 'gem-bright' style. This she certainly achieved. Part of her technique was to reuse certain words in many poems, which thus took on an almost symbolic meaning: smiles, hooks, element, dissatisfaction, vowels, shriek, horse, sea.

'Black Rook in Rainy Weather' is a good example of her earlier control of language and form. In it the language is clear and precise, creating a series of carefully worked out pictures.

'Pheasant' is a later example of her skilled control of descriptive language. The form here is less dominant, and the poet's feelings are reflected in the personal voice that speaks throughout. The words are simple, the descriptions are vivid, and the poem is crystal clear. It is a good example of Plath's descriptive powers at their best.

'Elm' shows her powerful response to loss, pain and terror. The feeling of despair, for example, is conveyed through a number of highly charged nouns and verbs.

Imagery

Certain images recur in Plath's poetry, taking on a symbolic meaning that gains added force through repeated use.

- The moon symbolises barrenness, coldness and the negation of life. In 'Elm' it is merciless, cruel and barren, associated with pain and suffering.
- The mirror often symbolises the hidden alter ego (the 'other self'), as in 'Mirror'.
- The horse is a symbol of vitality. In 'Elm', love gallops off like a horse.
- Blood symbolises vitality, life force and creativity, as in 'Poppies in July'. In a later poem, Plath states:

The blood jet is poetry,
There is no stopping it

• The sea is often associated with undefined menace or hidden threat, as is so graphically evident in 'Finisterre'.

She uses many other images, however, that are not symbolic, images that add to the vividness and immediacy of what she is describing. One of the most distinctive features of her work is her use of metaphors, many of which are visual. Examples abound:

• Mists are 'souls', which 'bruise the rocks out of existence' ('Finisterre').
• The pheasant is 'brown as a leaf', a 'little cornucopia' ('Pheasant').
• Poppies are 'little hell flames', 'wrinkly and clear red, like the skin of a mouth | A mouth just bloodied', 'little bloody skirts' ('Poppies in July').
• The bee box is 'square as a chair', a 'midget's coffin' ('The Arrival of the Bee Box').
• Bees are like 'African hands, | Minute and shrunk for export' ('The Arrival of the Bee Box').
• A life of boring regularity is like a 'stuck record' ('The Times are Tidy').
• The baby's mouth opens 'clean as a cat's' ('Morning Song').
• Her crying is 'a handful of notes', which rise 'like balloons' ('Morning Song').

Plath attached great importance to colours, often identifying them with specific attributes. The repeated use of colour to suggest certain qualities links her poems to one another, giving added force to her meaning.

• Red signifies vitality, life force: the red poppies are animated, vital, unlike the colourless life of the narrator. The pheasant's vitality is envisaged largely through its vivid colouring.
• Green too signifies the positive, creativity, life force: the pheasant is red and green.
• Black is associated with death, anger, depression, aggression and destruction: the black headland that opens 'Finisterre' underlines the sinister mood.
• The depressed mood of the speaker in 'Black Rook in Rainy Weather' is conveyed through the repetition of black and the dominating presence of the rook.
• Surprisingly, white too is sinister: the white faces of the dead, the white mists in 'Finisterre'.

Humour

Running through her work is Plath's humour, sharp and ironic at times, at other times mocking and black. She uses ironic humour to challenge self-importance, to mock what she found ridiculous and pompous, and often to mock herself.

'The Times are Tidy' ridicules the politicians and the life of the 1950s. The smug satisfaction of this decade was all-pervasive. Plath ironically contrasts this era with that of dragon-slayers and witches (created by myth-makers). The rich cream – wealth and material possessions – is an ironic substitute for adventure and excitement. The inch-thick cream suggests fat cats 'creaming' it.

In 'Finisterre' the ironic description of the monument shows how remote formal religion is from the concerns of ordinary people. The giant statue of Our Lady of the Shipwrecked ignores the plight of the little people at her feet. The introduction of the shell-toy women makes the reader wonder whether they don't offer more comfort than their gigantic marble sister.

In 'Morning Song' she uses gentle self-irony, creating an amusing picture of the mother in the small details given: she stumbles from her bed, cow-like in her flowery nightdress.

'Mirror' opens with the mirror's unintentionally comic description of itself, giving the poem an ironic twist.

Plath's romanticism

Sylvia Plath was a lyric poet in the Romantic tradition. She wrote poems that drew on her own experience of life and explored a range of emotions from love and joy to terror and despair. Like the Romantics, she looked inwards rather than outwards; her experience is gauged by what she has lived through.

'Elm' is perhaps the most striking example of this. It is one of a number of poems she wrote around the same time, expressing agonising emotions. Some of these emotions were quite 'acceptable', provided they were not shown too openly: the grief and loneliness expressed in 'Elm', for example. However, less acceptable was the intensity with which she voiced them; it was considered 'over the top', too revealing. She also voiced the other, far less 'acceptable' feelings (those not talked about in public) here and in other poems: gleeful destructiveness and hatred ('Daddy') or intense resentment ('The Zoo-Keeper's Wife').

The writer and critic Joyce Carol Oates sees in these poems the seeds of Plath's eventual suicide.

> Her poems have that heart-breaking quality about them that has made Sylvia Plath our acknowledged Queen of Sorrows, the spokeswoman for our most private, most helpless nightmares; her poetry is as deathly as it is impeccable; it enchants us almost as powerfully as it must have enchanted her.

Not everyone agrees with this estimate, however. Janice Markey sees Plath's writings as life-affirming:

The enduring success and greatness of Plath's work lies in its universal appeal and in an innovative, effective presentation. Plath was the first writer in modern times to write about women with a new aggressive confidence and clarity, and the first to integrate this confidence and clarity in a sane, honest and compassionate vision.

Forming a personal view or response

1. What did you like best about Sylvia Plath's poems?
2. Choose one poem that you enjoyed and identify what appealed to you about it.
3. In what way is Plath different from the other poets on your course?
4. Plath's poetry reflects many facets of life. Which of these did you find most interesting?
5. What did you learn about Plath as a person from studying her poetry?
6. Is there anything you particularly like or dislike about her poetry?
7. Are the themes and issues in her poetry relevant to young people today?
8. Plath's unique and distinctive voice has often been praised. Do you find her voice – her way of writing, of expressing her ideas – unique?
9. Is there any particular image or description that remains with you from reading Plath's poetry? If so, identify why it impressed you.

Questions

1. 'Sylvia Plath created a language for herself that was utterly and startlingly original.' How true is this statement of the poems by Plath that you have studied?
2. Discuss Plath's treatment of nature in her poems. Support your discussion by quotation from or reference to the poems by her that you have studied.
3. 'Plath's poetry is a reflection of the era in which she lived.' Discuss this statement, supporting your discussion by quotation from or reference to the poems by Plath that you have studied.
4. Write a short essay on the aspects of Sylvia Plath's poems (content or style) that you found most interesting. Support your discussion by reference to or quotation from the poems by Plath that you have studied.
5. 'Sylvia Plath: a personal response'. Using this title, write an essay on the poetry of Plath, supporting your points by quotation from or reference to the poems on your course.
6. 'Sylvia Plath's taut language and startling images make her poems unique.' Discuss this statement, supporting your discussion by quotation from or reference to the poems by Plath that you have studied.

7. 'Sylvia Plath's poetry reflects a wide range of emotions.' Discuss this statement, concentrating on at least two different emotions that are evident in her poetry.
8. 'Despite the seriousness of her themes, Plath uses humour to devastating effect at times.' Discuss this statement, supporting your discussion by quotation from or reference to the poems by Plath that you have studied.
9. 'Recurring themes of loneliness, separation and pain mark the poetry of Sylvia Plath.' Discuss this statement, supporting your discussion by quotation from or reference to the poems by Plath that you have studied.
10. 'The use of brilliant and startling imagery gives a surreal quality to the poems of Sylvia Plath.' Discuss this statement, supporting your discussion by quotation from or reference to the poems by Plath that you have studied.

7 *Derek* MAHON

Mary Shine Thompson

Biographical note

Derek Mahon was born in Belfast in 1941. The previous year the German air force bombed the city as part of its offensive against Britain during the Second World War, and his earliest days were darkened by the shadow of hostilities. He grew up in the suburb of Glengormley on the north side of the city, near the Antrim Road. Glengormley was a mixed part of Belfast, home to a range of social classes, from working class to upper middle class. Mahon's father worked in the Harland and Wolff shipyard, his mother in the Flax Spinning Company, two industries central to the Northern economy of the period but whose significance was already waning.

His first memories of the war years are of sirens and blackouts and sleeping under the stairs during air raids. Recollections of ration-books give way to milk bars and images of Jews released from concentration camps as the war ended. From an early age much of his school holidays were spent cycling, often to the seaside town of Portrush and sometimes as far afield as Co. Donegal. He was a choirboy in St Peter's Church, and he says that this experience fostered his interest in language. While at school he discovered poetry, but that did not deter him from being a 'fairly nifty' scrum half. The cinema also attracted him, especially war films and *A Night to Remember,* the film about the sinking of the *Titanic* (built in Belfast). He remembers

> the exquisite pleasure of spending sunny afternoons at the cinema watching really bad films and emerging virtuous and refreshed. Other pastimes: golf (all the men in the family played golf), climbing the Cave Hill, learning the piano (which I have since forgotten), listening to 'The Goon Show' and Radio Luxembourg. Staring out my bedroom window at the rain. Spying on Eileen Boyd. Writing Dylan Thomas poems.

Even as a child he seems to have had a poetic sensibility and a capacity to see the world from an oblique, distinctive angle. Consider this scene:

> In the back garden there was a coal-shed in which Mahon kept his bicycle .... The little boy felt pity for the coal in the coal-shed and each

> time he closed the coal-shed door he felt regret, if not guilt. Why should all that glittering coal be shut away and live an imprisoned anti-social life of its own?

He attended the Royal Belfast Academical Institution; then, when he failed the eyesight test for ship's officer, he prepared to enter Trinity College, Dublin, where he studied French, English and philosophy; later he studied at the Sorbonne College, University of Paris. While a student at Trinity he struck up a friendship with Michael Longley, another Belfast poet, and began writing poetry in earnest.

On leaving university Mahon earned a living from freelance journalism (including a period as a feature-writer and reviewer for *Vogue,* the women's magazine), teaching, and radio and television work, and has been writer in residence in several universities. He has adapted for television the novels and short stories of twentieth-century writers, including Elizabeth Bowen and Jennifer Johnston. For years his literary reviews in the *Irish Times* attracted a regular following; always entertaining and energetic, they were humorous and insightful.

In addition to the Welsh poet Dylan Thomas, the first modern poets he encountered were Robert Graves, W. B. Yeats and, in his last year at school, Louis MacNeice, another Northern poet. The first poem he wrote that he considered successful is dedicated to MacNeice and is entitled 'In Carrowdore Churchyard', subtitled 'at the grave of Louis MacNeice'. He also acknowledges the influence of MacNeice's contemporary, W. H. Auden. He shares their erudition; like theirs, his poetry is urbane and lyrical and deals fluently with public matters. He also claims a cultural affinity with the writer Samuel Beckett, which relates to their shared Protestantism, and admires his mordant humour. Other poets he admires include the Americans Robert Lowell, Elizabeth Bishop and Hart Crane. French and Russian poetry also interests him, and he has been awarded numerous prizes for his translations; the best known of these are his versions of the work of the French poet Philippe Jaccottet.

Mahon has lived in Canada, the United States and England as well as in Kinsale. His relationship with his home place is complex. Not possessed of Séamus Heaney's sense of rootedness, he found it impossible to settle in the North of Ireland, yet he has admitted to feelings of guilt for having abandoned it. He is conscious of the limitations of the orderly, thrifty lifestyle of his people, but he refuses, as he says in one of his poems, 'to die their creature'. He recognises that the material affluence brought by industrialisation created its own coarseness, but that too is an aspect of his inheritance. As he writes in an early poem, 'Glengormley', 'By necessity, if not choice, I live here too.' Despite his reservations and ambivalence about Belfast, he is exasperated with people who do not accept that 'the Protestant suburbs of Belfast are part of Ireland.'

His poetry, therefore, issues from the cultural deprivation of his unionist background, but is not confined to it. He recognises that his urban middle-class background is culturally uninspiring and, unlike rural Ireland, has no mythology or symbolism that would nurture his imagination. The old mythologies that tell of the heroic deeds of giants and fighting men are irrelevant to his affluent community, which is preoccupied with talk of fitted carpets, central heating and automatic gear-change. If he has got a hidden myth it is what Terence Brown describes as 'the Protestant planter's historical myth of conquest, and careful, puritan self-dependence frozen to vicious, stupid bigotry which constricts personal identity'. So he creates his own symbols and myths, and his raw materials are the unresolved tensions and ironies of harsh, intolerant Belfast.

Mahon has rejected the idea that poetry should be socially relevant or that it should be politically engaged. 'Poems may appear to be about history or politics or autobiography, but [poetry] is essentially an artistic activity,' he wrote. For him it is about shape and form, about taking the formless and making it interesting. Notice the austerity of his poems: the few, precise details, the limited palette of colour, the controlled tone, the unyielding landscape, all fastidiously chosen. There is no slackness in the refined diction. However, that technical virtuosity must be matched by inspiration. 'You need soul, song and formal necessity, and you have to fly blind,' he has written. Living a life that pursues perfect form and technique is seductive, but it carries the danger of isolating the poet from the rest of humanity, and Mahon is aware of this. At his best, as the critic Séamus Deane has observed, Mahon balances his poetic nature with the demands the outside world makes on it. The early 'meta-poetic' pieces (that is, poems about poetry), such as 'Grandfather' and 'Ecclesiastes' and the poems that document personal, existential crises, such as 'Day Trip to Donegal', give way to the more engaged tone poems such as 'A Disused Shed in County Wexford'.

Mahon's interest in form is evident in his translations and versions of French and Greek classic drama. He has adapted French classical plays, including Molière's *High Time, The School for Husbands* and *The School for Wives* and Racine's *Phaedra,* as well as *The Bacchae,* after Euripides. As this interest in theatre might suggest, Mahon is visually aware, and he has also written several poems about painters and about specific pictures. Of these the most famous is his meditation on *Courtyards in Delft* by the Dutch artist Peter de Hooch, which celebrates the ordinary domestic lives of ordinary people. At their best, Mahon believes that poetry and painting can transform the ordinary into the marvellous. 'It's the most familiar things,' he writes, 'which exercise the strongest hold upon the imagination.'

You will encounter Mahon's early poetry in the selection here; the most recent poem included was published in 1985. In later poems, in particular in

'The Hudson Letter' and 'The Yellow Book', he has adopted a less tense, less minimalist style, using a more relaxed, contemporary conversational idiom, an informal frankness, longer lines and playful lists. The form of the verse letter has attracted him. Favoured by MacNeice and Auden, it has strongly autobiographical overtones and establishes an intimate bond with the reader. It is a form spacious enough to accommodate almost any subject. Many of Mahon's prose letters from New York were published in the *Irish Times*; his best-known verse letters include 'Beyond Howth Head', 'The Yaddo Letter', and 'The Hudson Letter'.

Nowadays Mahon lives in Dublin, and is a member of Aosdána. He is a retiring, reticent man who shuns publicity and has isolated himself from literary politics. In MacNeice's phrase, he has stayed 'outside the cliques, unbothered with the fashion', yet his work is highly acclaimed, especially by his fellow poets.

Principal volumes of poetry

Listed below are Derek Mahon's principal volumes of poetry. The volumes from which the poems on this course are taken are also shown. (Versions of some of these poems are included in more than one volume.)

Night-Crossing (1968)	'Grandfather'
	'Day Trip to Donegal' (stanza 3 omitted subsequently)
	'As God Is My Judge' (a version of 'After the Titanic')
Lives (1972)	'Ecclesiastes'
	'As It Should Be'
The Snow-Party (1975)	'A Disused Shed in County Wexford'
Poems, 1972–1978 (1979)	All the poems named above
	'The Chinese Restaurant in Portrush'
Courtyards in Delft (1981)	'Rathlin Island' (later 'Rathlin')
The Hunt by Night (1982)	'Rathlin Island'
Antarctica (1985)	'Antarctica'
	'Kinsale'
Selected Poems (1991)	All the poems named above
Selected Poems (1993) [A slightly different version, one new poem added, one deleted]	
The Hudson Letter (1995)	
The Yellow Book (1997)	
Collected Poems (1999)	All the poems named above

Grandfather

Text of poem: New Explorations Anthology page 406
[*Note: This poem is also prescribed for Ordinary Level 2008 exam*]

This poem is from Mahon's first collection, *Night-Crossing,* which also contains a poem about another relative, 'My Wicked Uncle', as well as poems about Belfast and Glengormley, the district in which he grew up. In this book he is marking out as his poetic territory industrialised, urban Belfast. By the time he writes it he has already left the North behind and is trying to come to terms with his background. Mahon's grandfather worked as a foreman-boilermaker on the *Titanic,* and he has written that he sometimes wonders whether his grandfather was responsible for the sinking of the ship.

FORM AND IMAGERY

Like Grandfather with his block of wood and box of nails, Mahon mischievously toys with his poetic apparatus, the sonnet form. A sonnet compresses a great deal of information and emotion into a conventional form, and makes considerable demands on a poet. It is generally defined as a fourteen-line poem, usually in *iambic pentameter* (containing lines with five feet, with the stress on the second of the two syllables in each foot), divided into units of eight and six lines. Among the most accomplished sonneteers were Petrarca and Shakespeare. Petrarca's rhyming scheme, which was adopted by Philip Sydney and other English poets of the sixteenth century, is *abba, abba, cde, cde* (or *cdc, dcd*); Shakespeare's was *abab, cdcd, efef, gg.* Mahon displays his virtuosity by taking elements from both forms and then making his own of them. His rhyming scheme alludes to both masters: *abab* in the first stanza is Shakespearean, *abba* in the second is Petrarchan and the sestet, *cde, ced,* is a variant of the Petrarchan form. (The rhymes themselves are playful, and sometimes require the reader to elide the mid-syllable '*r*': 'world' rhymes with 'rolled'; with a little sleight of hand the last syllable of 'childhood' is echoed in 'recovered').

Lines 2, 3, 5, 6, 9 and 14 open with the heavy stress of the *trochee* rather than the more predictable *iamb*. Where the *volta* (or 'turn' of the sonnet) lies is debatable. The expected place is after the caesura in line 9 (before 'But after dark'); however, until the next caesura (before 'Each night'), Grandfather remains the character we see in the octet, now thumping about in great boots where earlier he was banging round the house. Only near the end of line 11 do we discern a shift in the tone of the poem, as he bolts the door against the future. So it could be argued that the volta comes before 'Each night'. The final line is symmetrical in structure: its second part mirrors the first and puts Grandfather at its centre. The *spondees* (successive stressed syllables) 'he' and 'him' serve to emphasise his achievement.

The poem sustains throughout the image of a man who has learnt his craft and now, withdrawn from the world, uses his skill for his own pleasure. It no longer serves any useful purpose. The image of this old craftsman might be seen as a metaphor for the poet as self-possessed craftsman.

This early poem establishes Mahon's formal standards. It displays his technical expertise and his playfulness with form.

Day Trip to Donegal

Text of poem: New Explorations Anthology page 408

This poem comes from Mahon's first book, *Night-Crossing* (1968). It was republished in *Poems, 1962–1978,* in which he dropped a stanza and made four verbal changes. He made two additional adjustments before including it in *Selected Poems* (1991). This repeated revision suggests both that the poem is an important element in Mahon's work and also that he has experienced difficulty in capturing his precise meaning.

The excluded stanza is as follo

How could we hope to make them understand?
Theirs is a sea-mind, mindless upon land
And dead. Their systematic genocide
(Nothing remarkable that millions died)
To us is a necessity
For ours are land-minds, mindless as the sea.

Here the speaker draws our attention to the huge gap in understanding between human and fish minds. We are not moved by their slaughter: in fact we see it as a necessity. Defining fishing as 'systematic genocide' also draws our attention to the metaphorical possibilities of the image. Thousands of human beings too have been systematically murdered, because others regarded it as necessary and failed to recognise their humanity. In this respect the poem's preoccupations resemble those of another poem on the course, 'A Disused Shed in County Wexford', but in the latter poem they are amplified and intensified.

In the original version of the poem this stanza went some way towards explaining the speaker's profound desolation in the last two stanzas. Without it, the reader must struggle to understand and articulate the unspeakable agony of another species, the dying fish in stanza 2.

Form and imagery

The poem takes the form of five six-line stanzas, each composed of three rhyming couplets, primarily in pentameter. The presentation of the central images is symmetrical. In stanza 2 the writhing fish, violently plucked from the water that is their element, are contorted in attitudes of heartbreak and agony. This image finds its echo in the fourth stanza, where the speaker now is suffering as the sea enters his consciousness. The contrast between the first and last stanzas is pointed. First the speaker approaches the shore; at the close he is far out to sea. He is busy, purposeful, confident at the beginning, but later the bustle is replaced by uncertainty. Stanza 3, at the heart of the poem, has the poet returning to his familiar urban home. Images of movement abound: towards Co. Donegal, back home, and then into the uncharted spaces of the troubled mind, whose metaphor is the sea.

After the Titanic

Text of poem: New Explorations Anthology page 411

[*Note: This poem is also prescribed for Ordinary Level 2008 exam*]

A version of this poem was first published under the title 'As God Is My Judge' and signed 'Bruce Ismay', and another as 'Bruce Ismay's Soliloquy'. The speaker is Bruce Ismay (1892–1937), manager of the White Star Line, owner of the *Titanic*. He was one of the relatively few men to have escaped from the sinking *Titanic*, and he was strongly criticised for allegedly failing to help the drowning passengers.

The *Titanic*, built in Belfast in the Harland and Wolff shipyard, was named after the Titans, the gigantic gods of Greek mythology who were the offspring of heaven and earth; the word 'titanic' hence came to mean colossal, and indeed this ship was immense. According to Ismay it was also 'the latest thing in the art of ship building'. However, it sank dramatically when it collided with an iceberg on its first voyage to America in 1912, with the loss of 1,500 lives – the greatest peacetime loss of life in maritime history.

This grim catastrophe was a mortal blow to the self-confidence of its age; it quickened the sense of impending doom already widespread at the turn of the century. The period since the sinking of the *Titanic* could be seen as a phase of post-history. Progress and technology no longer offer a blueprint for the future, and neither do human beings: their self-absorption precludes optimism.

The mythology of the *Titanic* is intimately linked to Mahon's past, as several members of his family worked in the shipyards, and his grandfather in fact worked on building the ship.

Diction

Notice how often the personal pronoun 'I' or 'me' and the possessive adjective 'my' are used, accentuating Ismay's preoccupation with self. Every sentence of the poem relates to him. His address is direct, a series of mainly short statements that testify to his life after the loss of the Titanic. There are two relatively long sentences, 'As I sat …' and 'The shower …' One depicts graphically the chaos and turmoil of the sinking, with a catalogue of items incongruously thrown together; the other describes its aftermath and Ismay's long drugged isolation.

The diction of the final two sentences contrasts strongly with those preceding them. 'My poor soul | Screams' and 'heart | Breaks loose and rolls down like a stone' seem hyperbolic, exaggerated, out of character for Ismay and removed from the tone of the earlier address. Are you convinced that they express genuine emotion? By contrast, the unadorned admonition of the final line strikes a dry note, world-weary, perhaps even cynical.

INTERTEXTUALITY

The term 'intertextuality' relates to the ways in which texts connect with each other. Many poems contain echoes of other texts, and these echoes take a variety of forms. Some quote directly from other poems, some are parodies (humorously imitating and exaggerating other texts), and some poems have similar structures to others. Take the example of the television programme 'The Simpsons'. It makes a wide range of intertextual allusions: to other television programmes and films, to stories, to the discourses of politics and advertising, and so on.

Let us take an example from poetry. Séamus Heaney's poem 'Casualty' has as its central character a fisherman who becomes a heroic example, a man with an independent mind who pays for his independence with his life. Our understanding of this figure is enhanced when we recall the idealised fisherman in a famous poem by W. B. Yeats, 'The Fisherman'. This is one type of intertextual link that exists between Heaney's poem and Yeats's. The same poem, 'Casualty', describes how the Parachute Regiment of the British army killed thirteen people in Derry in 1972: 'PARAS THIRTEEN, the walls said, | BOGSIDE NIL.' This is another example of intertextuality. The poem appropriates graffiti, which in turn adopted the idiom of football scores, to summarise the killing; by using that language it suggests that for some, killing is merely a game.

Some critics believe that all texts are woven out of other texts, whether the writers themselves are aware of it or not. After all, nearly all the words, phrases and images a poet (or a novelist, dramatist or journalist) employs have previously existed in other literary works. A new poem conveys meanings or traces from those former texts that it echoes. So we must look beyond the formal limits of a poem if we are to explore its full import.

INTERTEXTUALITY IN 'AFTER THE TITANIC'

The last line of 'After the Titanic' links it to the Book of Lamentations from the Old Testament, which is an outpouring of grief at the destruction of Jerusalem. The Christian churches have used it as an expression of generalised sorrow. Its anonymous speaker is one 'who has seen affliction', and through this persona the reasons why the city has fallen are explored. It ends with an appeal to God for help. A parallel is implied between Ismay (whom this poem does not name) and the Book of Lamentations' anonymous speaker.

This intertextual reference widens the scope of the poem in several directions. It directs us to examine the cause of so great a tragedy, comparable to the fall of Jerusalem. The contrast between Ismay's self-absorption and the empathy of the speaker in the Book of Lamentations is notable. It also implies the perversion of religion that has been a feature of Northern history, which is echoed in 'Ecclesiastes'.

Tone

Ismay, the reviled outcast, stresses that he has seen affliction, and he identifies with the Biblical speaker. For the reader aware of how the negligence of his company contributed to the disaster, this is ironic. The irony is again evident when he compares himself to 'any | Hero', and is intensified by the puns 'I turned to ice' and 'my costly | life'; the speaker seems unaware of it.

Metre

In 'lament metre', the form associated with the Book of Lamentations, the second of two lines is shorter than the first. Mahon has alternated *hexameters* and *tetrameters* (lines with six and four stresses), so approximating this form.

Ecclesiastes

Text of poem: New Explorations Anthology page 414

This poem was published in 1972 in the collection called *Lives*. At this time the violence that had begun with civil rights marches in 1969 was increasing, and the unionist and nationalist communities were increasingly distrustful of each other. In this poem the speaker does not shirk from describing the intolerance and extremism to which some of his people were prone: indeed he recognises the tendency within himself to prefer language to love. He addresses his poem, which consists of a series of exhortations, to a preacher or *ecclesiastes*. However, the preacher's love and command of impressive diction mirrors the speaker's own, and so he is implicitly criticising his own tendencies.

Imagery

The poem is a tissue of images of darkness and bleakness: the cold silence of Belfast, 'cold' hearts, the black garb of the preacher, which is also the colour of mourning, the deprivation, the dark. The only depiction of colour and freedom of personal choice is to be found in the 'red | bandana and stick, that banjo,' but they are swiftly buried. Only the rhetoric is expansive. The speaker shows his awareness of rhetorical devices – the repetition of words and forms of speech, the lists, the persuasive tone. The seductiveness of language is placed in opposition to human values, to understanding and forgetting.

Mahon dexterously weaves Biblical and other religious images into the poem. References to afflatus (divine inspiration), puritans, locusts and wild honey, dank churches and fierce zeal combine to evoke a soulless religiosity.

Mood

The mood is profoundly satirical. The portrait of the preacher is grotesque and exaggerated but still close to the real, and the poet is intolerant of his limitations. He despairs of the ideal way of life that is warmed by 'the heat | of the world,' and he relies on the reader to compare his way of life with an ideal.

Tone

The tone of the poem varies. Declarative and exhortatory to begin with, it urges the preacher forward. It is transparently ironic when it charges him to bury his bandana, to close one eye and be king. There is an irony too in the repeated calls on God – not the God of love and compassion but a figure constructed out of a narrow, black imagination. These are not the poet's values. However, this call is followed by a pronouncement in a conflicting mood. It seems all too likely that the preacher will recruit followers in the housing estates, and so there is a trace of irony in this statement. The Book of Ecclesiastes in the Old Testament lends its title to this poem, and its scepticism and dry wit inform the poem.

The tone of this poem might be described as parodic. Parody – the humorous exaggerated imitation of a style – is a 'knowing' form, highly critical of its subject, which it attacks indirectly. 'Ecclesiastes' mimics the preacher's style and, in the process, deflates it, exposing his and his people's pretensions and lack of self-awareness.

Structure

The poem takes the form of one paragraph, which consists of five sentences. The first, second and fifth whip up enthusiasm with a direct address: you could grow to love this way of life, you could punish yourself, you could promise the people nothing. The third sentence exhorts the preacher to 'be king'; the fourth reminds him that he has a credulous following. The repetition of the sentence form unifies the address and increases its intensity. 'God' is strategically placed at the beginning and end of the poem, and 'feel' and 'speak' occur right in the centre, as if to alert the reader to the poem's main concerns. The long vowel sounds of the occasional rhymes ('wiles and smiles', 'fierce zeal') and of the many assonantal line endings ('streets', 'heat', 'zeal', 'bleak', 'heaped') are emphatic and evoke the preacher's uncompromising tone.

As It Should Be

Text of poem: New Explorations Anthology page 416

The poem, published in 1972, is based on the story of Denis Johnston's play *The Moon in the Yellow River,* first produced in 1931. The play is set in 1927 and concerns the building of a new hydroelectric scheme. When a revolutionary, Blake, tries to blow up the generator an officer of the Free State army, Lanigan, shoots him. The persona of the poem is a spokesman for the Free State, which condoned the killing of Blake. In the poem the revolutionary is shot among lorries beside an electricity generator – monuments to progress. Material improvement comes at a price, in this case brutal killing.

Though Johnston's play is based on a fictional incident, the Free State government did indeed quell republican agitation by shooting prisoners, with little legal or moral justification. As one of the characters in the play comments, the birth of a nation is never immaculate. There is little room in the modern world, it seems, for those who cannot or will not adapt to progress. The play also questions whether industrialising Ireland, and violating the landscape in the process, is desirable.

The play was revived in the Abbey Theatre, Dublin, in 1971, about the same time that the poem was written. Denis Johnston, in his author's note for the theatre programme, remarked that

> with the passage of time the play has become not less but more up to date. Its concern is what is now not an Irish but a universal problem – Industrialisation versus the Human Race.

This conflict has a particular resonance for Mahon, whose roots in industrialised Belfast alerted him to the limitations of material progress.

The title of the play came from Ezra Pound's image of a drunken poet, Li Po, who grasps at illusory ideals and was drowned while trying 'to embrace the moon in the Yellow River'. This image comes to symbolise Blake's hopeless romantic dream. The story suggests that the world of the imagination (in this case allowing oneself believe in a reflection) is perilous. If society is to prosper, people like this character and Blake from the play must not be allowed to flourish.

The poem deliberately imports aspects of these two stories. Its first stanza is a summary of the action of the play; the second contains an overt reference to both the play and the story. By doing this it stresses that its full significance must be found beyond the poem's own formal boundaries. Knowledge of its intertextual references (its relationship to other texts) is essential, and it enriches our reading of the poem.

Preoccupations

This poem consists of four self-contained stanzas of varying line lengths. The first stanza is five lines long; the remaining three contain three lines. The extended first stanza enacts the pursuit and murder of the unnamed offender and contains opposing images. The west of Ireland, where the hunt takes place, has traditionally been associated with natural energy and ancient spirituality and has been the setting of much Irish literature. Describing it as 'starlit' adds to its romantic ambience. This serene, unspoilt rural landscape is juxtaposed with images of power and progress – the lorries and the electricity generator. The relatively long second line and its list of places evoke the wide spaces of the countryside, and this contrasts with the 'blind' yard: it is closed up, concealed. We are also alerted to the speaker's lack of understanding, through the pun on the word 'blind'.

In the second stanza the speaker dismisses the romantic ideals of the murdered man with a caustic reference to the Johnston play that his own story re-enacts and to Li Po. Note that he uses a euphemism, 'departure', to refer to cowardly murder. The body is unceremoniously cast into the water, in broad daylight. The speaker concludes emphatically that ridding the community of people such as his victim – a dreamer and a romantic – will ensure his children's happiness. The cold, curt certainty of the last stanza brooks no disagreement.

In another poem published at the same time as 'As It Should Be', entitled 'Rage for Order', Mahon has a character pronounce: 'Now watch me | As I make history, | Watch as I tear down | To build up.' This speaker too is a maker of history, believing that compulsion and suppression will build a better world. He believes that any means are acceptable if they serve his objective.

Irony

The poem is full of ironies, but the speaker appears blithely unaware of them. This type of irony – where the reader (or the audience) is conscious of the full import of a speaker's words – is called *dramatic irony*. The speaker's statement that 'the air blows softer since his departure' implies that violent killing can lead to a milder, more benign atmosphere, and he sees no contradiction there. He elevates 'method' over human life. In his rage for order, he is blind to the price of progress.

Though the no-nonsense tone gives the impression of straight talk, the speaker deludes himself by using terms like 'departure' and 'tide-burial' to dress up the brutal truth. The ringing tones of his address expose the hollowness of his values. The poem leads the reader to reflect on the dangers to society of people who speak in absolute terms. It draws our attention to the precariousness of civility, and so it functions like an address from an Old Testament prophet, railing against the arrogant certainties of humanity. Its subtle rebuke of its readers might be compared with that of other poems on the course, such as 'After the Titanic' and 'Day Trip to Donegal'.

A Disused Shed in County Wexford

Text of poem: New Explorations Anthology page 418

This is Derek Mahon's best-known and perhaps finest poem. John Banville believes it will outlive us all; the critic Declan Kiberd remarked in 1982 that it was 'arguably the finest poem to come out of Ireland in the past twenty years'.

The poem was inspired by an imagined anecdote about a forgotten shed in the grounds of a burnt-out hotel somewhere in Co. Wexford. Mahon dedicated it to his friend J. G. Farrell, author of the novel *Troubles*. The book and the poem evoke the period of the Civil War (1922–23), when British rule had ended and Ireland began a long period of cultural and economic isolation, which ended fifty years later. However, it refuses to be limited to this circumstance and reads as a meditation on injustice, lost and wasted lives, and our human fear of death, decay and silence.

Preoccupations

The poem begins 'Even now', suggesting that even though traumatic events have overtaken us there are still places where a thought might grow, where a new beginning is possible, but they are places abandoned and forgotten by humans. Among these is a disused shed in Co. Wexford, where, unknown to the world, a forgotten and unlikely community of *anthropomorphic* mushrooms (that is, possessing the attributes of human beings) lives and dies in the confined universe of a shed, disengaged from history. The only source of light, the sun in their sky, is the keyhole, and they strain towards it. Though they yearn for another life, they endure their anguish in patience and silence.

The third stanza tells how they have lived thus since Civil War days, since the mycologist (expert on mushrooms) – possibly a metaphor for deposed rulers – departed. Now their world slowly disintegrates.

The fourth stanza creates a surreal image of the misery of captivity, with those strong enough bullying their way towards the light, and the weaklings reduced to inarticulate groans. Their longing for liberation has been thwarted for so long that now they are left with only the posture of desire. Deprived of light and freedom, they have become contorted, deformed and frail, like 'triffids' or moonmen. They are hardly prepared for life outside their prison. They silently beg the tourist passer-by to do something for them, to save them, not to shut the door on them.

The achievement of the poem

Though the poem is set in a particular place, it transcends its context. Its references to the sites of holocaust and natural disasters extend its scope to include all victims silenced by history, the disappeared masses, the nameless exterminated multitudes everywhere and in every era. At one level it may be read as a comment on the fate of those loyal to Britain after the foundation of the Irish state. Mahon himself has related it to the decay of the culture of the Big House, a subject popular with Anglo-Irish writers. Equally it may be interpreted as a reflection on victims of the holocaust (the reference to Treblinka invites such a response) and all those who are beyond redemption politically and psychologically. It charges those who can record the horror, personified here as tourists with cameras, to act on behalf of the less fortunate. However, the victims may find little consolation in this action. 'We too had our lives to live,' the mushrooms say – 'had,' not 'have'. It is too late to change the legacy of their past. Only the posture of desire and expectancy remains.

Tone

One aspect of the achievement of this poem is its complex tone. It is a public meditation conducted in a vein just short of despair. As one critic, Seán O'Brien, put it, 'it takes the weary facts – death, decay, fear, solitude – and reanimates them for the reader's contemplation.' It projects its desolation onto inanimate objects: echoes are trapped and doors lack confidence. The sense of loss and betrayal felt by the voiceless mushrooms is made explicit, as is the horror of their daily life.

However, the presence of another figure, the cameraman, adds an additional dimension to the poem. This watcher is nominated the agent of change. He has the capacity to effect some limited transformation, and so invested in him is the lingering, diminishing hope of the silenced masses. His presence generates regret for the lives of quiet desperation. He and the mushrooms are irrevocably separated – by their silence, by his power to change their lives.

Above the mood of regret, however, hovers a strain of celebration. The power of art, the poem's capacity to represent the mushrooms' plight, is expressly commended. By presenting us with exemplary images and the best words in the best order, a poem becomes an articulate witness, a space where a thought might grow. However, the poem is also conscious of the limitations of poetry and the fact that it has its own, formal agenda. Note the use of 'light meter', at once a piece of photographic equipment and a pun on 'light metre', a type of airy, insubstantial verse rhythm. Poetry has its own priorities – it is light metre – and may seem frivolous to sufferers. The poet recognises this. Indeed the poem's formal excellence, the subtlety of the rhyme and assonance, the discipline and sophistication of the ten–line stanzas and the vigour of its language, are a world away from the 'naïve labours' of the mushrooms. The poet accepts the implicit rebuke.

The Chinese Restaurant in Portrush

Text of poem: New Explorations Anthology page 422

In the second stanza we are given a hint about how this poem might be approached. Here a yacht hoisting its sail becomes 'an ideogram on sea-cloud'. The phrase may be read in two ways. It suggests the visual image of a Chinese character set against a background of sea and cloud. However, the phrase could also mean a character or letter that represents the concept of sea-cloud, just as the phrase 'a discussion on school' could be said to explore the concept of school. 'An ideogram on sea-cloud' is an image inscribed with meaning beyond that which it articulates. This poem works obliquely, offering the reader a succession of ideograms containing the merest traces of meaning. The reader is then obliged to work on making sense of those traces.

'The Chinese Restaurant in Portrush' calls forth the idea of home, but home itself is either unattainable or a dream, or both. The word itself appears only at the poem's end, and within the context of a Chinese emigrant's dream. The evocation takes three forms. First is the seaside town of Portrush itself. On this balmy day it is at its best, the weather temperate, the wintry atmosphere giving way to good humour. There is even a touch of frivolity in the window-shopping gulls. This is prelapsarian Portrush (that is, as it might have been before the fall of humankind). And yet the dozing wolfhound in the foreground of the stanza is a reminder of old, dormant mythologies. The past is only temporarily obscured. The openness and welcome implicit in the open doors is a phenomenon rare enough to be remarked upon. Portrush is 'as it might have been,' and the poem's use of the conditional past tense underlines the nostalgic awareness that it cannot ever be Eden. There is an added irony in setting a reflection on home in a tourist resort, the site of brief, transient stays.

With the opening of the second stanza we realise that our focus has been directed by a speaker who is seated beneath a framed photograph of Hongkong, home to a Chinese restaurateur. The photograph, like the image of home framed within the previous stanza, is also fixed, idealised. When this poem was written, Hongkong was a British colony, its political status loosely comparable to that of Northern Ireland. Home for the Chinese restaurateur is therefore a complex entity, the reality removed from the idyllic tourist image captured in a photograph.

The arrangement of the two men in the second stanza creates a complex dynamic. While the speaker is under the photograph of the restaurateur's 'home', the eye of the Chinese man is directed towards Co. Donegal. It is bathed in 'the light of heaven', and it is seen across the watery divide of the Foyle estuary. The subtle logic of the poem's symmetry suggests that Co. Donegal too may be an idealised representation of home, as illusory and seductive an image as Portrush without its tourists. This reading is further underlined by the proximity of the words 'Donegal' and 'home' near the end of the poem.

Governing these images is the wry presence of the speaker, who is aware of the incongruity of his cosmopolitan meal. He is set apart from this place, which he might have made his home, by his analytical, probing eye. To this urbane, cosmopolitan speaker 'home' is an ideogram, a concept that cannot be adequately articulated. It belongs to the realm of the 'might have been'.

Mahon has identified the north Antrim coast, on which Portrush is situated, as his 'home landscape' – not, as might be predicted, the Belfast in which he grew up. His speaker's affection for the place is evident, yet he is a 'tourist in his own country', to borrow MacNeice's phrase.

As displaced as the restaurateur, the speaker maintains a critical distance, which enables him to reflect on the nature of home. Home is a romantic topic and even in this poem is imbued with yearning and nostalgia reminiscent of the work of a poet such as the German romantic Holderlin. However, there is a significant difference in the way Mahon and romantic poets treat the topic of home. Whereas romantic poets tried to reconcile their inner vision and outer experience, the probing, unsentimental presence of the speaker in 'The Chinese Restaurant' compels us to face the reality that home, whether it is viewed in a national, local or personal sense, is utopia, literally 'no place'. The poem therefore is a *valediction*: it bids farewell to the glimpse of the ideal homes it offers. As the critic John Kerrigan remarked, Mahon uses Romantic rhetoric to realise emptiness.

Rathlin

Text of poem: New Explorations Anthology page 424

(Early editions of this poem, published in 1981 and 1982, were entitled 'Rathlin Island'.)

The remains of ring-forts, underground passages and a fortified castle on Rathlin Island suggest something of its besieged past. Danish invaders ransacked it in 973; but the worst atrocity it endured was the slaughter of the entire population of six hundred people by Walter Devereux, Earl of Essex, in 1575. For years after this atrocity the island remained uninhabited. The slaughter, like the more conclusive Battle of Kinsale, signalled the decline of independent Irish power – the end of one kind of history.

IMAGERY

The first stanza indicates how the sounds of nature gradually erode the memory of the island's barbarous history. Now the engine of the boat carrying the tourists to the island shatters the dream-time, the sense that this is a place outside ordinary, chronological time. The island is characterised by a lack of boundaries; the haze and the limitless ocean create a blank space, punctuated only by a sleepy, slow-moving boat. Mahon repeats a phrase here from another poem, 'The Last of the Fire Kings': this place is 'through with history', unlike the housing estates of the mainland that harbour bombs.

What sordid tale of history has Rathlin forgotten? A tale of the gratuitous massacre of innocents in 1575, as one chapter of the past, was savagely cut short. Rathlin embodies the 'infancy of our race,' the primal act of violence from which the present destruction ensued. The meditation on Rathlin's past leads the speaker to speculate on whether the future resembles the violent past.

MOOD AND DICTION

Rathlin Island is a metaphor for universal desolation, and the mood of the poem is apocalyptic. It senses the end of civilisation. We are in this one place, but we could be anywhere. The world seems destined to replay the violence of the past. While Rathlin Island may be 'through with history', the townspeople are not; the bombs in the housing estates could shake off their drowsiness and burst into action at any moment. The speaker's bleak insight into the future is hinted at in the pun on the word 'report': it means a loud noise, the explosive crack of a rifle shot, say, as well as an account or record of events. The reference to the 'amazed' birds forces us to look at the event from their perspective, and so we are jolted into confronting our complacent understanding of past and future. The shearwater's cry, the sound that dominates the opening lines, also commands the end.

ASSONANCE

The skilful, inventive assonance and rhyme underline the speaker's concerns. The slant or off-stress rhyme of 'shearwater' and 'motor' draws attention to their incompatibility. The assonantal echo of the final syllable of 'history' in 'repeats' and 'sea' creates its own story – that history repeats itself, giving land back to the dominion of the sea.

Antarctica

Text of poem: New Explorations Anthology page 427
[*Note: This poem is also prescribed for Ordinary Level 2008 exam*

This poem was published in a collection entitled *Antarctica* in 1986. It relates to an incident that took place during Captain Robert Scott's third expedition to Antarctica in 1911–12. His plan was to be the first person to reach the South Pole. Eventually, and after much hardship and mismanagement, he and three others, including Captain Lawrence Oates (1880–1912), attained their goal, only to find that an expedition led by a Norwegian, Roald Amundsen, had succeeded just three weeks before them.

Scott's return journey was dogged by misfortune. The expedition's dogs and horses perished, food was in short supply, and temperatures reached as low as –50°. One member of the team, Edgar Evans, suffered a bad fall and died a fortnight later.

Oates's frostbitten feet became gangrenous, and he begged the others to abandon him. They refused. To avoid being a burden, he walked out into the night, to his certain death, with the words 'I am just going outside and may be some time.' A cross was placed near the spot where he left the tent, inscribed *A very gallant gentleman.* The other three struggled to within a mere eleven miles of their base camp, where plentiful provisions awaited them, but then a blizzard struck. Their bodies were found in their tent eight months later.

Critical commentary

Ostensibly this poem is about Lawrence Oates, a member of Scott's failed expedition to the South Pole. His existential drama is played out against a backdrop of an uninhabitable empty space, devoid of cultural or geographical definition. As a free and responsible agent, he determines his own future, with none of society's structures to support him. He chooses certain death in an Antarctic blizzard rather than be a burden to his fellow-explorers.

The opening stanza sets the scene, as Oates departs from their shelter, and introduces two refrains that are repeated throughout the poem. Of these, the first consists of Oates's understatement as he goes to his death; the other is the speaker's judgment on such a deed. Stanzas 2 and 3 enable the reader to identify with Oates as he loses his sense of direction and is lost for ever in the freezing conditions. The final three stanzas elaborate on the speaker's statement that there is at 'the heart of the ridiculous, the sublime.' At once absurd and noble, Oates comes to embody the foolishness and the greatness that only human beings are capable of. The poem's speaker dismisses the argument that Oates's suicide was a criminal act, seeing his solitary death instead as a catalyst for change in humankind. The word 'enzyme', used to describe Oates, is a scientific term meaning a living organism that can cause another to change but is not changed itself.

This poem is evidence that Oates's death did transform the engagement of others with the world. Though there was for him no glimmer of light in the darkness on that fateful night, his quiet, dignified departure becomes a beacon to those, like the poem's speaker, who know the tale. The poem therefore celebrates those moments of heroism of which humans are capable. And yet it repeatedly suggests that Oates's gesture is as ridiculous as it is sublime.

Form

The poem is a marvel of tight construction and control. It is an example of a form known as the *villanelle,* a nineteen-line poem that follows a strict pattern and in its original pastoral form contained a refrain. It is considered a particularly demanding form in English. (Dylan Thomas's 'Do Not Go Gently into the Dark Night' is one well-known villanelle.)

Consisting of five three-line stanzas and a concluding quatrain, 'Antarctica' accommodates two refrains. Both appear in the first and last stanzas and alternate in the remaining stanzas. Juxtaposed in this way, the refrains interrogate each other. Mahon retains the *aba* rhyme throughout 'Antarctica', except for the last stanza, where it is *abaa.* Some line endings are *homonymic* (pronounced the same but spelt differently), such as 'know' and 'no'; this kind of rhyme is called *rime riche.* Others are expanded homonyms: 'no' and 'snow', or 'crime' and 'rime'.

Mahon takes few liberties with the discipline. There are some off-rhymes (rhymes in which the stress does not fall on the rhyming syllable in one word); examples are 'pantomime' and 'time', or 'vertigo' and snow'. In each case the stress is on the first syllable of the first word here and not on the rhymed last syllable.

This formality of 'Antarctica' may be interpreted in conflicting ways. It may reflect the speaker's view that the sublime inhabits the ordinary. Seen in this manner, the discipline of the villanelle invests the event described – Oates's death – with a ritual and ceremonial importance. However, the element that is paralleled by the ostentatious style may be the emptiness of Oates's gesture, and not its grandeur. There is also an irony in creating a wasteland Antarctic setting within a pastoral form (the villanelle) that connotes a romantic, idealised country life, idyllic and harmonious. The tone of the poem, therefore, is unstable, and this adds to its complexity.

Kinsale

Text of poem: New Explorations Anthology page 430

Kinsale is important from the point of view of Ulster's history, because in the battle fought there in 1601 Queen Elizabeth's soldier, Mountjoy, routed the Ulster chieftains Hugh O'Neill and Hugh O'Donnell. This defeat signalled the end of native rule in Ireland and the decline of native Irish civilisation. Ulster, which had been the most resistant province to English rule, was colonised by

Scots and English settlers and became in time the most Anglicised. Kinsale, therefore, is the site of cultural and political failure and, like Rathlin Island, is a post-historical place.

Nonetheless the mood of this poem is buoyant, even celebratory. It captures the existential joy of that moment when tragedy is excluded and optimism prevails. The rain acts as a metaphor for darkness, deliberation, and the laborious probing (the 'deep-delving') that characterised the past, with its institutionalised religion and dull poverty (the spire and bogland). The images associated with 'today' contrast sharply with the almost sinister brooding rain. Now, clear skies and colourful leisure-boats dominate this site of former failure. Roof slates, normally grey-blue, radiate the lustre of the blue sky. 'Tinkling' and 'dancing' are the present participles that replace the more sluggish 'browsing', with its connotations of feeding off the people. Windows – the lens through which we see the world – emit and reflect light and optimism. Further optimism may be adduced from the repetition of the personal pronoun 'we', with its implicit suggestion of common purpose and community.

However, a certain caution is implicit in the expression 'a future forbidden to no-one', with which the poem ends. An enabling future is not forbidden, but it is not guaranteed either. It has yet to be created. Furthermore, the 'we' of the poem 'contemplate' shining windows, that is, consider the idea, mull over or entertain the notion of the future, rather than create it. Finally, any realist knows (and we must credit the speaker with such knowledge) that rain ceases only temporarily in Ireland. The logic of the metaphor suggests that 'we' will encounter more darkness in the future.

Several of Mahon's other poems evoke images of unlikely places where future civilisations might evolve (as he writes in 'A Disused Shed in County Wexford', 'even now there are places where a thought might grow'): in the hub-cap of a wheel, a disused shed in Co. Wexford, or in Kinsale. In a poem entitled 'Christmas in Kinsale', published in 1997, as the speaker takes out the rubbish on Christmas morning he is conscious that new life can evolve even in such post-historical times and places. The measured optimism of both these poems about Kinsale confronts failure and limitation and yet avoids despair.

Overview

Mahon's poetry does not flinch from exposing human inadequacy, especially, but not exclusively, the pathology of the Northern Protestant people. Oates's heroic gesture in 'Antarctica', the naked aggression in 'As It Should Be', the narrow bigotry of 'Ecclesiastes', and Bruce Ismay's self-absorption in 'After the Titanic' – all are testaments to human shortcomings. However, while Mahon deplores the 'stiff rhetorical intransigence' of his people (as Séamus Deane puts it), he also sympathises with them in their isolation and fading presence.

Poetry is essentially an artistic activity for him: it is more concerned with shape and form than with content or politics. Like the great modernist poets T. S. Eliot and W. B. Yeats, he takes pleasure in and is consoled by the order and formality of poetry – an order that is notably absent from many of the lives he describes. This might suggest that his poetry is removed from everyday concerns, and indeed he sometimes yearns for what he calls poetry's 'palace of porcelain' – a place or state that is elegant, decorative and decorous.

However, this desire is only one of the warring instincts within him. Mahon has also suggested that poetry is capable of improving humankind. He has invoked Shelley's claim that poetry enlarges the circumference of the imagination, which is 'the great instrument of moral good'. Looked at in this way, poetry is an unacknowledged legislator of the world, not isolated from it.

In the opinion of one critic, Gerald Dawe, Mahon's primary concern is to understand the imagination and find a place for it in the modern world. Mahon himself maintains that poetry can contribute to the creation of a life that is nearer the ideal. 'A good poem is a paradigm [model] of good politics,' he has written – 'of people talking to each other, with honest subtlety, at a profound level. It is a light to lighten the darkness.'

Séamus Deane remarks that Mahon's poetry 'expresses a longing to be free from history'; but his poems on civility and barbarity (the greatest of which is probably 'A Disused Shed in County Wexford') contradict that longing. He has had good reason to yearn to be 'through with history', since he belongs to a country that has violently enacted its versions of history, with deadly effect. However, history is not his only preoccupation. His themes also include the age-old conflict between the individual and his community. In Mahon's case, poetry is also especially a statement about what it means to be a poet today, distanced from, but implicated in, the historical world. So he does not escape from history; instead it is incorporated or woven into the oasis of peace and aesthetic order that is each poem.

The poems in this selection are sufficient evidence of Mahon's superb poetic technique and the seriousness of his subject matter. What are the characteristics of his style? He displays a combination of brevity and detail, and this is achieved with a cadenced precision. How effective and economical a description is 'a writhing glimmer of fish' in 'Day Trip to Donegal', for example! In addition, his elegant and playful rhymes and adroit control of assonance are impressive. He endorses traditional poetic forms, such as the sonnet and the villanelle, and yet subverts them. His pared-down vernacular idiom is combined with a prodigious learning, which Mahon wears lightly and which makes an oblique and understated appearance in the poems.

The voices of his poems – and they are many – are sophisticated yet possessed of a heartfelt, if weary, empathy with their subjects. They are often still, small voices, educated but understated, learned but not pedantic, always self-aware and often self-mocking. They are the voices of men of conscience who are implicated in the guilt of being human beings. (Women figure only peripherally or by implication in the poems that are on the course.) Their agonised intelligence is often close to despair, but they still go on. The critic Terence Brown uses the phrase 'terminal pathos' to describe this distinctive note in Mahon's poetry, which can also be found, incidentally, in the work of Samuel Beckett. Brown is referring to that quality of poetic speech that can excite in the reader extreme pity or sorrow.

However, the poems are not all delivered in a tone of mortal sadness. Central to Mahon's tonal repertoire is the use of an urbane irony. Often his meanings have a different or opposite tendency to that expressed by the words used. When he rails against bigotry and hatred in 'Ecclesiastes', and against violence in 'Rathlin', he is stringently critical, but his gentle mockery in 'Grandfather' is impish and mischievous. He tempers the cruel precision of his observations with compassion, amusement and pain. Witty and darkly humorous, he relishes the absurd and the lyrical simultaneously, as this extract from 'After the Titanic' illustrates:

> a pandemonium of
> Prams, pianos, sideboards, winches,
> Boilers bursting and shredded ragtime.

Settings range from the precisely identifiable Portrush and Belfast to the metaphorical sites of past political failures and violence, like Kinsale and Rathlin Island, and the psychic wasteland of Antarctica. Harshness predominates. Surfaces are unyielding, climates are bracing. Even cities may be empty, as in 'Ecclesiastes', or their citizens voluntarily withdraw into isolation, as in 'Grandfather'. We sense that, although the poems are set 'in one place only', the feelings they evoke are universal. Always there is a consciousness of the vastness of the universe and the limitations of human struggle. The reader is aware that, whatever the setting of a particular poem, it engages in dialogue with or provides a foil to that desperate, barren place, Belfast, which so informs Mahon's imagination.

Frequently places are viewed from elsewhere, from a distance that may be historical, geographical or ironic. The titles of the first and last books from which the poems here are taken, *Night-Crossing* and *Antarctica,* testify to his shifting ground. Frequently too the speaker is a traveller, a tourist or a reporter, traversing difficult country. The unyielding terrain becomes a metaphor for the existential, regional or global anxieties from which he suffers.

In certain poems there is an inkling of an 'elsewhere' that is nearer the ideal state than that now inhabited. That place or state is suggested by, for example, post-historical Rathlin Island, now a bird sanctuary, or by the glimpse of Co. Donegal beyond the shores from Portrush, or by those faraway places where a thought might grow. It is beyond reach, and the speaker is often aware of its fictiveness, as he is in 'The Chinese Restaurant in Portrush'.

Estranged loners crowd the poems. In works such as 'After the Titanic' and 'Rathlin' their distance from other humans, whether temporal or spatial, gives some idea of the extent of their isolation. Sometimes, as in 'Day Trip to Donegal' and 'A Disused Shed', their alienation is suggested by their anthropomorphic otherness (that is, by attributing human personality and feelings to entities as unlikely as fish and fungi). Whatever solidarity these characters find is fleeting. Note, for example, how the 'we' in 'Day Trip to Donegal' gives way to the tortured 'I'. Note too the absence of any sense of fellowship or community among the oppressed mushrooms in 'A Disused Shed'.

Mahon holds an especial affection for scapegoats and failures, such as the murdered dreamer in 'As It Should Be', or Bruce Ismay in 'After the Titanic', seeing in their particular brand of failure a kind of successful avoidance of the mundane. As he writes in a 1997 poem, 'The greatest men fail, or seem to have failed.'

A distinctively Mahon outsider is the detached observer, at one remove from reality yet part of it. He is to be found, for instance, in 'A Chinese Restaurant in Portrush', 'Day Trip to Donegal' and 'A Disused Shed in County Wexford'. His role is to interpret and comment obliquely on the poem's action, as would the chorus of a classic Greek play, or to lament man's inhumanity, as did Old Testament prophets such as Jeremiah. Unlike a Greek chorus, however, Mahon's outsider is implicated in the conditions and predicaments the poems express. His watchful presence also ignites an inquiry into the relationship between the poet and the historical world around him.

Mahon has a special gift for selecting telling images of the commonplace, material world and investing them with resonance. Tied-up swings, Peruvian mines, burnt-out hotels, a red bandana – the images are acutely visual and activate a series of associations in our minds. Mahon is at pains to catch the quality of light that falls on his landscapes and has a visual artist's awareness of shape and colour. 'The Chinese Restaurant in Portrush', for example, is replete with precise visual detail – such as open doors, the girl swinging her bag, the chow mein, the photograph of Hongkong, the yacht – which he then invests with significance.

Derek Mahon is one of the most important poets writing in Ireland today. His poetry is memorable because his technical excellence, contemporary idiom and serious subject matter combine with an urbane yet passionate sensitivity.

Questions

1. 'Derek Mahon's landscapes are more than mere setting: they are a source of value.' Give your response to this view, with supporting quotation from or reference to the poems by Derek Mahon on your course.
2. 'Suffering and violence offer the greatest challenge to poetry.' Discuss this view, supporting your answer by quotation from or reference to the poems by Derek Mahon on your course.
3. Discuss Derek Mahon's exploration of place in some of the poems on your course, supporting your answer with quotations from and reference to specific poems.
4. 'Derek Mahon's poetry is more concerned with the future than with the past.' Discuss this statement, supporting your view with reference to and quotations from the poems on your course.
5. 'Derek Mahon demonstrates that poetry can reaffirm hope, love and tolerance.' In your reading of Derek Mahon's poetry, did you find this to be true? Support your answer by reference to, or quotation from, the poems on your course.
6. 'People, more than places, preoccupy Derek Mahon.' How far do you agree with that statement? Support your answer by reference to, and quotation from, the poems by Derek Mahon on your course.
7. 'Derek Mahon's poetry explores the relationship between the poet and the world around him.' Discuss this view, supporting your answer by quotation from or reference to the poems by Derek Mahon on your course.
8. 'Derek Mahon's poetry reports on life lived at the margins.' In your reading of Derek Mahon's poetry, did you find this to be true? Support your answer by reference to, or quotation from, the poems on your course.

Bibliography

Battersby, Eileen, 'Made in Belfast' (interview with Derek Mahon), *Sunday Tribune,* 26 August 1990.

Brown, Terence, 'An interview with Derek Mahon,' in *Poetry Ireland,* vol. 14 (autumn 1985).

Cooke, Harriet, 'Harriet Cooke talks to the poet Derek Mahon,' in *Irish Times,* 17 January 1981.

Dawe, Gerald, 'Icon and Lares: Derek Mahon and Michael Longley,' in *Across a Roaring Hill: The Protestant Imagination in Modern Ireland* (Gerald Dawe and Edna Longley, editors), Belfast: Blackstaff Press 1985.

Deane, Séamus, 'Derek Mahon: freedom from history,' in *Celtic Revivals: Essays in Modern Irish Literature, 1880–1980,* London: Faber and Faber 1985.

Kelly, Willie, 'Each poem for me is a new beginning' (interview with Derek Mahon), in *Cork Review,* vol. 2, no. 3 (1981).

Kerrigan, John, 'Ulster Ovids,' in *The Chosen Ground: Essays on Contemporary Poetry of Northern Ireland* (Neil Corcoran, editor), Bridgend (Glamorgan): Seren Books 1992.

Murray, Christopher, and Donnelly, Brian (editors), *Irish University Review,* special issue: Derek Mahon, vol. 24, no. 1 (spring–summer 1994).

O'Brien, Seán, 'Derek Mahon: the world as exile,' in *The Deregulated Muse,* Newcastle-upon-Tyne: Bloodaxe Books 1998.

Scammell, William, 'Derek Mahon interviewed,' in *Poetry Review,* Irish issue, vol. 81, no. 2 (summer 1991).

8 *Eavan* BOLAND

John G. Fahy

A literary life

Eavan Boland was born in Dublin in 1944. Her mother was the painter Frances Kelly and her father was the diplomat Frederick Boland, whose career moves resulted in her roving childhood and youth. From the age of six to twelve she lived in London, then in New York for a number of years, to return to Dublin when she was fourteen.

She was educated at Holy Child Convent, Killiney, County Dublin, then went on to Trinity College, first as a student and later as a lecturer in the English Department. After a few years she embarked on a career as a literary journalist with the *Irish Times*, and she also presented a regular poetry programme for RTE radio.

'New Territory'

New Territory, her first book of poetry, published in 1967, contains the early poems, written between the ages of seventeen and twenty-two, which were critically acknowledged at the time as talented, well-crafted work. Among its main concerns, this volume showed some preoccupation with the role of the poet, in pieces such as 'The Poets' and 'New Territory'. It also contained the first of her poems about paintings and so introduced what was to become an important theme of Boland's work: the stereotyped view of women in art and literature. 'From the Painting *Back from Market* by Chardin' shows the peasant woman, defined by love and domestic duties, 'her eyes mixed | Between love and market.'

The poet feels that artists throughout the centuries have ignored the real lives of women:

> I think of what great art removes:
> Hazard and death, the future and the past,
> This woman's secret history and her loves …

In general this volume is in the mainstream of the Irish political – romantic poetic tradition, with its themes of exile ('The Flight of the Earls') and political martyrdom ('A Cynic at Kilmainham Jail'); poems about Irish poets ('Yeats in Civil War' and 'After the Irish of Aodhagán Ó Rathaille'); and the retelling of legends ('Three Songs for a Legend' and 'The Winning of Etain'). But her outlook was soon to change, under pressure of the unfolding political situation.

Religious and political antagonism in Northern Ireland exploded into violence from 1969 onwards. Few people were unmoved or unaffected by this. The violence spread southwards with the bombing of Dublin and Monaghan in May 1974. Eavan Boland conducted a series of interviews in the *Irish Times* with Northern writers concerning their views on the situation, its effects on the work of the writer, and in general concerning the function of art in a time of violence. In a seminal article on 7 June 1974 entitled 'The Weasel's Tooth', she questioned the whole notion of cultural unity and accused Irish writing, influenced by Yeats, of fostering lethal fantasies for political activists:

> Let us be rid at last of any longing for cultural unity in a country whose most precious contribution may be precisely its insight into the anguish of disunity ... For there is, and at last I recognise it, no unity whatsoever in this culture of ours. And even more important, I recognise that there is no need whatsoever for such a unity. If we search for it we will, at a crucial moment, be mutilating with fantasy once again the very force we should be liberating with reality: our one strength as writers, the individual voice, speaking in tones of outcry, vengeance, bitterness even, against our disunity but speaking, for all that, with a cool tough acceptance of it.

'The War Horse'

The second volume of poetry, *The War Horse,* published in 1975, reflects Boland's concerns with violence and conflict in both private and community life. She deals with many types of conflict: the Irish–English struggle, worrying families, and the conflict between lovers. The development of this theme ranges from a recognition of the killer instinct inherent in all nature, however domesticated ('Prisoners'), to a consideration of notorious historical public moments of conflict and death ('The Famine Road', 'The Greek Experience' and 'Child of Our Time', which was written after the Dublin bombings of 1974) and the archetypal deadly conflict of fathers and sons ('The Hanging Judge' and 'A Soldier's Son'). The latter poem, in which a father kills his own son, has been read as 'an image of a society at war with its own inheritance and future'. 'The War Horse', both a private and a political poem, brings a vivid personal awareness of destruction and war to leafy Dublin suburbia.

The feminine vision and view of the world is also a force in this volume. In 'The Famine Road' Boland equates the callous official lack of understanding of the famine victims with the offhand, male medical attitude meted out to a contemporary woman suffering from sterility. Racial suffering is equated with female suffering. In 'Suburban Woman' and 'Ode to Suburbia' she deals with the daily grind of the housewife and the conflict between a woman's traditional role and her identity as a poet and creative artist:

> Her kitchen blind down – a white flag –
> the day's assault over, now she will shrug
>
> a hundred small surrenders off as images
> still born, unwritten metaphors, blank pages;
>
> and on this territory, blindfold, we meet
> at last, veterans of a defeat
>
> no truce will heal, no formula prevent
> breaking out fresh again. Again the print
>
> of twigs stalking her pillow will begin
> a new day and all her victims then –
> hopes unreprieved, hours taken hostage
> will newly wake, while I, on a new page
>
> will watch, like town and country, word, thought
> look for ascendancy, poise, retreat,
>
> leaving each line maimed, my forces used.
> Defeated we survive, we two, housed
>
> together in my compromise, my craft –
> who are of one another the first draft.

Boland had by this time married and moved from her city flat and literary lifestyle to the Dublin suburb of Dundrum, where she was rearing her two daughters. These poems and others such as 'The Other Woman' and 'Child of Our Time' reflect an attempt to find and bring together her identity as wife, Irishwoman, poet and mother with her life in the suburbs.

In this volume also there are some beautiful and honest personal poems on family, love and friendship: 'Sisters', 'The Laws of Love', and 'The Botanic Gardens' – all demonstrating peaceful alternatives to conflict.

'In Her Own Image'

In 1976 she began to work simultaneously on her next two volumes of poetry, *In Her Own Image*, published in 1980, and *Night Feed*, published in 1982. *In*

Her Own Image deals with individual private female identity, 'woman's secret history'. The poems explore taboo issues: anorexia, infanticide, mastectomy, menstruation, masturbation and domestic violence. Here is a cry to look at the reality of woman, her sexuality, desires, feelings of degradation, and failure to be understood.

'Anorexia' explores female suffering; 'Mastectomy' and 'In His Own Image' explore feelings of degradation and see the female body as the object of man's desire and of his need to control and shape:

> He splits my lip with his fist,
> shadows my eye with a blow,
> knuckles my neck to its proper angle.
> What a perfectionist!
> His are a sculptor's hands:
> they summon
> form from the void,
> they bring
> me to myself again.
> I am a new woman.

'Solitary' suggests that only a woman knows the real sensual rhythms of her own body. 'Tirade for the Mimic Muse' and 'Witching' undermine the accepted conventional image of woman. 'Tirade' in particular deflates the traditional male-created image of the muse as a beautiful girl, choosing instead to deal with the less picturesque reality:

> I've caught you out. You slut. You fat trout.
> So here you are fumed in candle-stink
> Its yellow balm exhumes you for the glass.
> How you arch and pout in it!
> How you poach your face in it!
> Anyone would think you were a whore –
> An ageing out-of-work kind-hearted tart.
> I know you for the ruthless bitch you are:
> Our criminal, our tricoteuse, our Muse –
> Our Muse of Mimic Art.

These are angry poems, featuring degraded states of women, in a sort of anti-lyric verse, yet they goad the reader into considering the reality of woman, not the image.

'Night Feed'

If *In Her Own Image* featured the dark side of 'woman's secret history', *Night*

Feed features the suburban, domestic and maternal: the ordinary, traditional, everyday aspects of woman's identity. The main sequence of poems, 'Domestic Interior, 1–11', focuses on the close bond between mother and child and explores the intensity of that maternal experience. It includes the now familiar 'Night Feed'.

Night Feed

This is dawn.
Believe me
This is your season, little daughter.
The moment daisies open,
The hour mercurial rainwater
Makes a mirror for sparrows.
It's time we drowned our sorrows.

I tiptoe in.
I lift you up
Wriggling
In your rosy, zipped sleeper.
Yes, this is the hour
For the early bird and me
When finder is keeper.

I crook the bottle.
How you suckle!
This is the best I can be,
Housewife
To this nursery
Where you hold on,
Dear life.

A silt of milk.
The last suck.
And now your eyes are open,
Birth-coloured and offended.
Earth wakes.
You go back to sleep.
The feed is ended.

Worms turn.
Stars go in.

Even the moon is losing face.
Poplars stilt for dawn
And we begin
The long fall from grace.
I tuck you in.

Also in this volume is a group of poems examining artistic images of women: 'Degas Laundresses', 'Woman Posing', 'On Renoir's *The Grape Pickers*' and 'Domestic Interior'. These women are either defined in relation to their work in field or kitchen or else are putting on a false, decorative pose, fulfilling the stereotyped image man created for them. Woman's perceived need to comply with this idealised image of timeless beauty is satirised in such pieces as 'The Woman Turns Herself into a Bush', 'The Woman Changes Her Skin' and 'A Ballad of Beauty and Time'. In this last poem plastic surgery is under the poet's satirical knife:

A chin he had re-worked,
a face he had re-made.
He slit and tucked and cut.
Then straightened from his blade.

'A tuck, a hem, he said –
'I only seam the line,
I only mend the dress.
It wouldn't do for you:
your quarrel's with the weave.
The best I achieve
is just a stitch in time.'

These fake images of woman, romanticised stereotypes, are set against the real defining moments in a woman's history in the 'Domestic Interiors' sequence. On the one hand Boland is saying that it is these family relationships that are real and important, that identity can be found among the washing-machines and children's toys in suburbia. But she is also protesting that, traditionally, a woman has not had a choice about this. She has been imprisoned at hearth and home and so kept to the margins of society, removed from the centre of history-making and power. Boland seeks a more equitable balance between 'hearth and history'.

It's a Woman's World

Our way of life
has hardly changed
since a wheel first

whetted a knife.
Maybe flame
burns more greedily,
and wheels are steadier
but we're the same

who milestone
our lives
with oversights –
living by the lights

of the loaf left
by the cash register,
the washing powder
paid for and wrapped,

the wash left wet:
like most historic peoples
we are defined
by what we forget,

by what we never will be –
star-gazers,
fire-eaters,
It's our alibi

for all time:
as far as history goes
we were never
on the scene of the crime.

So when the king's head
gored its basket –
grim harvest –
we were gristing bread

or getting the recipe
for a good soup
to appetise
our gossip . . .

'The Journey'

Boland's fifth collection, *The Journey*, was published in 1982 and republished in *The Journey and Other Poems* in 1986. Prominent among its many and complex themes is the quest for identity: the poet's national identity, suburban identity, feminist identity, and identity as mother and wife. Childhood memories in England and the feeling of being different in such poems as 'I Remember', 'An Irish Childhood in England: 1951' and 'Fond Memory' provoked a consciousness of the poet's own nation and how language defines a person:

> ... the teacher in the London convent who
> when I produced 'I amn't' in the classroom
> turned and said – 'you're not in Ireland now.'
> ['An Irish Childhood in England: 1951']

This consciousness of language as part of one's identity prevails throughout the volume. Yet her relationship with her history and the women of history is not an easy one, and she resists going back to it in 'Mise Éire'. She finds the grim reality of Irish women in history, soldiers' whores or helpless immigrants, difficult to confront:

> No. I won't go back.
> My roots are brutal:
>
> I am the woman –
> a sloven's mix
> of silk at the wrists,
> a sort of dove-strut
> in the precincts of the garrison –
>
> who practises
> the quick frictions,
> the rictus of delight
> and gets cambric for it,
> rice-coloured silks.
>
> I am the woman
> in the gansy-coat
> on board the 'Mary Belle',
> in the huddling cold,
>
> holding her half-dead baby to her
> as the wind shifts East

and North over the dirty
waters of the wharf

mingling the immigrant
guttural with the vowels
of homesickness who neither
knows nor cares that

a new language
is a kind of scar
and heals after a while
into a passable imitation
of what went before.

Yet these are the real women of the past, not those images created by many previous male poets, who idealised women and moulded them into metaphors of national sentiment and so created mythic national female figures.

'Outside History'

Outside History (1990), Boland's sixth volume, is divided into three sections: 'Object Lessons', 'Outside History: A Sequence' and 'Distances'. The object lessons, in the main, are what woman has learned about life. Some poems, such as 'The Black Lace Fan My Mother Gave Me' and 'The River', reflect on the puzzling, almost inexplicable relationship between men and women and on their different perspectives on the world ('Mountain Time'). Couples growing apart and breaking up are the focus of 'Object Lessons'. We are made to feel in this sequence how fragile and transient is all human interaction, particularly in 'We Were Neutral in the War' and 'Mountain Time'.

... darkness will be only what is left of
a mouth after kissing or a hand laced in a hand ...
['Mountain Time']

The female speaker senses that she is not regarded as significant, that she is marginalised, forced to the sidelines and excluded from the centre of happening history in 'We Were Neutral in the War'.

Your husband frowns at dinner, has no time
for the baby who has learned to crease three
fingers and wave 'day-day.' This is serious,
he says. This could be what we all feared.

You pierce a sequin with a needle.
You slide it down single-knotted thread
until it lies with all the others in
a puzzle of brightness. Then another and another one.

The female voices in these poems resemble 'The Shadow Doll', a mere replica of a bride, a protected image, locked in a vacuum. But the speaker is a poet, with her own recognised space, metaphorically represented as a room, and she reaches out to other women writers, trying to imagine 'the rooms of other women poets'. She knows that the literary and creative world has been male-dominated, but the gift has passed into her hands.

Bright-Cut Irish Silver

I take it down
from time to time, to feel
the smooth path of silver
        meet the cicatrice of skill.

These scars, I tell myself, are learned.

This gift for wounding an artery of rock
was passed on from father to son,
        to the father
of the next son;

is an aptitude
for injuring earth
        while inferring it in curves and surfaces;

is this cold potency which has come,
by time and chance,

into my hands.

Boland's response to being marginalised as a woman poet is to explore alternative history. 'So much that matters, so much that is powerful and frail in human affairs seems to me, increasingly, to happen outside history: away from the texts and symmetries of an accepted expression. And, for that very reason, at a great risk of being edited out of the final account' (*Poetry Book Society Bulletin*, winter 1990).

Boland feels that significance is to be found in the margins of life also, that the unrecorded history of individuals is important too. And it is this alternative history that is the focus of the central section of the volume *Outside History*. In it she explores her own history, but this operates at both a personal and a universal level. Her own history can be read as a metaphor for the unrecorded female history of the nation. She explores her own personal history as a developing writer and poet. She is the young immature poet in 'The Achill Woman' who does not fully comprehend the significance of what she has experienced. She attempts to understand her developing self and to make connections between her present persona as a woman poet and her student past in 'A False Spring'. She is forging an identity as a woman poet in 'The Making of an Irish Goddess', and she is the suburban woman seeking to re-establish contact with her natural and cultural roots in 'White Hawthorn in the West of Ireland'. She finds real significance in moments of human experience, not in symbolic happening, in 'We Are Human History. We Are Not Natural History'. She feels trapped by time, and as a woman she is alienated from the male-dominated version of history in 'An Old Steel Engraving'. She feels powerless and unable to influence history in 'We Are Always Too Late'.

Many of the poems record a sense of incompleteness, such as 'A False Spring', which records the failure to find again her younger, student self and integrate that phase of her life with the embodied now. The lost cultural heritage, passed from mother to daughter but forgotten, is recorded in 'What We Lost'.

There is a keen sense of displacement in the poems. The au pair girls in 'In Exile' signify displaced woman, isolated by the barriers of language and by age and cultural differences. In the sequence we see Boland attempting to recover a sense of belonging and completeness by making connections with her personal history and her cultural history, but also by shedding the myth and the stereotyped image:

> out of myth into history I move to be
> part of that ordeal . . .

The third section, 'Distances', focuses mostly on the past, the distant past of her childhood memories and the more recent past of occasional moments of insight. These memories are connected to the present as if the poet is at last achieving a kind of quiet wholeness in her life. She is linked to the past, to family, to moments of love and insight, even to the future, in 'What Love Intended', where she imagines herself coming back like a ghost to a radically altered suburb.

'In a Time of Violence'

In a Time of Violence, her seventh collection, was published in 1994. It is divided into three sections, the first of which is entitled 'Writing in a Time of Violence'. The poems in this section touch on specific national and historical issues and events, such as the Famine ('That the Science of Cartography is

Limited' and 'March 1, 1847. By the First Post'), agrarian violence and the Peep o' Day Boys ('The Death of Reason'), the Easter Rising ('The Dolls Museum in Dublin'), nineteenth-century women emigrants ('In a Bad Light') and language and nationality ('Beautiful Speech'). But each is examined from an interesting and unusual angle, such as the unsympathetic and insensitive view of the Famine from a woman of the ascendancy class in 'March 1, 1847. By the First Post'.

Many of the meditations are inspired by a visit to a museum or an exhibition. For example, the dress in a museum in St Louis featuring the work of Irish dressmakers sparked off thoughts of women's servitude in exile in the nineteenth century ('In a Bad Light'). But each event is re-created with authentic realism and each tale narrated with sympathy and affection. The poems offer fresh insights into old history as the poet focuses on the human experience behind these historical artefacts.

The poems in the second section, 'Legends', focus on women as mothers for the most part. The fierce protectiveness and the maternal side of women is portrayed in poems such as 'This Moment' and 'The Pomegranate'. Woman as mother is playing an age-old role and has universal significance. The ageing woman features in 'Moths', 'The Water Clock', and 'Legends'. Some of the poems stretch back to the poet's own mother and grandmother through remembrance of a particular skill ('The Parcel') or a link with an heirloom ('Lava Cameo'). Some, such as 'Legends', establish continuity with the next generation:

> Our children are our legends.
> You are mine. You have my name.
> My hair was once like yours.
> And the world
> is less bitter to me
> because you will re-tell the story.

The main work of the third section is the title poem, 'Anna Liffey'. It is, in the words of the author, 'about a river and a woman, about the destiny of water and my sense of growing older'. This section concludes with four poems examining the unsatisfactory portrayal of women in myth, art and literature. The idealised images and the stereotypes are false and suffocating.

She appeals for realism and release in 'A Woman Painted on a Leaf':

> This is not death. It is the terrible
> suspension of life.
>
> I want a poem
> I can grow old in. I want a poem I can die in.

'Object Lessons'

Her prose collection, *Object Lessons: The Life of the Woman and the Poet in Our Time*, appeared in 1995. In autobiographical mode, Boland traces her own development as a woman poet, recounts her search as a woman for some kind of arrangement with the male-dominated concept of the nation, and reviews the status of women in poetry and history

Main volumes of poetry

	Poems in this selection
New Territory (1967)	
The War Horse (1975)	'The War Horse' 'The Famine Road' 'Child of Our Time'
In Her Own Image (1980)	
Night Feed (1982)	
The Journey (1982)	
The Journey and Other Poems (1986)	
Selected Poems (1989)	
Outside History (1990)	'The Black Lace Fan My Mother Gave Me' 'The Shadow Doll' 'White Hawthorn in the West of Ireland' 'Outside History'
In a Time of Violence (1994)	'This Moment' 'Love' 'The Pomegranate'
Collected Poems (1995)	

The War Horse

Text of poem: New Explorations Anthology page 434

Themes and issues

The poem stems from an encounter with a roving horse and also the excerpt from *Object Lessons* (page 304), which occurred, coincidentally, during an upsurge of disruption and violence in Northern Ireland. The poet's response is a metaphor poem with political overtones. The horse became the poetic incarnation of all those statistics of violence and death that were pouring nightly from the television screens. ★NB★

The poem operates on a number of levels of significance. At an immediate level it confronts the issue of violence. We notice the seeming casualness of it, the arbitrary nature of this violence: ‘the clip, clop, casual | Iron of his shoes as he stamps death | Like a mint on the innocent coinage of earth.’ The treatment of the violence may be metaphorical, yet there is an awareness of the reality of death and wanton injury, which is carried in the imagery. The beheaded crocus is ‘one of the screamless dead’, the uprooted vegetation ‘like corpses, remote, crushed, mutilated’, and the eaten leaf merely ‘of distant interest like a maimed limb’. The ungainly and often directionless nature of violence is suggested in the motion of the animal as ‘he stumbles on like a rumour of war’. The overtones of the language become more overtly political as the poem proceeds: the rose is ‘expendable … a volunteer’; and ‘atavism’, ‘cause’ and ‘betrayed’ are the verbal coinage of revolutionary groups.

Could we read this poem as reflecting a Southern view of the Northern conflict – a middle-class, slightly nationalist Southern view? The speaker feels threatened by the ‘casual iron of his hooves’, vulnerable with ‘only a rose’ to form ‘a mere | Line of defence against him’, and afterwards breathes a sigh of relief that this only partly understood phenomenon is gone:

> But we, we are safe, our unformed fear
> Of fierce commitment gone …

Lack of interest in this intrusive violence is at first feigned by the speaker. Others pretend he isn’t there, ‘use the subterfuge | Of curtains.’ Yet for all that danger and disruption the speaker faintly admires the beast:

> I lift the window, watch the ambling feather
> Of hock and fetlock …

She is also slow to blame him: ‘No great harm is done. | Only a leaf of our laurel hedge …’ But most significantly of all, at the end of the poem he stirs her race memory (‘my blood is still | With atavism’) of colonial injustice, English aggression, and the cycle of failed rebellions:

> Of burned countryside, illicit braid:
> A cause ruined before, a world betrayed.

The speaker’s attitude to the animal is a complex one and is perhaps contradictory at times, incorporating fear, resentment and relief but also furtive admiration.

Examine what Boland has to say about political poetry in the extract from *Object Lessons* below (page 304).

So, on another level the poem demonstrates how history impinges on the domestic and the artistic, which are frail in comparison. We are made aware, forcefully, of how fragile the domestic is. Boland herself has described the tension in the poem as that of 'force against formality'. The race memory of fighting against imposed order is conjured up by the modern parallel of conflict in a suburban garden, where wild nature reasserts itself over humankind's attempts to tame it. And the speaker can empathise. The rebel is not far beneath the surface of the psyche, despite the suburban veneer.

'The War Horse' is among the first of Boland's poems of the suburbs. The irony is that suburbia was really designed as slumberland, but even in safe, leafy, middle-class dormer territory the 'rumour of war … stumbles down our short street,' awakening age-old conflicts. Boland is legitimising suburbia as a place of real experience and insight, a fit location and subject matter for poetry.

'The War Horse' is a private 'coming to awareness' of public violence, an intimate 'thoughts inside the head' reflection on the theme. In this aspect it differs from the more public scrutiny of violence in 'The Famine Road' and 'Child of Our Time'.

These notions concerning the influence of history, the relationship between art and society and the search for meaning in suburbia become important and frequently examined issues in Boland's poetry.

Features and style

Versification

The poem is composed in open rhyming couplets. Unlike closed couplets, the sense here often runs from one couplet to the next. This gives a flowing rhythm, a fluid energy to the verse, which might be said to reflect the unpredictable energy and purpose of the horse. For example, the sequence of lines from 'I lift the window' to 'his snuffling head | Down', ending two couplets further on, must be read in one breath and might suggest the animal's forward momentum. Following that, the speaker's short gasp of relief ('He is gone') makes an effective contrast and also points up Boland's use of rhythm for effect.

The rhyming is very casual, composed of half-rhymes and off-rhymes for the most part: death – earth, fear – care, limb – climb, huge – subterfuge, street – wait, etc. This offhand casualness accords well with the beast's casual destruction.

Sound effects

This poet is not deaf to the music of language. Everywhere there are echoes and internal rhymes: 'hock – fetlock', 'Blown from growth', 'fear | Of fierce', etc. The alliteration of 'stumbles down our short street' emphasises the ungainly movement in the confined space. The unobtrusive musical assonance of 'Then to breathe relief lean', with its long *e* sounds, effectively conveys the speaker's sense of release, of escape.

Sound effects are an integral part of the animal portraiture here. The onomatopoeia of 'breath hissing' and 'snuffling head' conveys the threatening unfamiliarity of this beast that has invaded the suburban garden.

Imagery

The poet employs vivid graphic visual imagery, whether to convey fearsome destructive power ('Iron of his shoes ... stamps death') or beauty ('ambling feather | Of hock and fetlock'). Similes and metaphors are often striking and unusual: the torn leaf is 'Of distant interest like a maimed limb'; the broken crocus is 'one of the screamless dead'. These comparisons are very disturbing and have a nightmarish quality, which brings to consciousness the suppressed terrors that have been unleashed in the speaker by this violent visitation. Altogether the imagery and the language are vigorous and muscular, as befits the scene: 'stamps death | Like a mint'. Notice also the violence of the verbs: stamps, smashed, uprooted, stumble, etc.

Boland's recollections on the origins and significance of the poem

This extract is taken from her prose collection *Object Lessons* (1995) (chapter 8):

> It was the early seventies, a time of violence in Northern Ireland. Our front room was a rectangle with white walls, hardly any furniture and a small television chanting deaths and statistics at teatime.
>
> It was also our first winter in the suburb. The weather was cold; the road was half finished. Each morning the fields on the Dublin hills appeared as slates of frost. At night the street lamps were too few. And the road itself ran out in a gloom of icy mud and builders' huts.
>
> One evening, at the time of the news, I came into the front room with a cup of coffee in my hand. I heard something at the front door. I set down the coffee, switched on the light and went to open the door.
>
> A large, dappled head – a surreal dismemberment in the dusk – swayed low on the doorstep, then attached itself back to a clumsy horse and clattered away. I went out and stood under the street lamp. I saw its hindquarters retreating, smudged by mist and darkness. I watched it disappear around a corner. The lamp above me hissed and flickered and finally came on fully.
>
> There was an explanation. It was almost certainly a travellers' horse with some memory of our road as a travelling site and our gardens as fields where it had grazed only recently. The memory withstood the surprises of its return, but not for long. It came back four or five times. Each time, as it was startled into retreat, its huge hooves did damage. Crocus bulbs were uprooted. Hedge seedlings were dragged up. Grass

seeds were churned out of their place.

Some months later I began to write a poem. I called it 'The War Horse'. Its argument was gathered around the oppositions of force and formality. Of an intrusion of nature – the horse – menacing the decorous reductions of nature which were the gardens. And of the failure of language to describe such violence and resist it.

I wrote the poem slowly, adding each couplet with care. I was twenty-six years of age. At first, when it was finished, I looked at it with pleasure and wonder. It encompassed a real event. It entered a place in my life and moved beyond it. I was young enough to craft and want nothing more.

Gradually I changed my mind, although I never disowned the poem. In fact, my doubts were less about it than about my own first sense of its completeness. The poem had drawn me easily into the charm and strength of an apparently public stance. It had dramatised for me what I already suspected: that one part of the poem in every generation is ready to be communally written. To put it another way, there is a poem in each time that waits to be set down and is therefore instantly recognisable once it has been. It may contain sentiments of outrage or details of an occasion. It may invite a general reaction to some particular circumstance. It may appeal to anger or invite a common purpose.

It hardly matters. The point is that to write in that cursive and approved script can seem, for the unwary poet, a blessed lifting of the solitude and scepticism of the poet's life. Images are easily set down; a music of argument is suddenly revealed. Then a difficult pursuit becomes a swift movement. And finally the poem takes on a glamour of meaning against a background of public interest.

Historically – in the epic, in the elegy – this has been an enrichment. But in a country like Ireland, with a nationalist tradition, there are real dangers. In my poem the horse, the hills behind it – these were private emblems which almost immediately took on a communal reference against a background of communal suffering. In a time of violence it would be all too easy to write another poem, and another. To make a construct where the difficult 'I' of perception became the easier 'we' of subtle claim. Where an unearned power would be allowed by a public engagement.

In such a poem the poet would be the subject. The object might be a horse, a distance, a human suffering. It hardly mattered. The public authorisation would give such sanction to the poet and the object would not just be silent. It would be silenced. The subject would be all-powerful.

At that point I saw [that] in Ireland, with its national traditions, its bardic past, the confusion between the political poem and the public poem was a dangerous and inviting motif. It encouraged the subject of the poem to be a representative and the object to be ornamental. In such a relation, the dangerous and private registers of feeling of the true political poem would be truly lost. At the very moment when they were most needed.

And yet I had come out of the Irish tradition as a poet. I had opened the books, read the poems, believed the rhetoric when I was young. Writing the political poem seemed to me almost a franchise of the Irish poet, an inherited privilege. I would come to see that it was more and less than that, that like other parts of the poet's life, it would involve more of solitary scruple than communal eloquence. And yet one thing remained steady: I continued to believe that a reading of the energy and virtue of any tradition can be made by looking at the political poem in its time. At who writes it and why. At who can speak in the half-light between event and perception without their voices becoming shadows as Aeneas's rivals did in the underworld of the Sixth Book.

In that winter twilight, seeing the large, unruly horse scrape the crocus bulbs up in his hooves, making my own connections between power and order, I had ventured on my first political poem. I had seen my first political image. I had even understood the difficulties of writing it. What I had not realised was that I myself was a politic within the Irish poem: a young woman who had left the assured identity of a city and its poetic customs and who had started on a life which had no place in them. I had seen and weighed and struggled with the meaning of the horse, the dark night, the sounds of death from the television. I had been far less able to evaluate my own hand on a light switch, my own form backlit under a spluttering street light against the raw neighbourhood of a suburb. And yet without one evaluation the other was incomplete.

I would learn that it was far more difficult to make myself the political subject of my own poems than to see the metaphoric possibilities in front of me in a suburban dusk. The difficulty was a disguised blessing. It warned me away from facile definitions. The more I looked at the political poem, the more I saw how easy it was to make the claim and miss the connections. And I wanted to find them.

The Famine Road

Text of poem: New Explorations Anthology page 436

A READING OF THE POEM

Boland is drawing parallels between certain aspects of the famine experience and the experience of woman today. The famine road, symbol of purposeless, thwarted lives, is equated with female sterility. The supercilious treatment of the suffering people she sees as akin to the unfeeling arrogance meted out to the childless woman.

> You never will, never you know
> but take it well woman, grow
> your garden, keep house, goodbye.

Boland feels that being a woman gives her a unique perspective on Irish history, as she elaborated in response to the question, 'What does being Irish mean to you?'

> Apart from the fact that it connects me with a past, I find it a perspective on my womanhood as well. Womanhood and Irishness are metaphors for one another. There are resonances of humiliation, oppression and silence in both of them and I think you can understand one better by experiencing the other. [From the interview in *Sleeping with Monsters*]

If we explore the poem's comparison in detail we find that both the Irish in history and women in society are generalised about and so misunderstood: 'Idle as trout in light Colonel Jones | these Irish …' The woman in the monologue is a mere faceless statistic ('one out of every ten …'). Neither are treated rationally ('could they not … suck | April hailstones for water and for food'). The cruel indifference of these people's treatment is linked to the nonchalant lack of medical explanation ('Anything may have caused it, spores … one sees | day after day these mysteries'). Both groups are different, physically or mentally segregated, condemned to an isolated life or death.

> They know it and walk clear. He has become
> a typhoid pariah, his blood tainted, although
> he shares it with some there …
>
>> Barren, never to know the load
>> of his child in you, what is your body
>> now if not a famine road?

Boland links this oppression and humiliation of the sterile woman with that of the famine people. Their blood too is wasted ('could | they not blood their knuckles on rock'). This image is an impotent echo of that authoritative gesture of Trevelyan's ('Trevelyan's | seal blooded the table') as they too put their seal on their work.

The following bleak humorous image conveys their humiliations, shows the primitive state to which they were reduced: 'cunning as housewives, each eyed – | as if at a corner butcher – the other's buttock.' Both woman and famine people are silent sufferers. Disenfranchised, they are allowed to make no contribution. The superior discussion is carried on above their heads and is quite dismissive: 'Might it be safe | Colonel, to give them roads,' and 'grow | your garden, keep house, goodbye.'

The lack of understanding, the unfeeling treatment, the callous oppression, the silent suffering, the feelings of humiliation, of uselessness, the pointlessness of it all, the sense of failure – these are the links between womanhood and Irishness in this poem.

Child of Our Time

Text of poem: New Explorations Anthology page 440

[*Note: This poem is also prescribed for Ordinary Level 2008 exam*]

Background note

The poem was inspired by a press photograph showing a firefighter carrying a dead child out of the wreckage of the Dublin bombings in May 1974.

A reading of the poem

First and foremost this is an elegy for the untimely death of a child. It bemoans the senselessness and irrationality of the child's slaughter in an act of public violence.

> This song, which takes from your final cry
> Its tune, from you unreasoned end its reason;
> Its rhythm from the discord of your murder …

In the second stanza the keen sense of loss is encouraged by the mournful litany of the literary rituals of childhood, naming again the associations of intimate moments, the rituals around sleeping and waking:

> rhymes for your waking, rhythms for your sleep,
> Names for the animals you took to bed,
> Tales to distract, legends to protect …

This sense of loss is compounded by guilt, in that it is the adults who should have been the guardians and guides of the child:

> We who should have known how to instruct
> With rhymes for your waking ...

The elegy finishes in a prayer that adult society will learn from this horror, expressed in the paradox 'And living, learn, must learn from you dead,' and so construct a better method of social interaction so that the death will not have been in vain ('find, for your sake whose life our idle | Talk has cost, a new language.') The poem is also a searing condemnation of violence. Society stands accused ('our times have robbed your cradle'), accused also of this barbarous irrationality ('your unreasoned end' ... 'the discord of your murder'). The only hope is that society would awaken to the reality of its actions and that the child might 'Sleep in a world your final sleep has woken.'

The poem could also be read as a comment on the failure of communication. The entire poem is couched in language terminology. It is a 'lullaby', a 'song', inspired by a 'final cry', a 'tune' with 'rhythms'. In the second stanza, loss is expressed in terms of language deprivation and child rearing seen in terms of language fostering: 'rhymes for your waking', etc. The only way forward from this conflict and violence is described as 'a new language'.

So the failure of language is associated with death and destruction. But language is the only bulwark against chaos, and this is the positive message of this bleak poem. Poetry, the most artistic expression of language, can be created out of this pain – this 'tune' from 'your final cry'. It signals a victory of order over chaos, reason 'from your unreasoned end', rhythm from 'discord'. It offers a chance to rebuild broken images and visualise a better society.

Feelings

A delicate balance of emotions is achieved in this poem. The brutal reality of the killing is never denied, and the fact of death is faced squarely, as in 'And living, learn, must learn from you dead,' where the placing of the last word in the line gives it finality and emphasis. But the references to death are sometimes veiled in poetic terms: 'your final cry' and 'your final sleep'. Or they are intellectualised, as in 'the discord of your murder'. Here the aspect of death dwelt on is its discordance, its out-of-tuneness, the disharmony of death. Or the child's broken body is rendered as 'your broken image'. The inversion of the natural order of life and death, in the killing of a child, is expressed in the paradoxes 'from your final cry | Its tune,' 'from your unreasoned end its reason;' and 'Its rhythm from the discord of your murder'. Consideration of this death is poeticised or intellectualised to some degree.

But this is no anodyne reaction. Feelings of grief, loss, guilt and resolution to learn a better way are all conveyed. Yet there is a delicacy and gentleness to the mourning, made all the more poignant by the fact that the poem is a sort of final lullaby. So the slightly euphemistic treatment is appropriate. Death is a kind of sleep. 'Sleep in a world your final sleep has woken.' Altogether the poem seems to be an interesting combination of dirge and lullaby.

The Black Lace Fan My Mother Gave Me

Text of poem: New Explorations Anthology page 442

A READING OF THE POEM

The poem focuses on courtship and deals with the messy and sometimes enigmatic relationship between the sexes. Just as the blackbird engages in its courtship ritual, human lovers too participate in a sort of courting dance.

> She was always early.
> He was late. That evening he was later.
>
> She ordered more coffee. She stood up.

The staccato rhythms of the verse here, created by the short sentences, draw attention to a choreographed sequence of movements, as a ritual to be played out. There is evidence too of disharmony, never the perfect entry together but rather of fretting and bad timing. If the weather is a barometer of the emotions, then the indications are of a stormy relationship, oppressive and explosive: 'stifling'; 'A starless drought made the nights stormy'; 'the distance smelled of rain and lightning'; 'An airless dusk before thunder.'

The fan is seen as a symbol of courtship, both with humans and in nature. It is a thing of beauty, associated with sensual allure, a romantic symbol. And so it functions here, but it also has darker associations of plunder and violation. The tortoiseshell has been pillaged from its natural habitat, killed off, and 'keeps … an inference of its violation.' As Boland herself saw it, 'as a sign not for triumph and acquisition but for suffering itself' (*Object Lessons*). It becomes a symbol of pain rather than an erotic sign. Still, in nature it retains its sensual overtone, 'the whole, full, flirtatious span of it.' So it carries these contradictory associations, reflecting the real-life complexity of the love relationship, not some stereotyped romantic image.

In other ways too it is an unusual love poem. There is no clear perception of the lovers, no clear recollection of the emotions, no detail of the moment:

> And no way to know what happened then –
> none at all – unless, of course, you improvise.

It is an oblique love poem that focuses on the love token that has lost much of its particular significance, yet is somehow still linked (by means of the blackbird) to their perennial courtship in nature. Its most positive statement is to assert the eternity of courtship, of love gestures. It makes no claims about eternal memories or the triumph of love against time. Rather the opposite, as the particulars of the emotional encounter are lost, eroded by time. Time erodes significance, and even cherished keepsakes lose their importance. There is emphasis also on the darker undertones of love, the tempests and the suffering.

Imagery and symbolism

The style of communication in this poem is somewhat oblique. Nothing is actually said: rather, we come gradually to apprehend the nuances and feelings. The core of meaning is communicated through the connotations of the images and symbols. And these images manage to transmit something of the complexity of the emotions and relations.

The fan itself, as the poet has mentioned, is not just an erotic object but also carries some notion of the violations of love, through the pain and plunder of its past. So the symbol deepens the understanding of love in the poem. The parallel image of the blackbird's wing restores some of the sensuality to the love symbol.

The tempestuous nature of the relationship is suggested in the weather imagery, as the atmosphere parallels the emotion: 'An airless dusk before thunder.' It is interesting too that all the references are to dusk or night, not the romantic kind but 'a stormless drought'. The poem explores more the darkness of the emotions than the starry insights of love.

Some ideas in the poem

- The love relationship is mysterious, inaccessible to outsiders and to history.
- The sensual courtship gestures in a love affair are universal, common to humans and nature.
- But here the symbol of courtship is not just an erotic object, but also a sign of pain.
- What remains are the gestures; the particular emotions are forgotten, eroded by time.
- History and memory fail us in the search for truth: we are forced to invent.
- Yet nature remains flirtatious always.

The Shadow Doll

Text of poem: New Explorations Anthology page 445

A reading of the poem

This poem has similarities with 'The Black Lace Fan My Mother Gave Me', in that it too uses a symbol to tease out some truths about the image of woman and the nature of the male–female relationship. We are offered the bride's perspective, a female insight on the wedding, which is portrayed in all its turmoil, an occasion 'to be survived'.

Boland uses the symbol of the doll to point up the discrepancy between the image of woman, particularly nineteenth-century woman, and the less glamorous reality. The manufactured image is elegant, in virginal white ('blooms from the ivory tulle'; 'oyster gleam', etc.), a model of discretion and sensitivity, devoid of sexual appetites ('discreet about | visits, fevers, quickenings and lust'), certainly too polite to talk about these taboo subjects. The reality is that of real-life emotional woman ('feeling satin rise and fall with the vows') and nervous repetition of vows amid the chaotic clutter of wedding preparations.

There may even be a slight envy of the doll's calmness; yet somehow the fevered reality is more appealing than the 'airless glamour' that is 'less than real', like the stephanotis. However, speaker and doll share a sense of confinement: the doll 'Under glass, under wraps,' the speaker restrained by vows and, like the suitcase, pressed down and locked.

Views of woman

- The false image versus the reality: the pure, asexual creature of 'airless glamour' is set against the emotional and physical turmoil of the reality.
- Oppressed woman is emphasised: woman confined, repressed, under glass, under vows, locked in.

Imagery

The imagery mediates the theme very effectively. The delicacy of 'blooms from the ivory tulle' and the 'shell-tone spray of seed pearls' helps create the notion of frail beauty, elegant if bloodless. The unreality is reinforced by the flowers ('less than real | stephanotis'). The colours, too, help to create this lifeless perfection: ivory and oyster. And of course the symbolism of the doll, which is a mere replica, underlines the falsity of this image of woman. Both the glass dome and the locked case carry, in their different ways, suggestions of oppression, secrets to be locked away, lack of true freedom.

White Hawthorn in the West of Ireland

Text of poem: New Explorations Anthology page 448

A reading of the poem

This is one of a group of poems from the volume *Outside History,* in which the poet is attempting to 'make connections' with her world – to establish continuity in her personal life, family traditions and lore, to find a working relationship with her cultural history and, here, to re-establish the age-old connection with the natural world.

In this poem she is going back to nature, fleeing 'suburban gardens. | Lawnmowers. Small talk.' This toy-house neatness and inconsequential chatter of suburbia is contrasted with the wild, uncultivated beauty, the primitiveness and the naturalness of life in the west:

> Under low skies, past splashes of coltsfoot,
> I assumed
> the hard shyness of Atlantic light
> and the superstitious aura of hawthorn.

She identifies immediately with the naturalness, is at home with the earth. Her enthusiasm is communicated in the energetic rhythms of the language, the flowing, run-on lines:

> All I wanted then was to fill my arms with
> sharp flowers,
> to seem, from a distance, to be part of
> that ivory, downhill rush. But I knew . . .

Contrast this enthusiasm with the minimalist staccato phrases of lines 3 and 4: 'I left behind suburban gardens. | Lawnmowers. Small talk.'

The hawthorn is associated with supernatural forces, primitive beliefs, the strange sub-rational powers of the earth. The power underneath the ordinary benign face of nature fascinates the poet here. Like hawthorn, water has a gentle fluency combined with enormous power ('able | to re-define land'), a power that is usually veiled under the river's more usual appearance of a recreational amenity or a landscape bearing for lost travellers. Nature dominates all human exchange – 'the only language spoken in those parts.'

Themes

- The poem contrasts two ways of life, the 'cultivated' suburban versus the natural primitiveness of life in the country.
- The superiority of the natural is proclaimed, with its excitement and energy.
- This is an 'earth poem', exploring the power beneath the ordinary face of nature, the hidden sub-rational depths.
- It might also be read as a symbolic journey, of the deracinated poet, the suburban dweller, searching for her real roots – her roots understood in both a geographical and a metaphysical sense. She is searching for a place and also for a philosophy. The undefined time of year, the 'season between seasons', seems to point up the poet's sense of 'out-of-placeness,' her unsettled state of mind.

Outside History

Text of poem: New Explorations Anthology page 450

A READING OF THE POEM

Boland rebelled against the mythicisation of Irish history: the songs, the ballads, the female icons of the nation, the romantic images. Myth obscures the reality, manipulates history. It is outside real lived history, a remote, unchanging image, a false construct.

Here Boland, as a poet, rejects myth in favour of real history as the proper authority for her poetry and her idea of nation.

The stars are symbolic of outsiders, remote and unreal, 'whose light happened | thousands of years | before our pain did'. Paradoxically, though they appear unchanging and are symbols of eternity, their illumination is thousands of years out of date when it reaches us. Ironically, it is the light that is an illusion: the darkness is real. The stars' unrelenting, cold, hard wintry light is shown in direct contrast to human vulnerability ('our pain'). The alternative to this remote, unchanging mythical framework for viewing life is the vantage point of human history, with its real suffering and mortality:

> Under them remains
> a place where you found
> you were human, and
> a landscape in which you know you are mortal.

It is necessary to choose between the two outlooks. Boland has chosen to move 'out of myth into history', to be part of the real pain and suffering of life. Only now does she begin to experience the real torment of lives endured by countless people throughout the years. In a nightmarish, Armageddon-type image suggestive of famine disaster ('roads clotted as | firmaments with the dead') she invites us in to comfort all the dying in history, real history:

> How slowly they die,
> as we kneel beside them, whisper in their ear.

The critic Jody Allen-Randolph has described it as follows: 'In a moment of power and dignity, the dead are finally allowed to die, however slowly and painfully, as both poet and audience move in to whisper the rite of contrition. Their deaths are not manipulated to serve any cause beyond their suffering which survives in the poem as a moment of collective grief.' It is a final laying to rest of the nationalist dead. But it is too late ('And we are too late. We are always too late'). This melancholic ending echoes an awareness of the suffering caused by this mythical view of history and realises that it cannot be undone fully.

This Moment

Text of poem: New Explorations Anthology page 452

[*Note: This poem is also prescribed for Ordinary Level 2008 exam*]

A READING OF THE POEM

At one level this is a simple nature lyric celebrating the moment of dusk in the suburbs. The scene is filled with the usual furniture of a suburban evening: darkening trees, lighted windows, stars, moths, rinds, children, and mothers calling them in. It is a romantic evocation of suburban twilight, creating an atmosphere of calm, of continuing growth, ripeness and natural abundance: 'One window is yellow as butter ... Moths flutter | Apples sweeten in the dark.' Boland is celebrating the ordinary, having discovered that even banal suburban routines can stimulate the poetic in her.

Yet for all its outward ordinariness there is a hint of the mysterious:

> Things are getting ready
> to happen
> out of sight.

This might refer simply to nature's continuing growth in the secrecy of night ('Apples sweeten in the dark') or to some deeper significance of this scene.

Notice that the really significant part of the moment is the reuniting of mother and child. There is a subtle dramatic build-up to this, with intimations that something is being held back slightly: 'Things are getting ready | to happen ... But not yet.' The intervening images serve to heighten the wait for the finally revealed moment:

> A woman leans down to catch a child
> who has run into her arms
> this moment.

This stanza is emphasised by having the only significant activity in the poem: 'leans', 'to catch', 'runs'. With that activity 'this moment' has arrived. So the moment celebrated is maternal, a physical demonstration of the bond between mother and child, with all its connotation of love, security and protection.

The fact that this is happening everywhere, in suburbs all over the world, gives it a universal significance, lends a mythic quality to the gesture. The woman in the poem is connected to all women in history who must have performed a similar action.

So the poem is about dusk, a moment of transition in nature; but it is also about a universal moment in woman's experience: the confirmation of maternal love.

Ideas in the poem

- The ordinary beauty and richness of nature at the mysterious hour of dusk
- That the suburbs can be poetic
- That significant moments are moments of human encounter
- A woman sharing in the universal experience of motherhood.

Love

Text of poem: New Explorations Anthology page 454

Background note

'Love' is one of a sequence of poems entitled 'Legends' that explores parallels between ancient myths and modern life. In some of the poems, such as 'Love' and 'The Pomegranate', the exploration of myth is used to deepen an understanding of woman as mother. Other poems explore themes of faithfulness, the creation of images of love, the fragility of all life, etc. In general, the point being made is that legends, myths and such stories point up the similarity of human experience throughout the ages and show a line of continuity from present days to ancient past.

Towards the end of the sequence Boland examines the end of this continuum line, her own family history, when she is prompted by personal memories or significant objects, such as an heirloom brooch or other keepsake.

In classical Greek and Roman mythology a number of the stories feature visits by the living to the underworld, Hades, the kingdom of the dead. So 'the hero' who 'crossed on his way to hell' might be the hero Odysseus, who conjured up the spirits of his dead companions by offering sacrifice on the banks of the river Ocean. But it is even more likely that the speaker refers to the story of Orpheus and Eurydice, a tale of the anguished separation of ardent lovers found in Virgil's fourth 'Georgic'. Orpheus went down into Hades to rescue his beloved Eurydice, who had been killed by a snake bite. His songs to her on his lyre had held all spellbound, and he was allowed to leave with her on condition that he did not look back. But

> He halts. Eurydice, his own is now on the lip of
> Daylight. Alas! he forgot. His purpose broke. He looked back.
> His labour was lost, the pact that he had made with the merciless king
> Annulled. Three times did thunder peal over the pool of Avernus
> 'Who', she cried, 'has doomed me to misery, who has doomed us?'
>
> Thus she spoke: and at once from his sight, like a wisp of smoke
> Thinned into air, was gone.

Wildly he grasped at shadows, waiting to say much more,
But she did not see him; nor would the ferryman of the Inferno
Let him again cross the fen that lay between them.

The story goes on to chart the months of weeping and mourning suffered by Orpheus, wandering through caves and forests, where his sorrow touched even the wild animals and the trees. Boland uses the myth as a framework for exploring ideas of love and loss and the impossibility of recovering the passionate intensity of first love.

Layers of meaning

As with many a Boland poem, this has a number of layers of significance. At one level it is a love poem, in which the speaker reflects on her present loving relationship with her husband but still yearns for the intensity of their early love, when they first lived in this American town with their young family many years before. But the speaker's thoughts are drawn continually to classical myths and legends, in which she finds experiences parallel to her own. She uses these mythical allusions to explore the infant's brush with death, the nature of her relationship with her husband, and her female consciousness and role. She identifies with the female voice in the myth, thereby establishing the continuity and importance of the female experience throughout the ages.

So this is a poem about love, about family, about female experience, and about the centrality of myth to our lives.

The poem has a number of overlapping time frames: present, recent past, and ancient time.

Themes and issues

Love

Different facets of love are touched on in this poem. The passion and delicacy of first physical love is most keenly registered.

And we discovered there
love had the feather and muscle of wings
and had come to live with us,
a brother of fire and air.

The bird metaphor conveys the elemental nature, the naturalness, the strength and grace of love. Indeed there is an almost nostalgic yearning for the intensity of this early love: 'Will we ever live so intensely again?' etc. With great honesty she admits her need to cast her lover in a heroic mould, to see the beloved as hero. Here she is creating myths, manufacturing an image of love and lover, a classical hero in suburban America: 'I see you as a hero in a text . . . with snow on the shoulders of your coat | and a car passing with its headlights on . . . the image blazing and the edges gilded . . .' The love she speaks of in the present tense is described in terms of language – love seen as communication:

> We love each other still . . .
> we speak plainly. We hear each other clearly.

Yet a problem is hinted at here. We have less than perfect communication:

> But the words are shadows and you cannot hear me.
> You walk away and I cannot follow.

The underlying mythical allusions augment this sense of failure, as they all deal with separation and loss and the creation of insufferable barriers between lovers. So the love between speaker and husband here carries connotations of failure, of unheard words.

She also deals with love in a family context, amid kitchen tables and threatened tragedy:

> We had two infant children one of whom
> was touched by death in this town
> and spared;

This is the quiet familial love of the suffering mother who can only watch and wait.

The significance of myth and legend

Human affairs are seen in the long tradition of history, even prehistory and mythology. Love, death, pain and separation are the universal human experience. The poet uses mythical allusions to create an awareness of the continuity of human experiences and to deepen an understanding of some of them. For example, the threatened loss of her child is explored through a parallel myth. The sense of loss, the separation of death, the awful failure of communication and the waste of life's opportunities are all evoked by reference to myth.

> When the hero
> was hailed by his comrades in hell
> their mouths opened and their voices failed and
> there is no knowing what they would have asked
> about a life they had shared and lost.

Is the effect of this to distance and lessen the mother's anguish?

The experience of love is seen in the heroic terms of myth and legend, as we have seen: 'I see you as a hero in a text', etc. It is as if the ordinary, everyday reality of love is insufficient and there is a need for the heroic, the superhuman, the extraordinary quality of myth in human lives. She imagines the hero-husband edged with an aura like a god of mythology, though it is merely the effect of car headlights behind him – 'the image blazing and the edges gilded'.

But perhaps the most significant aspect of myth is that it allows the speaker to tap into female experience and the universal female voice.

THE FEMALE VOICE

The secondary role of woman is much in evidence here, yielding precedence and importance to the male hero, viewing her partner as a 'hero in a text', etc. She is silent, voiceless, but longing 'to cry out the epic question | my dear companion'. She is the unheard voice of woman, throughout myth and history: 'But the words are shadows and you cannot hear me.'

Even her role as mother here is essentially powerless in the face of the threatened death of her infant. She adopts a passive, stoical attitude, as if life and death are completely in the hands of fate. The child 'was touched by death . . . and spared . . . Our child is healed.' Perhaps this episode could be seen as referring back to an earlier theme of Boland's in 'The Journey': the fears of women with sick children.

Overall, the poet is asserting the universality of female experience, whether it be in Ancient Greece and Rome or modern America, on the banks of the mythical river Styx or a bridge over the Iowa river. By identifying with female voices of myth, and particularly with that of the abandoned Eurydice in the last lines ('You walk away and I cannot follow'), she again registers the powerlessness of women.

Imagery

The poem opens and closes with images of darkness and shadow. The prevailing darkness and Stygian gloom of the first stanza ('Dark falls . . . Dusk has hidden the bridge . . . hell') recurs in the final lines ('words are shadows'). So the poem is bracketed by gloom, which qualifies and balances the enthusiasm of the love theme. In contrast to this darkness, the hero is silhouetted in light ('the image blazing and the edges gilded'). So we get a very primal contrast of colours, reflecting love and death, good and evil. Family love and life are mediated in images of ordinary domesticity: an old apartment, a kitchen, an Amish table, a view. References to speech and dumbness abound. Death is pictured as voicelessness, love as plain speaking, and the failure of love as a failure of speech.

Perhaps the most exciting metaphor is that of love as a bird, communicating the natural energy and beauty of the emotion ('love had the feather and muscle of wings').

Form

The poem is written in loose, non-rhyming stanzas, in which the natural rhythms of speech are employed to carry the reminiscences and the personal narrative. Might it be significant that the stanzas gradually diminish in size? The first three are of five or six lines, then one of five lines, three stanzas of four lines, and finally a two-line stanza to finish. Might this mirror the diminishing scope of love as treated in the poem?

The Pomegranate

Text of poem: New Explorations Anthology page 456

A READING OF THE POEM

This poem deals with the value of myth to life, with the universal truth of legend. The poet explores this theme by recalling the interlinking of life and legend in her own experience.

She first encountered this particular legend when she was a child in exile in London, 'a city of fogs and strange consonants'. The story of separation and confinement in an alien world must have resonated powerfully with her own experience then. Another facet of the legend's theme, the mother's anguish for her lost child, struck a chord with the poet at a later stage in her life, when she 'walked out in a summer twilight | searching for my daughter at bed-time.' She also takes to heart one of the myth's bitter truths: the ravages of time and the seasons on nature and humankind.

> But I was Ceres then and I knew
> winter was in store for every leaf
> on every tree on that road.
> Was inescapable for each one we passed.
> And for me.

The legend assists the poet in understanding her daughter. Insights so gained vary from the startlingly banal fact that 'a child can be | hungry' to the deeper understanding that she must allow her daughter space, the freedom to grow up: 'I will say nothing.' The stories of legend are archetypal and run parallel to human experience in all ages, and it is a worthwhile experience, an enrichment, to move in and out of the different worlds and time zones through 'such beautiful rifts in time'.

The poem also explores the relationship between mother and daughter. It paints a picture of intimate moments, as the mother views the teenage clutter with eyes of love:

My child asleep beside her teen magazines
her can of Coke, her plate of uncut fruit.

The poet shares with Ceres that fierce maternal protectiveness. And moving through the beautiful rift in time, the images of Persephone and her own daughter fuse, and the poet's maternal instinct is to warn and protect the child then and the child now:

I could warn her. There is still a chance
The rain is cold. The road is flint coloured.
The suburb has cars and cable television.
The veiled stars are above ground.
It is another world.

Yet she realises that the girl must experience the truth of the legend for herself, must be free to experience the temptation ('the papery flushed skin in her hand'), to make mistakes, to suffer pain. If the mother protects her too much the wisdom of the legend (the gift) will mean little: 'If I defer the grief I will diminish the gift.' And what better inheritance can a mother bequeath than the eternal wisdom of myth and legend?

But what else
can a mother give her daughter but such
beautiful rifts in time?

Issues raised in the poem

- The value of myth to life: how legend embodies universal truth, conveys vital understanding, and illuminates the present.
- The relationship between mother and daughter: the intensity of the bond, the fierce protectiveness, but also an awareness of the independence of the child and her need to experience life, truth, love and passion for herself.

Imagery

Some images are used in a symbolic way. The pomegranate, for instance, has mythological significance, a fruit sacred to the underworld, drawing those who eat it down into darkness. Here it fulfils a similar function, with overtones, perhaps, of sexual temptation.

She will hold
the papery flushed skin in her hand
And to her lips.

Has the uncut fruit connotations also of the temptation and loss in the Garden of Eden? Is the mother attempting to protect her daughter from the griefs associated with sexuality?

Much of the imagery is of darkness, twilight, the underworld, etc.: 'hell', 'the cracking dusk of the underworld', 'a city of fogs', 'twilight', 'it is winter | and the stars are hidden', and 'The road is flint-coloured.' This motif of darkness is associated with both the legend and the poet's present experience and creates a somewhat bleak atmosphere. But it is a fitting setting for the poet's anxiety and the pain she suffers in conferring freedom on her daughter. The modern bedroom, if not 'a place of death' as in the legend, is still 'full of unshed tears'.

Overview of the issues in this selection of Boland's poetry

Boland's view of Irish history and the idea of nation

- Boland deals with the reality of Irish history, the familiar story of oppression, defeat and death ('The Famine Road'). The sense of national identity that comes across from 'The Famine Road' speaks of victimisation, being downtrodden and living out pointless lives: see also the suffering in 'Outside History'.
- Opposed to that view is the male-created myth, involving heroic struggle, battle and glorious defeat: see the image of the dying patriot immortalised by art in 'An Old Steel Engraving'. The woman poet feels excluded from that cultural tradition – 'One of us who turns away.'
- Boland resists this mythicisation of history, insists on the necessity of confronting the reality, facing the unburied dead of history and laying them to rest ('Outside History').
- She shows concern for the unrecorded history, for the significance of lives lived on the margins of history, away from the centre of power, far from the limelight of action. She mourns the forgotten lives in 'That the Science of Cartography is Limited'.
- In her prose writings Boland explores the idea of nation and the difficulties it produces for her as a woman poet.

> So it was with me. For this very reason, early on as a poet, certainly in my twenties, I realised that the Irish nation as an existing construct in Irish poetry was not available to me. I would not have been able to articulate it at that point, but at some preliminary level I already knew that the anguish and power of that woman's gesture on Achill, with its suggestive hinterland of pain, were not something I could predict or rely on in Irish poetry. There were glimpses here and there; sometimes more than that. But all too often, when I was searching for such an inclusion, what I found was a rhetoric of imagery which alienated me: a fusion of the national and the feminine which seemed to simplify both.

It was not a comfortable realisation. There was nothing clear-cut about my feelings. I had tribal ambivalences and doubts, and even then I had an uneasy sense of the conflict which awaited me. On the one hand, I knew that as a poet I could not easily do without the idea of a nation. Poetry in every time draws on that reserve. On the other, I could not as a woman accept the nation formulated for me by Irish poetry and its traditions. At one point it even looked to me as if the whole thing might be made up of irreconcilable differences. At the very least it seemed to me that I was likely to remain an outsider in my own national literature, cut off from its archive, at a distance from its energy. Unless, that is, I could repossess it. This proposal is about that conflict and that repossession and about the fact that repossession itself is not a static or single act. Indeed, the argument which describes it may itself be no more than a part of it.

VIOLENCE IN SOCIETY

- 'The War Horse' explores suburban, middle-class attitudes to political violence. It is really a psychological exploration of the theme 'how we respond to violence'.
- Race memory and the old antagonisms to English colonial rule still exist just beneath the surface ('The War Horse').
- The real human consequences of political violence are portrayed in 'Child of Our Time'. The poet acts as conscience of our society here.
- Violence is seen as the result of a failure of language, an inability to communicate ('Child of Our Time').

THE SIGNIFICANCE OF MYTH

- In one sense myth is seen to play a positive and enabling role, even in modern life. It gives the poet a framework for exploring human truths such as themes of love and death ('Love'). The wisdom of myths enables her to deal sensitively with her growing daughter ('The Pomegranate'). Mythical stories demonstrate the universality of human experience. The poet sometimes feels part of this tradition by doing the ordinary things and so shares in the long history of woman's experience and becomes a part of myth or universal truth ('This Moment').
- But created images can be false, limiting and confining. Idealised or mythicised images of woman are fixed in time, unable to love, breed, sweat or grow old (see 'Time and Violence').
- Boland often challenges the image of woman in mythology (also in art and literature), particularly when it shows woman as marginalised, silenced, subservient to her husband the hero, as in 'Love'.

- History is laced with myths. The unreality, the coldness and the distance of myth from real lives is symbolised in the stars of 'Outside History'.

THE EXPERIENCE OF BEING A WOMAN

Boland's strong feminine perspective lends an extra dimension of insight to all her themes. But she also considers specific issues relating to the portrayal and the treatment of women.

- The image versus the reality: 'The Shadow Doll' explores that false image of woman, specifically nineteenth-century woman, but it has universal relevance. The image is one of elegance, dignified control of emotions ('an airless glamour'), and suppressed sexuality ('discreet about | visits, fevers, quickenings and lust'). Women are forced to conform to a false image, repressed, metaphorically enclosed in glass, locked away ('The Shadow Doll').
- The image of woman in art, literature and mythology is often idealised or stereotyped. The mythological allusions in 'Love' conjure up an image of woman as powerless and silent, yearning in vain for a heroic love.
- The sufferings of woman are equated with the oppression of the nation ('The Famine Road').
- The traditional role of woman is validated in such poems as 'This Moment', which show woman as mother. That maternal gesture of catching the child in her arms is the key to the poem. The protectiveness of mothers features in 'The Pomegranate'. Also her wisdom is displayed in allowing the daughter freedom to learn for herself.
- Woman as lover features in 'The Black Lace Fan My Mother Gave Me' and 'Love'.
- Suburban woman features in many of the poems: e.g. 'The War Horse' and 'This Moment'.
- The puzzling relationship between men and women features in 'The Black Lace Fan My Mother Gave Me': the mistimings, the tempests of love, the sensual allure. Love diminishes in time, like the importance of the fan. This makes an interesting alternative view to the blinkered one of idyllic romance.
- Boland challenges the patriarchal tradition of Irish poetry. In *Object Lessons* she elaborated on her objections to the images of woman in literature.

> The majority of Irish male poets depended on women as motifs in their poetry. They moved easily, deftly, as if by right among images of women in which I did not believe and of which I could not approve. The women in their poems were often passive, decorative, raised to emblematic status. This was especially true where the woman and the idea of the nation were mixed: where the nation became a woman and the woman took on a national posture.
>
> The trouble was [that] these images did good service as

ornaments. In fact, they had a wide acceptance as ornaments by readers of Irish poetry. Women in such poems were frequently referred to approvingly as mythic, emblematic. But to me these passive and simplified women seemed a corruption. For they were not decorations, they were not ornaments. However distorted these images, they had their roots in a suffered truth.

What had happened? How had the women of our past – the women of a long struggle and a terrible survival – undergone such a transformation? How had they suffered Irish history and rooted themselves in the speech and memory of the Achill woman, only to re-emerge in Irish poetry as fictive queens and national sibyls?

The more I thought about it, the more uneasy I became. The wrath and grief of Irish history seemed to me, as it did to many, one of our true possessions. Women were part of that wrath, had endured that grief. It seemed to me a species of human insult that at the end of all, in certain Irish poems, they should become elements of style rather than aspects of truth.

Ageing

- In the later poems, such as 'The Pomegranate', Boland is conscious, in a personal sense, of the ageing process.

Representation in art

- In other poems Boland is particularly concerned with the representation of women in painting.

Striving for truth

- In all these areas explored – history, art and love – Boland is striving for truth and searching out the reality rather than the glittering image.

Poetry in the suburbs

- A good deal of her poetry is set in the suburbs, a setting not associated traditionally with poetic aspiration.
- The fragile nature of the beauty and order created in the suburbs is brought out in 'The War Horse'.
- The toy-house neatness of suburbia is no match for the wild, elemental attractions of nature in 'White Hawthorn in the West of Ireland'.
- In the later poems we encounter a romantic evocation of a suburban twilight ('This Moment'). Nature has colonised the suburbs ('Stars rise. | Moths flutter.' and 'One window is yellow as butter').

- But the real bleakness of the suburban street is not hidden: 'The rain is cold. The road is flint-coloured' ('The Pomegranate').

Forging a personal understanding of Boland's poetry

Think about the following points and make notes for yourself or discuss them in groups.

1. On reading Boland, which poems do you particularly like?
2. On reading Boland, what were the main issues the poems raised for you?
3. What settings, colours and moods do you associate with Boland's poetry?
4. What general understanding of the poet did you form?
   - What is important in her life?
   - How does she see herself?
   - Is she a happy or a sad person? etc.
5. Did reading her poetry add anything to your understanding of Irish history? What, and in which poems?
6. Consider her thoughts on the treatment of women in society and in history. Do you consider that she makes an important contribution to feminist thinking?
7. What insights did she give you into suburban life?
8. Would you consider her a radical poet? Explain your views.
9. Why do you think we should read her poetry?
10. What aspects of Boland's poetry strike a chord with you: particular themes; settings; point of view on the world; the images she creates; the feeling and tones in the poems? What appeals to you?

Questions

1. Outline three significant issues dealt with in the poetry of Eavan Boland. Explore, in detail, the poet's treatment of any one of these issues.
2. Do you find the poet's view of Irish history particularly bleak? Comment.
3. 'The attempt to shed the constricting husk of myth and enter the nightmare of history is an important theme in Boland's poetry' (R. Smith). Discuss.
4. 'Boland's poetry shows a consciousness of the sustaining power of cultural heritage, whether through primitive Irish superstition or classical mythology.' Discuss this statement in the light of the poems you have read.
5. 'Boland's poetry shows how idealised images of women need to be set beside the reality.' Discuss.
6. 'While she takes a feminist line, maternity and suburbia feature prominently in Boland's poetry.' Consider this statement in the light of at least two poems you have read.

7. 'The relationship between mother and daughter is an important preoccupation in Boland's' poetry.' Discuss, with reference to at least two of the poems you have read.
8. 'Boland is always conscious of the natural context in which human events occur.' Consider Boland as a nature poet.
9. 'Boland's imagination thrives in the shadows.' Would you agree?
10. 'Finding significant moments of human experience is the goal of much of Boland's poetry.' Discuss this statement, with reference to at least three poems.

Bibliography

Allen-Randolph, Jody, '*Écriture féminine* and the authorship of self in Eavan Boland's *In Her Own Image*', *Colby Quarterly,* vol. 27 (1991), 48–59.

Allen-Randolph, Jody, 'Private worlds, public realities: Eavan Boland's poetry, 1967–1990', *Irish University Review,* vol. 23 (1993), no. 1, 5–22.

Boyle Haberstroh, Patricia, *Women Creating Women: Contemporary Irish Women Poets,* Syracuse (NY): Syracuse University Press 1996, 59–92.

Dawe, Gerald, 'The suburban night: Eavan Boland, Paul Durcan and Thomas McCarthy' in *Against Piety: Essays in Irish Poetry,* Belfast: Lagan Press 1995, 169–93.

Denman, Peter, 'Ways of saying: Boland, Carson, McGuckian' in *Poetry in Contemporary Irish Literature* (Irish Literary Studies, 43), edited by Michael Kenneally, Gerrards Cross (Bucks): Colin Smythe 1995, 158–173.

Kiberd, Declan, *Inventing Ireland,* London: Jonathan Cape 1995.

Longley, Edna, 'From Cathleen to anorexia: the breakdown of Irelands' in *A Dozen Lips,* Dublin: Attic Press 1994, 162, 187.

McGuinness, Arthur, 'Hearth and history: poetry by contemporary Irish women poets' in *Cultural Contexts and Literary Idioms in Contemporary Irish Literature* (Irish Literary Studies, 31), edited by Michael Kenneally, Gerrards Cross (Bucks): Colin Smythe 1988, 197–220.

Mahoney, Rosemary, *Whoredom in Kimmage: Irish Women Coming of Age,* New York: Houghton Mifflin 1993.

Matthews, Steven, *Irish Poetry: Politics, History, Negotiation: The Evolving Debate, 1969 to the Present,* Basingstoke: Macmillan 1997.

Meaney, Geraldine, 'Sex and nation: women in Irish culture and politics' in *A Dozen Lips,* Dublin: Attic Press 1994, 188–204.

Ní Chuilleanáin, Eiléan (editor), *Irish Women: Image and Achievement,* Dublin: Arlen House 1985.

Roche, Anthony, and Allen-Randolph, Jody (editors), *Irish University Review Special Issue: Eavan Boland,* vol. 23, no. 1 (spring–summer 1993).

Ward, Margaret, 'The missing sex: putting women into Irish history' in *A Dozen Lips,* Dublin: Attic Press 1994, 205–24.

Ordinary Level, 2008 EXAMINATION

Explanatory note

Candidates taking the Ordinary (Pass) level exam in 2008 have a choice of questions when dealing with the prescribed poems. They can answer either (*a*) a question on one of the poems by a poet prescribed for Higher Level for the 2008 exam, or (*b*) a question from a list of other prescribed poems (i.e. the alternative poems discussed on pages 305–325).

(a) The poems by Higher level poets that may also be answered by Ordinary level candidates in the 2008 exam are as follows:

Donne	The Flea (p. 2) Song: Go, and catch a falling star (p. 4)	**Rich**	Aunt Jennifer's Tigers (p. 272) Storm Warnings (p. 278) Power (p. 305)
Frost	'Out, Out–' (p. 102) The Road Not Taken (p. 104) Acquainted With the Night (p. 108)	**Plath**	The Arrival of the Bee Box (p. 372) Child (p. 375)
Larkin	At Grass (p. 205) An Arundel Tomb (p. 212) The Explosion (p. 228)	**Mahon**	Grandfather (p. 406) After the *Titanic* (p. 411) Antarctica (p. 427)
Montague	The Cage (p. 228) Like dolmens round my childhood. . . (p. 257)	**Boland**	Child of Our Time (p. 440) This Moment (p. 452)

(*b*) The alternative poems that Ordinary level candidates sitting the exam in 2008 may choose to study instead are discussed on pages 305–25.

CONTRIBUTORS
Carole Scully
John McCarthy
John G. Fahy
David Keogh
Bernard Connolly

Ordinary Level, 2008 Examination

Alternative poems

William Shakespeare
Fear no more the heat o' the sun

Text of poem: New Explorations Anthology page 461

A reading of the poem

This is a very moving dirge that nevertheless manages to convey a measured statement about death. Death is a refuge from the extremes of weather, from political tyranny and social injustice, and from the day-to-day struggles of life. Death is comfortable and familiar, a well-earned rest after work.

> Thou worldly task hast done,
> Home art gone and ta'en thy wages.

Death is seen as the consummation of life.

There is also the reminder that death is inevitable for all ages and all ranks in society: golden lads and girls; all young lovers; chimney-sweepers; kings, scholars, and doctors. Beauty and youth, the powerful and the learned, as well as the socially insignificant – all must succumb.

It ends with a moving prayer that the dead be protected from all evil of witchcraft or spirits and be allowed a quiet return to the earth, and that the grave be honoured and respected.

Percy Bysshe Shelley
Ozymandias

Text of poem: New Explorations Anthology page 471

A reading of the poem

'Ozymandias' explores a common theme of Romantic poetry: the passing of all human creations, the vanity of the works of humankind, and so the pointlessness of life. Perhaps it is also sneering at the arrogance of rulers – a favourite theme of Shelley's. There is a hint here too of the relative superiority of art over life (in that it lasts slightly longer).

Unusually for a sonnet, this poem is structured as a narrative. It tells the story of a traveller who returned from visiting the remains of an ancient civilisation and described what he saw. The place has been reconquered by the desert, and all that remains as an indication of a once-great power are the ruins of an enormous statue – 'Two vast and trunkless legs of stone', and some pieces of its shattered face. Yet the shattered head still preserves the king's features, particularly the expression of arrogance and of unchallengeable authority ('frown, | And wrinkled lip, and sneer of cold command'). This shows the perceptiveness of the sculptor, who managed to capture the king's emotions or passions in the stone ('its sculptor well those passions read | which yet survive, stamped on these lifeless things').

The syntax is quite involved here and makes understanding less immediate. In the eighth line, 'hand' refers to the sculptor's hand, and 'the heart that fed' refers to the king's heart, which gave life and energy to all this in the first place. Shelley uses this technique of *synecdoche* (where a part stands for the whole) to reinforce the sculptor's excellence at recording the king's inner emotions. Hand captures heart. The pedestal also survives, ironically still proclaiming its message of arrogant superiority ('Look on my works, ye mighty, and despair!').

In fact it is mainly by the use of irony right through the poem that Shelley reinforces his theme of the vanity of human endeavour. For example, the once-great civilisation is now a desert, and even its precise name is no longer used ('an antique land'). The haughty superiority of the king, while still visible in the sculpture, is nevertheless shattered ('Half sunk, a shattered visage'). The fact that all that remains of a civilisation renowned for its architecture and art is this grotesque piece of statuary ('Two vast and trunkless legs') adds a further twist to the irony. It is now disparagingly referred to as 'that colossal wreck'. The inscription on the pedestal too is deeply ironic, as time has made the king's boast a hollow one.

The final statement, by sound and image, reinforces the theme: we see that the works of humans are merely a disfiguring, decaying wreck spoiling the serene emptiness of the natural landscape. The insignificance of human civilisation when compared with the vastness of time is caught in that beautiful image of rolling desert sands, stretching as far as the eye can see and back through history. The long vowel sounds reinforce this sense of the emptiness of time: decay, boundless, bare, lone, far away.

As a sonnet

This poem has been highly praised by critics, who suggest that it displays the best features of sonnet form. Its simplicity is often remarked on. It has a single idea and one simple point to make. The language is simple yet effective (Think of the 'sneer of cold command'). The only change from octave to sestet is a deepening of the tone of irony with the reference to the king's foolish boast. The epigrammatical summary in the final lines reinforces the theme visually and definitively, as we expect from a good final couplet.

The sonnet is structured as a narrative, so the run-on lines are entirely appropriate, the first long sentence holding the atmosphere of the story. Subsequently, the dramatic effect of the single short sentence is all the greater: 'Nothing beside remains.' We hardly notice that the rhyming scheme is slightly irregular, with some off-rhymes (stone – frown; appear – despair) and an unusual rhyming scheme.

Christina Rossetti
Remember

Text of poem: New Explorations Anthology page 474

Structure

This poem is written in the Sonnet form. It is made up of fourteen lines. The first eight lines are divided by the rhymes at the ends of the lines and the punctuation into two groups of four, known as quatrains. The final six lines are called a sestet.

A reading of the poem

Rossetti opens the poem by telling her companion to 'remember' her when they are no longer together. She emphasises the idea of separation by repeating the words 'gone' and 'away' and adding in the word 'far'. She uses two vivid images to help the reader to understand the effects that this parting will have on the couple: they will no longer be able to hold hands or to turn around to be together. So, in the first quatrain, the couple are seen as being forced to give up their close physical intimacy and, instead, to be 'far away' from each other.

In the second quatrain, she uses the phrase 'remember me' twice as if she is growing increasingly agitated. These lines also develop our understanding of just how close the couple's relationship is. They speak together of their 'future' in detail. We realise that they are not only physically close, but also intellectually and emotionally close: they share their thoughts and hopes and dreams. This conversation contrasts with the terrible quietness of 'the silent land' that Rossetti imagines in the second line of the poem. The feeling that the couple are helpless to resist this separation is suggested in the phrase 'It will be late to counsel then or pray'.

The sestet reveals just how much Rossetti cares for her companion. Although she has repeated her hope that she will be remembered in the first eight lines of the poem, she now reveals her concern that her partner should not feel sad nor grieve for her going. In the final two lines of the poem she makes it clear that her desire to be remembered after she is gone is not as strong as her desire for her partner to be happy without her. In words that are simple yet deeply moving, she says that she would rather her companion forgot about her and be happy than remember her and be sad.

Siegfried Sassoon
On Passing the New Menin Gate

Text of poem: New Explorations Anthology page 480

A READING OF THE POEM

Sassoon launches us straight into the central theme of the poem in the first two lines of the first stanza, where his questions place 'this Gate' alongside the 'Dead who fed the guns'. It is the relationship between these two that he explores in the remainder of the poem.

Initially, in the first stanza, he focuses on the 'Dead'. He comments on the 'foulness of their fate' and describes how they 'endured' the nightmarish environment of a 'sullen swamp' before being 'fed' to the guns. His pity for these unfortunate men is heightened by the fact that they had no choice about being in such a dreadful situation, as they had been 'conscripted' into this bloody and brutal war.

Balanced against these horrifying images is 'this Gate'. He tells us, contemptuously, that it has been 'Crudely renewed', suggesting that it has been put together roughly. To Sassoon it seems to be 'a pile of peace-complacent stone'. This image of a 'pile' does not suggest a structure that would create the sense of 'pomp' that Sassoon links it to in line 7.

His repetition of the word 'Paid' communicates his feelings of disgust that such a construction could be seen as a suitable way of paying for all the suffering and death that occurred around it. It becomes evident that his use of the words 'unheroic', 'unvictorious' and 'dim' does not reflect his opinion of the 'Dead', but rather those of their military leaders. To these men, safe and secure far away from the fighting, the 'Dead' were no more than 'cannon fodder', nameless bodies to be hurled at the enemy.

In the second stanza, Sassoon continues to express his feelings of disgust and contempt for the 'Gate' and the military leaders who caused it to be erected; and his pity and sympathy for the 'Dead'. To him, the horrifying experiences of the 'Dead' represent 'the world's worst wound'. Here again, he follows an image of suffering with an image of 'the Gateway'. Just as in the first stanza it was linked to 'pomp', here it is connected to 'pride'. The inscription on the 'Gate' promises immortality for all those who perished nearby. Sassoon sees all too clearly the terrible irony behind these words, for the 'Dead' who are now named for eternity with 'pride' were 'nameless' nonentities to the military leaders when they were alive.

Sassoon ends his poem with an image that vibrates with the bitterness of his emotions. The nightmare experiences of the 'Dead' worsen as he describes how they 'struggled in the slime'. Sassoon expresses his belief that the hypocrisy of the 'New Menin Gate' is so great that the bodies of these men will surely rise from the dead to ridicule it. In Sassoon's view, the military commanders have committed an act of crime against the 'Dead' by erecting this monument, since it does nothing to acknowledge what these men had been forced to endure. On the contrary, as far as he is concerned, it simply serves as a memorial to the pomposity, complacency and, above all, the pride of the military leaders.

Tone

There is an incredible intensity of emotions in the tone of this poem. Sassoon achieves this by his skilful use of word sounds. He employs alliteration of the letter 'f' (alliteration: where two or more words close together begin with the same letter) in line 4, to convey his disgust about the way the 'Dead' were forced to suffer and die in battle: 'Who shall absolve the **f**oulness of their **f**ate'. Similarly, the alliteration in lines 6–7 suggests that Sassoon feels such contempt for this memorial and those who ordered it to be built that he is almost spitting out these words: '**P**aid are its dim defenders by this **p**omp; / **P**aid, with a **p**ile of **p**eace-complacent stone'.

His uncompromising imagery conveying the horror of the battle scene often combines the sounds of the words with their meanings, as in the terrible image of dying men 'who struggled in the slime'. Here, the alliteration of the letter 's' reinforces the meaning of the word 'slime' by suggesting the slippery unpleasantness of the mud that sucked the last of the fading life out of the 'Dead'.

Richard Wilbur
The Pardon

Text of poem: New Explorations Anthology page 495

A Reading of the Poem

This poem explores a young boy's experience of death. The aspect of it borne in on him most forcefully is that the dead are so different. 'Sad or strange' are the words from a child's vocabulary used to describe the difference or 'otherness' of death. The sense of distance involved also strikes him: 'In my kind of world the dead were out of range.' The strangeness of death and its completely different nature register strongly on the boy.

The poem also records the boy's inability to cope with it. Straightforward fear is the repeated response: 'I was ten and very much afraid . . . I felt afraid again . . .' The nightmare images manifest this: 'still he came . . . clothed in a hymn of flies, | And death was breeding in his lively eyes.' There is also the inability to comprehend death – inadequately described as 'strange', as we saw. Death is somehow seen as a failing, a hurt, an injury to the living: 'I could not forgive the sad or strange | In beast or man.' And this leads to an inability to mourn.

Consequently the boy is consumed with guilt; but the horror of the dream is cathartic for him and opens the flood-gates of emotion: 'I started in to cry and call his name.' The guilt is faced and named, and so he is free of it.

> Asking forgiveness of his tongueless head.
> . . . I beg death's pardon now. And mourn the dead.

There is emotional release in mourning.

Some knowledge of the imperfections of the world and strange contradictions of life are among the powerful insights gained from this experience. Death and beauty exist side by side: the honeysuckle smell and 'another odour heavier still.' This is a traumatic growing-up experience, a moment of realisation concerning the discordance of the world that Wilbur talks about. Death has invaded the child's Eden. Nature shows its other frightening, less beautiful face; and the boy must learn to cope with this less than perfect world.

The poem also explores the power of dreams to communicate truth. The nightmare or vision results in the beneficial release of bottled-up feelings and emotions: 'whether this was false or honest dreaming | I beg death's pardon now.'

Themes and issues

- Coping with the experience of death: the inability to comprehend it; the inability to mourn; the resultant guilt; and finally the release of tears
- Discovering the discordance of the world and the imperfections of nature
- A moment of growth and development
- The function and power of dreams.

Structure

The poem is structured as a first-person narrative, which develops into a reflection on the psychological nature of the experience. In some ways this is a typical Wilbur poem, as he often begins by describing a scene or an object, then goes on to make a moral or philosophical point about it, thereby gaining insight and wisdom from the event. Often, as happens here, the poem grows by drawing him into an emotional relationship with the subject. This poem is framed by the first and final lines: 'My dog lay dead . . . And mourn the dead.' In between is the process whereby he came to mourn.

Conventional in form, the poem has regular four-line stanzas with a loose and barely noticeable rhyme. The second and third lines rhyme fully, while the first and fourth often manage a looser off-rhyme (grave – alive, was – buzz, grass – confess), as well as the full head – dead, etc. The general effect is of naturalness, totally appropriate to the narrative reminiscence.

A SENSUOUS POEM

One of the most striking features of Wilbur's style is the sensuous evocation of death. The earliest intimations are through the sense of smell, where the odour of death mingles with the scent of summer honeysuckle. The suggestion is delicately rendered yet real: 'another odour heavier still.' The sounds are more explicit, 'the flies' intolerable buzz' communicating something of the boy's revulsion; further down, the startling combination of the religious and the rotten, 'clothed in a hymn of flies,' communicates something of the discordance of death. It is a sort of bizarre dirge or requiem that evokes all the horror that the boy experiences. Nor is the sense of sight neglected. The nightmare image 'glowed a fierce and mortal green' and 'death was breeding in his lively eyes,' suggesting the horror of maggots without actually mentioning it. Altogether, the boy's memories of the event are powerfully sensuous.

TONE

From the matter-of-fact, conversational opening (My dog lay dead five days . . .') we are swiftly introduced to powerful, if still controlled, emotions and suggestions of guilty feelings ('I who had loved him while he kept alive | Went only close enough . . . '). This reflective tone of the first three stanzas gives way to something verging on panic in the final stanza; so we can see a growing emotional involvement as the poem progresses.

Elizabeth Jennings
The Ladybird's Story

Text of poem: New Explorations Anthology page 504

A READING OF THE POEM

This is a narrative poem, as it tells a story. The poet, Elizabeth Jennings, tells the story from the point of view of the ladybird. The small size of the ladybird is suggested by the metaphors (metaphor: comparing one thing to another without using 'like' or 'as') and similes (simile: comparing one thing to another using 'like' or 'as') that are used to describe the human being. So, to the ladybird the hand is 'a roadway'; the eyes are 'Glassy moons' and the nose is a 'peak'.

Jennings effectively conveys the vulnerability of the ladybird by directly contrasting it with the human. While the harmless ladybird has 'no sting', the human has a threatening nose like the 'beak' of the ladybird's greatest enemy, a bird. While the ladybird is 'frightened', the human is not. Significantly, the ladybird hears the human voice as 'a siren', often a sound signalling danger. It is clear that the ladybird is totally at the mercy of the human, able to do no more than cling to the giant hand as she is observed.

But more than anything else, Jennings contrasts the ladybird's innocence with the knowing awareness of the human being. At first, the ladybird does not understand what is preventing the human from carelessly destroying her with a 'blow'. In fact, the human immediately sees the ladybird as a sign of 'Good luck' in the form of 'some money'. Gradually, the ladybird realises that the kind treatment she receives as she is 'Gentled' off the hand is due to the human's greed and superstition. Luckily for the ladybird, the human being regards her as being of possible benefit, and it is this selfishness that saves her life.

However, in the brief moments of the incident described in the poem, the ladybird has come to 'understand' a great deal about human nature. She realises that humans are dangerously brutal and that her survival has not been motivated by any great moral appreciation of the preciousness of all life on the human's part. The ladybird remembers all too clearly the equally small and vulnerable 'flies' killed by the same human without a second thought. She knows that she has been saved by the self-centred greed and superstition inherent in human nature.

Tone

Jennings successfully controls the tone of this poem so that we can feel and hear the changing emotions in the ladybird's voice. Initially, the ladybird is quietly and calmly going about her life, choosing the possibilities that were offered to her: 'So many meeting-places and directions.' She is self-confident: 'But I did not tumble off.'

In an instant those possibilities are cut off and the ladybird feels afraid as she is observed by this giant: 'Suddenly, I was frightened, fearful of falling.' Jennings' use of alliteration with the 'f' (alliteration: where two or more words close together begin with the same letter) and the quicker rhythm of this line suggest the ladybird trembling with fear. There is a pleading tone in the phrases 'I have / No sting. I do not wound.' Here the full stops break up the words into short, breathless phrases reflecting the speech of someone who is begging for mercy.

Finally, there is a tone of growing confidence and acceptance in the concluding two lines of the poem, as the ladybird realises that she owes her life to the greed and superstition of humans. Now assured of survival, her focus moves away from herself and onto the 'you' of the human. She accepts the reality of human nature in all its self-centred greediness. Indeed, there is even a hint of contempt in the ladybird's voice as she says, 'You see I have watched you with flies.' Suddenly it is she, not the human, who is in the powerful position of being 'the observer'.

Richard Murphy
The Reading Lesson

Text of Poem: New Explorations Anthology page 508

Critical commentary

'The Reading Lesson' is based on a dialogue between two people. The speaker in the poem is a reading teacher who is trying to help a fourteen-year-old traveller boy to read. The poem describes the boy's struggle to come to grips with the world of letters and the teacher's frustration at his lack of progress, and it also shows the rest of society's reaction to their attempts. The poem uses images that are part of the boy's world to describe the struggle that goes on between them.

The boy either doesn't want to read or he is finding it so hard that he has almost given up. The first metaphor that is introduced by the poet to describe the situation is the dog hunting the hare. This gives the reader an image of a great wild chase – that he is trying to trap and tie down the boy's wild nature and bring it to a passive trap. There is a sense here, understood by both the teacher and the boy, that if he is 'tamed' he may lose something in the trade-off between them. The hunt is brought up to a climax when the teacher finally becomes so frustrated that he challenges the boy with a stern question. The teacher may think he is being rhetorical, but the boy takes him very literally and gives an equally stern reply:

> 'Don't you want to learn to read?'
> 'I'll be the same man whatever I do.'

The teacher compares this riposte to an animal that has been cornered and comes out with his teeth bared on his release.

The second verse continues with the nature imagery. The poet uses a mule, a goat and a snipe to describe the way the boy looks at the page. He explains that the atmosphere is tense and says that if there is

> 'A sharp word, and he'll mooch
> Back to his piebald mare and bantam cock.'

He finishes by explaining that his task is as difficult as catching mercury.

The third verse shows us that they have all but given up; the boy will not be using his fingers to follow words on a page, but he will use them to go hawking scrap or even to go pickpocketing. The teacher says that the boy could easily revert to the stereotype that the chuckling neighbour ascribes to him. The neighbour says that the boy is untameable, that he will always have a yearning to escape and go back to being his natural, wild self as soon as he has the chance.

The final verse finishes with some images that are specific to travellers. He says that books are something that the boy feels will restrict him and stop him from making his own way. They are as restrictive and separate from him as the idea of settling on a small farm to live for the rest of his life. He says that his life will be one of petty theft and poaching. He ends by comparing this book learning to the wren. The wren became The King Of All Birds by being clever enough to sit on the back of an eagle and therefore fly the highest in the sky. To the boy, that is how unobtainable to him books are.

Maya Angelou
Phenomenal Woman

Text of poem: New Explorations Anthology page 511

A READING OF THE POEM

Angelou has pretty much signalled the direction of this poem in her title, 'Phenomenal Woman'. She embarks on a series of images that show her being the focus of attention. So she describes 'Pretty women' who want to know her 'secret', and the way that her entrance into a room results in men gathering around her like 'A hive of honey bees.' Even more importantly, she relates how men take the time and trouble to try to understand her.

But, in spite of all their efforts, none of these people can understand what it is that makes her have such an effect. Angelou tries to explain her 'secret' to them, saying, 'It's in the reach of my arms'; 'It's the fire in my eyes'; and 'It's in the arch of my back'. But the 'Pretty women' cannot understand, because in their terms she is not exceptional – she is 'not cute or built to suit a fashion model's size'. The men cannot understand either, because their terms of judgment arise out of their male gender.

Angelou, however, knows that her 'secret' lies in the fact that she is her own woman. She is very definitely female, but she keeps emphasising that she is a unique female with a unique identity. She speaks of her physical uniqueness: 'my arms'; 'my hips'; 'my eyes'; 'my feet'; 'my breasts'; 'my hand'. She also describes how her behaviour is unique to her: 'The curl of my lips'; 'I walk into a room | Just as cool as you please'; and 'The grace of my style'.

This belief and faith in her individuality give her quiet, but indestructible, confidence and composure: 'I don't shout or jump about'. She encounters the world positively with 'joy' in her 'feet', because she knows that her 'head's not bowed.' She has faced terrible obstacles in her life, but these contributed to her own uniqueness, as did her triumph over them. She moves through life with the greatest support of all – she loves and values her own personhood. This enables her to celebrate her sense that she is a 'Phenomenal Woman'. Because she feels like this about herself she has an inner glow and the 'sun' is in her smile. This draws other, less secure people to her in the hopes that they too may learn to be as comfortable with their own uniqueness. But, although Angelou acknowledges that others should feel proud when they see her survival, because it represents what they too could do, she knows that she cannot make others feel as she does. Just as she did, they must each find their own uniqueness and love it.

Mood

This poem is filled with verbs that create a wonderful mood of energy and confidence. Angelou is able to 'stride' through life, to 'swing' her hips and to 'click' her heels. This mood is strengthened by her use of images that suggest activity – 'A hive of honey bees' – and warmth – 'The sun of my smile'.

There is also a mood of great good humour. Angelou may not need all the fuss to boost her confidence, but she certainly enjoys it. It is evident that she is amused by the 'Pretty women' asking for her advice. There is also a suggestion of humorous exaggeration in her descriptions of men who react to her entrance by falling 'down on their knees.'

Roger McGough
Bearhugs

Text of poem: New Explorations Anthology page 519

A reading of the poem

McGough opens the poem with a warm and affectionate image of him and his two sons hugging each other. There is something charming about the way that the two big, strong sons are expressing their love for their father in such an open way. Although they are his sons, McGough conveys an image of their being physically much larger than he is, when he describes how they lift him off his feet and crush him with their hugs. The title of the poem, 'Bearhugs', seems very appropriate for this very 'male' demonstration of affection.

McGough is immediately struck by the adult smells that cling to his two sons: aftershave, beer, tobacco and women. Although the three seem to genuinely care for each other, they evidently do not share intimate stories about their relationships. McGough does not know who these women are and whether his sons really care about them, and neither does he ask them. Perhaps this indicates some feeling of reserve between the men, but, again, it could just be indicative of a 'male' approach to love and affection.

The intensity of their hugging is explained in the third stanza, where we learn that McGough did not live with his sons as they grew up. The implication is that because of this he did not see the continuity of their daily development, nor could they express their love for each other on an ongoing basis. Their meetings were special, intensely emotional occasions, not the casual encounters that occur when a father lives with his children.

Clearly, McGough is anxious about the ways in which his separation from the boys affected his relationship with them and the influence that he had on them. As they do not seem to look like him physically, he tries to find some resemblance between them and his side of the family. By discovering 'something' of his father and uncles in them he is reassured that he did pass some inheritance on to them.

The resemblance of his sons to his father and uncles has another effect on McGough. He recalls a childhood memory of being hugged by these men while they were on leave from the war. Again we have the suggestion of father and son being separated, meeting only on special, intensely emotional occasions.

As his sons leave, McGough's confidence in their shared love is restored. He did not live with his father and uncles for a part of his youth, but the 'Bearhugs' that were shared between the child McGough and his adult relatives left him in no doubt that he was loved. Similarly, the 'Bearhugs' that he shares with his sons have a positive effect on him because they let him know that his two boys also love him deeply, and that his connection to them is safe.

Theme

McGough explores the nature of the connection that exists in families, particularly among the male members. He realises that this connection is not really based on living together, or on discussing intimate details, or on looking like each other. Rather, the male members of McGough's family are connected by the deep and enduring love that they share for each other, expressed in the 'Bearhugs'.

Seamus Heaney
Postscript

Text of poem: New Explorations Anthology page 522

A reading of the poem

This poem begins quietly enough, with Heaney's opening three lines having an understated tone. His language is conversational. It is as if we have just met him at a party and we are engaged in some pleasant social chatting. The specific details that he gives regarding the best area and time to go to this part of the 'west' suggest that it is a treasured place for him.

Significantly, Heaney does not use any full stops until line 11, and this creates a sense of sequence that smoothly moves us, the readers, in place towards the 'west' and in time to 'September or October'. The pace begins to quicken with the final three words of the third line, 'when the wind', and, in the next eight lines, we find ourselves actually travelling in a car through this wonderful countryside.

Bright, vivid images flash by us as we speed along the coast road. Snatches of the world of 'the Flaggy Shore' snapshot into our vision for a few seconds and then vanish. We glimpse the 'foam and glitter' of the ocean. Suddenly, we see 'a flock of swans', luminous against the 'slate-grey lake'. Heaney describes the swans in four lines of breathtaking imagery that convey both their 'flesh and blood' reality and their mythical 'magic' qualities; their embodiment of 'feathers roughed and ruffling' and 'earthed lightning'.

And then, with the suddenness of a full stop, the swans are gone. But Heaney wisely warns us not to try to turn back for another look at them. For this is the way of car journeys. We 'hurry through' a place. It is the unpredictability of whether the next thing we see will be 'known' or 'strange' that makes the experience exciting. Each new kilometre brings the possibility of a stunning image, made even more special because of its fleeting presence.

In this way Heaney encourages his readers to think again about travelling by car: to see that a car journey can be so much more than simply a movement in place and time. As he has so wonderfully demonstrated, it can also be a movement in our hearts and souls.

Imagery

This poem is an excellent example of the way in which poetry can paint vivid 'word' pictures that not only describe a scene, but also convey the sensations and emotions connected to it.

So, for example, we have his use of alliteration with the letter 's' (alliteration: where two or more words close together begin with the same letter) in the lines 'and inland among stones | The surface of a slate-grey lake is lit'. This alliteration creates a slick, watery sensation that reinforces Heaney's use of colour, 'slate-grey'. So we not only 'see' the lake, we 'feel' it as well.

Similarly, with the final two lines of the poem, 'As big soft buffetings come at the car sideways | And catch the heart off guard and blow it open', Heaney links the physical sensation of the car being blown by gusts of wind to the emotional effects of what is being seen on the car journey. In this way, he emphasises the theme of this poem by making us 'feel' the concrete, physical movement of a car journey alongside the intangible, inner changes that, he believes, can also take place.

Sharon Olds
Looking at Them Asleep

Text of poem: New Explorations Anthology page 529

A READING OF THE POEM

Sharon Olds uses an everyday situation of a mother watching her daughter and son sleeping to explore the nature of a mother's love for her children. By placing such an exploration in a commonplace setting, she encourages her readers to reassess the importance of such moments that may all too easily become lost in the rush and activity of present-day life.

Olds briefly sets the scene for her poem in the opening line and gives a short summary of what the experience means to her in the final two and a half lines. However, most of the poem is focused on Olds' marvellously detailed descriptions of how her two children sleep and what this reveals about their characters.

Her daughter sleeps with 'her arm curled about her head', lying 'on her back in abandon and sealed completion'. Olds acknowledges both her daughter's strengths and weaknesses. Her ability to rest easy is related to her awareness of her own 'self', of what she wants and the ways to satisfy those wants. However, this 'self' awareness also leads her to continually want more, so that she is never fully satisfied.

Her son is a much more restless sleeper, with his 'thin quivering eyelids' and his 'breathing hard'. Once again, Olds recognises that her son has strengths and weaknesses. He is passionate and active, always embarking on some 'quest'. But his 'crumpled' forehead and his 'wide open' eyes behind the closed lids indicate that he is also anxious and nervously alert.

Because of this full knowledge that she has of her children, Olds is able to predict exactly how they would react it she were to awaken them. Her daughter would 'smile and turn her face toward me though | half asleep'; while her son would 'jerk and say Don't and sit | up'.

Finally, Olds' recognises that this full knowledge comes from the fact that she is a mother who truly loves her children. It is this love that enables her to observe their different strengths and weaknesses, and yet still regard each of them as uniquely precious.

LINE STRUCTURE AND LINE MEANING

Olds skilfully uses the structure of her lines to reinforce their meaning. Thus the length, rhythm and sounds of the lines are connected to their sense.

If we look at one of the lines describing her daughter sleeping – 'her eyes so closed you would think they have rolled the' – we can see that this is a long line. It also has a slow, steady pace that is created by her use of single-syllable words and her use of assonance with the letter 'o' (assonance: where two or more words close together have the same vowel sound): ' her eyes so closed you would think they have rolled the'. All of this serves to convey the calm and contented way in which her daughter sleeps.

On the other hand, her description of her son's sleeping is very different, as in 'and panting a bit, his brow is crumpled'. This is clearly a much shorter line, broken by a comma in the middle. The rhythm is quicker and jerkier because Olds uses a mixture of single- and two-syllable words. There is also a similar variety in the sounds of these words with the vowels, a, i, o and u and the consonants p, b, h, b, c all jumbled together. So, we have the impression of a restless, nervy sleeper that mirrors the meaning of this line.

Paul Durcan
Going Home to Mayo, Winter, 1949

Text of poem: New Explorations Anthology page 531

A READING OF THE POEM

The poem deals directly with the contrast between urban life and rural culture, between present and past. The village is a romantic, welcoming place, with an old-fashioned, magical charm about it – 'all oil-lamps and women'. It has a gentle, feminine identity, in contrast to the hard, powerful, masculine city: 'blocks after blocks of so-called "new" tenements'. The country is a known place, a place of heritage, where they belonged: 'my father's mother's house'. This is in marked contrast to the impersonal 'alien, foreign city of Dublin'.

The village is an exotic place, particularly to a child. There is the novelty of the unusual: 'my bedroom over the public bar below'. It is all beautifully chaotic, with an animal wildness, a naturalness, that is quaintly appealing.

> And in the morning cattle-cries and cock-crows:
> Life's seemingly seamless garment gorgeously rent
> By their screeches and bellowings.

Contrast this with the rigid divisions and barren orderliness of the city, with its 'railings and palings and asphalt and traffic-lights'.

The village is a place that fostered intimacy between father and son:

> I walked with my father in the high grass down by the river
> Talking with him – an unheard-of thing in the city.

The city is associated with loneliness, isolation, and death. The tenements are seen as graveyards, with 'thousands of crosses of loneliness' that somehow become a reminder of actual death for the father. For him, death is more real, perhaps because it is more immediate – and so the shape of the grave is more clearly defined as 'the narrowing grave'. But the city carries an aura of death even for the child, for whom death is less immediate and obvious: 'In the wide, wide cemetery of the boy's childhood.' Perhaps there is a hint, too, that the city proved the cemetery of the boy's dreams.

The poet displays a yearning for the village of Turlough that is almost religious in its intensity. Like a religious exile, he is 'going home', with all the excitement and anticipation that entails. Consequently he is deeply disappointed when he realises that it is a temporary stay, that 'home was not home'. Turlough means life and excitement for him; the city means exile and death.

A child's view of the world

Part I communicates a child's view of life, a magical world full of possibilities:

> 'Daddy, Daddy,' I cried, 'Pass out the moon.'

The journey becomes a symbolic quest for the promised land: names of towns are reeled off as in a religious litany. And in this magic place, all is transformed, and children are no longer treated as inferior.

> I walked with my father in the high grass down by the river
> Talking with him . . .

Father and son

The relationship with his father provided a good deal of grief for Paul Durcan, but we see little of that here. The portrait of the father is typically masculine, associated with driving, energy, direction and with going places. There is a hint of aloofness, in that the intimacy of conversation is unusual, 'unheard-of thing in the city'. Yet on this occasion father and son collaborate on the quest ('no matter how hard he drove he could not pass out the moon'). An interlude of closeness and cooperation is provided by the return to the village; it is as if the ideal relationship is attainable only in this hallowed place.

Imagery

The image of a journey, which is central to the poem, achieves a certain symbolic significance here. It is both a real journey and a magical quest for origins, for the perfect place, for happiness. The drive through the night has its counter-image in the 'daylight nightmare of Dublin city' and so helps to link both halves of the poem, the perfect dream and the hard-working reality. The images evoking rural life have a biblical quality to them: 'oil-lamps and women', 'cattle-cries and cock-crows'; and the metaphor of most obvious biblical significance, 'Life's seemingly seamless garment gorgeously rent.' The effect is to suggest that this is a good and holy place, as well as a place obviously teeming with life.

In contrast, pictures of the city are cold, non-human, and divisive rather than fostering life: railings and palings, blocks of flats; and in some surreal way they become associated with crosses and death.

Paul Muldoon
Anseo

Text of poem: New Explorations Anthology page 541

Critical commentary

'Anseo' describes how things happen in cycles and how the abused can often become the abuser.

The initial scene is a typical Irish primary school. The poet describes the roll-call system by which everybody would answer 'Anseo' as their name was called out. This word 'was the first word of Irish I spoke', as was the case and possibly still is for many Irish schoolchildren. The poet remembers what would happen at the start of every class, when the teacher would call out the last name on the roll – which belonged to Joseph Mary Plunkett Ward. This name is significant for a number of reasons. Joseph Mary Plunkett was one of the leaders of the Easter Rising in 1916. The Mary part of it is also significant, in so far as it is usually a name associated with girls rather than boys, and certainly not with a military leader – which the 1916 leader was and that this boy was about to become.

Finally, the name is also important because it gives the teacher a chance to make a pun on the boy's name. Every day he would ask the same question: 'And where's our little Ward–of–court?' There was a sense of expectancy around this question; the other students would look at each other to see the reaction to it. The teacher was obviously having fun at Ward's expense.

In the second verse we see the twisted nature of the teacher, as he would send

Ward out to find his own stick to be beaten with. The teacher would refuse different options, until he got the right one to beat him with. This is the sort of ritual that Ward was seeing and, as we see later on, he was learning from it as well. The poet gives us fine detail as he outlines exactly the trouble that Ward would go to when he was preparing his own tormentor. We can almost imagine Ward taking pride in his work or being given a lecture about it from the teacher. We can see the engraving being like a commemoration on a gift:

> Its twist of red and yellow lacquers
> Sanded and polished,
> And altogether so delicately wrought
> That he had engraved his initials on it.

The poet then brings us further along in time. Joseph Mary Plunkett Ward is now doing what his part namesake had also done. He is leading a secret IRA battalion and had obviously risen through the ranks. There are many contradictions in his life when we see that

> He was living in the *open*,
> In a *secret* camp

He is no longer the boy who is being bullied and victimised. Instead he is 'Making things happen.' He has become an important person in a vicious world. He has also learned from his old schoolteacher. He calls a roll, just like in primary school. One feels the punishment for not answering the roll call this time could be much more severe than getting beaten by a hazel-wand.

He is now the one in the position of authority. He is able to put people in their place and tell them what to do. People have fear of him now.

Muldoon makes a simple point in a clever way and uses the simple Irish word 'Anseo' to illustrate it. He says that power must be used carefully. He also says that if not cared for properly, the bullied can become the bully.

Kerry Hardie
May

Text of poem: New Explorations Anthology page 544

A READING OF THE POEM

Here, Kerry Hardie creates a wonderful 'word picture' that not only vividly describes the reality of the month of May, but also conveys the emotional impact that this time of year has both on her and on the world of nature.

The first line of the poem sets the tone for the following breathtaking descriptions of the effects that May has on the countryside. Hardie's opening words, 'The blessèd stretch and ease of it –' not only speak of things relaxing and opening out; they also create these feelings. She achieves this through her use of assonance with the letter 'e' (assonance: where two or more words close together have the same vowel sound) along with sibilant (hissing) 's' sounds. Hardie continues to link the meaning and sounds of her words together in the same way. So, we have the marvellous lines: 'The **b**irdsong | **b**ouncing **b**ack out of the sky.' The alliteration of the letter 'b' (alliteration: where two or more words close together begin with the same letter) acts to re-create the way that the birds' singing echoes around the sky. Similarly, her use of onomatopoeia (onomatopoeia: a word made up of an actual sound) in 'The horses **swishing** their tails', again with sibilant 's', helps the reader to 'hear' the sounds made by the horses' tails. These lines also illustrate another method that Hardie uses to make her descriptions of May come alive: she uses imagery that appeals to a number of our senses.

Many of Hardie's images call on more than just our sense of sight, although she does use colour most effectively in this poem. In her image 'Balm in the air', she appeals to the sense of touch with her use of the word 'Balm', because a balm is a soothing, healing ointment. Thus it conveys the soothing sensation of the warm May air on the skin and all the other surfaces in nature. We have already seen in the previous paragraph her use of the sense of hearing with the birdsong and the horses' tails.

The final two lines of the poem convey Hardie's view of the emotional effects brought about by the month of May. Briefly she returns to winter, listing in short, harsh-sounding words the unpleasant effects that it produces: 'hardship, hunger, treachery'. These stand in stark contrast to May causing everything to 'stretch and ease'. Happily, May's arrival wipes out any memories of such a negative and depressing time. The warmer air, the brighter days, the flourishing world of nature – all serve to create a much more positive atmosphere. Hardie is aware that this 'conviction', this firm belief that all will be much better, may be 'unfounded', in that it has no provable basis. However, as she looks at the countryside around her she senses a force that impels the natural world to move on from winter by offering 'forgiveness' for its 'hardship, hunger, treachery' and by finding 'hope' for the future.

Mood

Hardie succeeds in creating a very positive mood in this poem. She does so in a number of ways. Firstly, her poem glows with bright colours: blue, yellow and cream are mentioned, and there is also a lot of green implied. Secondly, the poem echoes to joyous sounds: 'birdsong', 'horses swishing their tails'. These are pleasant sounds that we enjoy hearing. Thirdly, she uses verbs that vibrate with energy and life, such as 'bursting' and 'bouncing', alongside verbs that suggest relaxation: 'stretch', 'lain' and 'rests'. This combination conveys a feeling of having the energy to enjoy life, but in a very relaxed manner. Fourthly, her imagery is of the world of nature, beautiful and blooming, as in 'And the first cream splatters of blossom'.

It is no wonder that the one intrusion of negative feelings, 'All hardship, hunger, treachery of winter' is brief and quickly forgotten. At such a time, in such a place, 'forgiveness' and 'hope' can only come easily.

Carol Ann Duffy
Valentine

Text of poem: New Explorations Anthology page 548

A READING OF THE POEM

This is a love poem, but it is not a straightforward, romantic love poem. Indeed in the first line we see that the poet is putting great emphasis on the fact that her love (the emotion and the person) is not ordinary, and therefore she is not going to give a traditional gift for St Valentine's Day, like a 'red rose or a satin heart'; instead she is going to give her lover an onion.

The rest of the poem explains why she feels she should give an onion to her lover. The onion becomes an *extended metaphor.* She points out that the onion can give light in a time of darkness, just like the moon. She examines the erotic nature of an onion. She compares the onion to a lover who brings out the truth regardless of the price. She says that a love affair, like an onion, can make the protagonists see sides of themselves that they'd rather not see. She talks about its taste, which is difficult to shift; but, like the taste of an onion, a love affair can eventually end as well. Then she compares the inside of an onion to a wedding ring; but then she says that this is lethal.

All these images are harsh, and in a way they are cold. The poet seems to be bringing a 'wake-up call' to her lover. The implication could be that they have not got a traditional romantic relationship, and therefore to give a traditional romantic present would be the wrong thing to do and would be dishonest.

At the end she adds her own caution: getting too close is dangerous; love can be 'lethal'.

TONE

She uses a forceful, matter-of-fact tone. There is little ambiguity. Note her use of the definite 'I will' and 'I give,' instead of 'It could' or 'I offer.' There is a sense of 'these are the facts; if you don't like them – tough'; though there is a little hint of teasing in the poem as well.

STRUCTURE AND LANGUAGE

She uses very few formal traditional poetic devices, though she is careful with her use of sound, especially in such lines as

> Its fierce kiss will stay on your lips.

The metre in the poem seems to be purpose-built. She varies her line lengths a lot, even giving one word to one line. What do you think the significance of these small lines is?

Simon Armitage
It Ain't What You Do, It's What It Does To You

Text of poem: New Explorations Anthology page 555

This is a beautifully simple poem about the difference people can make and about how people can be important, even if they are not living exotic lives. The poet sets up four exotic scenarios and contrasts them with four seemingly banal instances, giving each equal credence. This poem could easily be compared with Patrick Kavanagh's poem 'Epic' in the way that it contrasts the local with the universal.

The first contrast is between a Bohemian travelling across the USA, living 'with only a dollar to spare, one pair | of busted Levis and a Bowie knife', and simply living with 'thieves in Manchester'. The banality of the place Manchester, which is local and drab, compared to the living-on-the-edge lifestyle in the States, is also emphasised by the simplicity of the line.

Next, he tells us that he doesn't get his spiritual wholeness from one of the wonders of the world, but from the energy used in skimming stones across an old lake in northern England. He finds himself at one with the energy of the Black Moss, instead of with the glamorous Taj Mahal. He points out here that what is important is the feeling it gives him, rather than the location.

Finally he refers to two different actions. The first is daring and brave – getting ready to take a parachute jump where life and limb are seemingly risked. The second is simply caring for a mentally handicapped boy in a help centre. He obviously feels that the latter is more important. He goes on to assess what this does to him, and finds that it gives him a 'tightness in the throat' and a 'tiny cascading sensation'. He thinks that these feelings give him a purpose in life. They give him a 'sense of something else'.